FRENCH COOKING AT HOME

For Jérôme

FRENCH COOKING AT HOME

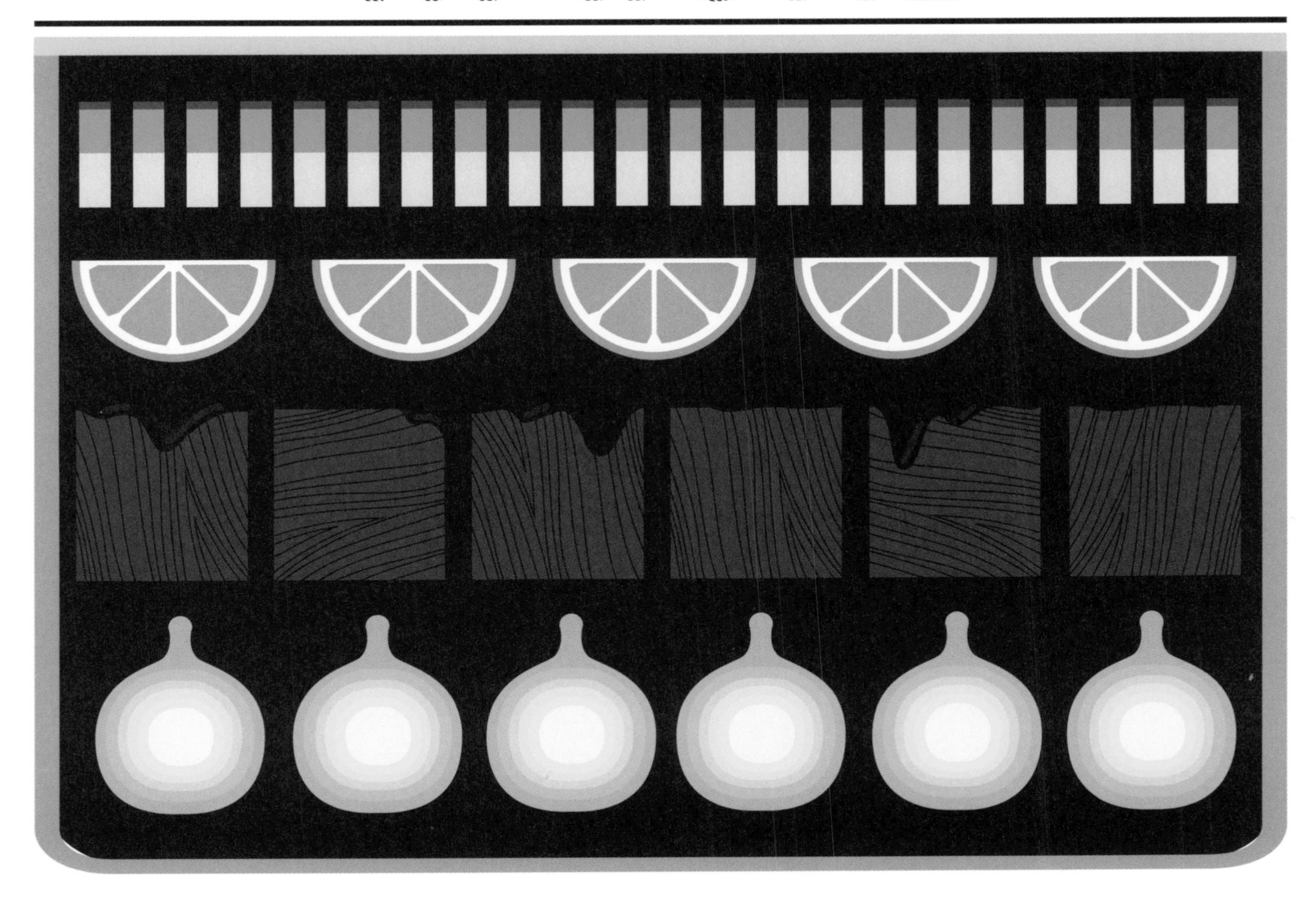

MARIANNE MAGNIER-MORENO
CUISINE AND INSTRUCTIONS

PHOTOGRAPHS BY PIERRE JAVELLE
ILLUSTRATIONS BY YANNIS VAROUTSIKOS
SCIENTIFIC EXPLANATIONS BY ANNE CAZOR

An Imprint of HarperCollinsPublishers

CONTENTS

BASE RECIPES

RECIPES

ILLUSTRATED GLOSSARY

HOW TO USE THIS BOOK

BASE RECIPES

Discover all the basic recipes of French cooking,
categorized into stocks, sauces, mixtures, pastries, ingredients, and cooking methods.
Each base recipe includes a diagram and explanation
of the specific preparation techniques.

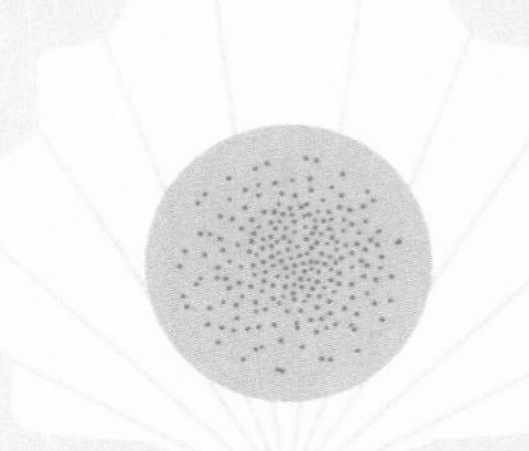

RECIPES

Put the base recipes to work to make appetizers, main dishes, and side dishes.
Each recipe cross-references to the base recipes, with a diagram for understanding
the concept of the dish, and step-by-step photos of each stage of the recipe.

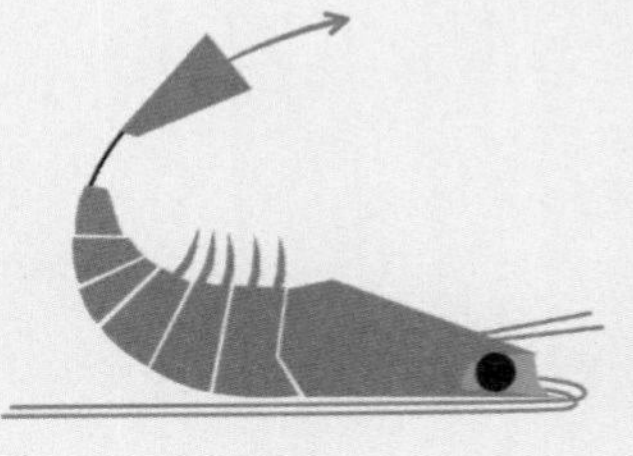

ILLUSTRATED GLOSSARY

Learn additional information on the ingredients and main
techniques presented in each of the recipe sections.

CHAPTER 1
BASE RECIPES

STOCKS

BASIC SAUCES

EMULSIONS

BASIC PREPARATION TECHNIQUES

PASTRY

BASIC INGREDIENTS AND THEIR PREPARATION

COOKING TECHNIQUES

WHITE POULTRY STOCK

Understand

WHAT IS IT?

A decoction (see below) of poultry bones and vegetables that make an aromatic poultry-flavored stock

TIME TO MAKE

Preparation: 10 minutes
Cooking: 2 hours

EQUIPMENT

Dutch oven, stockpot, or large saucepan
Skimmer
Fine-mesh sieve

USES

Cooking liquid for braised meats, vegetables, or stews
Base for sauces and gravies

VARIATIONS

Brown poultry stock

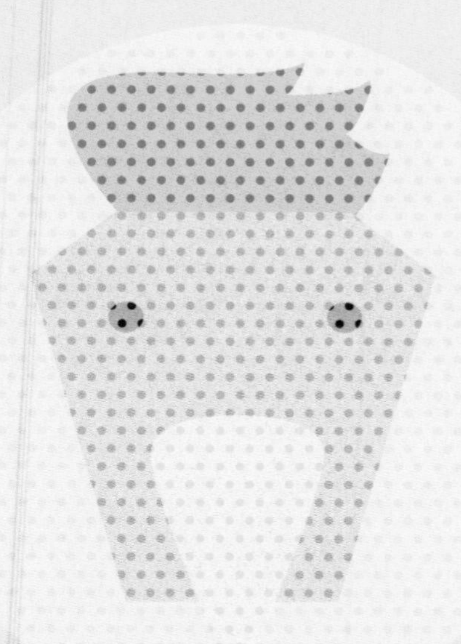

DERIVATIVES

Poultry velouté sauce (roux + white poultry stock)
Sauces (suprême, allemande)
Soups (veloutés, cream soups)

TECHNIQUES TO MASTER

Crushing spices (page 280)
Skimming (page 283)
Degreasing a Broth (page 283)
Straining through a sieve (page 281)

IT'S READY . . .

When the stock is lightly aromatic and golden.

STORAGE

3 days in the refrigerator or 3 months in the freezer. Bring to a boil before use.

WHY "WHITE" STOCK?

Unlike "brown" stock, the bones aren't browned before being covered with water. The brown molecules that result from the Maillard reaction (page 282) are therefore absent and the stock isn't dark.

WHAT IS A DECOCTION?

A mixture made by extracting the components of its ingredients through boiling. The ingredients are covered with cold water, then brought to a boil. From this, broths are made.

WHAT GIVES A STOCK ITS FLAVOR?

During cooking, the proteins are broken down in the water into amino acids, which provide flavor. The fat extracted from the meat also captures and enhances the flavors from the aromatic ingredients.

Learn

MAKES 2 QUARTS

POULTRY STOCK

3 lb 5 oz whole chicken or chicken wings
2½ quarts water

AROMATICS

½ onion
1 carrot
1 celery stalk
1 leek
1 thyme sprig
1 bay leaf

SEASONING

½–¾ teaspoon black peppercorns

1 Remove any fatty or bloody parts from the chicken. Peel, trim, and wash the vegetables. Crush the peppercorns.

2 Put the chicken in a stockpot and cover with cold water. Bring to a boil, then skim off any foam.

3 Add the vegetables, thyme, bay leaf, and peppercorns. Cook at a gentle simmer for 2 hours, skimming off any foam and degreasing from time to time.

4 Strain the stock through a fine-mesh sieve.

BROWN VEAL STOCK

Understand

WHAT IS IT?

A decoction (page 10) of bones and trimmings from roast veal and vegetables to obtain an aromatic beef broth

TIME TO MAKE

Preparation: 20 minutes
Cooking: 4–5 hours
Resting: 3 hours

EQUIPMENT

Roasting pan
Dutch oven, stockpot, or large saucepan
Skimmer
Fine-mesh sieve

USES

Cooking liquid for braised meats or stews
Base for sauces and gravies

VARIATIONS

White veal stock

DERIVATIVES

Glaze (reduced stock)
Thickened brown veal stock (brown stock reduced, then thickened with potato flour)
Brown sauces (e.g. pepper sauce)

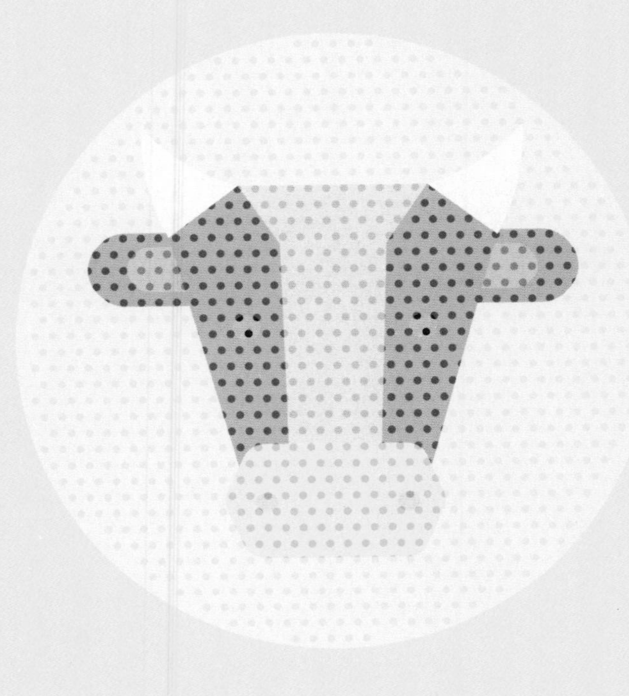

TRICKY ASPECTS

– Not burning the trimmings and bones
– Keeping an eye on evaporation

TECHNIQUES TO MASTER

Crushing spices (page 280)
Crushing garlic (page 280)
Cutting mirepoix (page 34)
Degreasing Broth (page 283)
Scraping the pan (page 283)
Deglazing (page 283)
Skimming (page 283)
Straining trhough a sieve (page 281)

IT'S READY . . .

When the stock is lightly aromatic and an orangey brown.

WHY "BROWN" STOCK?

A Maillard reaction (page 282) is a chemical process that creates brown molecules when the meat is roasted. The molecules provide aromatic notes to the dish. This is in contrast to "white" stock, where the poached element is raw.

WHY CHOP THE VEGETABLES IN MIREPOIX?

The bigger the pieces, the slower the extraction of the flavorful and aromatic elements. Since the cooking time for a stock is long, it's not necessary to chop finely.

WHY MUST THE BONES BE COVERED WITH WATER THROUGHOUT COOKING?

The extraction of the components of the bones (mainly collagen) occurs throughout cooking, even if it goes on for 4 hours. The extracted collagen is transformed into gelatin, which gives cold stock its jelly-like consistency.

TIP

Quick brown veal stock: brown the trimmings in a Dutch oven or stockpot in a little butter, then remove from the pan and sweat the vegetables in the same pot. Add the tomato paste, cook for 1–2 minutes, then deglaze with a little water, scraping any stuck-on bits off the bottom. Return the trimmings to the pot and cover with water. Cook at a very low simmer until you obtain the desired quantity of liquid (30 minutes to 1 hour). Strain through a fine-mesh sieve.

STORAGE

3 days in the refrigerator, 3 months in the freezer. Bring to a boil before use.

Learn

MAKES 1½ QUARTS

VEAL STOCK

3 lb 5 oz veal trimmings and bones cut into pieces 4 inches or smaller
1½ quarts water

AROMATICS

2 garlic cloves
3 carrots
1 large onion
¼ cup tomato paste
2 bay leaves

SEASONING

1 teaspoon black peppercorns

1 Preheat the oven to 430°F. Arrange the veal trimmings and bones in a roasting pan so that they don't overlap. Roast for about 45 minutes, until well browned. Peel, de-germ, and slice the garlic cloves. Peel and chop the carrots and onion for a mirepoix (page 34). Crush the peppercorns under the bottom of a saucepan.

2 Add the tomato paste to the roasting pan and mix. Add the carrots, onion, and garlic but don't mix. Roast for 10 minutes, then remove the pan from the oven. Reduce the oven temperature to 210°F.

3 Using a skimmer or slotted spoon, transfer the veal pieces and vegetables to a Dutch oven, so that they form two layers.

4 Degrease the roasting pan. Deglaze the pan with cold water (about 1 cup, page 283), scraping any stuck-on bits off the bottom, and pour it all into the Dutch oven.

5 Pour enough water into the Dutch oven to cover the meat by 2–4 inches. Heat to a simmer, then carefully skim and degrease. Add the peppercorns and bay leaves. Transfer to the oven, with the lid off, for 3–4 hours. Check halfway through cooking that the bones are still covered with water, adding more water if necessary.

6 Skim off any fat. Strain through a fine-mesh sieve, without pushing. Allow to cool, then degrease.

FISH STOCK

Understand

WHAT IS IT?

A decoction (page 10) of fish bones and vegetables to obtain an aromatic broth with a light taste of fish

TIME TO MAKE

Preparation: 15 minutes
Cooking: 20 minutes

EQUIPMENT

Chef's knife
Large saucepan
Skimmer
Fine-mesh sieve

USES

Poaching fish
Base for sauces and soups

VARIATIONS

Shellfish stock

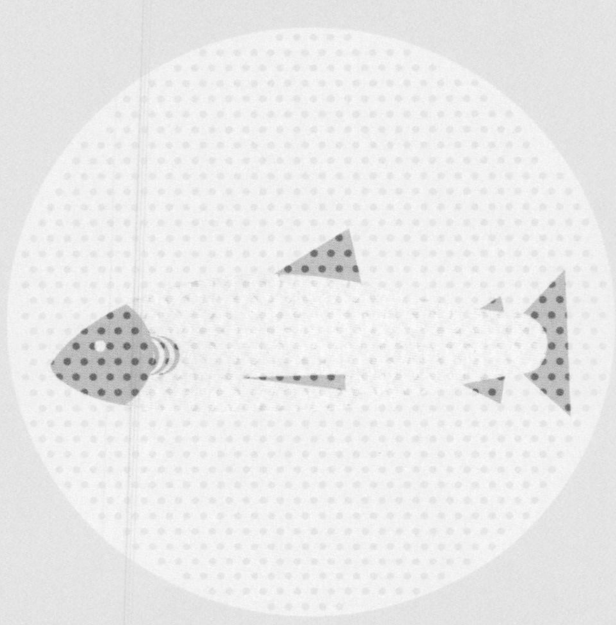

DERIVATIVES

Sauce américaine (fish stock [+ shellfish] + tomato)
Nantua sauce (fish stock + crayfish + tomato + cream)

TECHNIQUES TO MASTER

Crushing spices (page 280)
Crushing fish bones (page 279)
Thinly slicing (page 280)
Skimming (page 283)
Straining through a sieve (page 281)
Sweating (page 282)

IT'S READY . . .

When the liquid is lightly aromatic.

WHY THE SHORT COOKING TIME (LESS THAN 20 MINUTES)?

The longer the cooking time, the more chemical reactions occur, which can lead to off-flavors in the broth.

TIPS

- Reducing the quantity of liquid intensifies the stock (but make sure the bones and vegetables are still covered).
- Don't use more than 5 cups of liquid, or the stock will take too long to reduce and won't taste good.

STORAGE

2 days in the refrigerator
or 1 month in the freezer.

Learn

MAKES 1 QUART

FISH STOCK

1 lb 5 oz bones from thin fish (sole, flounder, whiting, cod, hake, etc.)
3 tablespoons butter
1 quart water
½ cup white wine or dry vermouth

AROMATICS

1 shallot
1 small onion
1 thyme sprig
1 bay leaf

SEASONING

5 black peppercorns

1 Peel and thinly slice the shallot and onion. Remove any remaining pieces of blood from the fish bones and crush the bones roughly using a chef's knife. Crush the peppercorns.

2 Melt the butter in a large saucepan over medium heat. Sweat the shallot and onion for 1–2 minutes.

3 Add the fish bones and allow them to sweat without coloring. Pour in the water and wine. Add the thyme and bay leaf. Bring to a boil, then simmer for 20 minutes. Skim off any foam. Add the crushed peppercorns 5 minutes before the end of the cooking time.

4 Strain through a fine-mesh sieve without pressing.

COURT BOUILLON

Understand

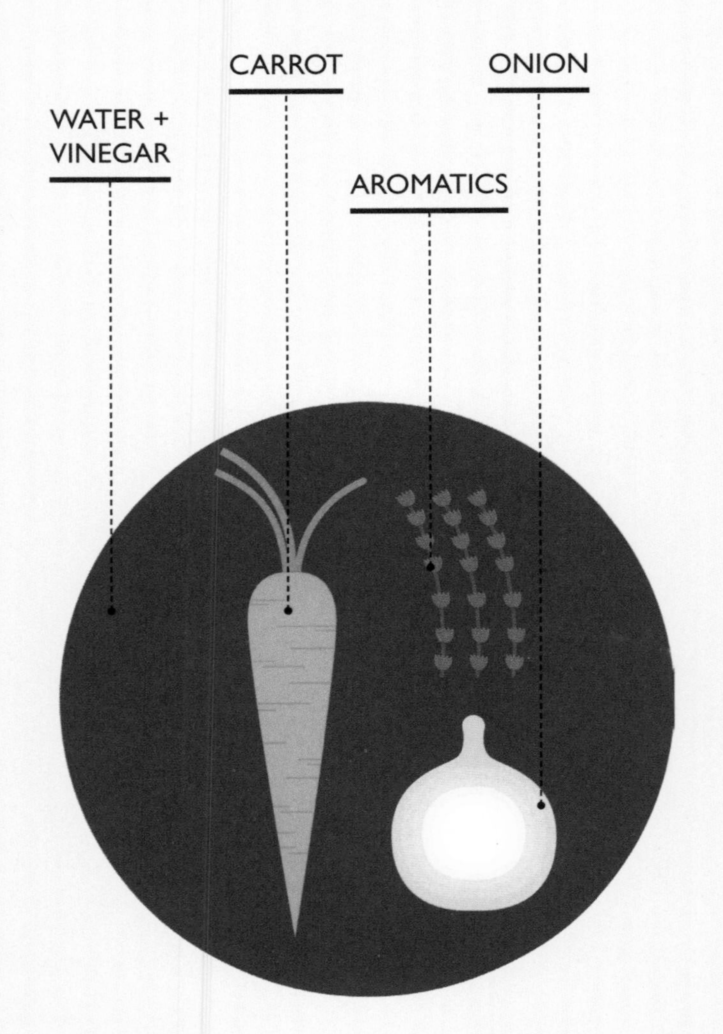

WHAT IS IT?

Aromatic broth with vinegar, used for poaching large proteins in a reduced volume of liquid (*court* in French means "short")

TIME TO MAKE

Preparation: 15 minutes
Cooking: 20 minutes
Resting: 1 hour

EQUIPMENT

Chef's knife
Large saucepan
Skimmer

USES

Poaching fish (whole or in pieces) and large shellfish

DERIVATIVE

Nage: court bouillon in which the vegetables are more finely cut; sometimes it is reduced before the butter is whisked in.

TRICKY ASPECT

Cutting the vegetables: They should not be too large or too fine. You want them to add flavor, but not dominate.

TECHNIQUE TO MASTER

Skimming (page 283)

TIP

Don't add vinegar when poaching salmon or trout, as it discolors the flesh.

IT'S READY . . .

When the liquid is cold, aromatic, and slightly acidic.

STORAGE

2 days in the refrigerator.

WHY FINELY CHOP THE AROMATICS?

The finer the vegetables are chopped, the greater the surface area exposed to the liquid. Extraction of the aromatic components is therefore greater when the pieces are small. We finely chop the vegetables for a court bouillon so that it has a stronger taste.

WHAT DOES THE VINEGAR DO?

The vinegar (or the wine) acidifies the court bouillon. This acidity improves the coagulation of the proteins and thus the texture of the fish.

WHY MUST COURT BOUILLON START WITH COLD WATER?

Starting with cold water allows the fish to firm up first due to the acidity in the vinegar, then more as the temperature rises. These two phases of firming up improve the texture of the fish and prevent overcooking.

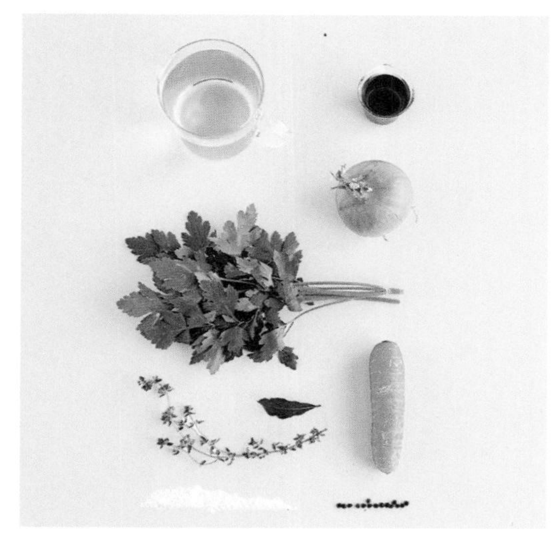

2

3

4

MAKES 1 QUART

COURT BOUILLON

1 medium carrot
1 quart water
¼ cup vinegar or ½ cup white wine
1 small bunch Italian parsley
3 thyme sprigs
1 bay leaf
1 small onion

SEASONING

½ teaspoon black peppercorns
2 teaspoons coarse sea salt

1 Peel, wash, and cut the carrot into thin (⅛-inch) slices.

2 Bring the water and vinegar or wine to a boil in a saucepan with the carrot, parsley, thyme, bay leaf, peppercorns, and salt. Skim off any foam, then simmer for 15 minutes.

3 Peel, wash, and cut the onion into thin (⅛-inch) slices. Add it to the pan and let it cook for 5 minutes more.

4 Allow the court bouillon to cool for 1 hour (without straining).

ROUX

Understand

WHAT IS IT?

A mixture of equal parts flour and butter, cooked for a short or longer time (white to blond to brown roux) to obtain a smooth base used for thickening

TIME TO MAKE

Preparation: 5 minutes
Cooking: 5 minutes

EQUIPMENT

Whisk
Saucepan large enough to contain the liquid to be thickened

USES

Thickening a soup or sauce in simmered dishes. Gradually pour the roux into the liquid to be thickened, whisking constantly. Bring to a boil, then let it cook for 1–2 minutes while whisking.

DERIVATIVES

Bechamel sauce (page 22)
Velouté sauce (page 20)

TRICKY ASPECT

Cooking time. Stop cooking as soon as you achieve the desired color; for a white roux, don't stop cooking too soon or the taste of the flour will remain in the final dish.

IT'S READY . . .

When the mixture is frothy and off-white. It "blooms."

TIP

For a very white roux, add the flour as soon as the butter has melted, otherwise the butter will color.

WHY MUST THE ROUX BE COOKED FOR A LONG TIME?

To break down the amylose molecules contained in the starch grains of the flour, thus dispelling their floury taste.

HOW DOES THE ROUX COLOR?

The flour contains proteins and sugars that react to heat. This process is known as the Maillard reaction (page 282). This reaction provides both color and aromatic components.

ROUX WITHOUT BUTTER

For some recipes for meat in a sauce, we sprinkle flour over the meat and toast it in the oven for a few minutes to color it before adding the liquid element; the cooking fats and the flour are then mixed to make a blond roux (or a brown one, depending on the roasting time).

Learn

TO THICKEN 1 QUART LIQUID

3–5 tablespoons unsalted butter
¼–½ cup all-purpose flour

The usual one-to-one mixture varies depending on the desired thickness of the final liquid: use 3 tablespoons butter and ¼ cup flour for a soup, and 5 tablespoons butter and ½ cup flour for bechamel sauce.

1 WHITE ROUX

Cut the butter into pieces and melt them in a saucepan over low heat.

Add the flour as soon as the butter has melted.

Whisk until the mixture is smooth.

Allow to cook over low heat, whisking constantly, until the mixture becomes frothy.

2 BLOND ROUX

Follow the directions for white roux, but continue cooking over low heat until the mixture becomes lightly golden.

3 BROWN ROUX

Follow the directions for white roux, but continue cooking until the preparation browns slightly.

VELOUTÉ SAUCE

Understand

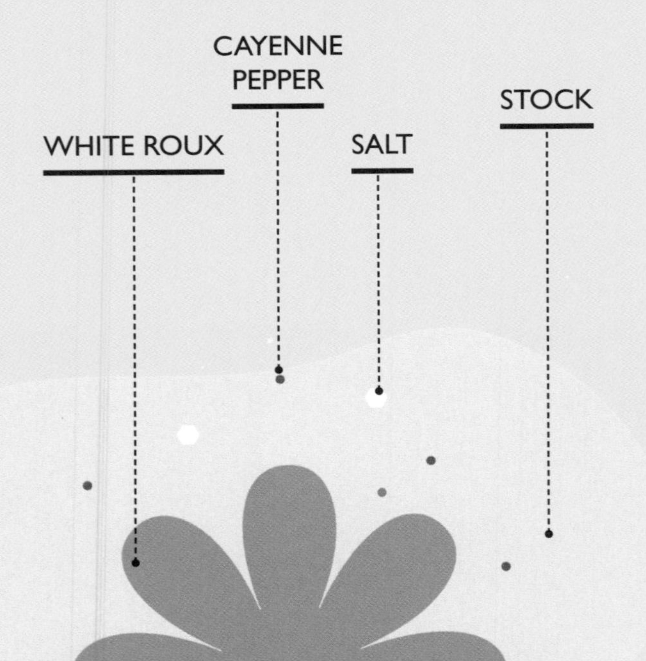

WHAT IS IT?

Sauce made by mixing a white roux with a white stock or fish stock

TIME TO MAKE

Preparation: 5 minutes
Cooking: 10 minutes

EQUIPMENT

Whisk
Large saucepan

USES

Base for sauces or soups
Added to mixtures: it provides cohesion to reduced sauces

DERIVATIVES

Suprême sauce (velouté sauce + cream)
Ivoire sauce (velouté sauce + cream + reduced veal stock)
Cream of vegetable soup (velouté + cream + vegetables)
Sauce for blanquette of veal (velouté sauce + cream + egg yolk)

TRICKY ASPECT

Preventing lumps

TECHNIQUE TO MASTER

Reducing a sauce (page 283)

IT'S READY . . .

When the stock has thickened and its flavors are concentrated.

TIP

Whisk vigorously as soon as you add the liquid, to avoid lumps forming.

STORAGE

1 hour covered in a hot water bath or 3 days in the refrigerator.

WHY DO LUMPS SOMETIMES FORM?

The starch in flour gelatinizes, absorbing water and swelling up in the heat. When we add water to flour, the flour clumps into "packets." The starch at the periphery of these packets absorbs the water and swells up. The water doesn't reach far enough to hydrate the center of the packet, and these partially gelatinized packets form the lumps.

Learn

MAKES 1 QUART

ROUX

5 tablespoons unsalted butter
½ cup all-purpose flour

WHITE STOCK OR FISH STOCK

1 quart white poultry stock (page 10) or fish stock (page 14)

SEASONING

1 teaspoon fine salt
pinch of cayenne pepper

1 Prepare the white roux: cut the butter into pieces and melt them in a large saucepan over low heat. Add the flour as soon as the butter has melted. Whisk until the mixture is smooth. Cook over low heat, whisking constantly, until the mixture turns pale and becomes frothy.

2 Pour the stock into the "blooming" roux all at once and whisk immediately.

3 Bring to a boil and continue to whisk until the liquid thickens.

4 Simmer the sauce for about 10 minutes until it reduces, whisking from time to time. Season with the salt and cayenne pepper.

BECHAMEL SAUCE

Understand

WHAT IS IT?
Thick sauce made by mixing a white roux with boiling milk

TIME TO MAKE
Preparation: 5 minutes

EQUIPMENT
Whisk
Large saucepan

USES
Soufflés (page 120)
Vegetable gratins
Lasagne

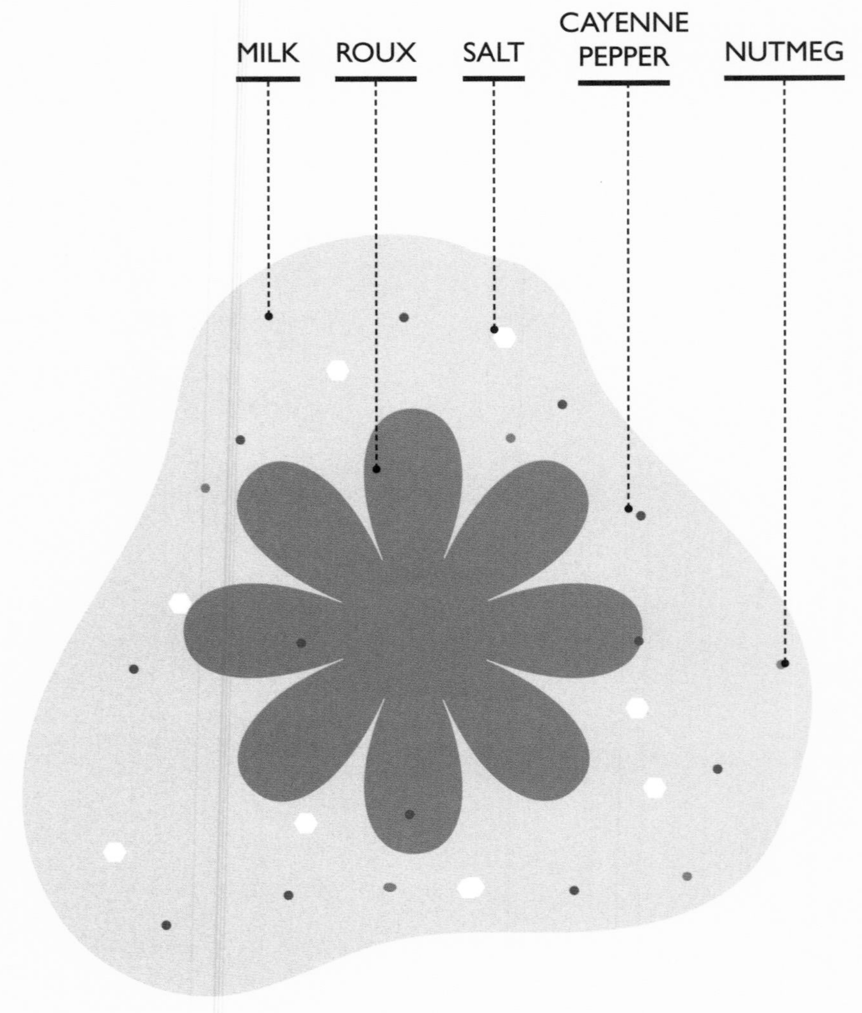

DERIVATIVES
Mornay sauce (bechamel sauce + egg yolk + Gruyère)
Cream sauce (bechamel sauce made with a mixture of milk + cream + lemon juice)

TRICKY ASPECT
Preventing lumps

IT'S READY . . .
When the mixture has thickened

TIPS
- Whisk vigorously as soon as you add the liquid, to avoid lumps forming.
- If the bechamel sauce is not perfectly smooth at the end of cooking, strain it through a sieve.

STORAGE
Cover with plastic wrap and set aside in a hot water bath.

WHY DOES THE ROUX THICKEN THE MILK?
The roux is a mixture of butter and flour. When we heat this mixture in milk, the starch in the flour swells up, which triggers a first thickening phase. If we continue to heat the mixture, the starch molecules break down and liberate their two constituent molecules—amylose and amylopectin—which bind the milk together and continue to thicken the mixture.

WHY NOT ADD THE MILK AT THE BEGINNING?
Before adding the milk, we first need to coat the flour in butter. This helps limit the lumps that may form when the milk is added because the butter separates the flour granules and prevents clumping.

Learn

MAKES 1 QUART

ROUX

5 tablespoons butter
½ cup all-purpose flour

LIQUID

1 quart milk

SEASONING

pinch of cayenne pepper
pinch of freshly grated nutmeg
1 teaspoon fine salt

1 Prepare the white roux: cut the butter into pieces and melt them in a large saucepan over low heat. Add the flour as soon as the butter has melted. Whisk until the mixture is smooth. Cook over low heat, whisking constantly, until the mixture turns pale and becomes frothy.

2 Pour the milk into the "blooming" roux all at once and whisk immediately.

3 Bring to a boil and continue to whisk until the liquid thickens.

4 Simmer while whisking constantly for 1–2 minutes. Season with the cayenne pepper, nutmeg, and salt.

TOMATO SAUCE

Understand

WHAT IS IT?
Puréed sauce made with tomatoes and aromatic vegetables

TIME TO MAKE
Preparation: 10 minutes
Cooking: 10 minutes

EQUIPMENT
Hand-held blender or food processor

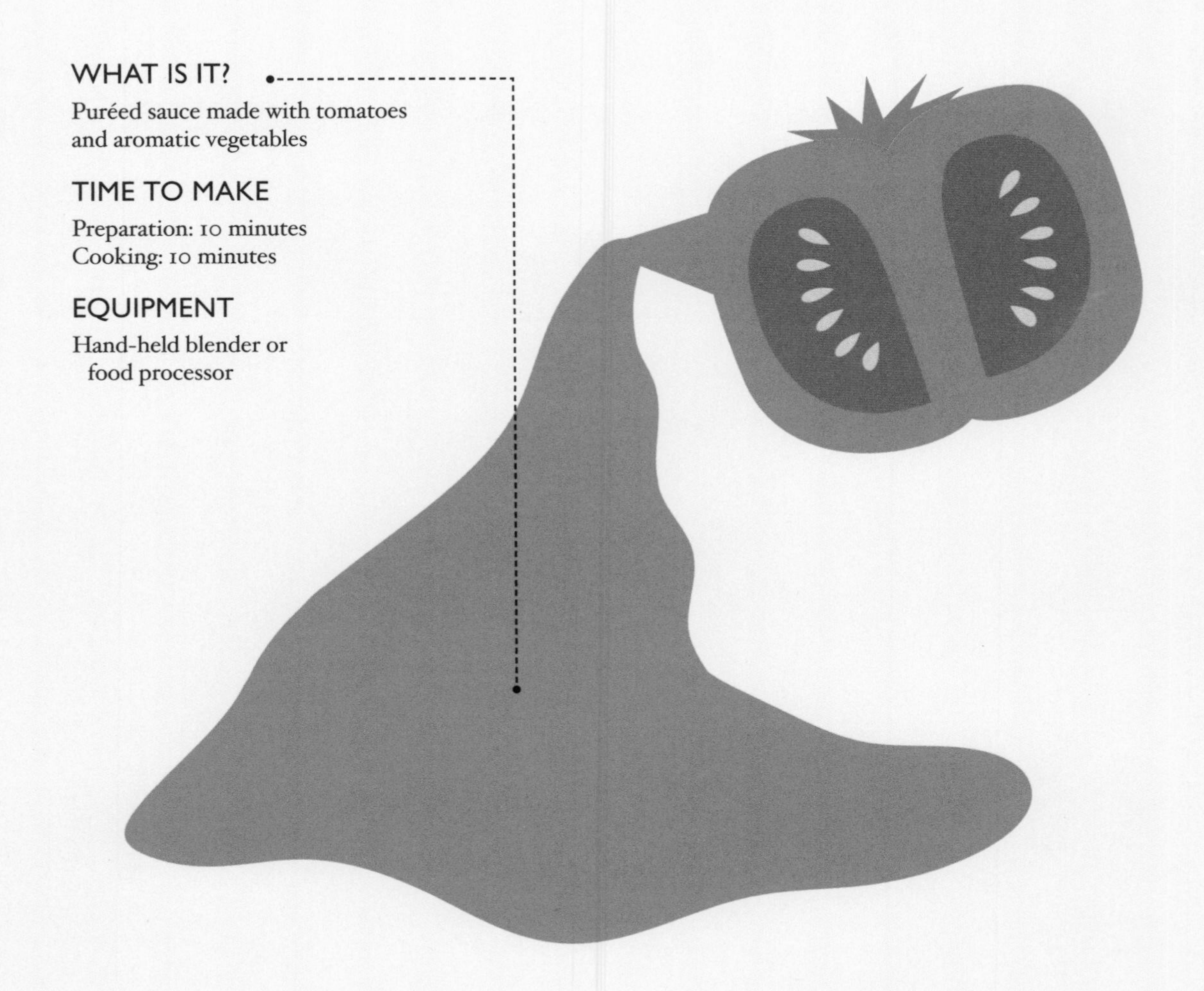

USES
Accompaniment for pasta, gnocchi, beans, lentils

VARIATIONS
Traditional tomato sauce made with a blond roux
Portuguese sauce
Provençal sauce

DERIVATIVES
Bolognese sauce

TECHNIQUES TO MASTER
Crushing garlic (page 280)
Mincing (page 280)
Sweating (page 282)

IT'S READY . . .
When the sauce is reduced and shiny.

STORAGE
2 days in the refrigerator or 3 months in the freezer.

WHY DOES THE COOKED SAUCE TAKE ON A SWEET TASTE?
During cooking, the water in the sauce evaporates, causing it to become concentrated. The sweet flavor becomes stronger during cooking because the sugars are also concentrated.

MAKES ABOUT 3½ CUPS

TOMATO SAUCE

1 garlic clove
1 medium onion
2 tablespoons butter
one 28-oz can chopped tomatoes
1 teaspoon sugar
2 tablespoons olive oil

AROMATICS

½ teaspoon dried oregano

SEASONING

½ teaspoon fine salt
¼ teaspoon freshly ground black pepper

1 Peel, de-germ, and crush the garlic. Peel and mince the onion. Melt the butter in a medium saucepan over medium heat. Add the onion, salt, and the oregano, crushed between your fingers. Sweat the onion until it begins to brown.

2 Add the crushed garlic and cook until it becomes aromatic (about 30 seconds). Add the tomatoes and sugar. Bring to a boil, then simmer for about 10 minutes, until it thickens.

3 Remove from the heat and add the olive oil and pepper. Purée with a hand-held blender or in a food processor, then adjust the seasoning if needed.

MAYONNAISE

Understand

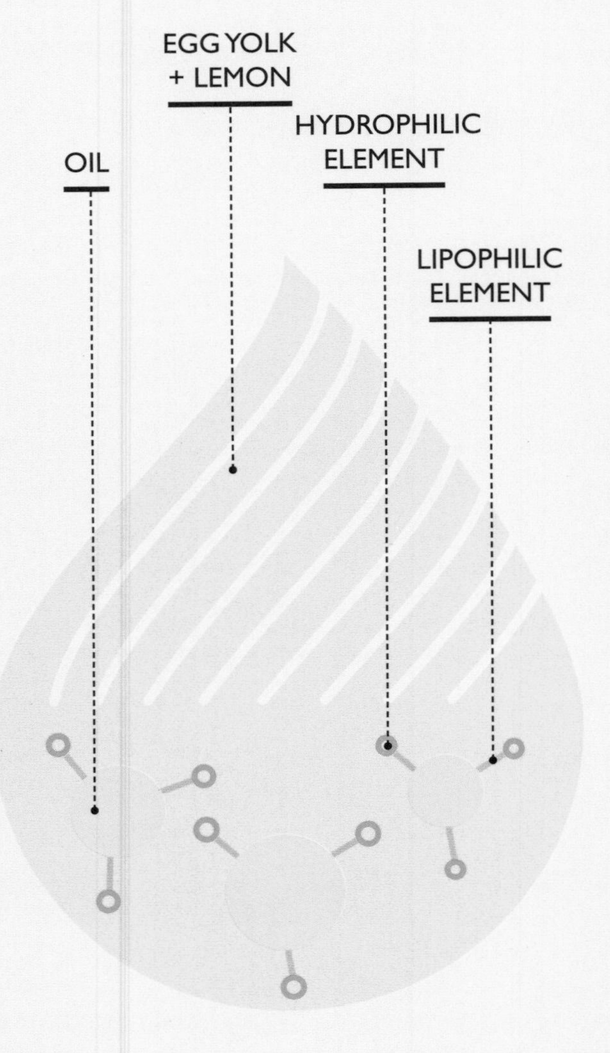

WHAT IS IT?

A cold emulsion of oil in egg yolk and lemon juice

TIME TO MAKE

Preparation: 10 minutes

EQUIPMENT

Whisk
Round- or flat-bottomed bowl
Electric mixer or food processor (optional)

USES

Accompaniment for cold preparations (meat, fish, shellfish, eggs, vegetables)
Dressing a salad

DERIVATIVES

Tartar sauce (mayonnaise + capers + cornichons + parsley + chervil + tarragon)
Cocktail sauce (mayonnaise + ketchup + Cognac + Worcestershire sauce + Tabasco sauce)

TRICKY ASPECT

Incorporating the oil

TIP

Season the egg yolk first, to avoid traces of salt at the end.

IT'S READY . . .

When the mayonnaise is creamy and firm enough for the whisk to leave a trace.

STORAGE

No more than 1 day in the refrigerator, covered with plastic wrap.

WHAT IS AN EMULSION?

A mixture of two ingredients that in principle do not mix. In mayonnaise, we combine oil with the water contained in the egg yolk and lemon juice.

HOW DOES AN EMULSION FORM?

The proteins in the egg yolk play the role of a surfactant: consisting of a hydrophilic part (attracted by the water in the egg yolk and lemon juice) and a lipophilic part (attracted by the fat content of the oil). They stabilize the oil in the water to form an emulsion.

WHY ADD THE OIL GRADUALLY?

When we add the oil gradually, it forms droplets and is incorporated into the water rather than the other way round.

WHY DOES THE MAYONNAISE SOMETIMES BREAK?

It happens when the oil can't break into fine droplets because it is added too rapidly, the bowl is too big, or the whisking is ineffectual.

THE IMPORTANCE OF WHISKING

To form a properly stable mayonnaise, there must be enough droplets of oil to bind the mixture and allow the egg proteins to thicken it. The whisking must therefore be thorough: the oil must be broken up into fine droplets.

SALVAGING A BROKEN MAYONNAISE

If the mayonnaise is too firm (using an electric mixer at too high a speed), thin it down by mixing in a little water.
If the ingredients are too cold, add a few drops of warm water.
If there's too much oil compared to egg yolk, add another egg yolk.

Learn

MAKES 1 CUP

1 tablespoon water
1 tablespoon lemon juice
½ teaspoon fine salt
¼ teaspoon freshly ground black pepper
1 egg yolk
¾ cup sunflower or peanut oil

1 Whisk the water, lemon juice, salt, pepper, and egg yolk in a round- or flat-bottomed bowl for 1 minute.

2 Pour in a few drops of the oil, whisking constantly.

3 Continue to add oil in a thin stream, still whisking constantly. After having added about a third of the oil (¼ cup), add the rest a little more quickly.

4 Whisk to thicken the mayonnaise. Cover with plastic wrap touching the surface of the mixture and refrigerate.

WITH AN ELECTRIC MIXER

Use a stand mixer with the whisk attachment, a hand-held mixer, or a food processor with the blade attachment to form the mayonnaise emulsion. Whisk by hand before adding the oil. Ensure that the blade or other attachment is in contact with the mixture from the beginning.

BEURRE BLANC

Understand

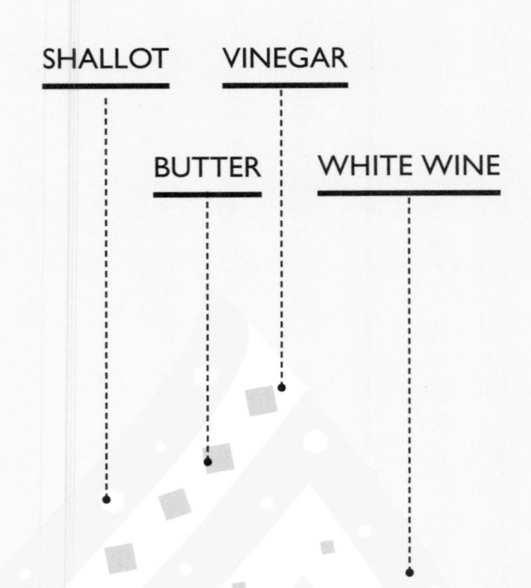

WHAT IS IT?

Hot emulsion of butter in a reduction of vinegar and white wine flavored with shallot

TIME TO MAKE

Preparation: 15 minutes
Cooking: 5 minutes

EQUIPMENT

Fine-mesh sieve

USES

Accompaniment for broiled or poached fish

VARIATION

Beurre nantais: beurre blanc with shallots (not strained)

TRICKY ASPECTS

The incorporation of the cold pieces of butter, cooking the butter gently

TECHNIQUES TO MASTER

Pushing through a sieve (page 281)
Straining through a sieve (page 281)
Reducing (page 283)
Finely chopping (page 280)

IT'S READY . . .

When the sauce is smooth and thick, but still fluid.

TIP

To help the emulsion form, add 1 tablespoon crème fraîche or heavy cream after reducing the white wine and vinegar, then reduce once more.

STORAGE

Use quickly. Cover and keep warm (over very low heat, at no more than 120°F) until using.

WHAT HAPPENS WHEN WE INCORPORATE THE BUTTER?

Mixing fats into the vinegar and wine base creates an oil-in-water emulsion: the butter is incorporated into the vinegar and warm wine base in the form of droplets. This emulsion has a different texture from a classic butter sauce: beurre blanc is "half-hard, half-melted."

WHY REDUCE THE VINEGAR AND WINE MIXTURE?

If the base is too liquid, the sauce will be too thin.

WHY ADD THE BUTTER GRADUALLY?

If it is added too quickly, the oil-in-water emulsion risks becoming a water-in-oil emulsion and the sauce may break.

WHY MUST WE USE BEURRE BLANC IMMEDIATELY?

Beurre blanc is an unstable emulsion. If it is reheated, it may destabilize and break.

Learn

MAKES ABOUT 1 CUP

1 small shallot
4 tablespoons white wine (preferably a Muscadet)
4 tablespoons white wine vinegar or sherry vinegar
18 tablespoons cold butter, cut into large dice

1 Peel and mince the shallot. Put it in a medium saucepan with the white wine and vinegar.

2 Reduce uncovered until only 1 tablespoon of liquid remains, 2–3 minutes.

3 Press the mixture through a fine-mesh sieve and return to the saucepan.

4 Over medium heat, add one or two pieces of the butter and swirl the saucepan to move the butter around, or whisk it, until the butter is almost melted.

5 Add another one or two pieces of butter and let it melt while whisking. Continue in this way until all the butter has been incorporated.

HOLLANDAISE SAUCE

Understand

WHAT IS IT?
Hot emulsion of butter in a sabayon (egg yolks + water), with lemon juice added

TIME TO MAKE
Preparation: 15 minutes

EQUIPMENT
Saucepan
Whisk
Thermometer

USES
Accompaniment for fish, eggs (Eggs Benedict), and poached vegetables

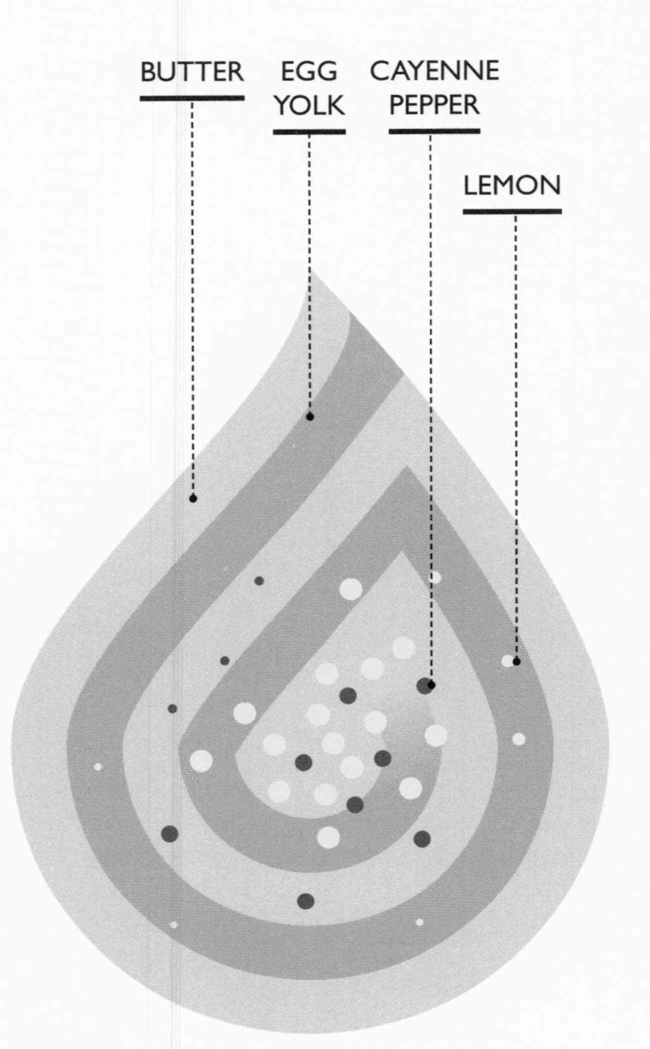

DERIVATIVES
Mousseline sauce (hollandaise sauce + whipped cream)
Maltese sauce (hollandaise sauce + orange zest and juice)
Mustard sauce (hollandaise sauce + mustard)

TRICKY ASPECT
Making the sabayon

IT'S READY . . .
When the sauce resembles a runny mayonnaise

STORAGE
No more than 1 hour, covered. Reheat over very low heat while whisking.

WHY ADD THE BUTTER GRADUALLY?
To favor the formation of a stable emulsion with small drops of fat that link easily, thus making a hollandaise sauce that doesn't break.

WHY MUST THE SABAYON NOT GO ABOVE 140°F?
The sabayon is made of eggs. The eggs contain proteins that coagulate above 140°F. The sauce will take on a grainy texture if it is heated above that temperature.

WHY ADD THE CLARIFIED BUTTER WHEN LUKEWARM?
If the butter is cold, the emulsion won't form easily. If the butter is too hot, the egg proteins will coagulate.

WHY DOES THE SAUCE SOMETIMES BREAK?
Either because of excessive coagulation of the egg yolks (cooking temperature too high) or because the water-fat emulsion breaks down.

SALVAGING A BROKEN SAUCE
If the sauce is too thick, loosen it with a little cold water. If the sauce breaks from the beginning, remix it with a little warm water and incorporate the butter slowly.

Learn

MAKES ABOUT 1½ CUPS

SAUCE

9 oz (1 recipe) clarified butter (page 51)
½ lemon
4 egg yolks
1 tablespoon water

SEASONING

1 teaspoon fine salt
pinch of cayenne pepper

1 Keep the clarified butter lukewarm (about 100°F) in a hot water bath. Juice the lemon half into a bowl.

2 Off the heat, quickly whisk together the egg yolks with the water and salt in a saucepan to form an emulsion. Set over low heat and whisk constantly to whip up the sabayon. The sabayon is ready when it is creamy and thick and the bottom of the pan is visible after each pass of the whisk (about 140°F).

3 Let it cool slightly. Remove the sauce from the heat, and gradually add the lukewarm clarified butter while whisking constantly (as for a mayonnaise).

4 Add the lemon juice and cayenne pepper while still whisking. Taste and adjust the seasoning as needed.

BÉARNAISE SAUCE

Understand

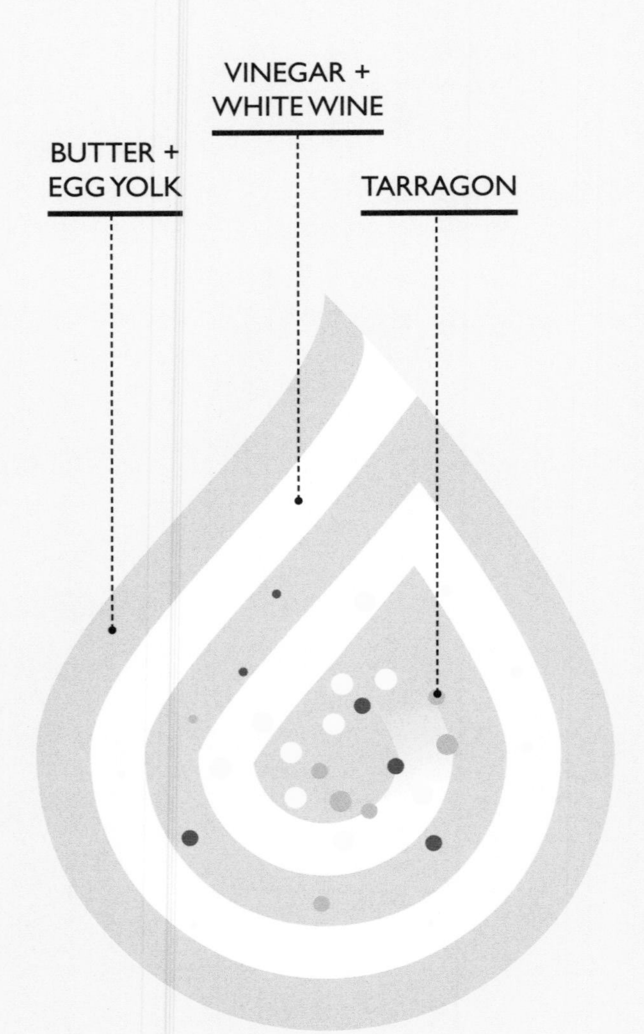

WHAT IS IT?

Hot emulsion of butter and egg yolk in a reduction of vinegar and white wine (flavored with shallots, chervil, and tarragon), with added chopped chervil and tarragon

TIME TO MAKE

Preparation: 25 minutes

EQUIPMENT

Whisk
Small saucepan

USES

Accompaniment for meats and broiled fish

VARIATIONS

Paloise sauce (replace the tarragon with mint)
Choron sauce (replace the tarragon and the chervil with tomato paste)

TRICKY ASPECT

Making the hot sabayon (adding the egg yolks to the reduction)

TECHNIQUES TO MASTER

Finely chopping (page 280)
Mincing (page 280)
Crushing spices (page 280)
Reducing a sauce (page 283)

IT'S READY . . .

When the sauce is creamy and light.

TIP

Use a small saucepan, otherwise the egg yolks will coagulate too quickly without gaining in volume.

STORAGE

No more than 1 hour, covered. Reheat over very low heat while whisking.

WHY ADD THE BUTTER GRADUALLY?

Béarnaise sauce resembles a mayonnaise made with butter rather than oil. By adding the butter a little at a time and whisking constantly, small fat bubbles form that contain egg (the proteins that stabilize the emulsion) and water (from the vinegar and wine). If we add the butter too quickly, the fat bubbles won't form and the emulsion will be reversed—that is, bubbles of water will form in the butter.

SALVAGING A BROKEN SAUCE

If the sauce is too thick, loosen it with a little cold water. If the sauce breaks from the beginning, remix it with a little warm water and incorporate the butter slowly.

Learn

MAKES ABOUT 1½ CUPS

BÉARNAISE SAUCE

1¼ cups (1 recipe) clarified butter (page 51)
3 tarragon sprigs
4 chervil sprigs
2 small shallots
2½ tablespoons white wine
2½ tablespoons red wine vinegar
4 egg yolks

SEASONING

1 teaspoon black peppercorns
½ teaspoon fine salt

1 Keep the clarified butter lukewarm (about 100°F) in a hot water bath. Wash, dry, pick, and finely chop the tarragon and chervil leaves. Peel and mince the shallots. Crush the peppercorns.

2 In a small saucepan, bring the white wine and vinegar to a boil with half the tarragon and chervil, the shallots, and the crushed peppercorns. Reduce the mixture by simmering for 2–3 minutes, until only ¼ cup of liquid remains. Let it cool.

3 Off the heat, quickly whisk together the egg yolks with the reduction and salt in a small saucepan to form an emulsion. Set over low heat and whisk constantly to whip up the sabayon. The sabayon is ready when it is creamy and thick and the bottom of the pan is visible after each pass of the whisk.

4 Let it cool slightly. Remove the sauce from the heat, and gradually add the lukewarm clarified butter while whisking constantly.

5 Stir in the remaining chopped herbs, then taste and adjust the seasoning if necessary.

AROMATICS

Understand

BOUQUET GARNI

WHAT IS IT?

Mixture of herbs tied together, used to flavor a liquid preparation (broth, stew, etc.)

EQUIPMENT

Kitchen string

USES

Aromatic base for stocks, sauces, meats, offal, and stuffed poultry
Cooking dried legumes

VARIATIONS

Bouquet garni for white stock: white part of a leek, thyme, bay leaf, and parsley stalks

INSTRUCTIONS FOR 1½–2 QUARTS WATER

10 parsley stems
2 thyme sprigs
1 bay leaf

Wash all of the ingredients. Group them into a bouquet. Hold it together firmly, then wind string around it two or three times high up (leaving about 8 inches of string free), then wind it around the bottom of the bouquet. Wind it around the middle and tie in a knot (this technique stops the bouquet from falling apart during cooking).

MIREPOIX

WHAT IS IT?

Aromatic base consisting of raw carrots and onions, cut into ⅜-inch pieces (short cooking time) or ⅝-inch pieces (long cooking time). The mirepoix is often retained as part of the dish

USES

Sauce bases and sauces (beef bourguignon)
Cooking dried legumes (purées and soups)

VARIATIONS

Traditional mirepoix: incorporates an equal weight of finely diced bacon.
Matignon: minced onions and carrots served as a garnish.

INSTRUCTIONS

Equal quantities of carrot and onion

Peel the carrot and the onion. Cut the carrot into 2½-inch lengths. Cut them into even lengthwise slices ⅜ inch thick. Put the slices on top of each other, then cut into even batons ⅜ inch thick. Bring the batons together, then cut them into ⅜-inch cubes. Cut the onion in half lengthwise. Lay the halves flat then slice them lengthwise every ⅜ inch, stopping before the root end. Cut crosswise into ⅜-inch dice.

Learn

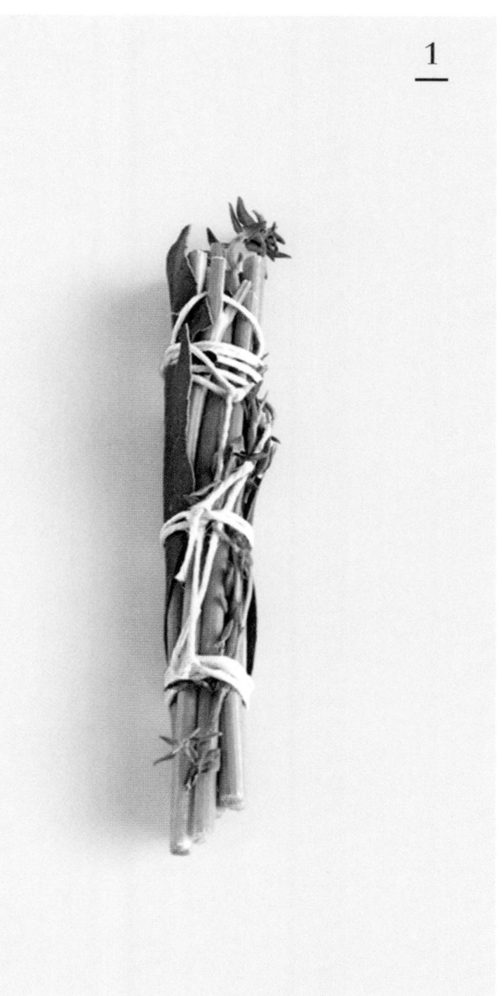

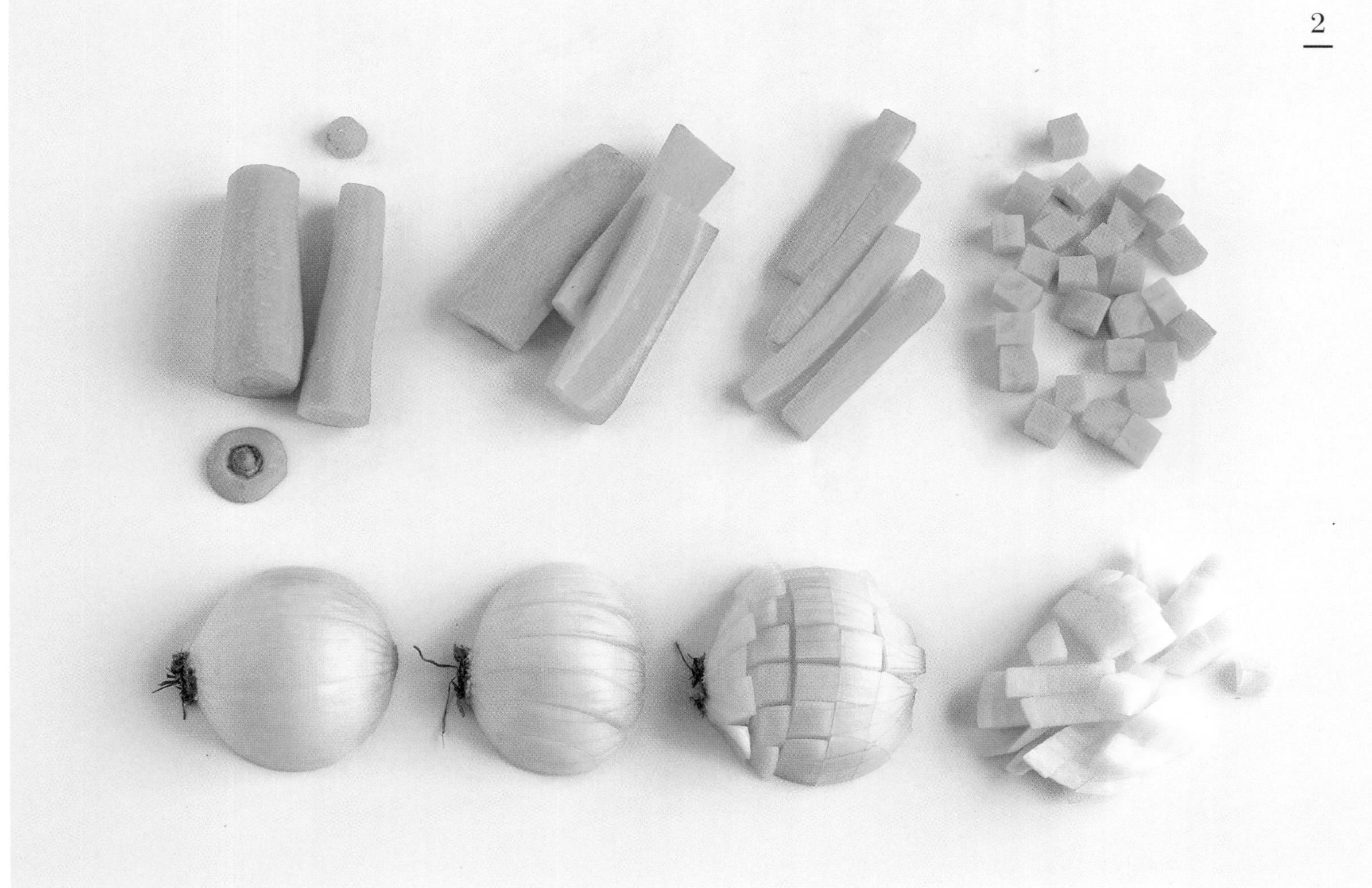

CUTTING VEGETABLES

Understand

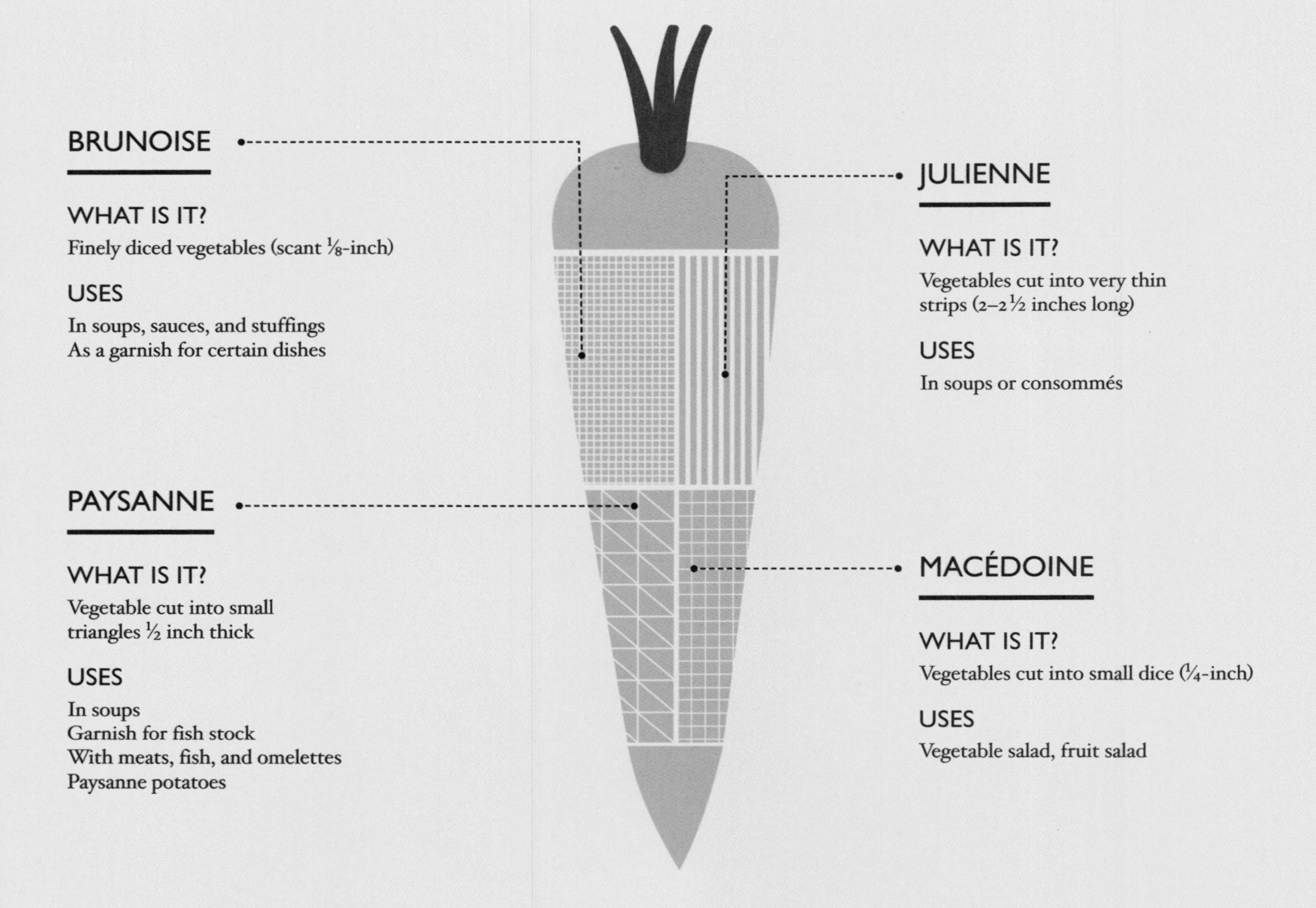

WHICH CUT FOR WHICH USE?

It all depends on the role of the vegetable in the dish. The finer a vegetable is cut, the faster it cooks, the more it diffuses its flavor, and the more it breaks up and thickens the mixture.

EQUIPMENT

Chef's knife
Mandoline (optional)

1 MACÉDOINE

Cut the vegetable into 2½–2¾-inch lengths. Cut a thin lengthwise slice off one side of each piece to stabilize it if needed.

Cut the lengths into even 1½-inch-thick slices, then 1½-inch-long batons, then ¼-inch dice.

2 JULIENNE

Cut the vegetable into 2½-inch lengths. Cut a thin lengthwise slice off one side of each piece to stabilize it. Slice them thinly lengthwise.

Put small groups of the slices on top of each other, then cut them lengthwise into very thin strips.

3 BRUNOISE

Cut the vegetable into 2½–2¾-inch lengths. Cut a thin lengthwise slice off one side of each piece to stabilize them.

Cut the lengths into even ⅛-inch-thick slices (or use a mandoline). Pile up a few slices then cut them into even ⅛-inch-wide batons.

Bring together small groups of batons, piling them up, then cut them into even scant ⅛-inch dice.

4 PAYSANNE

Cut the vegetable in half lengthwise, then in half lengthwise again.

Cut crosswise into ½-inch-thick slices.

TURNING VEGETABLES

Understand

TURNED ARTICHOKE

WHAT IS IT?
Artichoke trimmed of its darker and tougher leaves to reveal the more tender and edible parts of the artichoke

EQUIPMENT
Paring knife

USES
Artichoke (cooked)

TIP
Remove the choke after cooking.

TURNED CARROT

WHAT IS IT?
Small, even, elongated ovals of carrot

EQUIPMENT
Chef's or paring knife

USES
Turned carrots ¾–1 inch long: small vegetable presentation called *aux primeurs*
Turned carrots 1¼–1½ inches long: garnish called *aux primeurs mélangés*
Turned carrots 1½–2 inches long: *bouquetière* of vegetables (garnish of mixed vegetables)
Turned carrots 2–2½ inches long: vegetables for pot-au-feu and poule au pot (chicken in a pot)

WHY MAKE TURNED VEGETABLES?

Turned carrots, turnips, or potatoes have an aesthetic purpose: the vegetables are even and harmonious. In addition, sauces more evenly coat turned vegetables.

TURNING POIVRADE ARTICHOKES

These are small purple Provençal artichokes. Remove the outermost leaves by hand. Lightly peel the parts exposed by removing the leaves. Rub with lemon. Retain 1¼–1½ inches of the stalk. Lightly peel the stalk and rub it with lemon. Cut the leaves down to the level of the heart, so that only the tender part remains.

TIP
Baby artichokes are a good substitute for poivrade artichokes.

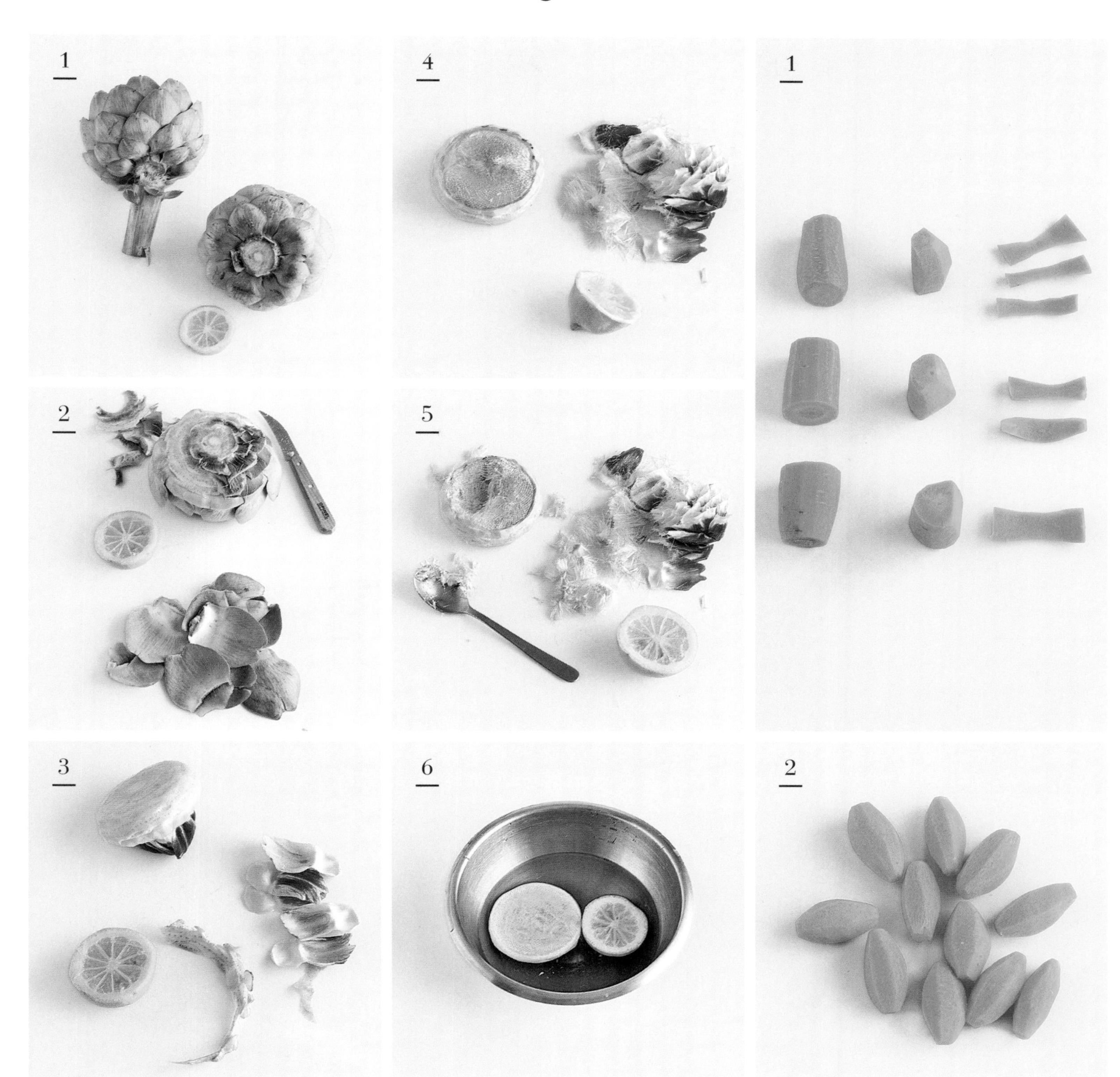

ARTICHOKE

1 Fill a bowl with cold water and the juice of half a lemon.

2 Snap off the fibrous stalk and trim it flat. Rub the other lemon half over the cut part. Progressively remove the leaves at the base as you turn the artichoke.

3 Whenever a significant amount of artichoke flesh is exposed, rub the cut surface with the lemon half to prevent it from browning. Continue to turn the artichoke and rub it regularly with lemon.

4 Remove all the leaves until you reach the choke. Trim down to the heart by removing any part that is too green, while giving the heart a round and even shape.

5 Remove the choke using a spoon.

6 Keep the artichoke heart in the cold lemon water until ready to cook.

CARROT

1 Cut the carrot into even lengths. Depending on the diameter of the carrot, leave the lengths as they are or cut in two, three, or four pieces lengthwise.

2 Using a paring knife, trim each length to give it an even football shape: hold the length in your left hand (if you're right-handed), with your right thumb resting against the end of the carrot piece, and the other four fingers holding the knife. The trimmings should be thick at the top and bottom, and very thin at the center.

COMPOUND BUTTERS

Understand

ESCARGOT BUTTER

WHAT IS IT?
Compound butter made by mixing cold butter with raw ingredients: garlic, parsley, shallot, and white breadcrumbs

EQUIPMENT
Tamis

USES
Served with snails, clams, and mussels

MAÎTRE D'HÔTEL BUTTER

WHAT IS IT?
Compound butter made by mixing cold butter with fresh lemon juice and parsley

USES
Cold: accompaniment for meats and broiled fish
Hot: to finish certain sauces

DERIVATIVES
Hôtelier butter (maître d'hôtel butter + duxelles; page 42)
Colbert butter (maître d'hôtel butter + meat glaze + tarragon)

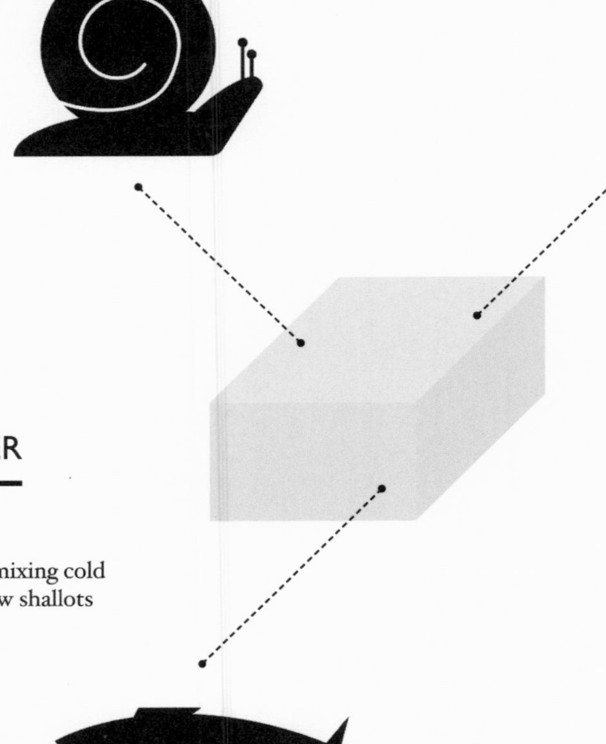

ANCHOVY BUTTER

WHAT IS IT?
Compound butter made by mixing cold butter with anchovies and raw shallots

USES
Accompaniment for fish

SOFTENING BUTTER

To make a compound butter, you will need to bring your butter to the right temperature. If the butter is too cold, it will be hard to incorporate other ingredients. If the butter is too warm, it will not have a creamy, spreadable texture. Keep these temperature ranges in mind when creating your compound butter:
- At 39°F, 70 percent of butter's fat content is in solid form.
- At 68°F, 20 percent of butter's fat content is in solid form; this is the perfect temperature to mix in other ingredients.
- At 86°F, 10 percent of butter's fat content is in solid form.

TECHNIQUES TO MASTER

Finely chopping (page 280)
Mincing (page 280)
Crushing garlic (page 280)

TIP

To prevent the roll of butter from being squashed, plunge it into ice water until firm before putting it in the refrigerator.

STORAGE

Softened butter: 2 hours at room temperature.
Rolled butter: 3 days in the refrigerator.

OTHER COMPOUND BUTTERS

Cold compound butters with raw ingredients: smoked fish butter, cheese butter
Cold compound butter with cooked ingredients: crayfish butter
Hot compound butter: beurre rouge (red wine butter)

Learn

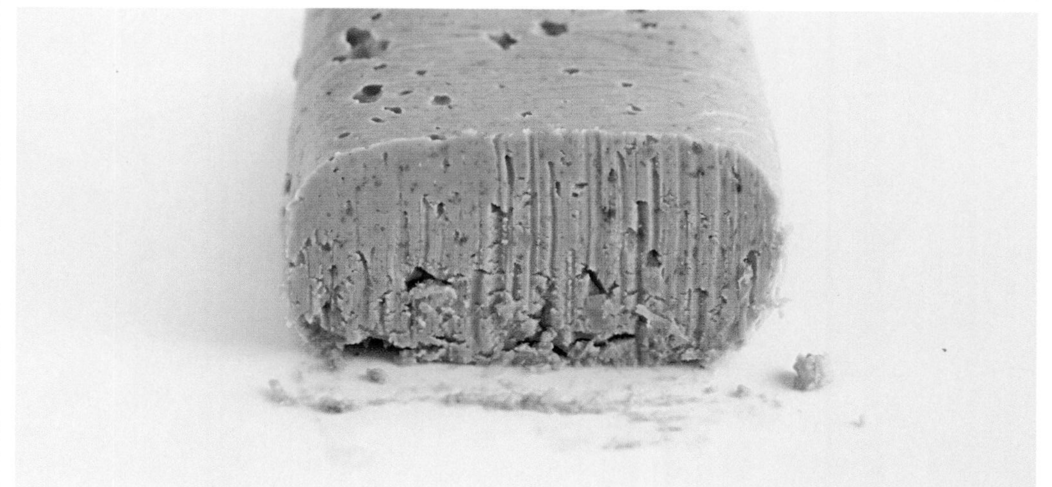

ESCARGOT BUTTER (¾ CUP)

1 shallot
1 small bunch Italian parsley
2 garlic cloves
1 slice day-old white bread (crusts removed)
11 tablespoons softened butter
½ teaspoon fine salt
freshly ground black pepper (8 turns)

1 Peel and mince the shallot. Wash, dry, pick, and finely chop the parsley leaves. Peel, de-germ, crush, and chop the garlic cloves. Crumble the bread and push it through a tamis (a flat-bottomed sieve). Combine everything in a large mixing bowl.

2 Using a silicone spatula that's not too flexible, add the butter and mix while crushing the ingredients into the butter. Season with the salt and pepper and mix again. Form a line of butter in the middle of a piece of plastic wrap, wrap it up, and seal the ends well to make a roll. Refrigerate, then cut into slices for each use.

MAÎTRE D'HÔTEL BUTTER (½ CUP)

½ small bunch Italian parsley
1 teaspoon fresh lemon juice
8 tablespoons softened butter
½ teaspoon fine salt
freshly ground black pepper (8 turns)

1 Wash, dry, pick, and finely chop the parsley leaves. Combine the parsley and lemon juice in a large mixing bowl.

2 Follow the second step for escargot butter.

ANCHOVY BUTTER (1½ CUP)

1 medium shallot
three 2 oz cans anchovies in oil, drained
1 tablespoon fresh lemon juice
11 tablespoons softened butter, cut into pieces
¼ cup almond meal

1 Peel the shallot and cut into quarters. In a food processor with the blade attachment, combine the anchovies, shallot, and lemon juice.

2 Pulse several times to obtain a purée. Add the butter. Continue to pulse until the mixture is creamy. Add the almond meal and pulse one last time to blend.

DUXELLES

Understand

WHAT IS IT?
Low-fat stuffing mixture made from chopped mushrooms

TIME TO MAKE
Preparation: 15 minutes

EQUIPMENT
Chef's knife
Medium saucepan or skillet

USES
Stuffed vegetables or poultry (page 218)
Poultry meatloaf

VARIATION
Duxelles for stuffing (duxelles + cream)

TRICKY ASPECT
Cooking without over-browning

TECHNIQUES TO MASTER
Finely chopping (page 280)
Mincing (page 280)
Sweating (page 282)

IT'S READY . . .
When the mixture is compact and light brown.

TIPS
- If you're not going to cook the chopped mushrooms right away, cover them with a paper towel that has been soaked in the juice of half a lemon to prevent them from oxidizing—the paper should be touching.
- When cooking, use a saucepan large enough to facilitate rapid evaporation of the water from the mushrooms.

STORAGE
2 days in the refrigerator, covered with plastic wrap.

WHY DO CHOPPED MUSHROOMS GO BROWN?
When we cut mushrooms, we cut their cells. The contents of these cells leak out and react with each other or with oxygen in the air. These interactions cause browning. We recommend using a very sharp chef's knife: the cuts will be cleaner, and this will reduce the crushing of the cells and thus the leakage of contents susceptible to oxidation.

WHY MUST THE MIXTURE BE DRIED?
So that the mixture is not soggy and holds together.

Learn

MAKES 1 CUP

DUXELLES

1 Italian parsley sprig
2 small shallots
2 tablespoons butter
2 cups white button mushrooms

SEASONING

¼ teaspoon fine salt
freshly ground black pepper (3 turns)

1 Wash, dry, pick, and finely chop the parsley leaves. Peel and finely chop the shallots. Sweat the shallots in the butter in a medium skillet over medium heat for 2 minutes, stirring from time to time. Remove from the heat.

2 Remove the mushroom stems, then peel the caps and, using a chef's knife, cut them in thin slices in one direction then the other, to obtain very small dice.

3 Add the mushrooms to the pan and cook for about 5 minutes over medium heat, stirring constantly until they are dry.

4 Add the parsley and stir well. Season with salt and pepper.

PIE DOUGH
(PÂTE BRISÉE)

Understand

WHAT IS IT?
A basic pastry dough made by rubbing butter into flour

TIME TO MAKE
Preparation: 15 minutes
Refrigeration:
1 hour 20 minutes

EQUIPMENT
Mixing bowl

USES
Base for tarts, quiches, or pies
Cooked after filling, or baked blind

VARIATION
Sweet pie crust: 1 teaspoon sugar for each ⅔ cup flour (pastry very lightly sweetened compared with pâte sucrée)

DERIVATIVES
Pâte sucrée (pâte brisée + sugar)
Pâte sablée (pâte sucrée + whole eggs)

TRICKY ASPECTS
- Rubbing in the butter without heating it up too much
- Not overworking the pastry

TECHNIQUES TO MASTER
Rubbing in butter (page 281)

IT'S READY . . .
When the pastry ball has a smooth, uniform consistency, without being elastic, and is still cold.

WHY AVOID OVERWORKING THE PASTRY?
When we knead pastry, a network of proteins develops: the gluten network. It lends elasticity to the pastry, which makes it difficult to roll out. It springs back like elastic when you pull on it.

WHY CHILL THE PASTRY?
To allow the butter to harden. During cooking, it will melt and lend softness to the pastry while minimizing shrinkage.

TIP
Rub the butter in with your hands a little bit above the bowl to keep the pastry from warming up too much.

STORAGE
2 days in the refrigerator. Let it warm up at room temperature for 15–45 minutes before rolling out.

Learn

MAKES 1 CRUST

1 cup plus 2 tablespoons all-purpose flour, plus extra for dusting
¾ teaspoon fine salt
6 tablespoons cold butter, cut into small dice
1 egg yolk
¼ cup water

1 Mix the flour and salt in a large mixing bowl.

2 Add the butter and rub it into the flour.

3 Stop when the flour has taken on an ivory color and the butter pieces are the size of peas.

4 Make a small well in the center of the mixture and pour in the egg yolk and water. Bring the mixture together using a fork until there is no more dry flour.

5 Turn the pastry out onto a lightly floured work surface. Knead until supple and no longer sticky.

6 Wrap the kneaded dough in plastic wrap, refrigerate, and let the dough rest for at least 1 hour, for best results.

SHAPING

Roll out the pastry and fit it into the pie plate. Refrigerate for at least 20 minutes to minimize shrinkage during cooking.

ROUGH PUFF PASTRY

Understand

WHAT IS IT?
A quick variation on the classic recipe: layered pastry made with flour, water, salt, and small pieces of butter

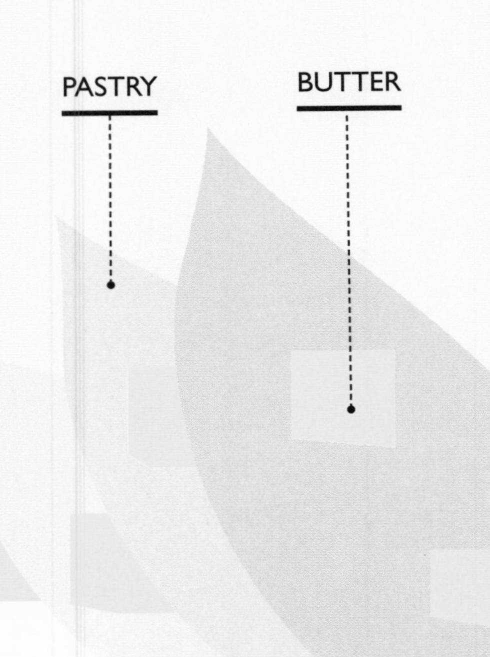

TIME TO MAKE
Preparation: 20 minutes
Refrigeration: 1 hour

EQUIPMENT
Food processor with blade attachment
Rolling pin

USES
Hot hors d'œuvre (cheese straws, small meat pies, vol-au-vents, etc.)
Coulibiac (page 174)
Beef Wellington (page 232)

VARIATION
Classic puff pastry: the butter is incorporated into the pastry through successive foldings and rest periods

TRICKY ASPECT
The temperature of the room: it should be cool (no more than 68°F)

IT'S READY . . .
When it starts to pull together in the food processor.

HOW DOES THE FLAKINESS HAPPEN?
This recipe produces puff pastry much more quickly than the traditional puff pastry recipe. Because it comes together so quickly, the very cold butter doesn't have time to melt as the pastry is worked, so it stays in small pieces. These specks of butter, as well as the final folding step, give the pastry its flakiness.

NOTE
Some butters, particularly organic butters, aren't hard enough—even when cold—for success with this recipe.

TIPS
- If the room is too warm (more than 68°F), refrigerate the flour before using.
- When buying the butter, press on it to ensure it is very hard.

STORAGE
2 days in the refrigerator or 3 months in the freezer, wrapped in plastic wrap. Thaw overnight in the refrigerator before using.

Learn

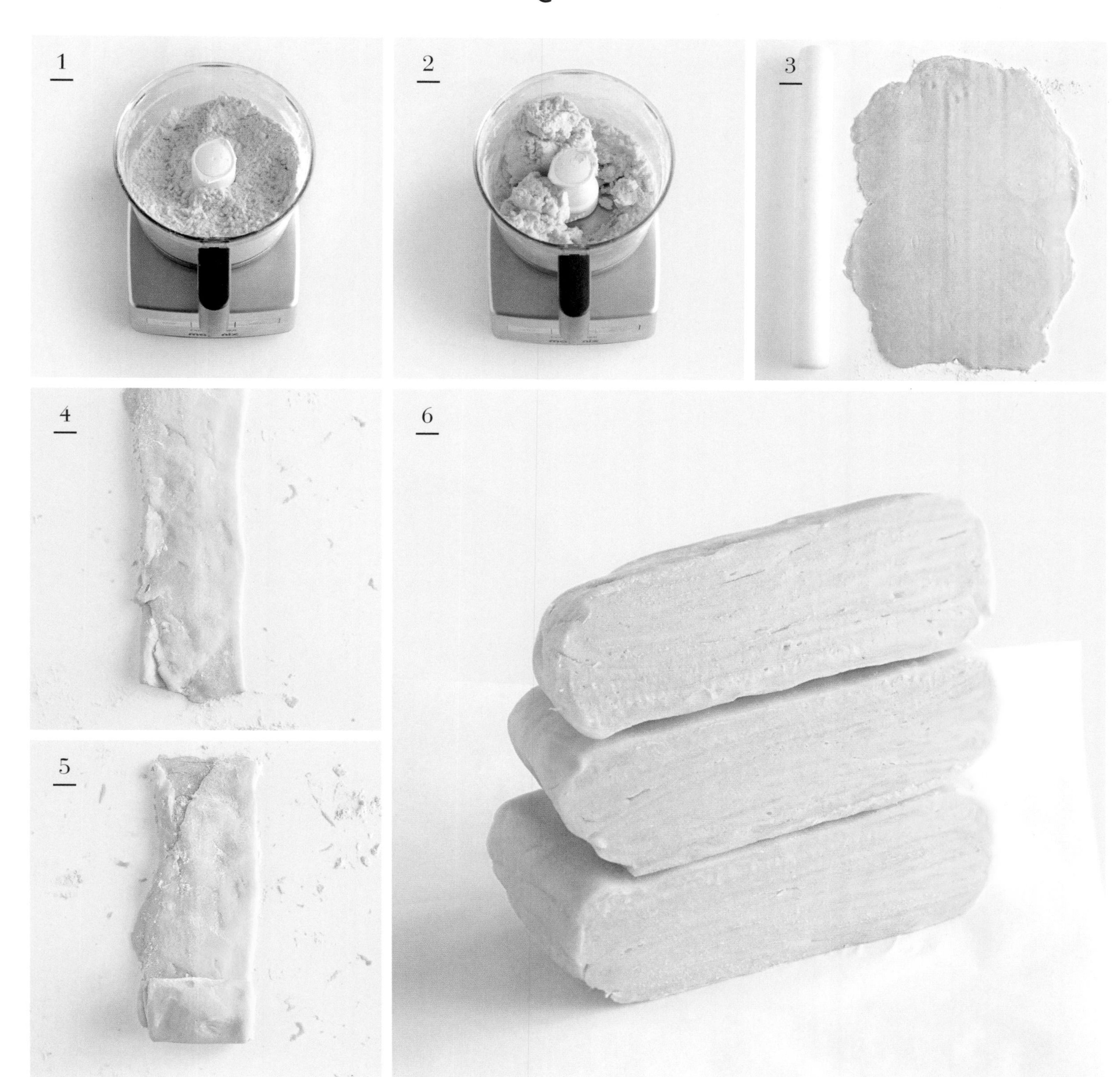

MAKES 1 LB 7 OZ

2 cups all-purpose flour, plus extra for dusting
20 tablespoons cold, very hard butter, cut into ⅜–⅝-inch dice
1 heaping teaspoon fine salt
6 tablespoons cold water

1 In a food processor, pulse the flour with 4 tablespoons of the butter for 1 second at a time, a dozen times, until the butter is absorbed. Add the rest of the butter, mixing a little with a spoon, then pulse once or twice to distribute the butter in the flour; it should still be in big pieces.

2 Dissolve the salt in the cold water, then pour it into the food processor. Pulse three or four times, until a dough just starts to form.

3 Turn the dough out onto a lightly floured work surface and press it into a rectangle. Roll it out to a rectangle about 12 inches × 18 inches. Regularly dust the pastry, work surface, and rolling pin with flour.

4 With a short side facing you, fold the upper third then the lower third toward the middle to obtain a rectangle of about 4 inches × 18 inches.

5 Roll the pastry up in a log, starting from one of the short sides. Tap the edges of this pastry packet to make a square shape. Wrap in plastic wrap and refrigerate for at least 1 hour, until the pastry is firm.

6 If you want to divide the pastry packet into pieces, cut it perpendicular to the direction of the coiled roll. Gently press each piece into a rectangle ¾–1¼ inches thick.

SALT

Understand

WHAT IS IT?

Mineral condiment composed of sodium chloride

FINE SALT

Small crystals. Use in both hot and cold dishes.
– Without additives: has a fresh, delicate taste, reminiscent of the ocean.
– With additives: "dry" and very smooth, it makes seasoning easy.
Role: seasoning evenly, before, during, and/or after cooking.

COARSE SEA SALT

– Gray (Atlantic) or white (Mediterranean), large crystals.
Role: seasoning cooking water, salt crusts, preserving.

FLEUR DE SEL

– White crystals that form at the surface of salt marshes.
Role: Used as a finishing salt for a plated dish to create contrasts in flavor and texture.

USES

Seasoning
Salt accentuates the flavors of a dish: it's a natural flavor enhancer.

Cooking
– Cooking in a salt crust: cooking a large item (fish, meat, vegetables) under an airtight layer of coarse sea salt in the oven (see opposite).
– Cooking in "half salt": used on raw fish with white, dense flesh (such as cod) to deeply season and firm up the flesh before cooking.

Preserving
Salt stops the growth of bacteria responsible for the deterioration of foods.

SHOULD YOU ADD SALT BEFORE OR AFTER COOKING?

Before cooking: in order to season completely or in a consistent fashion.
After cooking: for contrast.

Meats
Before cooking, to allow the formation of a "crust" that will add taste and texture.

Sauces, soups, stews
Throughout cooking. If the same quantity of salt is added at the end of cooking, the sauce will be less balanced and less complex, because the salt won't have the chance to be distributed throughout.

Fish
Just before cooking, to avoid "burning" the delicate flesh. For the same reason, avoid using coarse sea salt.

WHEN SHOULD YOU ADD PEPPER?

In contrast to salt, pepper should be added at the end of cooking. If it is added at the beginning, it can lose its piquant flavor.

SALTING WATER AND FAT

Salting cooking water
This allows ingredients to absorb seasonings. For pasta and other starchy ingredients: 1½ teaspoons per quart.
For green vegetables, potatoes: 1 tablespoon per quart.

Salting fat
Salt doesn't dissolve into fat. To salt fat, dissolve the salt first in a water-based ingredient (water, vinegar, lemon juice, etc.).

Cooking in a salt crust

CELERIAC IN A SALT CRUST

Celeriac cooked whole in the steam beneath an airtight layer of coarse sea salt, which renders it tasty and soft.

Preparation: 10 minutes
Cooking: 2 hours 30 minutes
Resting: 40 minutes
Equipment: Casserole or ovenproof saucepan

SERVES 4

1 large celeriac (2 lb), unpeeled
4 lb 6 oz coarse gray sea salt
4 tablespoons butter

1 Preheat the oven to 300°F. Wash the celeriac thoroughly, then dry it with a dish towel. Pour ¾–1¼ inches of salt into the bottom of a saucepan. Set the celeriac on the salt, then cover with the remaining salt. Bake for 2 hours 30 minutes. Leave the celeriac to cool inside the crust for 40 minutes.

2 Melt the butter in a saucepan. Break the crust and extract the celeriac. Cut it into four portions. Place each portion on a serving plate, then pour the melted butter on top.

WHAT HAPPENS UNDER THE CRUST?

The salt forms a barrier that allows the celeriac to cook in its own juices and absorb seasoning. At the same time, the salt absorbs the water on the surface of the celeriac. This mixture quickly reaches a higher temperature than the boiling point of water (212°F). The celeriac is well cooked on the surface, soft in the middle.

WITH OR WITHOUT EGG WHITE?

An egg white can give the crust a sturdier structure. The egg proteins coagulate and stiffen the crust. But if you support the crust with a rigid container, like a saucepan, and use a gray salt, which is wetter, the egg white isn't necessary.

FAT

Understand

WHAT IS IT?

Ingredients with a high fat content

FORMS

Oils (olive, peanut, sunflower, canola, etc.): fat of plant origin, 100 percent fat.
Butter (unsalted or lightly salted): fat of animal origin, 80 percent fat.
Cream: fat of animal origin: 30 percent fat.

ROLES

Butter
- Cooking: searing meat or fish, braising vegetables.
- Taste: depth, sweetness.
- Basting food with fat during cooking: concentrates flavors, cooks and colors evenly, gives body to a sauce.

Oil
- Cooking: frying, sautéing.
- Seasoning: flavors and adds smoothness at the end of preparation (a drizzle of olive oil).

USES

Butter
- Melting point (temperature at which it melts): between 86°F and 113°F.
- Toxic point (point at which some fats start to degrade to toxic compounds): 250°F.

For use at moderate heat.

Oil
- Smoke point of refined oils (cold-pressed): 400°F on average.
- For frying (which demands high temperatures).
- Smoke point of virgin oils (cold-pressed): 210–320°F.

Exception: extra virgin olive oil has the smoke point of refined oils.

WHAT IS THE SMOKE POINT?

The temperature at which the oil releases smoke and starts to become toxic.

WHY COOK IN OIL?

To achieve a good Maillard reaction (page 282) without burning the fat used (because oil can be used at higher temperatures). The fat itself doesn't pass its taste on to the food (except in dishes cooked at low temperature).

WHY COOK IN BUTTER?

Butter passes on its flavor to the food.

WHY COOK IN BUTTER + OIL?

Start cooking in oil for a Maillard reaction, then finish in butter for its taste. In addition, by mixing butter with oil, we modify its melting behavior. The oil allows us to cook with butter at a higher temperature without it burning.

WHY DOES FAT MEAN FLAVOR?

Because flavors dissolve into the fat, this amplifies the intensity of the taste of the dish.

CLARIFIED BUTTER

Understand

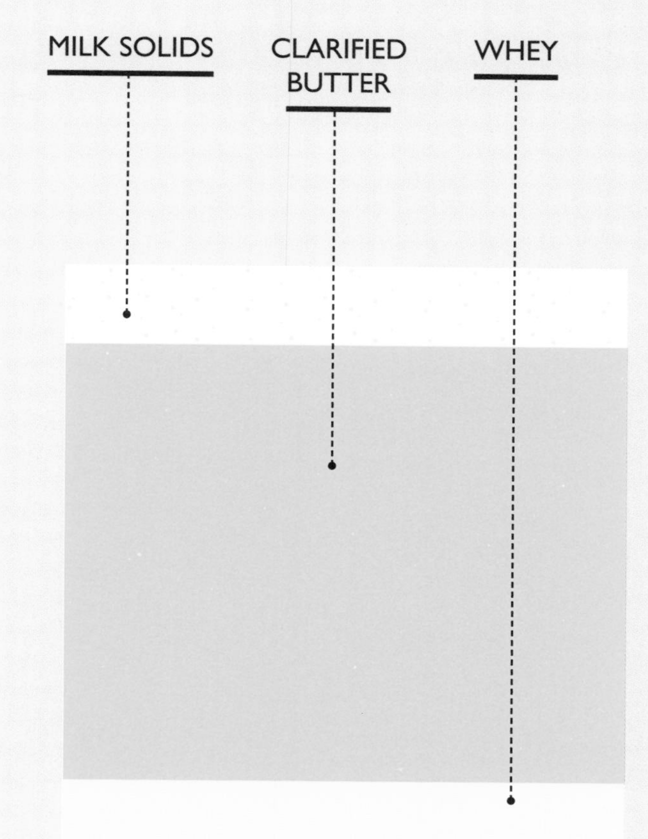

WHAT IS IT?

Melted butter with the whey and milk solids removed

TIME TO MAKE

Preparation: 15 minutes

EQUIPMENT

Fine-mesh sieve

STORAGE

Several weeks in the refrigerator in an airtight container.
Reheat over very low heat.

NOTES

- Butter loses 20–25 percent of its weight during the clarification process.
- Ghee: the Indian version of clarified butter.

FAST VARIATION

Melt the butter over medium heat. Pour it into a heatproof container and let it cool. Seal and refrigerate (or freeze) until the butter is set. Scrape the top to remove the foam. Press gently on the butter and let the whey underneath run out. Discard the whey. The clarified butter is all that remains.

MAKES 1¼ CUPS CLARIFIED BUTTER

1 Cut 24 tablespoons butter into cubes. Melt in a small saucepan over low heat without stirring.

2 After about 15 minutes, when the whey has separated to the bottom of the saucepan, skim off all the white foam that has risen to the surface.

3 Strain the butter through a fine-mesh sieve, taking care to leave behind all the whey at the bottom of the saucepan. You should have nothing but yellow fat. Use immediately or refrigerate.

WHAT HAPPENS WHEN THE BUTTER IS HEATED?

Butter is an emulsion with a fat content of 80 percent. The remaining 20 percent is made up of water, proteins, and lactose. When the butter is melted, the emulsion is destabilized: the fat content (clarified butter) rises to the top, while the water and proteins (the whey) are separated from the fat.

WHAT'S THE POINT?

When we remove the proteins from the butter, the temperature at which it first starts to smoke is higher (340°F) than for nonclarified butter (250°F) because it is the proteins that burn first. It can therefore be used for cooking at higher temperatures, and notably to replace oil for sautéing.

BEURRE FONDU

Understand

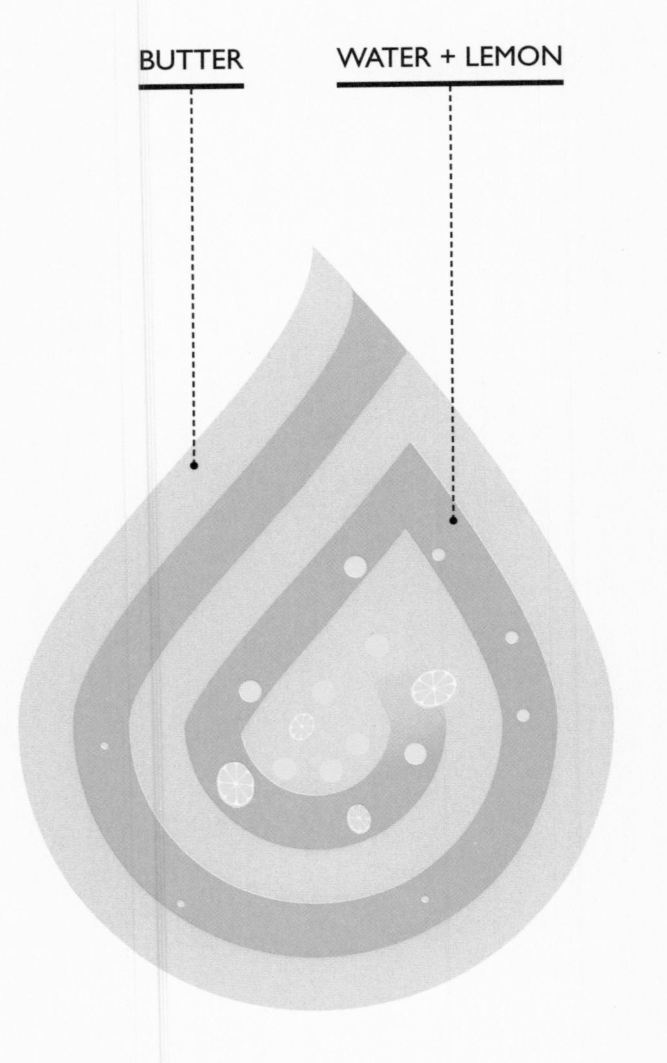

WHAT IS IT?

Butter emulsified with a lemon juice reduction

USE

Sauce for fish and shellfish

STORAGE

1–2 hours in a hot water bath over low heat.

MAKES 1 CUP BEURRE FONDU

EMULSFIED BUTTER

1½ tablespoons water
1½ tablespoons lemon juice
14 tablespoons cold butter, cut into large dice

SEASONING

½ teaspoon fine salt
pinch of cayenne pepper

1 Bring the water and lemon juice to a boil in a small saucepan. Let it reduce to three-quarters of its original volume, 30 seconds to 1 minute; 1 tablespoon of liquid should remain.

2 Add a cube of butter over medium heat and swirl the saucepan to move the butter around, or whisk it, until it is almost melted.

3 Add one or two cubes of butter and let them melt while swirling the pan or whisking.

4 When the butter is almost melted, add the other cubes until all the butter has been incorporated. Season with salt and cayenne pepper.

WHY START WITH A WATER + LEMON JUICE REDUCTION?

We add water to the lemon juice to soften the lemon flavor. This softened lemon mixture is reduced to limit the amount of water added to the final preparation (and therefore to stabilize the emulsion).

HOW DOES IT DIFFER FROM PLAIN MELTED BUTTER?

Emulsifying the butter with the lemon juice flavors the butter and gives it a thicker texture than simple melted butter.

BEURRE NOISETTE

Understand

WHAT IS IT?

Brown butter sauce: butter cooked until its color and taste are reminiscent of roasted hazelnuts

EQUIPMENT

Fine-mesh sieve

USES

Skate grenobloise (page 152)
Sole meunière (page 150)
Poached asparagus
Crepe batter (page 124)
Financiers

STORAGE

1–2 hours in a hot water bath over low heat.

WHAT HAPPENS WHEN THE BUTTER IS HEATED?

It develops brown, aromatic, and tasty molecules. Some caramelization reactions occur between the proteins and the lactose, adding caramel notes.

WHAT GIVES IT ITS "HAZELNUT" FLAVOR?

The proteins and the lactose in the butter react with each other to form the aromatic notes of roasted hazelnuts.

MAKES 11 TABLESPOONS

14 tablespoons butter

1 Cut the butter into large dice. Melt in a small saucepan over medium heat.

2 Scrape the bottom with a spatula from time to time to remove the residue at the bottom of the saucepan and watch its color.

3 When the residue turns brown, strain the butter through a fine-mesh sieve into a bowl to stop it cooking.

ACIDITY

Understand

WHAT IS IT?

Aromatic note that is a component of the balanced taste of a dish

ROLES

Freshness
The taste of a dish seems fresher with an acidic note.

Contrast
It contrasts with the sweetness of honey or the roundness of oil in a vinaigrette.

Flavor enhancement
Acidity (sourness) comes just after saltiness in the order we perceive each of the five tastes.

"Cooking"
Promotes the coagulation or setting of proteins and thus the "cooking" of a food (e.g., ceviche).

Storage
Pickling in acidic mixtures (e.g., pickled vegetables) reduces the development of bacteria. Acidity also prevents the oxidation of fruits and vegetables such as avocados, artichokes, bananas, Belgian endive, apples, etc.

FORMS

Vinegar (red wine, sherry, apple cider, etc.)
Lemon and lime juice
Other, sweeter citrus fruits (grapefruit, orange, citron, makrut lime, etc.)
Wines
Acidic dairy products: yogurt, crème fraîche, goat cheese, etc.
Pickled vegetables (capers, cornichons, etc.)
Mustards

WHY DOES FISH BROUGHT INTO CONTACT WITH LEMON JUICE SEEM COOKED?

The acidity in lemon juice promotes the coagulation or setting of the proteins, which gives the fish a "cooked" texture.

HOW DOES ACIDITY IMPROVE THE QUALITY OF A DISH?

Because acid lifts and balances a dish much like salt does.

WHEN SHOULD YOU ADD ACIDITY?

It can be incorporated at any time from the beginning to the end of preparation (like wine in a sauce, for example), but it is often added only at the end of cooking. For example: a drizzle of vinegar or squeeze of lemon juice added just before serving, to create contrast.

GASTRIQUE

Understand

WHAT IS IT?
A reduction of sugar and vinegar used as a base for sauces

TIME TO MAKE
Preparation: 5 minutes
Cooking: 5 minutes

IT'S READY . . .
When the liquid is thick and the color of caramel.

USES
Orange sauce
Sweet and sour sauce

DERIVATIVES
Glazes (reduced stocks)
Sauces

STORAGE
Use immediately.

WHY DOES THE SUGAR CRYSTALLIZE WHEN WE ADD THE VINEGAR?
Adding the vinegar at room temperature reduces the temperature of the caramel and makes it crystallize: it clumps together and returns to its crystal form. When the temperature of the mixture comes back up, the sugar dissolves once more.

MAKES 2 TABLESPOONS
3 tablespoons sugar
2 tablespoons sherry vinegar

1 Make a dry caramel: heat the sugar in a skillet over very high heat in a thin layer covering the whole bottom. When the sugar turns into a transparent syrup, stir gently with a wooden spoon. Continue to stir in this way until you have a golden caramel.

2 Remove from the heat and pour in the vinegar. It will crystallize.

3 Return to medium heat and cook until the sugar melts again.

ONIONS

Understand

WHAT ARE THEY?

Plants whose bulbs are harvested for use as a vegetable and condiment

ROLES

It provides both a sweet and savory note and it unifies different flavors (the word "onion" comes from the Latin *unio*, which means "one").

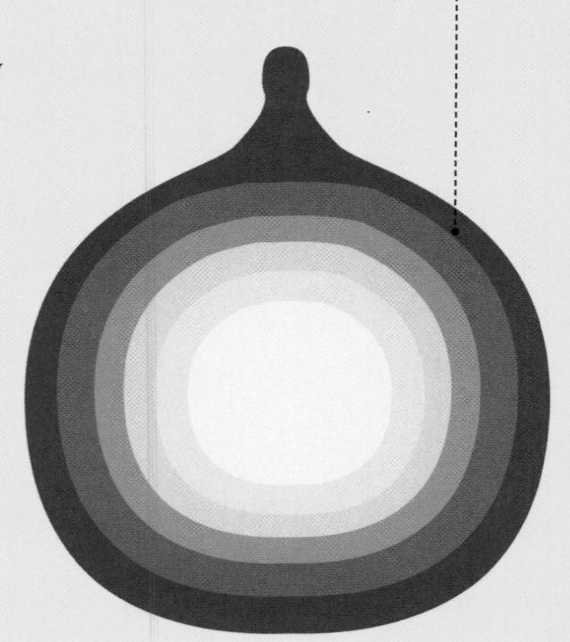

USES BY TYPE

White onion: raw (salads) or cooked (often stuffed)
Yellow onion: cooked (aromatic garnish, caramelized, "melted")
Scallion: raw or cooked (chicken consommé)
Red onion: raw or cooked (French onion soup, hamburgers)
Pearl onions: cooked, glazed (caramelized), pickled (with cornichons)

TYPES OF ONION

White onion: mild and crisp
Yellow onion: full-bodied flavor from slightly spicy flesh
Red onion: much milder in taste than yellow onions but also blander when cooked
Scallions and spring onions: mild and delicate
Baby or pearl onions: same flavor as yellow onions but eaten whole

USES BY CUT

Minced: fast-cooking preparations where the texture of the onion must disappear and leave only its flavor (tomato sauce)
Thinly sliced: slow-cooked preparations where the texture of the onion must remain (French onion soup)
Rings: decoration, raw (hamburgers) or cooked (poaching liquid)
Whole: side dish (baby onions)
Mirepoix: garnish

HOW DO RAW AND COOKED ONION DIFFER?

Raw onion: fresh, spicy flavor. Cooked onion: warm, sweet flavor.

WHY DOES SLICED ONION MAKE US CRY?

Because of the sulfur compound it contains, which is released during cutting. Using a very sharp knife crushes the plant cells less and so reduces the release of the compound.

WHY DOES ONION CARAMELIZE?

In response to the heat, the proteins in the onion release amino acids that react with the sugars to yield a sweet, savory, and nutty flavor.

HOW DO ONIONS DIFFER FROM SHALLOTS?

Shallots have all the characteristics of onions without their spicy, sometimes acrid taste.

Cutting and cooking onions

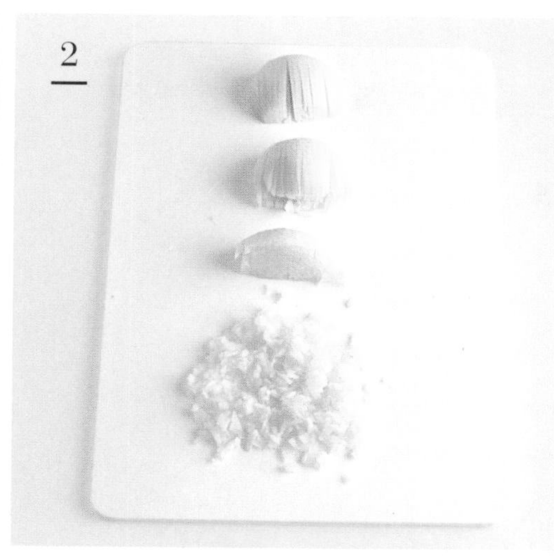

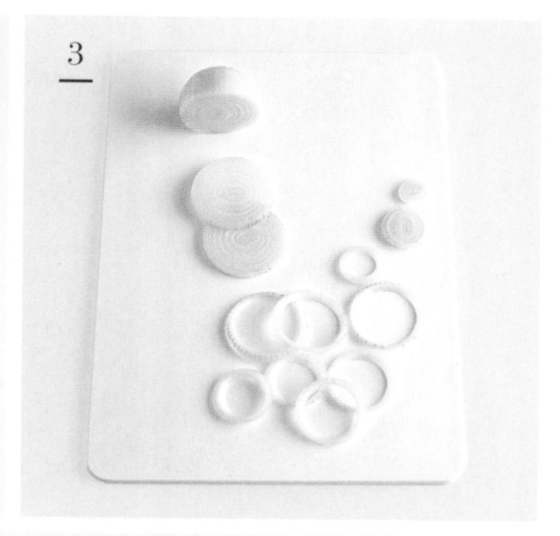

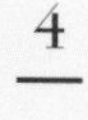

1 THINLY SLICED

What is it? Cutting into thin half-slices.

Cut the onion in half lengthwise. Place the flat side on the board, then slice off the root (bottom) end. Slice thinly, in the same direction as the natural lines (lengthwise).

2 MINCED

What is it? Cutting into small pieces.

Cut the onion in half lengthwise. Place the flat side on the board and slice thinly, in the same direction as the natural lines (lengthwise) using the point of the knife, without cutting through the root (bottom) end. Hold the onion on top with bent fingers. Slice across the thickness two or three times (parallel to the board), without cutting through the root end, then thinly slice perpendicular to the natural lines.

3 RINGS

What is it? Cutting into thin circles.

Lay the onion on its side and hold it at the root end, then cut into thin (⅛-inch) slices starting at the opposite end.

4 "MELTED" OR SWEATED ONIONS

What is it? Pieces cooked until completely soft (they are melted in the sense that they have lost their water content). The finer the cut, the faster they "melt." A pinch of salt accelerates the process.

Melt butter (1 tablespoon per onion). Add the chopped onion and sweat over medium heat, stirring occasionally, until it is completely soft but not colored.

5 CARAMELIZED ONIONS

What is it? Melted onions, cooked until they color.

Melt butter (2 ¼ teaspoons per onion). Add the onion and sweat until completely soft. Let it cook until the onion turns golden. Add sugar (½ teaspoon per onion) if you want to accentuate the caramelization.

POTATOES

Understand

WHAT ARE THEY?

Herbaceous plants, from the same family as tomatoes, of which we eat the tubers

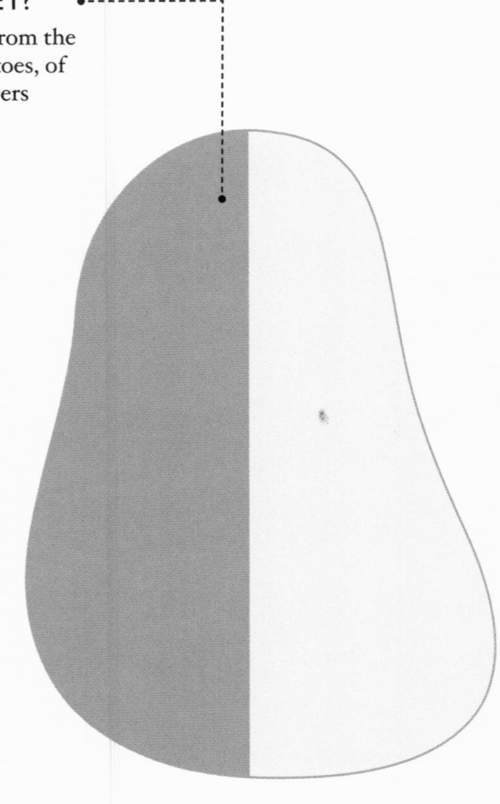

CATEGORIES

New potatoes: harvested in spring, before mature, eaten from April to mid-August. Thin skin, melting flesh, slightly sweet taste. To be eaten soon after purchase.
Storage potatoes: harvested at full maturity in September–October, they keep for several months in a dark room at 43°F.

ROLES

Binding (soups, green vegetable purées), thanks to their starch content
Base ingredient (for duchess potatoes, dauphine potatoes)
Accompaniment (mashed, steamed, sautéed)

VARIETIES

Boiling (waxy) potatoes
Characteristic: hold together during cooking.
– Uses: salads, steamed or sautéed.
– Examples: red skin, white, fingerling (various colors).

All-purpose potatoes
Characteristic: multi-purpose.
– Uses: stews (they absorb the flavor of sauces well), gratins.
– Examples: Yukon Gold (yellow skin and flesh).

Baking (starchy) potatoes
Characteristic: fall apart during cooking (they are thus very crumbly, without structure).
– Uses: fries, soups, baked potatoes.
– Example: russet.

RECIPES

Dauphinois (braised)
Allumettes (matchsticks), mignonettes, French fries (opposite)
Anna potatoes (baked in a mold)
Potatoes à la boulangère (braised in the oven)
Potato pancakes (sautéed in a skillet)
Potatoes fondantes (braised in a white stock)
Pommes noisettes (blanched)
Château potatoes (fried in butter and oil)
Mashed potatoes (boiled)
Baked potatoes (roasted in their skins)

PREPARATION

Peel them lengthwise. Remove all spots, but avoid digging in. Keep the potatoes in cold water in the refrigerator until ready to use.

WHAT ROLE DOES THE STARCH PLAY?

A complex sugar and potatoes' main energy storage, starch has a thickening property that can modify the consistency and structure of the liquids to which it is added.

Cutting potatoes

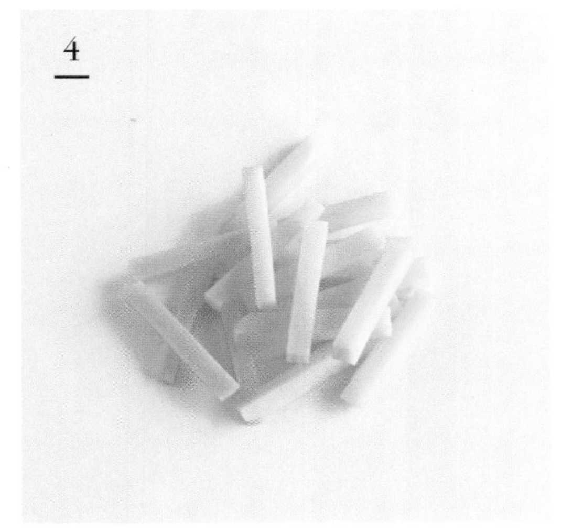

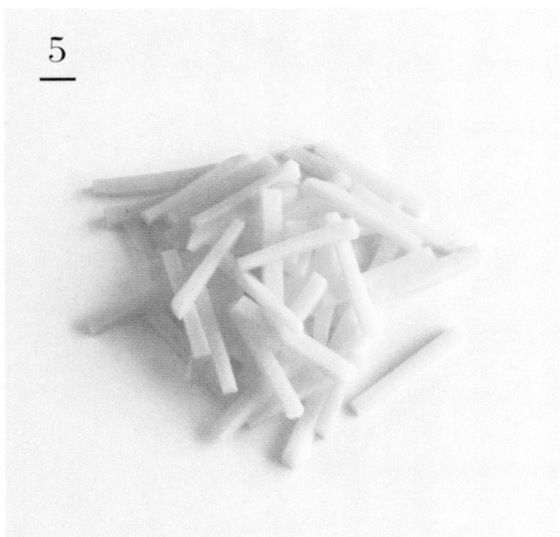

1 CHIPS

What are they? Paper-thin to 1/16-inch-thick rounds.

Lightly trim the ends of the potatoes to make them cylindrical. Slice them using a mandoline.

2 WAFFLE CHIPS

What are they? Thin rounds with a lattice pattern.

Use medium potatoes of an even shape. Peel them and round them off. Cut each with the wavy blade of a mandoline, rotating the potato a quarter turn between each pass to obtain an openwork lattice.

3 STRAWS

What are they? Thin batons 1/16 inch thick.

Using a mandoline, cut the potatoes in 1/16-inch-thick slices, then in even batons 1/16 inch thick.

4 FRENCH FRIES

What are they? Batons 3/8 inch thick and 2 1/2–2 3/4 inches long.

Trim the potatoes at their ends as well as along one side, to give them a stable base. Cut into even slices 3/8 inch thick and 2 1/2–2 3/4 inches long. Stack two or three slices on top of each other, then cut them lengthwise into even batons 3/8 inch thick.

5 MIGNONETTES

What are they? Batons 5/16 inch thick and 2 inches long.

Prepare as for French fries but make the batons 5/16 inch wide and 2 inches long.

6 MATCHSTICKS

What are they? Batons 3/16 inch thick and 2 inches long.

Prepare as for French fries but make the batons 3/16 inch thick and 2 inches long.

MASHED POTATOES

Understand

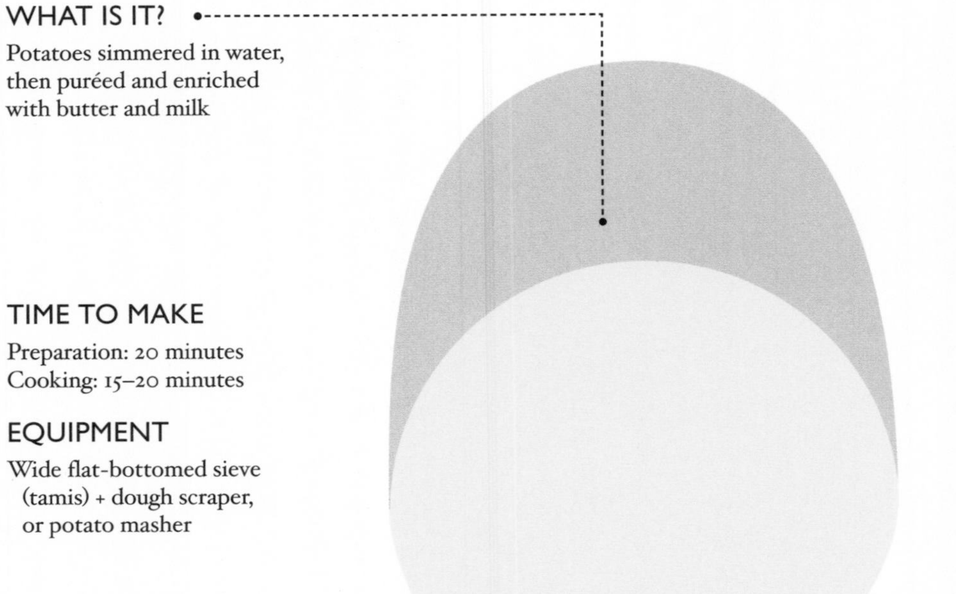

WHAT IS IT?

Potatoes simmered in water, then puréed and enriched with butter and milk

TIME TO MAKE

Preparation: 20 minutes
Cooking: 15–20 minutes

EQUIPMENT

Wide flat-bottomed sieve (tamis) + dough scraper, or potato masher

VARIATIONS

Infusing the milk with a small rosemary sprig and a sage leaf, or with a crushed garlic clove.
Mashed potato with beurre noisette: heat 7 tablespoons butter over medium heat until it becomes nutty. Strain through a fine-mesh sieve and add 5½ tablespoons of this butter to the warm milk. Pour the rest over the finished potatoes.

TRICKY ASPECT

Cooking the potatoes to the right texture

TECHNIQUES TO MASTER

Using a potato masher or a tamis with a dough scraper.

IT'S READY . . .

When the mash has a light, creamy texture.

WHY SHOULDN'T YOU USE A FOOD PROCESSOR TO MAKE MASHED POTATOES?

The blade cuts the starch grains in the potato. When these starch grains burst, they liberate components that make the purée gluey.

WHY ADD THE FAT?

The fat content of the butter and the milk adds creaminess. The fat also absorbs the flavors; the melted butter enhances the flavors of the thyme and bay leaf.

TIP

Prepare the mashed potatoes a few hours in advance and reheat over medium heat while adding up to 7 tablespoons of the potato cooking water.

Learn

SERVES 4

MASH

2 lb starchy potatoes (russet or Yukon Gold)
1 tablespoon coarse sea salt
1 garlic clove
¾ cup milk
6 tablespoons butter

AROMATICS

1 thyme sprig
1 bay leaf

SEASONING

½ teaspoon fine salt
freshly ground black pepper (6 turns)

TO FINISH

1½ tablespoons butter

1 Peel the potatoes and cut them into pieces about 2 inches square, then rinse.

2 Cover with 1¼ inches water in a large saucepan. Bring to a boil. Add the coarse sea salt and simmer (without boiling) for 15–20 minutes, until fork-tender.

3 Peel the garlic clove and cut in half. Heat the milk, salt, butter, pepper, thyme, bay leaf, and garlic clove in a small saucepan over medium heat until the butter has melted. Increase the heat to very high, then remove from the heat as soon as the mixture starts to simmer.

4 Drain the potatoes. Return them to the pan and dry them for 1 minute over low heat while stirring and shaking the pan.

5 Crush the hot potatoes with a masher or push through a fine-mesh sieve set over the saucepan.

6 Remove the thyme, bay leaf, and garlic from the milk with a skimmer or slotted spoon and gradually pour the infused milk over the potatoes while mixing with a wooden spoon. Adjust the seasoning.

7 Make a well in the top of the pile of mashed potato and place the final 1½ tablespoons of butter in it.

DUCHESS POTATOES

Understand

WHAT ARE THEY?

Duchess potatoes base: cooked and mashed potatoes, with butter and egg yolk added
Duchess potatoes: base mixture piped using a fluted decorating tip, then baked until golden
À la duchesse: a dish served with duchess potatoes

TIME TO MAKE

Preparation: 30 minutes
Cooking: 12–15 minutes

EQUIPMENT

Wide flat-bottomed sieve (tamis) + dough scraper, or potato masher
Pastry bag + ⅝ inch fluted decorating tip
Pastry brush

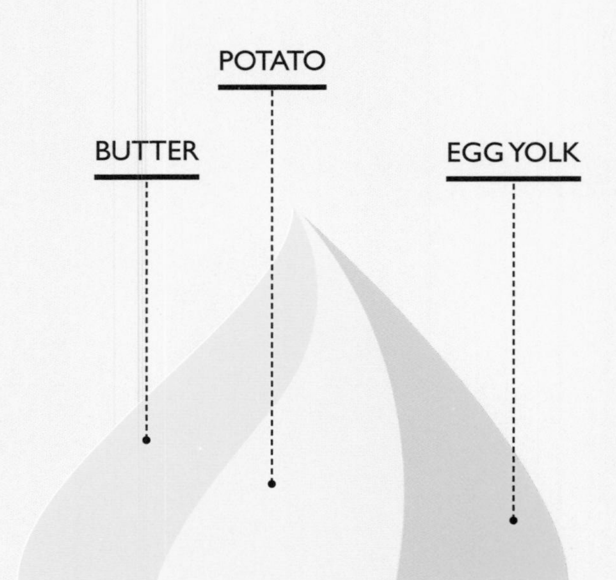

USES

Decoration of roast meat dishes
Small side dish

TECHNIQUES TO MASTER

Piping (page 281)

WHY COOK THE POTATOES ON COARSE SEA SALT?

This method takes longer than boiling, but results in the flesh being less moist (the salt absorbs water on the surface of the potatoes). With drier flesh, there is less chance of the mixture becoming gluey because the starch is less swollen with water.

VARIATIONS

Potato croquettes: duchess potatoes base shaped into cylinders, then coated with breadcrumbs and fried
Almond potato croquettes: duchess potatoes base shaped into almond shapes, then coated in flaked almonds
Dauphine potatoes (page 244): dauphine potato mixture + choux pastry

TIP

Use the duchess potatoes base hot; it will be easier to manipulate.

Learn

MAKES 35–40

DUCHESS POTATOES BASE

1 lb 2 oz potatoes (russet or Yukon Gold)
¼–½ cup coarse sea salt
5 tablespoons butter
3 egg yolks

SEASONING

pinch of freshly grated nutmeg
½ teaspoon fine salt
freshly ground black pepper (6 turns)

1 Preheat the oven to 400°F. Wipe the potatoes with a moist paper towel. Make a bed of coarse sea salt in an ovenproof cooking vessel and set the potatoes on top. Bake for 45 minutes to 1 hour, depending on their size. Check if the potatoes are cooked by cutting open the largest. Bake for a few more minutes if necessary.

2 Cut 3½ tablespoons of the butter into pieces and refrigerate. Melt the remaining butter and use it to grease a baking sheet with a pastry brush. Keep any remaining butter in the saucepan.

3 Remove the flesh from the potatoes using a spoon and push through a fine-mesh sieve with a dough scraper, or mash with a potato masher.

4 Dry the mashed potatoes in a saucepan over very low heat, stirring with a spatula to ensure they don't stick. Add the cold pieces of butter and stir them in until incorporated.

5 Remove from the heat, then add the egg yolks one at a time, mixing well after each addition. Season with nutmeg, salt, and pepper.

6 Quickly stir the mixture over low heat for 1–2 minutes until the mixture is smooth.

7 Fill a pastry bag with the mixture and use a ⅝-inch fluted decorating tip to pipe evenly spaced small heaps of the mixture on the greased baking sheet. Brush each one with a little of the remaining melted butter. Bake for 12–15 minutes, until lightly browned.

EGGS

Understand

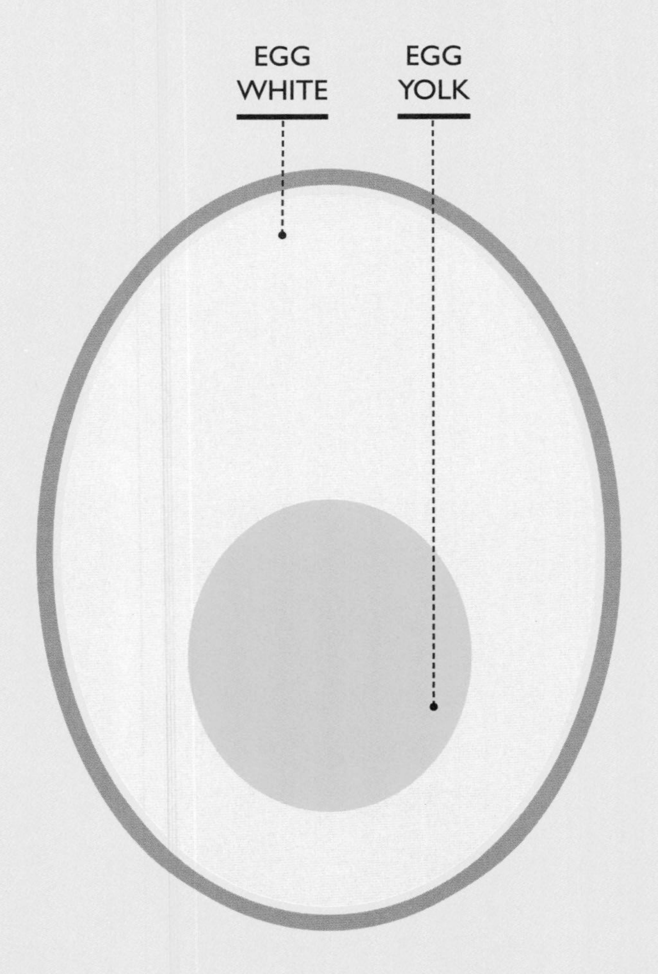

WHAT ARE THEY?

Products laid by hens and consisting of a shell containing two elements: the white and the yolk

PRODUCTS

- Weight (large egg) = 2 oz (¼ oz for the shell, 1¼ oz for the white, and ½ oz for the yolk).
- Egg white: proteins.
- Egg yolk: fats, including lecithin (which plays an important role in emulsions: binding oil and water).
- "Extra-fresh" egg: laid less than 9 days before the purchase date.
- "Fresh" egg: laid 9–28 days before the purchase date.

ROLES

Egg yolk
- Thickening, notably of sauces (blanquette of veal)
- Stabilization: promotes the formation of and stabilizes emulsions (mayonnaise, hollandaise sauce, etc.)

Egg white (whisked)
- Creates mousses and rises (cheese soufflé)

Whole eggs
- Binding cream mixtures (quiche)
- Binding doughs (choux pastry, pasta)
- Binding stuffings

TASTE

Eggs have a characteristic flavor that remains after they are mixed with other ingredients and that emerges in cooking. They have the ability to capture flavors formed during preparation.

HOW DO YOU STOP THE SHELL CRACKING DURING COOKING?

Even if the egg is cold, if you place it very carefully in simmering but not boiling water, the shell won't crack.

HOW DO YOU ENSURE WELL-BEATEN EGG WHITES?

Use perfectly clean equipment and whites without any trace of yolk—any presence of fat will inhibit the process.

AT WHAT TEMPERATURE DOES AN EGG COAGULATE (COOK)?

The white begins to coagulate at 142°F, the yolk at 154°F.

WHY DOES EGG YOLK PROMOTE THE FORMATION OF EMULSIONS ?

During whisking, the fats and proteins it contains are activated to create and stabilize an emulsion.

TIPS

To make peeling easier: cool the egg by plunging it into very cold water for 5 minutes, then break the shell very delicately and peel the large end of the egg first, removing the shell membrane under the air chamber. Extra-fresh eggs are harder to peel than fresh eggs (the air chamber is smaller).

COOKING VARIATIONS

With eggs at room temperature: allow 3 minutes for soft-boiled eggs, 5 minutes for medium-boiled eggs, and 10 minutes for hard-boiled eggs.

Cooking eggs

COOKING AN EGG IN ITS SHELL

Bring a large amount of cold water to a boil in a small saucepan. Take an egg straight out of the refrigerator and immerse it carefully in the water using a skimmer or slotted spoon. Reduce the heat to medium.

1 SOFT-BOILED EGG

White semicoagulated, yolk liquid. Cook for 4 minutes from when it starts simmering again.

2 MEDIUM-BOILED EGG

White coagulated, yolk creamy. Cook for 6 minutes from when the water starts simmering again.

3 HARD-BOILED EGG

White and yolk coagulated. Cook for 12 minutes from when the water starts simmering again.

COOKING A SHELLED EGG

4 FRIED EGG

Unbeaten egg: white coagulated, yolk creamy.

Break the egg into a ramekin or cup. Melt 1½ teaspoons butter in a small nonstick skillet over high heat. When it starts to turn noisette (page 53), pour in the egg. Reduce the heat to medium. Cook for 1–2 minutes, until the white is lightly browned. Season the white with a pinch of salt and a grind of pepper.

5 SCRAMBLED EGGS

Beaten eggs: soft and creamy.

Using a fork, beat 4 eggs with ¼ teaspoon fine salt and a grind of pepper. Melt 1½ teaspoons butter in a small skillet over medium heat. Add the eggs when the butter stops foaming. Stir quickly with a silicone spatula until it leaves a trace in the pan. Reduce the heat to low and stir for 1 minute. When the eggs are still runny, remove from the heat and add 1½ teaspoons butter. Stir to incorporate.

ROLLED OMELETTE

Understand

WHAT IS IT?

Beaten eggs cooked in a skillet without coloring, then rolled

TIME TO MAKE

Preparation: 5 minutes
Cooking: 1–2 minutes

EQUIPMENT

Nonstick skillet (8-inch diameter)
Silicone spatula

VARIATIONS

Omelette with fines herbes, cheese, onions, seafood, chanterelle mushrooms, etc.

TRICKY ASPECT

The temperature of the butter: if it is too hot, the side of the omelette that is in contact with the skillet will wrinkle

TECHNIQUES TO MASTER

Rolling the omelette.

IT'S READY . . .

When the omelette unsticks from the skillet but is not yet colored.

WHY SHOULD THE EGG NOT BE OVERBEATEN?

There is a risk that the base will be frothy, because the proteins capture air and create a foam that can give the omelette too airy a texture.

WHY MUST THE OMELETTE NOT COLOR?

The browner it becomes, the more the egg proteins coagulate, creating sulfur bonds between the overcooked proteins that emit an unpleasant aroma.

DEGREES OF COOKING

Runny (a thin "sauce" seems to coat the coagulated egg): allow 1–2 minutes.
Soft (there is no more "sauce" but the egg is still very soft): allow 1–2 minutes, remove from the heat, cover, and wait 1 minute.
Well cooked (the coagulated egg is firmer): allow 1–2 minutes, remove from the heat, cover, and wait 2 minutes.

TIPS

- Cook at medium heat and stir the eggs constantly to ensure they don't color.
- When cooking with gas, preheat the empty skillet over low heat for 5 minutes before melting the butter over medium heat, as gas has a tendency to brown the omelette where the flame hits the pan.

Learn

MAKES 1 ROLLED OMELETTE

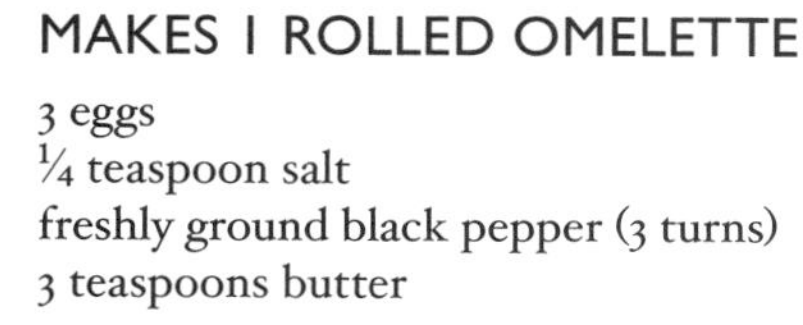

3 eggs
¼ teaspoon salt
freshly ground black pepper (3 turns)
3 teaspoons butter

1 Using a fork, beat the eggs in a mixing bowl with the salt and pepper until slightly foamy. Add 1 teaspoon of the butter, cut into small cubes.

2 Melt the remaining 2 teaspoons butter in a skillet over medium heat. Pour in the eggs all at once, wait a few seconds, then mix the eggs using a silicone spatula, with a rapid circular movement, for 1–2 minutes. Form the mixture into a round omelette without holes.

3 When the edges of the omelette can be lifted with the spatula, turn off the heat. Tip up the pan by lifting the handle, and fold over the third of the omelette nearest the handle. Slide the omelette slightly to the other side of the pan, fold the opposite third of the omelette over the first while turning it out onto a warm plate with the smooth side facing up.

4 Arrange the omelette with your hands if necessary so that it's slightly domed.

POACHED EGGS

Understand

WHAT ARE THEY?

Eggs cooked out of their shell in very hot water; the white is coagulated, the yolk creamy

TIME TO MAKE

Preparation: 5 minutes

EQUIPMENT

Small saucepan
Skimmer or finely slotted spoon

WHY DRAIN THE EGG BEFORE COOKING?

To remove the excess liquid of the white, which would form unattractive filaments during cooking, while retaining the viscous part of the white, which will coagulate better. This technique allows us to omit adding vinegar to the cooking water.

WHY IS VINEGAR SOMETIMES ADDED TO THE WATER?

The acidity provided by the vinegar accelerates the coagulation of the proteins and thus forms a neat white around the yolk. In this recipe, the excess liquid of the white is removed before cooking, so there is no risk of the white spreading out. The taste of the egg benefits from the absence of vinegar in the cooking water.

HOW DOES IT DIFFER FROM A SOFT-BOILED EGG?

For a soft-boiled egg, the egg is cooked in its shell (and so retains its shape during cooking).

WHY POACH AN EGG IN A WATER VORTEX?

The vortex gathers the white around the yolk and helps the egg retain its shape.

Learn

MAKES 1 POACHED EGG

1 cold, extra-fresh egg
pinch of salt
freshly ground black pepper (1 turn)

1 Heat a saucepan filled with water over medium-high heat. Break the egg into a small bowl.

2 Pour the egg onto a skimmer or finely slotted spoon set over a bowl. Let the excess white run through, then scrape the bottom of the spoon (the thick part of the white will cling to the yolk).

3 Pour the drained yolk back into the original bowl. When the water in the saucepan is simmering, reduce the heat to low and stir the water with a wooden spoon to create a small vortex. Pour the egg into the center of the vortex and let it cook for 90 seconds to 2 minutes, over low heat, gently pushing the white over the yolk until the white is cooked.

4 Remove from the heat and drain the egg using the slotted spoon, then place the spoon on a paper towel to drain. Carefully transfer the egg to a serving plate. Season with salt and pepper.

OIL-FRIED EGG

Understand

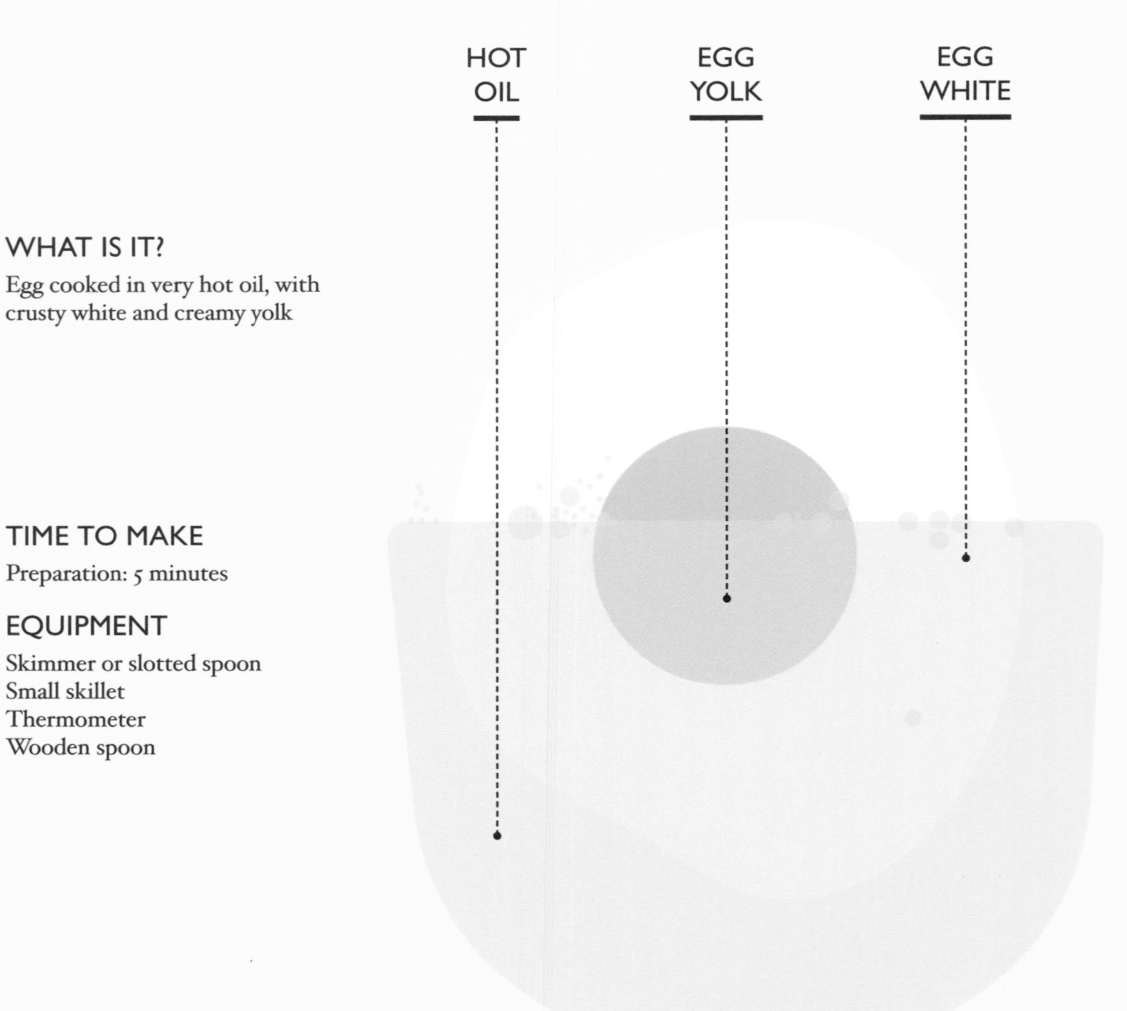

WHAT IS IT?

Egg cooked in very hot oil, with crusty white and creamy yolk

TIME TO MAKE

Preparation: 5 minutes

EQUIPMENT

Skimmer or slotted spoon
Small skillet
Thermometer
Wooden spoon

USE

Veal marengo

TRICKY ASPECT

"Shaping" the egg during cooking

IT'S READY . . .

When the white is golden.

WHY ARE EXTRA-FRESH EGGS PREFERRED?

In fresh eggs, the protein structure in the egg white is very tight so when fried it will not spread but retain its form around the yolk.

WHY IS THE COOKING TIME SO SHORT?

Oil can be heated to a much higher temperature than water, which doesn't go above 212°F. At 370°F, the egg cooks much more rapidly.

HOW DOES THE CRUST FORM AROUND THE EGG?

The high temperature dries out the protein network on the surface of the egg and makes it crusty.

Learn

FOR 1 OIL-FRIED EGG

1 cold extra-fresh egg
1 cup peanut oil
pinch of fine salt

1 Break the egg into a small bowl.

2 Heat the oil to 370°F in a small skillet. Tip it slightly to make the oil bath deeper, then gently pour in the egg.

3 The white will form large bubbles; push them quickly over the yolk using a wooden spoon while rolling the egg on itself to give it an even shape. Fry it for 1 minute maximum; the yolk should be soft and the white golden.

4 Pull out the egg using a skimmer or slotted spoon and drain it on a paper towel. Season with salt.

SAUTÉING

Understand

WHAT IS IT?

Sautéing: cooking small pieces at very high temperature in a skillet, in a small quantity of fat, uncovered (dry heat)

TIME TO MAKE

Quick (10–20 minutes)

EQUIPMENT

Skillet, straight-sided sauté pan, or slightly flared sauté pan to suit the size of the food to be cooked

TYPE OF COOKING

Constant: fast and well done on the outside, less cooked in the middle

INGREDIENTS TO SAUTÉ

Small cuts of tender meat (tournedos, veal cutlets, filet mignon, etc.)
Poultry pieces (cutlets, thighs, etc.)
Fish fillets
Offal
Eggs
Vegetables (potatoes, zucchini, mushrooms, onions, etc.)

USES

Sautéed potatoes
Sautéed chicken chasseur
Calf's liver à l'anglaise
Skirt steak with shallot sauce
Steak au poivre (pepper steak)
Sautéed veal chops à la crème
Sole meunière (page 150)
Fried eggs

WHY IS THE TECHNIQUE USEFUL?

It forms a very fragrant crust around the food during cooking in the skillet (Maillard reaction, page 282), which provides crispness without overcooking the center.

WHY BASTE THE FOOD DURING COOKING?

To improve the surface color and to moisten the food with its own flavorful juices and fat.

Learn

1

2

3

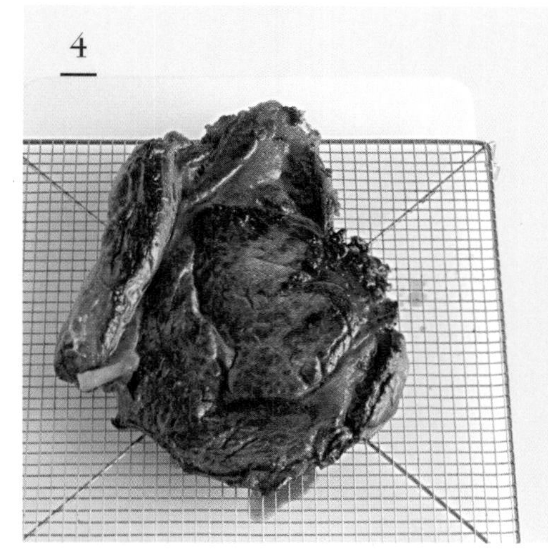

4

5

6

RIB-EYE STEAK WITH ROQUEFORT SAUCE

SERVES 2

1 shallot
2 packed cups arugula leaves
2 tablespoons olive oil
1 lb 5 oz boneless rib-eye steak
1 teaspoon fine salt
2 tablespoons butter
½ cup crème fraîche
½ cup crumbled Roquefort cheese
freshly ground black pepper (3 turns)
¼ teaspoon fleur de sel

1 Peel and mince the shallot. Wash and spin the arugula. Heat a skillet over very high heat and add the oil. Pat the meat dry with a paper towel then sprinkle with the fine salt. When the oil is just smoking, add the meat and sear for 2 minutes.

2 Turn it over, reduce the heat to high, and add the butter.

3 Cook for 2 minutes more, basting the meat with the foaming butter.

4 Transfer the meat to a wire rack and cover with foil.

5 Reduce the heat to medium and partially degrease (page 283) the pan. Add the shallot and let it sweat. Deglaze with ¼ cup cold water. Scrape any stuck-on bits off the bottom of the pan, bring to a boil, then reduce until almost dry.

6 Stir in the crème fraîche and Roquefort, then add half the arugula. Stir until wilted, then add the rest. Once all the arugula has wilted, adjust the seasoning.

7 Sprinkle the steak with the pepper and fleur de sel, then serve with the sauce.

ROASTING

Understand

WHAT IS IT?

Cooking a large piece of tender meat, a whole bird, or vegetables at high, dry heat in the oven

COOKING TIME

Medium (about 1 hour)

EQUIPMENT

Roasting pan (with a fitted wire rack for meats) that is both ovenproof and flameproof

Optional: meat thermometer with a probe you can leave in the oven during cooking. Insert the probe so that it passes through the center of the food.

TYPE OF COOKING

Fast and well done on the outside, then more gentle to continue cooking the center

INGREDIENTS TO ROAST

Whole poultry
Prime meats (page 278)
Certain vegetables (potatoes, squash, eggplants, etc.)

USES

Roast chicken
Roast leg of lamb
Roast pork
Roasted squash (page 254)

OVEN TEMPERATURE

Large pieces: cook at high temperature (430°F), then at low temperature (320°F).

Small pieces: cook at high temperature (430°F).

Avoid temperatures that are too high (460°F and over); put the meat under the broiler at the end of cooking to finish browning.

CORE TEMPERATURE

Take the meat out when the probe reaches 10°F below the desired final temperature.

Beef:
– very rare: 120°F
– rare: 130°F
– medium-rare: 140°F
– well done: 160°F

Pork:
– rare: 160°F
– medium-rare: 170°F

Lamb:
– rare: 140°F
– medium-rare: 160°F

Veal: 160°F
Poultry: 170–180°F
Fish: 120°F

WHY USE THIS TECHNIQUE?

To cook large pieces without them drying out. First at high temperature to sear the outside, then more gently to cook the center.

WHY BASTE THE MEAT?

To improve the surface color and to moisten the food with its own flavorful juices and fat.

WHY LET THE MEAT REST AFTER COOKING?

Resting the meat—on a rack to prevent it stewing in its own juices (which will soften the surface), relaxes the muscle fibers and evens out the internal color. Let it rest for 10–20 minutes, depending on the size of the piece.

VARIATION

Searing the meat on the stovetop before roasting to concentrate the flavor, and increase the color and crispness of the roast.

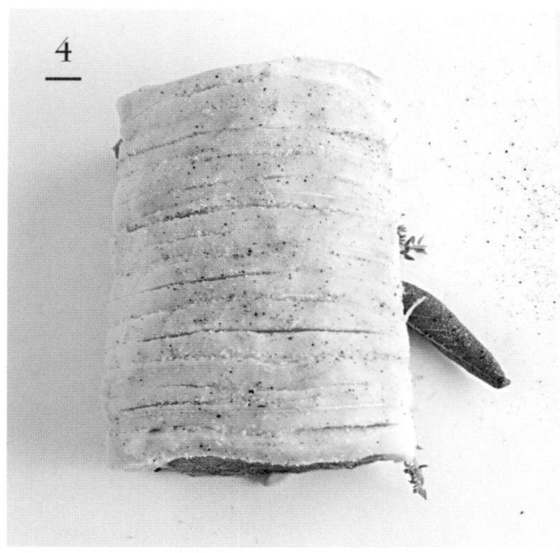

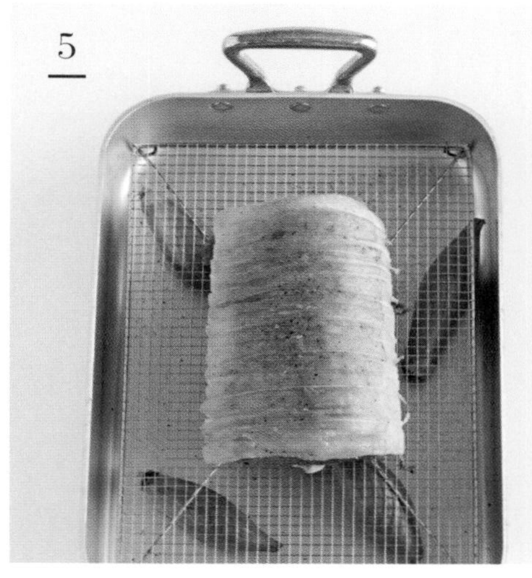

ROAST PORK

SERVES 4

4 large shallots
4 garlic cloves
5 sage leaves
5 thyme sprigs
2 lb 3 oz boneless pork loin, rolled and tied, with skin and fat left on
2 teaspoons fine salt
freshly ground black pepper (12 turns)
5 tablespoons olive oil

1 Preheat the oven to 430°F. Remove the outer layer of skin from the shallots. Peel and de-germ the garlic cloves, then cut each into two or three slices. Wash the sage and thyme.

2 Pat the pork completely dry with a paper towel. Score the fat with straight lines ⅜ inch apart, cutting through the entire thickness of the fat without touching the flesh.

3 Turn the roast over and rub it with the salt and pepper. Insert the garlic, thyme, and sage under the strings of the loin.

4 Turn it over again and then season the fat with salt and pepper, particularly between the cuts in the fat. Pour 2 tablespoons of the oil over the whole loin and massage it in.

5 Heat the remaining 3 tablespoons oil in a roasting pan over very high heat on the stovetop and brown the fat side of the loin. Transfer the loin to a wire rack, fat side up. Place the shallots in the bottom of the pan and place the rack with the loin on top. Roast for 20 minutes. Reduce the oven temperature to 320°F and roast for 35 minutes more. End by browning the fat for 1–2 minutes under the broiler, until it puffs up slightly and becomes crisp. Let it rest for 15 minutes on the rack, covered with foil.

6 Untie the loin. Discard the sage, thyme, and garlic. Remove the shallots from the pan. Partially degrease the cooking juices in the pan, then bring to a boil over very high heat on the stovetop. Pour in ⅔ cup of very cold water and scrape any stuck-on bits off the bottom. Bring to a boil and simmer for a few minutes, until reduced to your liking. Season to taste. Strain through a fine-mesh sieve. Serve the roast accompanied by the shallots and gravy.

GRILLING

Understand

WHAT IS IT?
Cooking over or under a source of very high direct heat

EQUIPMENT
Grill or grill pan: with a flat or ribbed plate, or grill grate (with barbecue-type bars)
Oven broiler

COOKING TIME
Small pieces of red meat (steaks, cutlets, etc.): fast cooking over very high direct heat
Small thick pieces of red meat (chateaubriand steaks, beef ribs): fast cooking over very high heat to sear, then medium heat (in the oven) to finish cooking
White meat, fish, or breaded foods: fast cooking over medium heat

TYPE OF COOKING
Constant: fast and well done on the outside, and less cooked in the middle

INGREDIENTS TO GRILL
Ribs (beef, veal, lamb, pork)
Fish steaks
Fast-cooking vegetables (mushrooms, tomatoes, etc.)
Shellfish

USES
Grilled chicken
Grilled steak with béarnaise sauce
Grilled sole with anchovy butter
Grilled corn on the cob

WHY USE THIS TECHNIQUE?
To form a flavorful crust around the food during cooking (Maillard reaction, page 282), which adds crispness without overcooking the inside.

WHY SHOULD WE NOT GRILL FOOD AT TOO HIGH A HEAT?
If overseared, grilled meats take on a metallic taste and toxic compounds form. The French call this meat ferrée *(tasting of iron).*

RESTING
Let small, thick pieces of red meat rest under foil for 5–10 minutes to even out the internal color and promote relaxation of the muscle fibers.

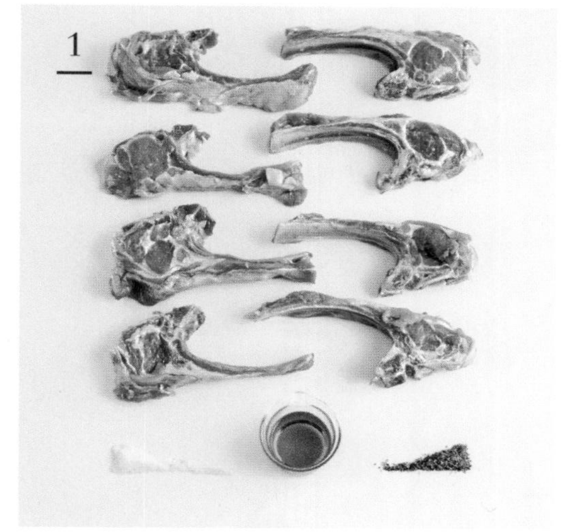

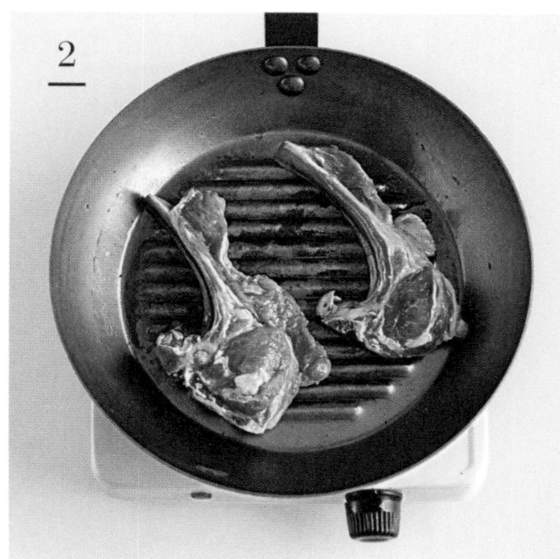

GRILLED LAMB CHOPS

SERVES 4

8 rib lamb chops
2 tablespoons olive oil
1 teaspoon fine salt
freshly ground black pepper (8 turns)

1 Coat the lamb chops in a thin layer of some of the oil. Season with the salt.

2 Lightly oil the grill or a grill pan using a paper towel soaked with the remaining oil. Heat the grill to very high or set the pan over very high heat.

3 Place the lamb chops diagonally across the grate or pan ridges and cook for 1 minute. Give them a quarter turn, then cook for another 1 minute, then turn them over and cook in the same way to give them a criss-cross pattern. Transfer the chops to a wire rack to rest, and season with the pepper.

BRAISING

Understand

WHAT IS IT?

Cooking a large piece of food slowly, covered, in liquid; with meat, it is either "brown braised" (browned first, to give it color) or "white braised" (oven cooked until firm, with no coloring)

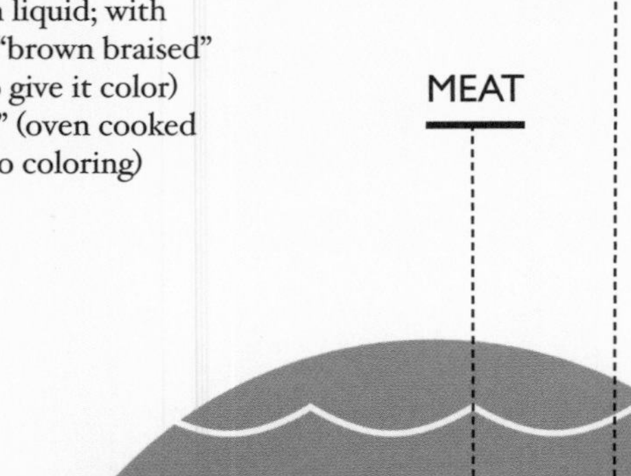

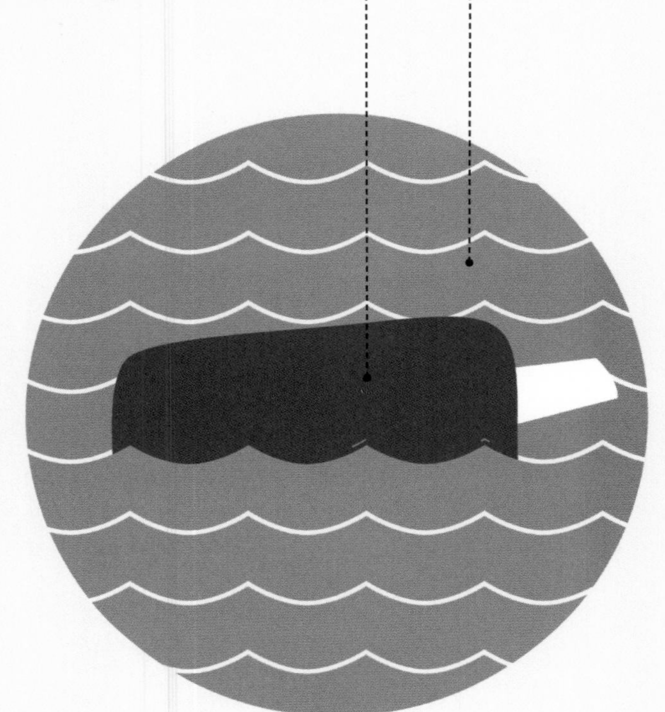

EQUIPMENT

Flameproof casserole or Dutch oven, or a straight-sided sauté pan: preferably heavy-bottomed (which retains the heat) and with a tight-fitting lid.

COOKING TIME

Choice or select meat (page 278): 4–5 hours in a 300°F oven
Fish and vegetables (high water content): 30 minutes maximum

TYPE OF COOKING

Fast and strong to color the outside, then in liquid to cook through

INGREDIENTS TO BRAISE

Large pieces of choice and select meat (page 278), which are firm and rich in collagen and need time to tenderize (chuck roast, veal shoulder, ham, etc.)
Whole fish or fish fillets
Leafy vegetables

USES

Beef pot roast with carrots
White- or brown-braised sweetbreads
Braised Belgian endive, lettuce, fennel, cabbage
Stuffed trout
Fillet of sole or turbot bonne femme

WHY USE THIS TECHNIQUE?

To form a very flavorful crust as food cooks in the oil (Maillard reaction, page 282). The cooking then continues in the liquid.
- Meat: to form a a very flavorful crust that then dissolves in the cooking liquid, flavoring and coloring the braising stock.
- Fish: to transfer its flavor to the cooking liquid, which allows the creation of very tasty sauces.
- Vegetables: to gain flavor from an aromatic cooking liquid (wine, stock).

DOES THE SIZE OF THE PIECES HAVE AN IMPACT ON TASTE?

When meat is cut into pieces, it gives more of its flavor to the cooking liquid than when cooked whole. In the latter case, the meat retains more of its own flavor.

HEIGHT OF THE COOKING LIQUID

The greater the volume of the cooking liquid, the thinner the braising stock will be. The less liquid there is, the more full-bodied the braising stock will be. Traditionally, a braising stock is rather thin.

BRAISED CHUCK ROAST

SERVES 8

3 large onions
3 garlic cloves
2 cups red wine (Côtes du Rhône)
4 cups white poultry stock (page 10)
1 thyme sprig
1 bay leaf
10 peppercorns
1 teaspoon fine salt
2½ tablespoons olive oil
3 lb 5 oz boneless chuck roast
3 tablespoons butter
½ teaspoon fleur de sel
freshly ground black pepper (8 turns)

1 Preheat the oven to 300°F with a rack placed as low as possible. Cut the onions in mirepoix (page 34). Peel, de-germ, and crush the garlic. Pour the wine and poultry stock into a saucepan. Add the thyme, bay leaf, and peppercorns, then bring to a simmer.

2 Pat the meat dry with a paper towel, then season with the fine salt. Heat the olive oil in a flameproof casserole or Dutch oven over very high heat. Brown the meat on all sides. Degrease the pan, then remove the meat to a plate.

3 Melt the butter in the casserole over medium heat. Add the onion and garlic, and sweat.

4 Deglaze with half the red wine and poultry stock mixture, scraping any stuck-on bits off the bottom. Bring to a simmer, then reduce by about one-third, skimming off any scum.

5 Return the meat to the casserole, then pour in the remaining wine and stock mixture. Bring to a simmer. Cover and transfer to the oven for 5–6 hours, or until the meat is very tender, turning the meat halfway through the cooking time.

6 Remove the meat and place it in a container that fits it. Strain the sauce through a fine-mesh sieve over the meat. Let it cool for at least 3 hours, or overnight.

7 Remove the cold meat from the sauce and set aside. Transfer the sauce to a saucepan, bring to a simmer and reduce by one-third. Strain through a fine-mesh sieve. Adjust the seasoning. Return the meat and reduced sauce to the pan, then bring to a simmer and reheat for 5 minutes over medium heat, basting the meat with the sauce.

8 Remove the meat and sprinkle with the fleur de sel and pepper. Serve the sauce in a gravy boat.

STEWING

Understand

WHAT IS IT?

Small pieces (meat, fish, vegetables) browned or cooked until firm without coloring, then immersed in a liquid thickened with flour, covered, and cooked

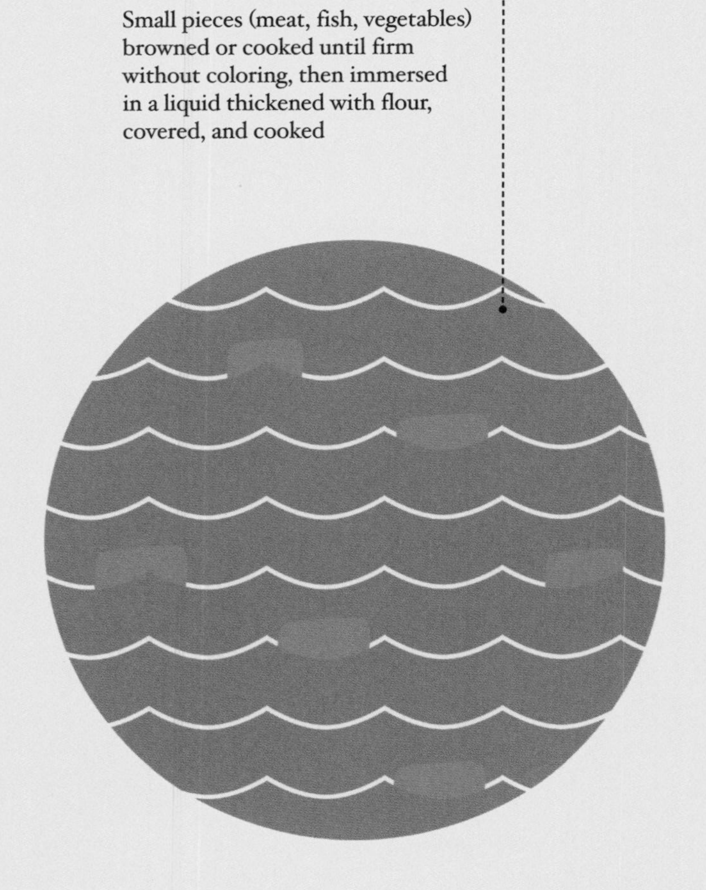

EQUIPMENT

Flameproof casserole, straight-sided sauté pan, or Dutch oven, preferably heavy-bottomed (which retains the heat) and with a tight-fitting lid.
The size of the cooking vessel should suit the volume of the ingredients so that not too much cooking liquid is required, which would dilute the sauce.

COOKING TIME

Firm pieces of beef: 3 hours in the oven
Shoulder of lamb or veal: 1 hour 30 minutes in the oven or on the stovetop
Fish and vegetables (high water content): 30 minutes maximum

TYPE OF COOKING

Fast and strong to color the outside, then in a liquid to finish cooking gently

INGREDIENTS TO STEW

Choice and select meats (page 278) that are firm and rich in collagen (neck, shoulder, etc.)
Chicken
Game
Shellfish
Firm-fleshed fish (monkfish, tuna, turbot, etc.)

USES

Beef stew
Monkfish à l'américaine (page 158)
Goulash
Veal Marengo
Navarin of lamb (page 196)
Coq au vin

WHY USE THIS TECHNIQUE?

To form a very flavorful crust (more or less brown depending on whether it is a white or brown stew) by cooking in oil (the Maillard reaction, page 282). The cooking then continues gently, by simmering in a liquid. The crust dissolves in the cooking liquid, flavoring and coloring the sauce.

DOES THE SIZE OF THE PIECES HAVE AN IMPACT ON THE TASTE?

When the meat is cut in pieces, it adds more flavor to the sauce.

WHY DUST THE MEAT WITH FLOUR?

Working on the same principle as a roux (page 18), the flour thickens the sauce.

HEIGHT OF THE COOKING LIQUID

The greater the volume of cooking liquid, the more the flavor of the sauce will be diluted. The less liquid there is, the more full-bodied it will be. The sauce of a stew should be quite full-bodied, so the cooking liquid should only fill the pan halfway.

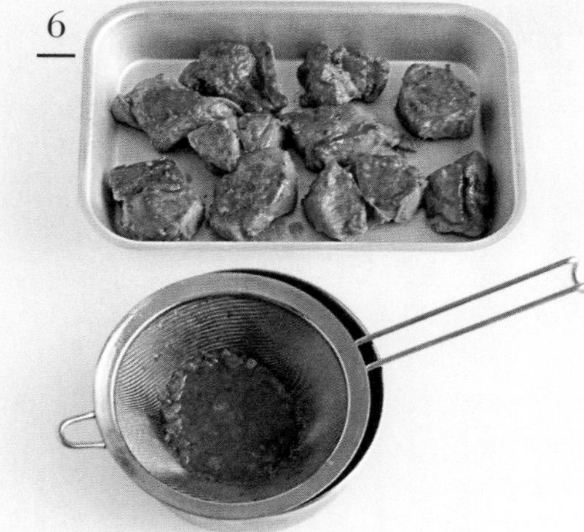

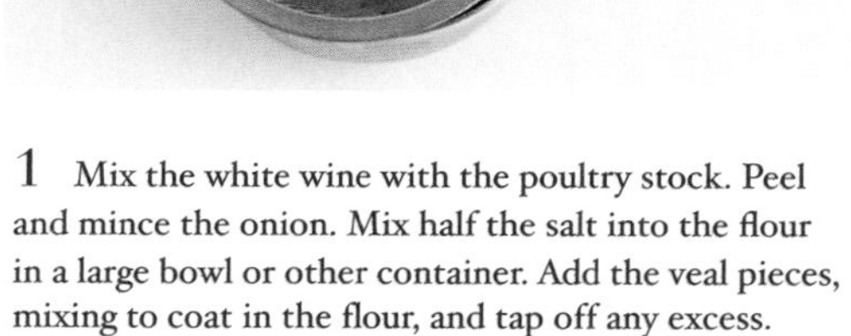

STEWED VEAL

SERVES 4

2 cups dry white wine
2 cups white poultry stock (page 10)
1 large onion
½ teaspoon fine salt
¼ cup all-purpose flour
2 lb 4 oz boneless veal shoulder, cut into 15–20 pieces
4 tablespoons butter
1 small bunch Italian parsley
1 garlic clove
1 lemon

1 Mix the white wine with the poultry stock. Peel and mince the onion. Mix half the salt into the flour in a large bowl or other container. Add the veal pieces, mixing to coat in the flour, and tap off any excess.

2 Melt the butter in a flameproof casserole or Dutch oven over high heat, then reduce the heat to medium and brown the veal on all sides.

3 Remove the veal from the casserole, degrease partially, then add the onion with the remaining salt. Sweat the onion, stirring.

4 Return the veal to the casserole, stir, then pour in the wine and stock mixture to halfway, while scraping the bottom of the dish with a flat spatula. Bring to a boil and skim. Cover and simmer for 2 hours.

5 Wash, dry, and finely chop the parsley. Peel, de-germ, and finely chop the garlic. Zest the lemon and chop the zest finely with a knife. Mix these three together.

6 Remove the meat and strain the sauce through a fine-mesh sieve without pushing on the solids. Adjust the seasoning.

7 Return the sauce to the casserole, add the meat and stir, then simmer for a few minutes. Top with the garlic, parsley, and lemon zest mixture.

COOKING AT LOW TEMPERATURE

Understand

WHAT IS IT?

Cooking a single piece in an oven at its lowest setting (200°F or lower)

EQUIPMENT

Ovenproof dish
Electronic thermometer with a probe

TIME TO MAKE

Preparation: 10 minutes
Cooking: 1 hour
Resting: 30 minutes

TYPE OF COOKING

Uniform cooking: cooking in an enclosed space that has a similar temperature to the core temperature desired in the final dish

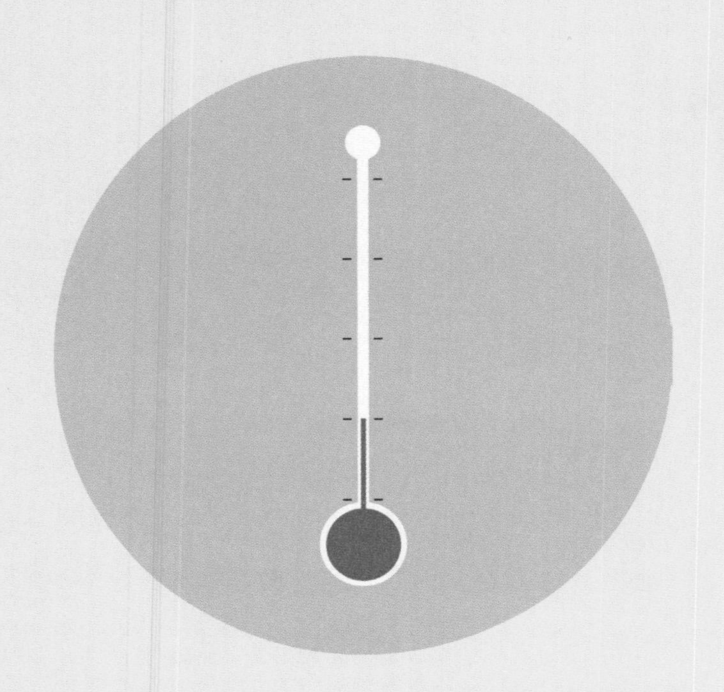

VARIATION

Finishing cooking by browning in a skillet

TRICKY ASPECT

The oven temperature

TECHNIQUES TO MASTER

Cooking with a thermometer probe (page 282)

TIP

To insert the probe, go through the middle of the piece, positioning it so it does not touch a bone.

WHY USE THIS TECHNIQUE?

Cooking occurs evenly from the outside to the inside, without the drying out associated with overcooking.

INGREDIENTS TO COOK AT LOW TEMPERATURES

Meat: loin of lamb, rib-eye steak, pork tenderloin, etc.
Fish: steaks of cod, salmon, tuna, etc.

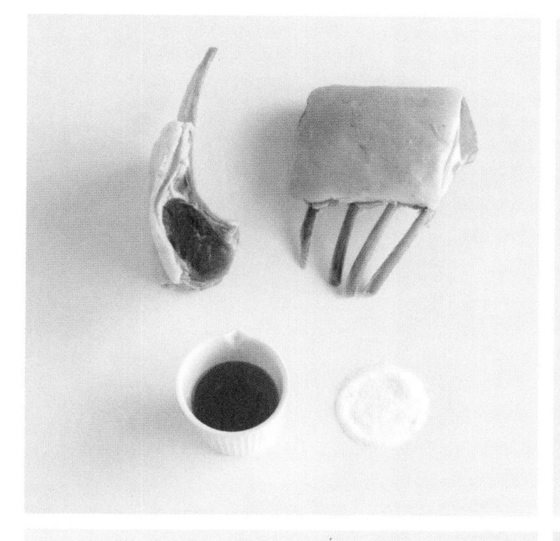

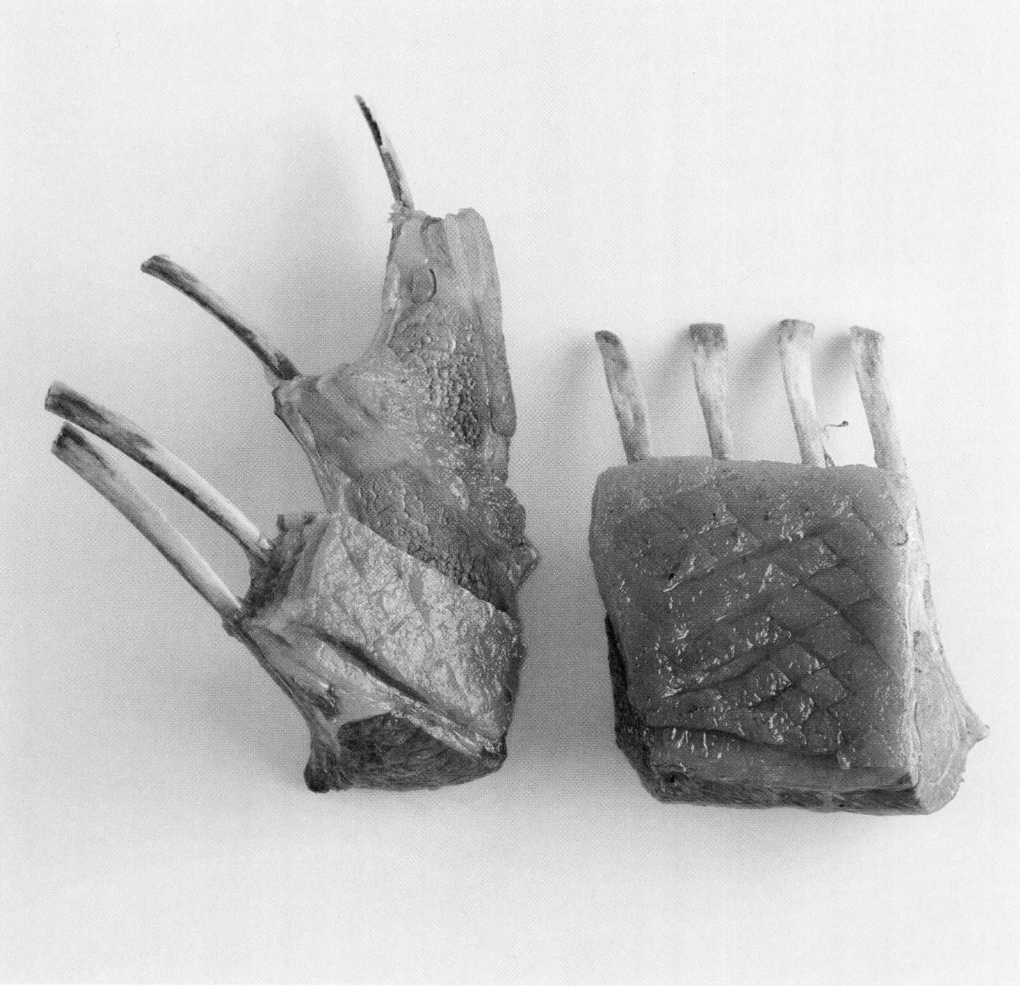

RACK OF LAMB

SERVES 4

two 14-oz frenched racks of lamb, refrigerated
1 teaspoon fine salt
4 tablespoons olive oil

1 Score the fat on the racks in a criss-cross pattern as soon as you remove them from the refrigerator, then leave them to come to room temperature, about 30 minutes. Preheat the oven to 250°F with your baking dish, meat probe, and four serving plates.

2 Season the racks with the salt and brush each with 1 tablespoon of the olive oil. Put them in the baking dish, insert the probe in one, and leave in the oven for 1 hour, or until the core temperature reaches 125°F.

3 Heat the remaining oil in a large skillet over high heat. Brown the racks of lamb on all sides, particularly on the fat side, so that it partially melts. Cut into chops by passing a knife between the ribs.

BLANCHING AND BOILING IN HOT WATER

Understand

WHAT IS IT?

Cooking by immersion in a large volume of salted boiling water

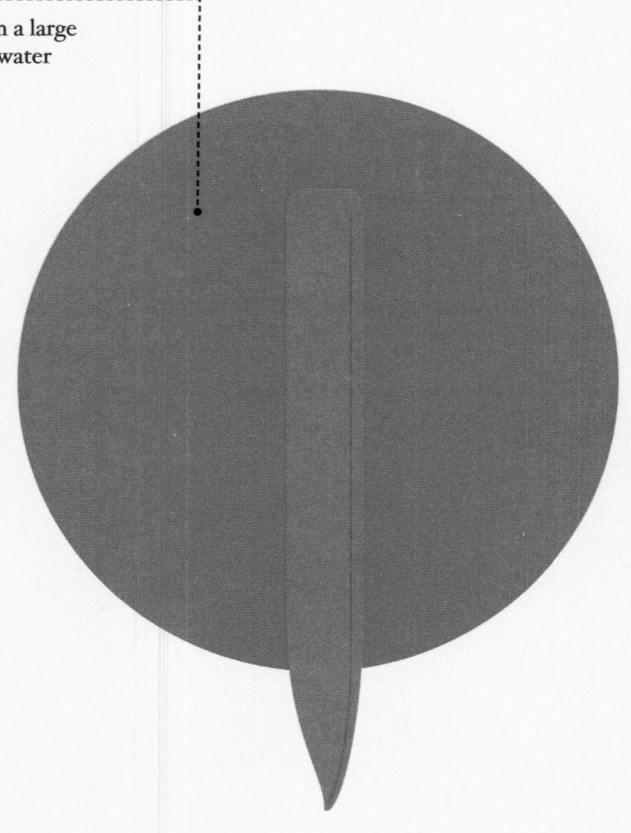

USES

Fast-cooking vegetables (green vegetables, cauliflower florets) that must stay al dente
Cooking eggs
Cooking pasta
Cooking rice

IT'S READY . . .

When the vegetable is still firm but not crunchy (you can crush it easily between two fingers).

VARIATION

Vegetables served cold: cooked in boiling water then refreshed in iced water (a large bowl of water and ice cubes)

BLANCHED GREEN BEANS

SERVES 4

1 lb 5 oz green beans, trimmed
1 tablespoon coarse sea salt per quart (4 cups) water
3 tablespoons butter
fine sea salt

1 Trim the beans, then wash and drain them.

2 Bring a large volume of water salted with the coarse sea salt to a vigorous boil. Plunge in all the beans at one time and cook for 5–10 minutes. Skim if necessary. Drain.

3 Transfer the beans to a large bowl, add the butter, and toss to coat well. Taste and add fine sea salt as needed.

WHY START WITH WATER THAT IS ALREADY HOT?

For fast tenderization of the food. For vegetables that don't need much softening and don't contain much starch, blanching in hot water is recommended because it is faster.

For meats, the temperature must be above 150°F to break down the collagen (and thus tenderize the meat). Boiling in hot water is thus recommended, because the meat benefits from a temperature that immediately tenderizes it.

COOKING WITH COLD WATER

Understand

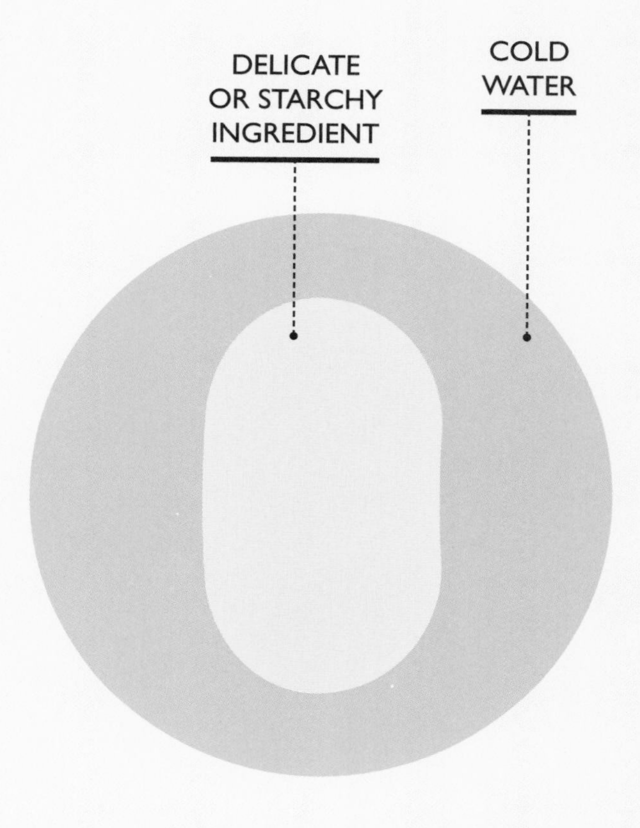

WHAT IS IT?

Cooking by immersion in a large volume of cold water that is then brought to a boil

USES

Cooking foods with delicate flesh (fish fillets)
Cooking foods containing starch (potatoes)
Making sauce (blanquette): starting with cold water allows an exchange of flavors between the main ingredient and the aromatics while enriching the cooking liquid

IT'S READY . . .

When the point of a knife plunged into the vegetable meets almost no resistance.

SIMMERED POTATOES

SERVES 4

2 lb 3 oz firm-fleshed potatoes, such as Yukon Gold
1 tablespoon coarse sea salt per quart (4 cups) water

1 Peel and wash the potatoes, then put them in a large saucepan. Cover with cold water (fill to at least 2 inches above the height of the potatoes).

2 Bring to a boil, then add the salt. Simmer for 20 minutes. Skim. Stop the cooking by pouring in a little cold water to keep them at about 190°F until ready to serve.

WHY START WITH COLD WATER?

For food containing starch: the gradual rise in temperature allows gelatinization of the starch before the cell walls break down. If potatoes were plunged into boiling water, the starch would form a "barrier" that would stop them cooking uniformly.

Fish: with the slow rise in temperature, the proteins coagulate less, and the flesh doesn't stiffen right away. It is close to the principle of cooking at low temperature. The flesh remains moist.

DOUBLE FRYING

Understand

WHAT IS IT?

Double cooking of foods that are completely immersed in hot oil, to ensure thorough cooking and the formation of a crust

EQUIPMENT

Heavy-bottomed saucepan
Thermometer
Frying basket

USE

Vegetable fries (sweet potato, parsnip, winter squash)

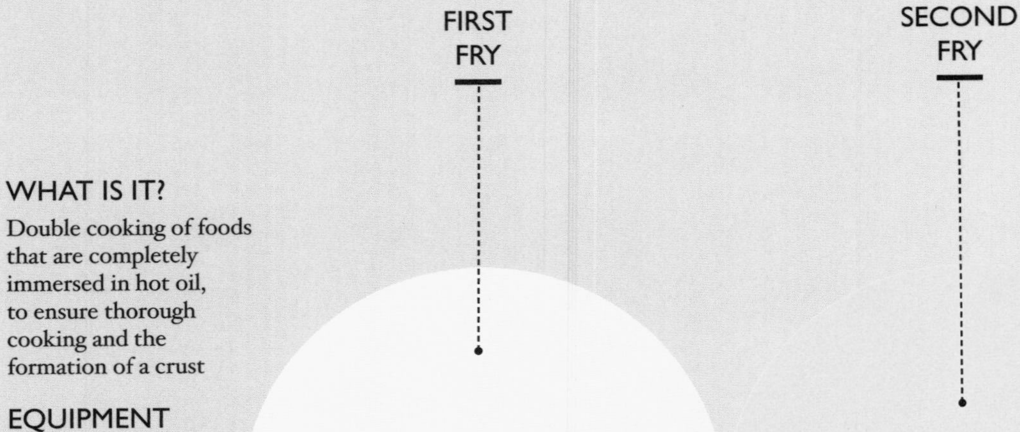

WITH AN ELECTRIC DEEP-FRYER

Same procedure.
– First fry: 270°F
– Second fry: 350°F

DEEP-FRYER TIP

If using an electric deep-fryer, check the temperature of the oil with a separate thermometer: the actual temperature is often below the temperature indicated by the deep-fryer.

WHY COOK TWICE?

First fry at 270°F: the potatoes cook. The starch they contain swells in the heat. Second fry at 350°F: the potatoes color. The surface of the potatoes is dried out by the high temperature of the oil, which makes the crisp crust.

WHY A DIFFERENT OIL TEMPERATURE EACH TIME?

The first bath, which is gentler, allows the potatoes to cook without burning; the second, which is hotter, forms the crust.

WHY ISN'T IT NECESSARY TO WASH THE CUT POTATO PIECES?

In double frying, the starch of the potatoes makes the fries crunchier.

FRENCH-FRIED POTATOES

SERVES 4

2 lb 3 oz starchy potatoes (russets)
1½ quarts (6 cups) peanut oil
1 teaspoon fine salt

1 Cut the potatoes into ⅜-inch-square French fry batons (page 59). Don't rinse them.

2 First fry: heat an oil bath to 360°F. Immerse the potatoes, let the temperature fall, then cook them until "blond" at 250–270°F. Remove the fries after 5–6 minutes: a fry pressed between two fingers (protected from the heat with a paper towel) should crush easily. Drain well in a colander or frying basket and let them return to room temperature.

3 Second fry: heat the oil bath to 370°F. Immerse the potatoes, let the temperature fall, then keep it at 350°F. Remove them after 2–3 minutes. The fries should be crisp, with a dark golden color.

4 Drain well, add the salt, mix, and turn out onto a paper towel.

MATCHSTICK POTATOES

Give them 3 minutes in the first oil bath (270°F), until a baton crushes easily when pressed between your fingers, then 1 minute in the second oil bath (350°F).

MIGNONETTE POTATOES

Give them about 4 minutes in the first oil bath (270°F), until a baton crushes easily when pressed between your fingers, then 2 minutes in the second oil bath (350°F).

SINGLE
FRYING

Understand

WHAT IS IT?
Cooking a food by completely immersing it in hot oil

EQUIPMENT
Heavy-bottomed saucepan
Thermometer
Frying basket

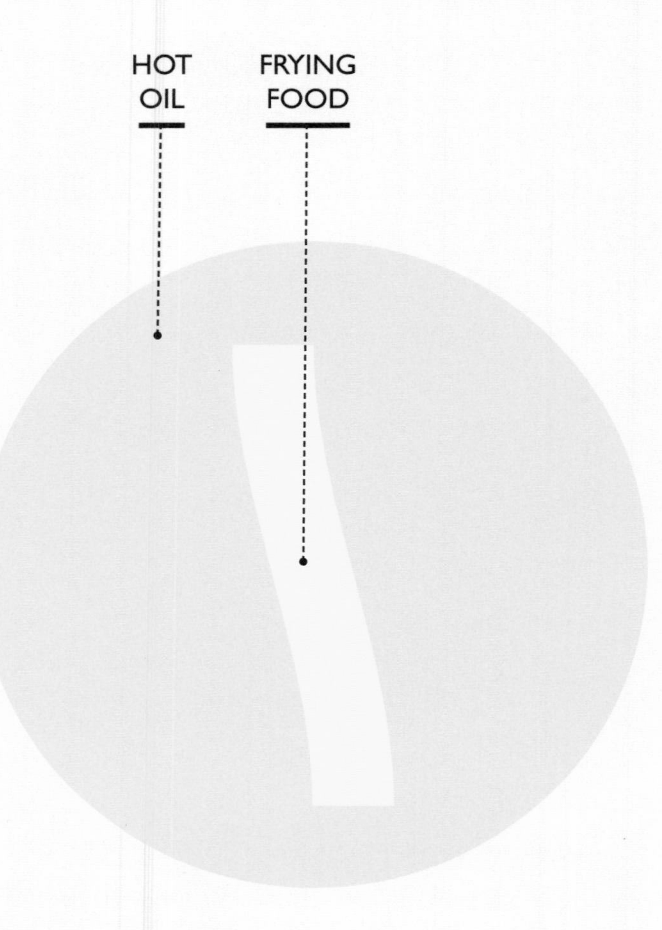

USES
Vegetable chips (beets, carrot, etc.)
Breaded food (flour, egg wash, and breadcrumbs)
Battered food (tempura, fish and chips, page 178)
Fritters

WITH AN ELECTRIC DEEP-FRYER
Same procedure but heat the oil to 270°F to start.

WHY COOK ONLY ONCE?
When the food being fried doesn't need a long cooking time (small pieces, soft vegetables), a single oil bath can suffice. It allows you to cook and brown at the same time.

WHY RUB THE POTATOES IN THE WATER?
To remove the starch released from plant cells during cutting. Instead of washing them, it is also possible to blot them with paper towels. This prevents the starch from getting into the oil and making it deteriorate faster.

1

2

3

POTATO CHIPS

SERVES 4

1 lb 2 oz starchy potatoes (russets)
1½ quarts (6 cups) peanut oil
1 teaspoon fine salt

1 Cut the potatoes into paper-thin rounds using a mandoline or very sharp knife. Soak them in cold water for 10 minutes. Rub them with your hands in the water. Drain them and dry them carefully with a clean dish towel.

2 Immerse the rounds, ten at a time, in an oil bath at 320°F, then let the temperature drop to 250–270°F. Stir the chips in the oil with a spatula, then drain them when they are golden and very dry (3–4 minutes of frying).

3 Add the salt and mix well. Drain on paper towels. Repeat with the remaining rounds.

WAFFLE CHIPS

Prepare the potatoes as indicated on page 59. Cooking time: 5 minutes.

STRAW POTATOES

Prepare the potatoes as indicated on page 59. Cooking time: 2–3 minutes.

CHAPTER 2

RECIPES

SOUPS

COLD APPETIZERS

HOT APPETIZERS

SHELLFISH

FISH

MEATS

ACCOMPANIMENTS

FRENCH ONION SOUP

Understand

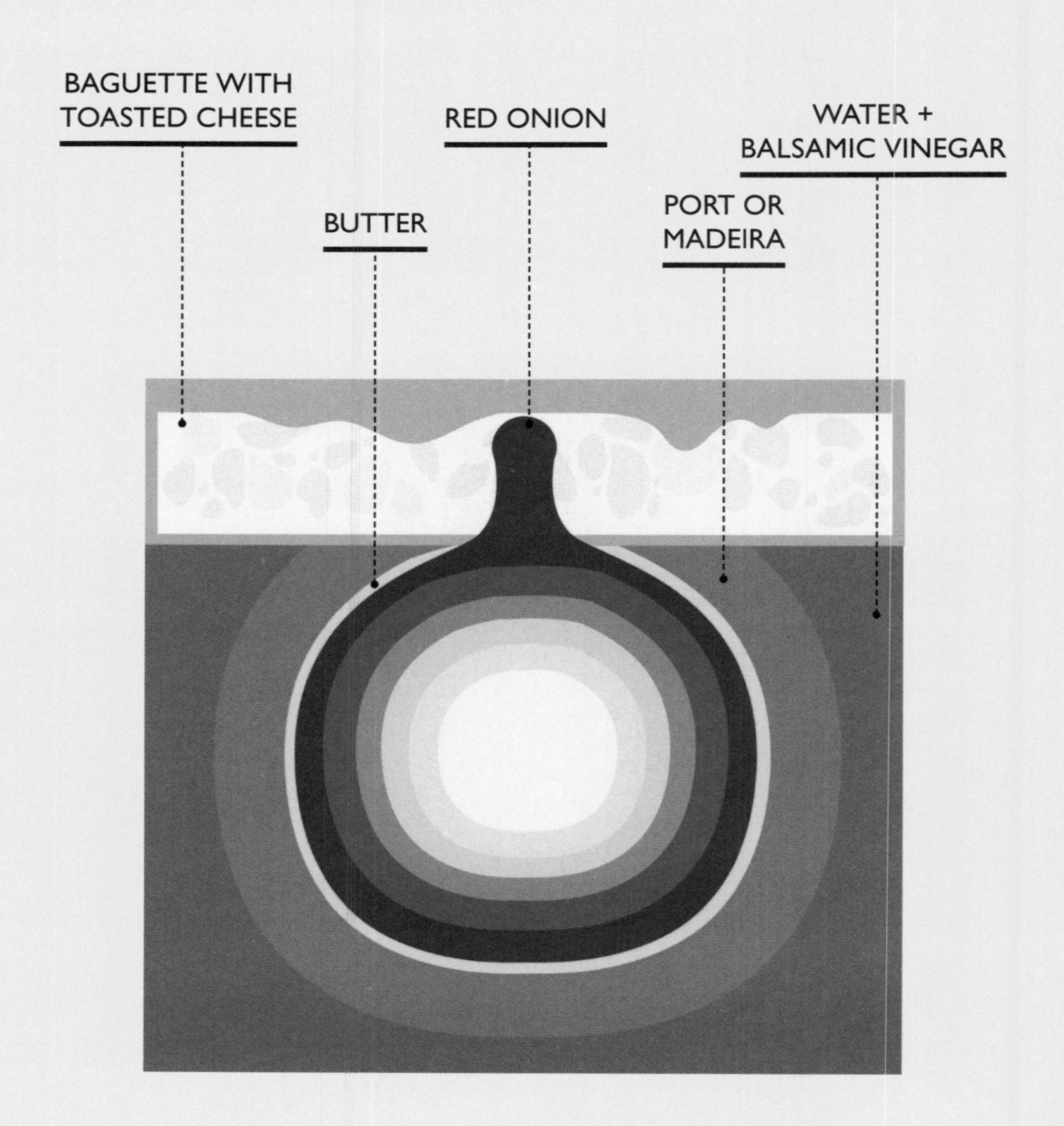

WHAT IS IT?
Onions stewed in butter, cooked in water with port or Madeira, and topped with toasted-bread-and-Gruyère croutons

TIME TO MAKE
Preparation: 25 minutes
Cooking: 50–55 minutes

EQUIPMENT
Heatproof serving bowls

VARIATIONS
Normandy-style onion soup: stewed onions thickened with flour (page 282), then mixed with milk and hard apple cider; croutons without cheese

TRICKY ASPECTS
– Stewing the onions
– The toasted cheese topping

TECHNIQUES TO MASTER
Scraping up stuck-on bits (page 283)
Thinly slicing (page 280)

TIP
If the browning onions stick to the bottom of the saucepan, add 1–2 tablespoons cold water.

IT'S READY . . .
When the soup is a dark golden brown.

STORAGE
3 days in the refrigerator (without the bread or cheese). Reheat by bringing to a simmer, and wait until the last minute to prepare the croutons.

Learn

SERVES 4

SOUP

3 large red onions
4 tablespoons butter
5 cups water
¼ cup port or Madeira

SEASONING

½ teaspoon fine salt
1 tablespoon balsamic vinegar
freshly ground black pepper, to taste

CROUTONS

½ baguette
⅔ cup grated Gruyère cheese

1 Peel the onions and cut them in ¼-inch slices. Melt 2 tablespoons of the butter in a large saucepan or flameproof casserole over medium heat. Add the onions and the salt. Cook for 25–30 minutes, stirring frequently, until they are a dark golden brown.

2 Pour in the water and the port or Madeira, bring to a boil, then scrape any stuck-on bits off the bottom of the pan. Reduce the heat and simmer for 20 minutes, uncovered, skimming as necessary.

3 Cut the baguette half in 8 slices about ⅝ inch thick. Melt the remaining 2 tablespoons butter in a large skillet until it foams. Fry the slices of bread until golden on both sides. Drain them on paper towels.

4 Preheat the broiler. Add the balsamic vinegar to the soup, then taste and adjust the seasoning. Pour the soup into ovenproof serving bowls set on a baking sheet, place one or two pieces of bread in each bowl and sprinkle with the Gruyère. Place under the broiler for 5 minutes, or until the cheese is golden.

SHRIMP BISQUE

Understand

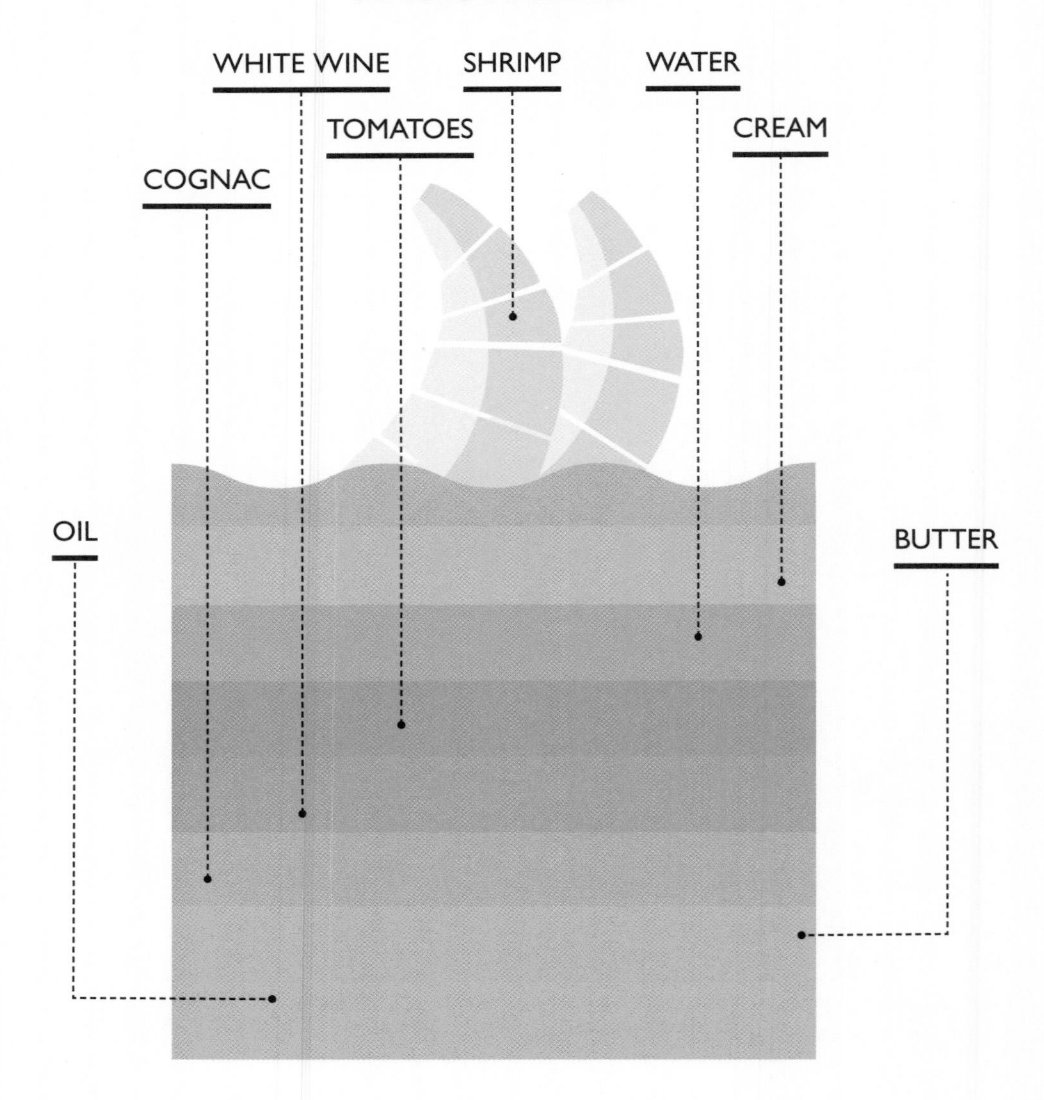

WHAT IS IT?
Shrimp browned with aromatic vegetables, then blended, strained, and enriched with cream

TIME TO MAKE
Preparation: 45 minutes
Cooking: 45 minutes

EQUIPMENT
Skimmer
Fine-mesh sieve
Blender or food processor

TRICKY ASPECT
The reduction

TECHNIQUES TO MASTER
Reducing a sauce (page 283)
Pushing through a sieve (page 281)
Thinly slicing (page 280)
Transferring (page 282)
Skimming (page 283)
Deglazing (page 283)
Sweating (page 282)

TIP
To sear the shrimp well, cook them in several batches.

IT'S READY . . .
When the bisque is creamy.

STORAGE
2 days in the refrigerator in an airtight container. Reheat over medium heat, stirring constantly, until it boils.

WHAT DO THE SHRIMP SHELLS ADD?
They contain chitin (a type of sugar molecule) that breaks down at high temperatures into powerful aromatic components.

Learn

SERVES 4

1 SHRIMP

2 lbs head-on shrimp, (30–50 shrimp, depending on their size)

2 BISQUE

2 large shallots
1 medium bulb fennel
4½ teaspoons olive oil
2 tablespoons butter, cut into dice
⅓ cup Cognac
1 cup white wine
2⅓ cups canned tomato purée
1 quart (4 cups) water
1 cup heavy cream

Making shrimp bisque

1 Wash the shrimp and dry them with a paper towel. Peel and thinly slice the shallots. Wash and thinly slice the fennel.

2 Sear the shrimp in the olive oil in a large saucepan over very high heat. Add the butter and let them caramelize over medium heat for 2–3 minutes. Remove 8 shrimp, peel them, then return their shells to the pan. Set the flesh aside in an airtight container.

3 With a slotted spoon or tongs, remove the remaining shrimp from the pan and set aside. Sweat the shallot and fennel in the same pan for a few minutes. Return the shrimp to the pan, then deglaze with the Cognac and white wine. Reduce until dry.

4 Add the tomato purée and cook for 1 minute. Pour in the water, bring to a boil, and simmer for 30 minutes, skimming regularly.

5 Blend or process the bisque into a smooth purée. Push through a fine-mesh sieve. You should have 4 to 5 cups of bisque.

6 Pour the strained bisque into a saucepan and reduce by half (10–15 minutes). Add the heavy cream and stir over high heat. Reduce for 3–5 minutes. Purée for a few seconds with a hand-held blender.

7 Divide the bisque among four serving bowls. Cut the reserved shrimp in half lengthwise, and place on top of the bisque.

CHICKEN CONSOMMÉ

Understand

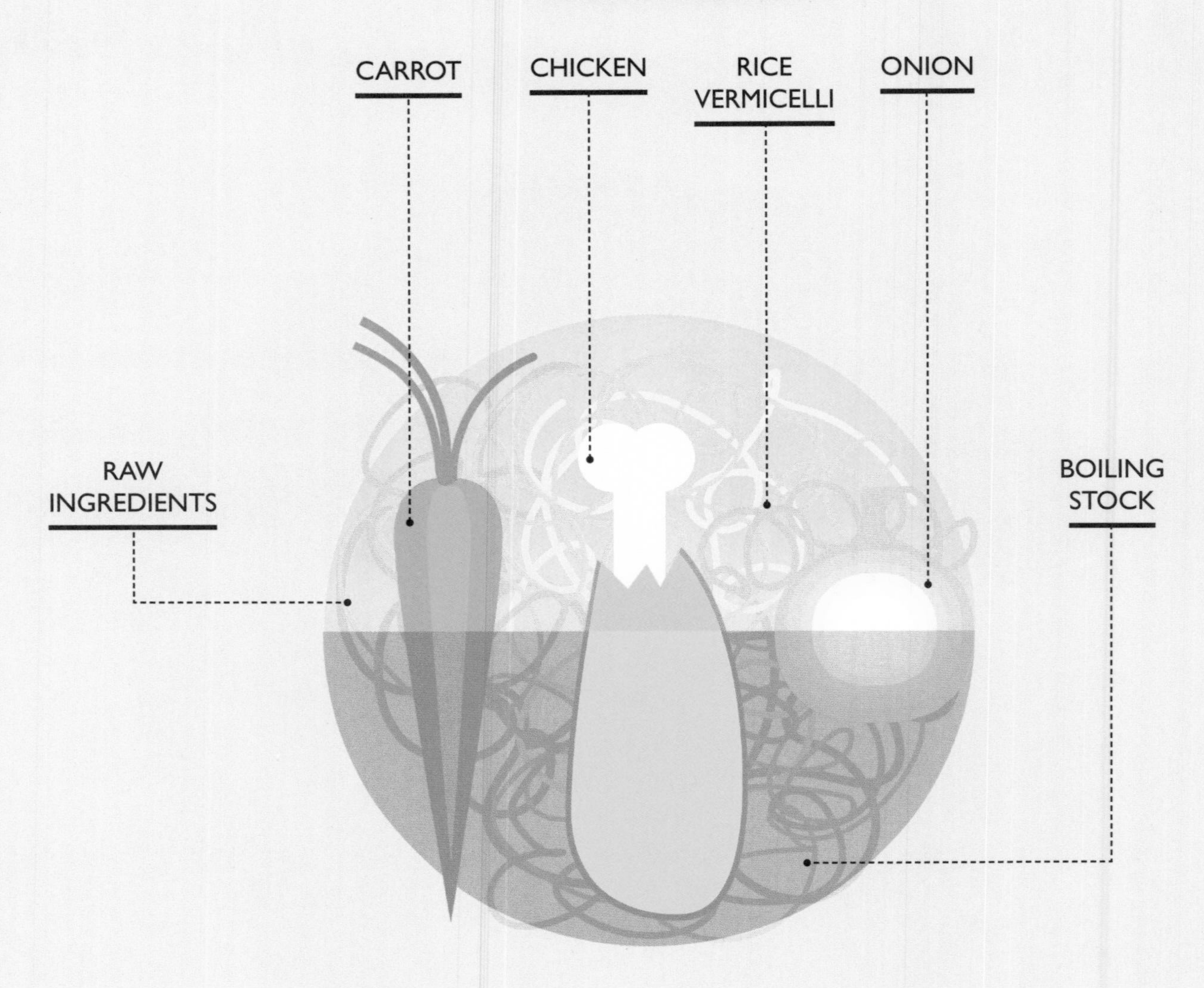

WHAT IS IT?
Boiling white poultry stock poured over raw chicken, carrot, and rice vermicelli

TIME TO MAKE
Preparation: 15 minutes
Resting: 5 minutes

EQUIPMENT
Meat tenderizer or heavy saucepan

VARIATION
Pot-au-feu broth

TRICKY ASPECT
The heat of the poultry stock must be very high to cook the vermicelli and the chicken, and soften the carrot.

TECHNIQUES TO MASTER
Flattening meat (page 278)
Cutting a brunoise (page 36)
Thinly slicing (page 280)
Mincing (page 280)

TIP
Let the stock boil for a few seconds so it comes to as high a temperature as possible.

IT'S READY . . .
When the rice vermicelli are soft and the chicken cooked.

STORAGE
2 days in the refrigerator. Bring to a boil when reheating.

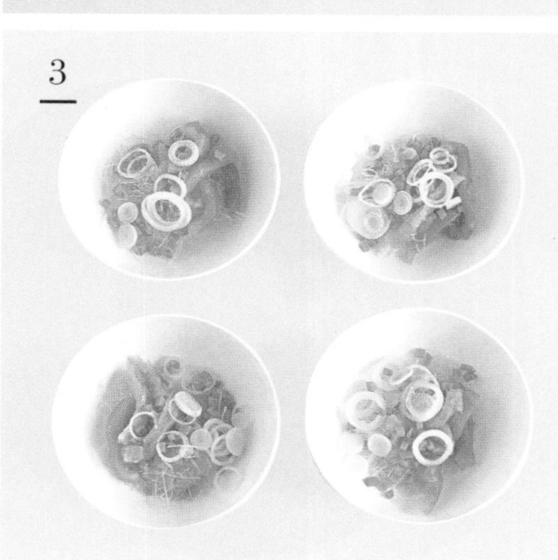

SERVES 4

SOUP

2½ oz clear rice vermicelli
1 carrot
2 scallions
1 large chicken breast
small handful Italian parsley
1 quart (4 cups) white poultry stock (page 10)

SEASONING

3 tablespoons nuoc mam (Vietnamese fish sauce)
½ teaspoon fine salt
freshly ground black pepper (2 turns)

1 Break the rice vermicelli in two. Peel the carrot and cut it in brunoise (page 36). Cut the green stalks and the roots off the scallions and remove the first layer of skin. Slice the bulbs thinly.

2 Flatten the thick parts of the chicken breast by hitting it with a meat tenderizer or the bottom of a heavy saucepan, then cut into thin strips 1½–2 inches long.

3 Divide the ingredients among four bowls. Wash, dry, pick, and finely chop or shred the parsley leaves.

4 Add the nuoc mam, salt, and pepper to the poultry stock and bring to a vigorous boil. Divide it among the four bowls, covering all the ingredients. Wait 5 minutes, then sprinkle with the chopped parsley.

MUSHROOM SOUP EN CROÛTE

Understand

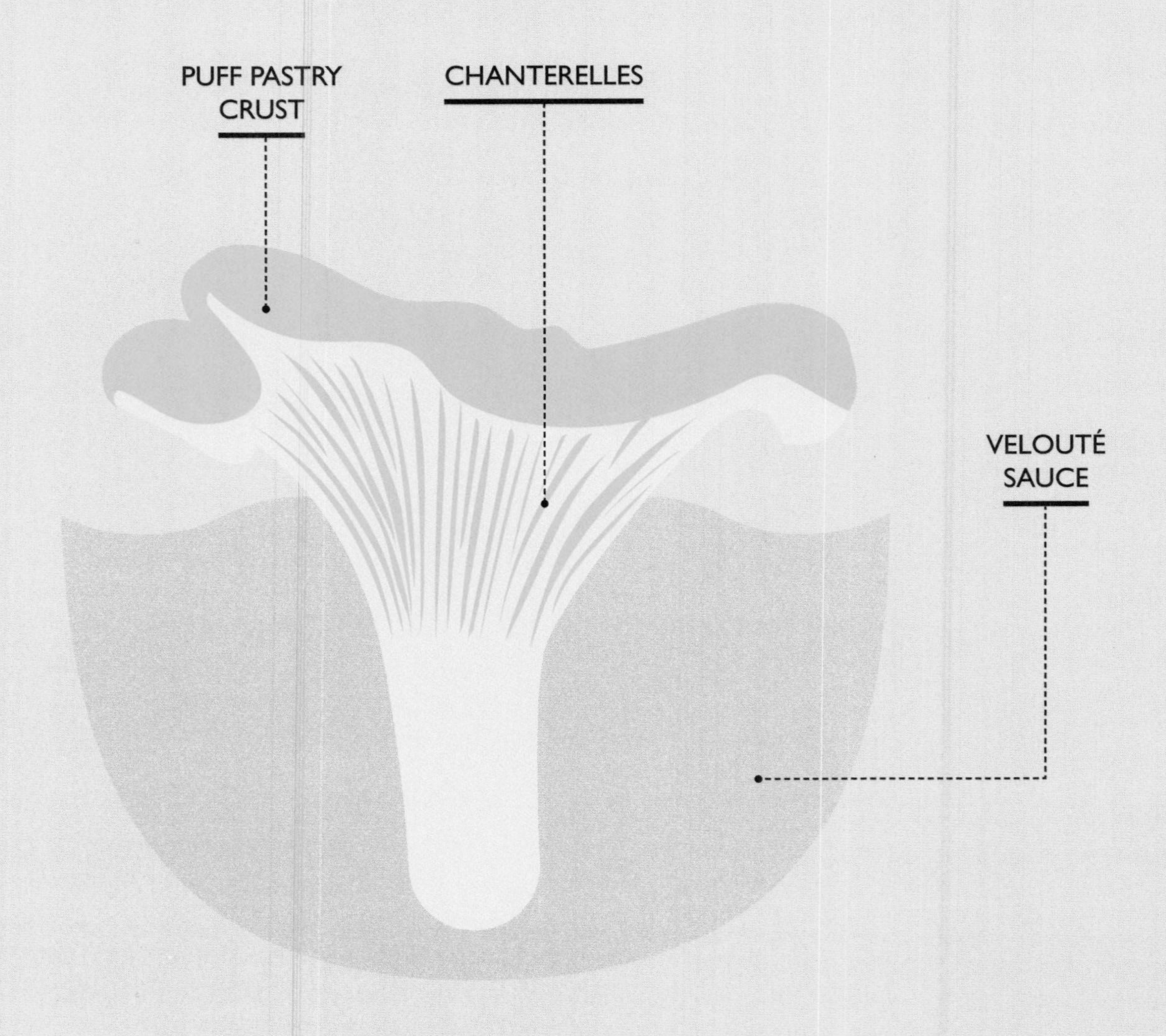

WHAT IS IT?
Velouté sauce of white mushrooms and chanterelles, enriched with cream, covered with a disk of puff pastry, then browned in the oven

TIME TO MAKE
Preparation: 35 minutes
Cooking: 40 minutes

EQUIPMENT
Ovenproof serving bowls
Pastry brush

VARIATION
Traditional velouté sauce: bechamel sauce base, thickened with cream and egg yolk

TECHNIQUES TO MASTER
Thinly slicing (page 280)
Mincing (page 280)
Finely chopping (page 280)
Cutting in scallops (page 280)
Sweating (page 282)

TIP
The puff pastry must be very cold to be worked easily.

WHY DOES THE PUFF PASTRY SWELL UP IN THE OVEN?
Puff pastry contains water, which vaporizes to steam during cooking. This change triggers the swelling of the pastry.

Learn

SERVES 4

1 VELOUTÉ SAUCE WITH MUSHROOMS

10 ½ oz large white mushrooms
7 oz chanterelles
1 shallot
1 garlic clove
3 tablespoons butter
2 ½ cups white poultry stock (page 10)
⅔ cup heavy cream

2 SEASONING

1 teaspoon fine salt
freshly ground black pepper (6 turns)

3 PASTRY

9 oz puff pastry (one-third recipe on page 46)
cold all-purpose flour, for dusting

4 TO FINISH

1 egg yolk, whisked with 1 teaspoon water

Making mushroom soup en croûte

1 Cut the stems off the white mushrooms and slice the caps into four or eight slices, depending on their size. Clean the chanterelles with a moistened pastry brush, then slice them thinly. Peel and mince the shallot. Peel and de-germ the garlic clove, then crush and finely chop (page 280).

2 Melt the butter in a large saucepan and sweat the shallot. Add the mushrooms, then stir constantly for 3–4 minutes, until the mushrooms have released their water. Add the garlic and cook for 30 seconds, or until fragrant. Season with salt and pepper.

3 In a separate saucepan, bring the white poultry stock to a boil, then pour it over the mushrooms. Simmer for 20 minutes. Preheat the oven to 360°F.

4 Remove about half the mushrooms. Add the cream to the saucepan, then blend with a hand-held blender to obtain a smooth creamy sauce.

5 Roll out the puff pastry on a floured work surface. Cut out four disks with a diameter 1¼ inches larger than the top of your ovenproof serving bowls. Set aside in the refrigerator.

6 Divide the reserved mushrooms among the serving bowls then pour in the cream sauce to ⅝ inch from the top.

7 Dampen the rim and the top of the bowls on the outside with a little water. Place a pastry disk over each bowl and fold down the edges over the top of the bowl, pressing a little to seal. Brush with the egg yolk mixture.

8 Bake for 20 minutes, or until the pastry is golden. Cut the crust with the tip of a knife.

SCALLOP CARPACCIO

Understand

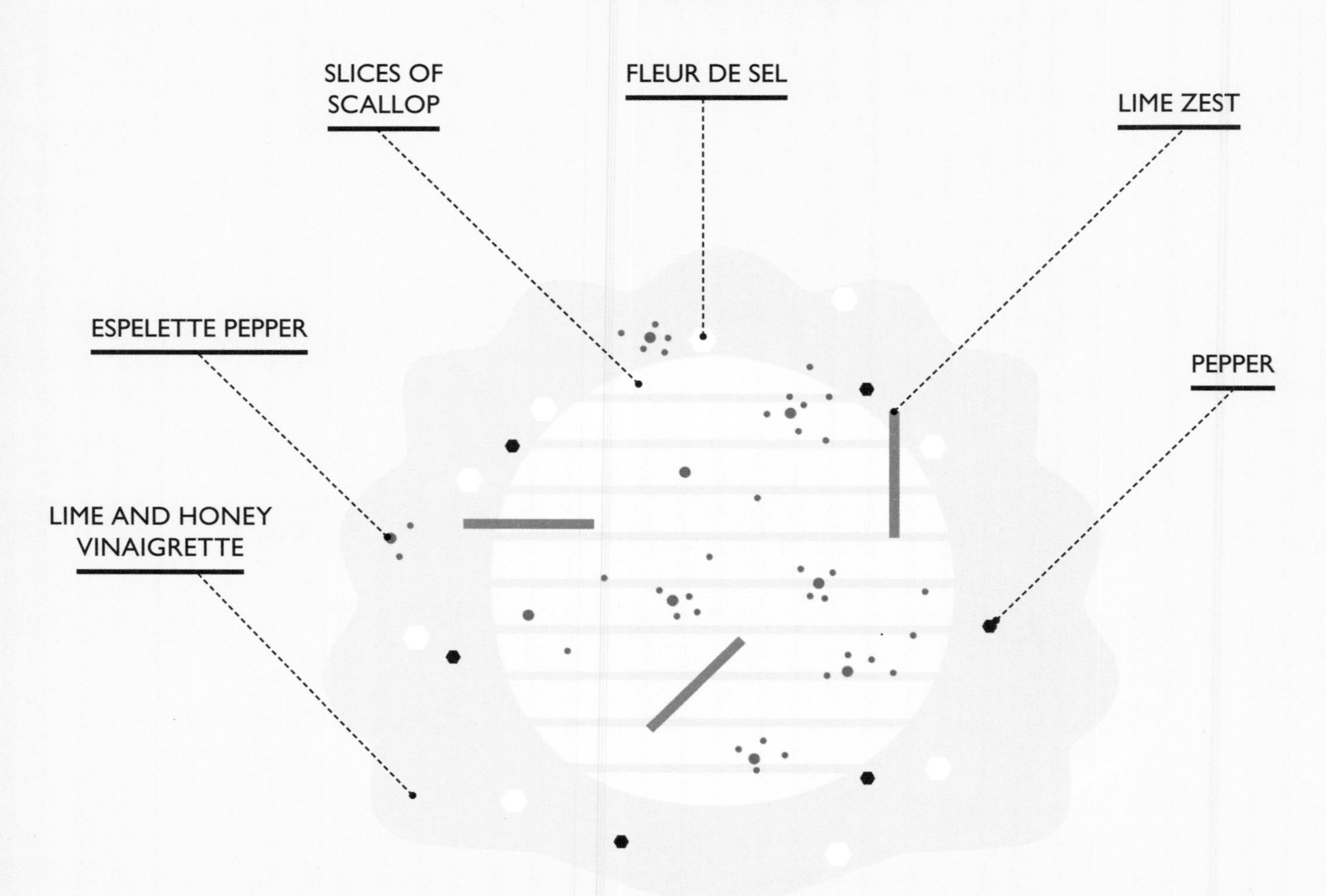

WHAT IS IT?
Thin slices of raw scallop, seasoned at the last minute with a lime vinaigrette

TIME TO MAKE
Preparation: 25 minutes
Resting: 30 minutes

EQUIPMENT
Very sharp, thin-bladed knife
French-style citrus zester

TRICKY ASPECT
Cutting the scallops

TECHNIQUES TO MASTER
Mincing (page 280)
Zesting (page 280)

TIP
With frozen scallops: slice them before they have completely thawed.

ORGANIZATION
Prepare the plates up to 30 minutes in advance. Cover with plastic wrap and refrigerate. Season at the last minute.

WHY FREEZE THE SCALLOPS?
Freezing firms up the flesh and makes it easier to cut.

WHAT EFFECT DOES THE VINAIGRETTE HAVE ON THE SCALLOPS?
Unlike a tartare or marinated fish, here the vinaigrette is added at the last minute; it doesn't change the texture of the scallop, simply dresses it.

Learn

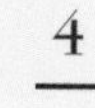

SERVES 4

SCALLOPS

12 sea scallops

VINAIGRETTE

1 lime
½ teaspoon fine salt
1 teaspoon honey
freshly ground black pepper (8 turns)
3½ tablespoons olive oil

TO SERVE

1 small shallot
pinch of Espelette pepper
¼ teaspoon fleur de sel

1 Wash the scallops and dry with a paper towel. Arrange on a plate, cover with plastic wrap, and freeze for 30 minutes.

2 Using a French-style zester, pull off fine shreds of lime zest and set aside. Squeeze the lime juice into a small bowl and dissolve the fine salt in the juice. Add the honey and pepper, then pour in the olive oil while mixing with a fork.

3 Peel and mince the shallot.

4 Cut the scallops horizontally into thin rounds, five or six slices per scallop.

5 Arrange the scallop slices on a plate. Mix the vinaigrette once more, then pour over. Sprinkle with the Espelette pepper, shallot, fleur de sel, and lime zest.

SALMON TARTARE

Understand

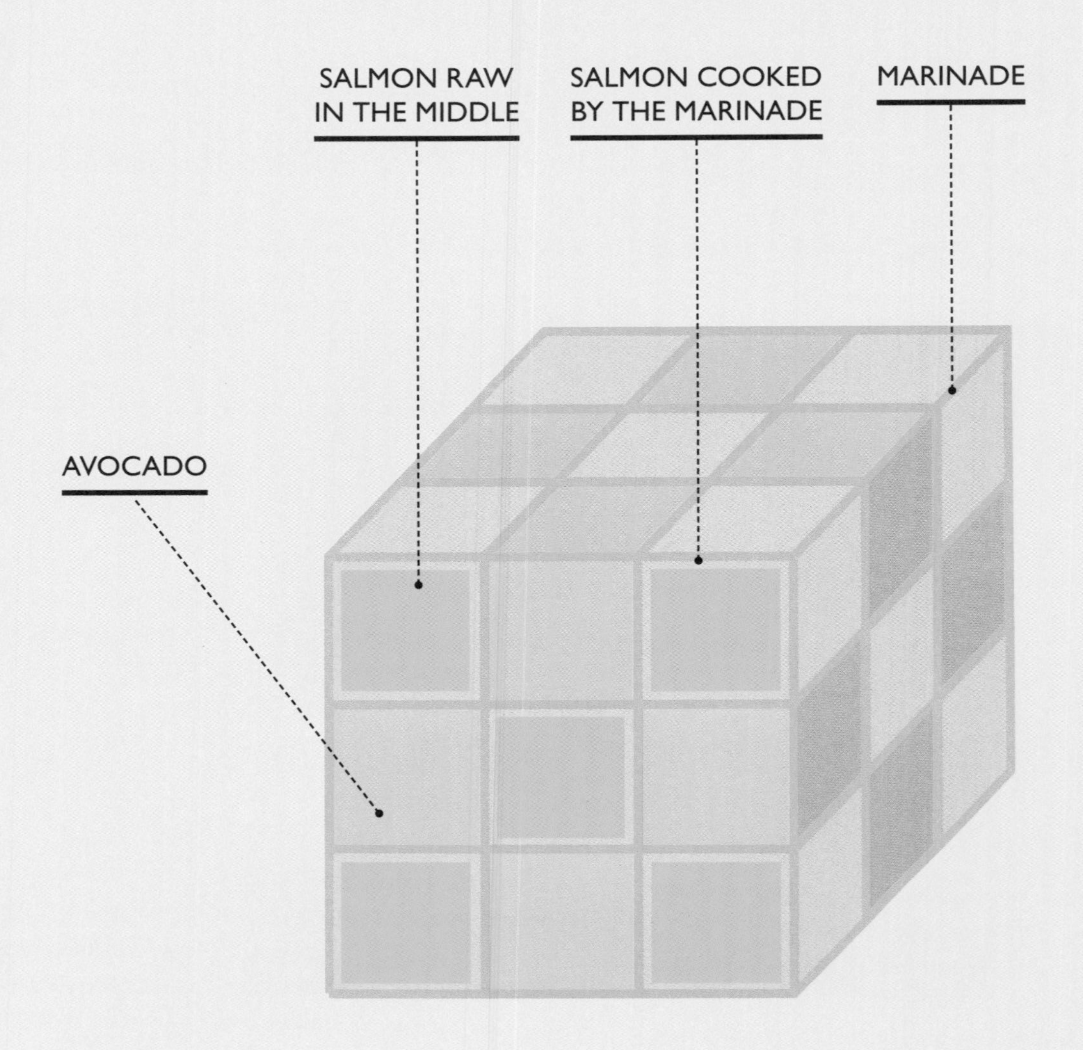

WHAT IS IT?
Diced raw salmon marinated in a mixture of lime juice, olive oil, shallot, and dill, adorned with diced avocado

TIME TO MAKE
Preparation: 25 minutes
Resting: 5 minutes

EQUIPMENT
Chef's knife, fine-mesh sieve

VARIATIONS
Tartare à la minute (without resting time)
Gravlax—24 hours in the marinade (page 108)

SERVING VARIATION
In a circle, alternating salmon and avocado

TRICKY ASPECT
Cutting the salmon

TECHNIQUES TO MASTER
Finely chopping and mincing (page 280)
Zesting (page 280)

TIP
Oil the knife to make cutting easier.

STORAGE
Prepare the salmon and the marinade separately, up to 1 hour before serving, and only bring them together 15 minutes before.

WHAT IS A MARINADE?
An aromatic liquid intended to tenderize and flavor large pieces before cooking or small pieces without cooking (instant marinades).

DOES THE ACIDITY OF THE LIME "COOK" THE FISH?
The French use the word coction *rather than cooking to describe the modification of the proteins by the acidity, since no heat is used.*

Learn

SERVES 4

TARTARE

14 oz skinless salmon fillets
1 avocado

MARINADE

a few dill sprigs
2 limes
1 shallot
2 tablespoons olive oil

SEASONING

½ teaspoon fine salt
freshly ground black pepper (6 turns)

1 Cut the salmon in very small dice. Set aside in the refrigerator. Wash, dry, pick, and finely chop the dill. Wash, dry, and zest one of the limes using a French-style citrus zester, then squeeze both. Peel and very finely mince the shallot.

2 In a large mixing bowl, dissolve the salt in the lime juice, then add the pepper, dill, and half the shallot. Pour in the oil and stir. Add the salmon, stir, then refrigerate for 5 minutes.

3 Cut the avocado in dice, then mix with the lime zest and the remaining shallot.

4 Drain the salmon over a bowl. Mix the avocado into the drained marinade, then drain the avocado, saving the marinade.

5 Carefully mix the salmon and drained avocado and dress with a little of the reserved marinade.

SALMON GRAVLAX

Understand

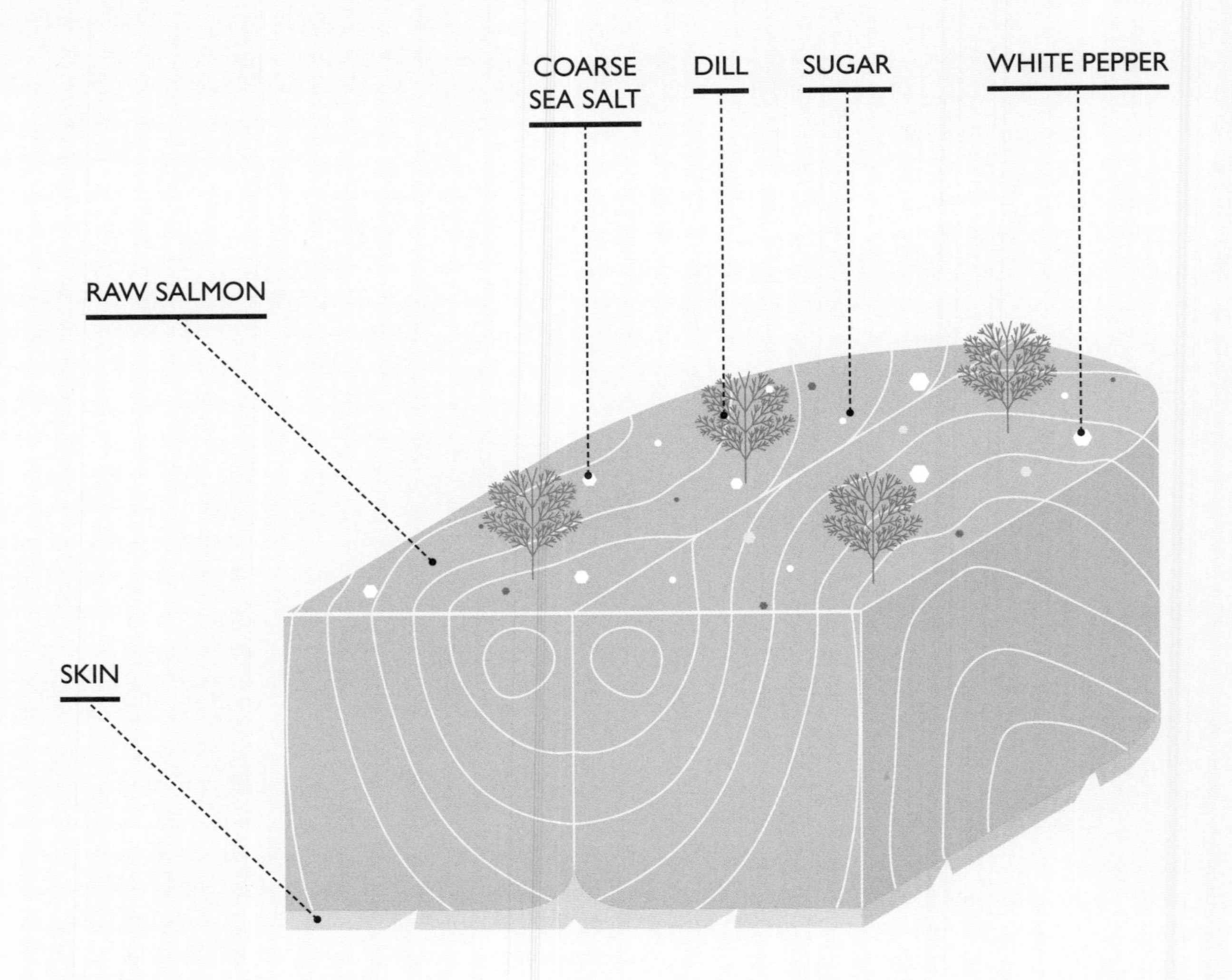

WHAT IS IT?

Raw salmon marinated in salt and sugar, and seasoned with pepper and dill

TIME TO MAKE

Preparation: 20 minutes (the day before) + 30 minutes
Maceration: 24 hours

EQUIPMENT

Fishbone tweezers
Very sharp thin-bladed knife

TRICKY ASPECTS

– Skinning the salmon
– Removing bones without tearing the flesh

TECHNIQUES TO MASTER

Crushing spices (page 280)
Finely chopping (page 280)

TIP

Dip the tweezers in water before removing each bone.

IT'S READY . . .

When the salmon has lost some of its water and firmed up.

STORAGE

1 week in the refrigerator wrapped in plastic wrap.

NOTE

For thicker, more uniform flesh, choose a piece from the center of the salmon.

WHAT ROLE DOES THE MARINADE PLAY?

The sugar and salt absorb water from the surface of the fish, which firms up the flesh. The dill, pepper, and coriander seed add aromatic notes that will be captured by the fat in the fish and flavor it deeply.

SERVES 4

GRAVLAX

- 1 small bunch dill
- 1 tablespoon coarse sea salt
- 4 teaspoons sugar
- ½ teaspoon peppercorns (preferably white), crushed (page 280)
- 1 teaspoon coriander seeds, crushed (page 280)
- 7 oz salmon fillet, pin bones removed

GRAVLAX SAUCE

- a few dill sprigs
- ½ lemon
- ½ teaspoon fine salt
- freshly ground black pepper (6 turns)
- 2 tablespoons Dijon mustard
- 1½ tablespoons maple syrup
- ⅓ cup peanut oil

1 To make the gravlax, wash, dry, pick, and finely chop the dill. Mix the coarse sea salt, sugar, dill, peppercorns, and coriander seeds.

2 Wash the salmon and dry with a paper towel. Score the skin with a sharp thin-bladed knife.

3 Spread one-third of the dill mixture in a baking dish. Place the fillet on top, skin side down, and cover with the remaining dill mixture, pressing with your hands to coat the fish well. Cover with plastic wrap. Set aside in the refrigerator for 24 hours. After 12 hours, pour off any liquid.

4 Rub the salmon with paper towels to dry it and remove the seeds. Remove the skin by sliding a sharp knife under it. Cut into thin slices on the bias, ⅜–⅝ inch thick.

5 To make the sauce, wash, dry, pick, and finely chop the dill. Squeeze the lemon half. Mix the lemon juice with the salt and pepper to dissolve the salt. Stir in the mustard and maple syrup, then gradually pour in the oil while whisking, to obtain a smooth mixture. Stir in the chopped dill.

6 Place three slices of salmon on each plate, with a little sauce to one side.

EGGS IN ASPIC

Understand

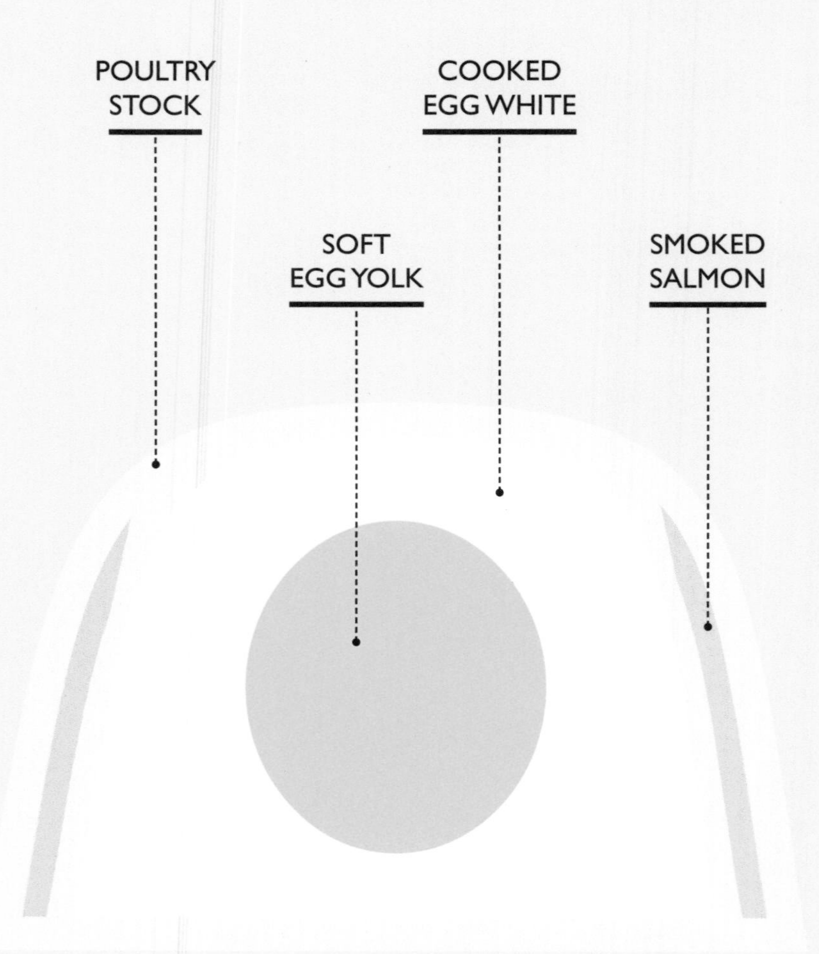

WHAT ARE THEY?

Medium-boiled eggs set in a molded flavored jelly and decorated with smoked salmon

DEFINITION

Aspic: cooked food suspended in a molded savory jelly. Egg, meat, and fish are all traditionally prepared this way.

TIME TO MAKE

Preparation: 45 minutes
Resting: at least 1 hour

EQUIPMENT

Eggs-in-aspic molds (or 6-ounce ramekins)

ALTERNATIVE

With a poached egg (page 68) instead of a medium-boiled egg

VARIATIONS

Eggs in aspic with ham
Dressed eggs in aspic
(cornichons + tarragon + capers)
Jelly flavored with port, Madeira, or Cognac

TRICKY ASPECTS

- The temperature of the jellied stock (if too hot it cooks the salmon, if too cold it starts to set)
- Turning out the molds

WHY REST FOR 1 HOUR IN THE REFRIGERATOR?

Once the gelatin is dissolved in a hot liquid, it must set into a jelly. This occurs at 50°F. With the cold, the gelatin molecules bind together to form a network characteristic of gels.

Learn

SERVES 4

EGGS

4 medium-boiled eggs, shelled (page 65)

JELLY

2 cups white poultry stock (page 10)
½ teaspoon fine salt
1 envelope powdered gelatin (2½ teaspoons), or 3 gelatin sheets

TO GARNISH

1¾ oz smoked salmon, sliced
4 dill sprigs

1 Wash, dry, and pick the dill. Cut the slices of salmon into strips 1½ inches wide and long enough to wrap around an egg the long way.

2 Heat the poultry stock. Add the salt (unless you're using purchased stock). Soften the gelatin in a small bowl following the instructions on the package, then add it to the hot stock. Whisk to dissolve it completely. Leave to cool.

3 Place three or four dill leaves in the bottom of each mold. Pour some still-warm gelatin mixture over the leaves to a depth of ⅛ inch. Refrigerate to set. Dip the salmon slices in the gelatin mixture. Stick them to the sides of the mold without overlapping (trim if necessary).

4 Cut a thin slice of egg white from one long side of each egg to stabilize it. Place an egg, sliced side down, in the center of each mold. Cover with the lukewarm gelatin mixture and refrigerate for at least 1 hour.

5 To unmold, slide a thin-bladed knife around the edge of the mold, then turn it out onto a plate.

LIGHTLY COOKED FOIE GRAS

Understand

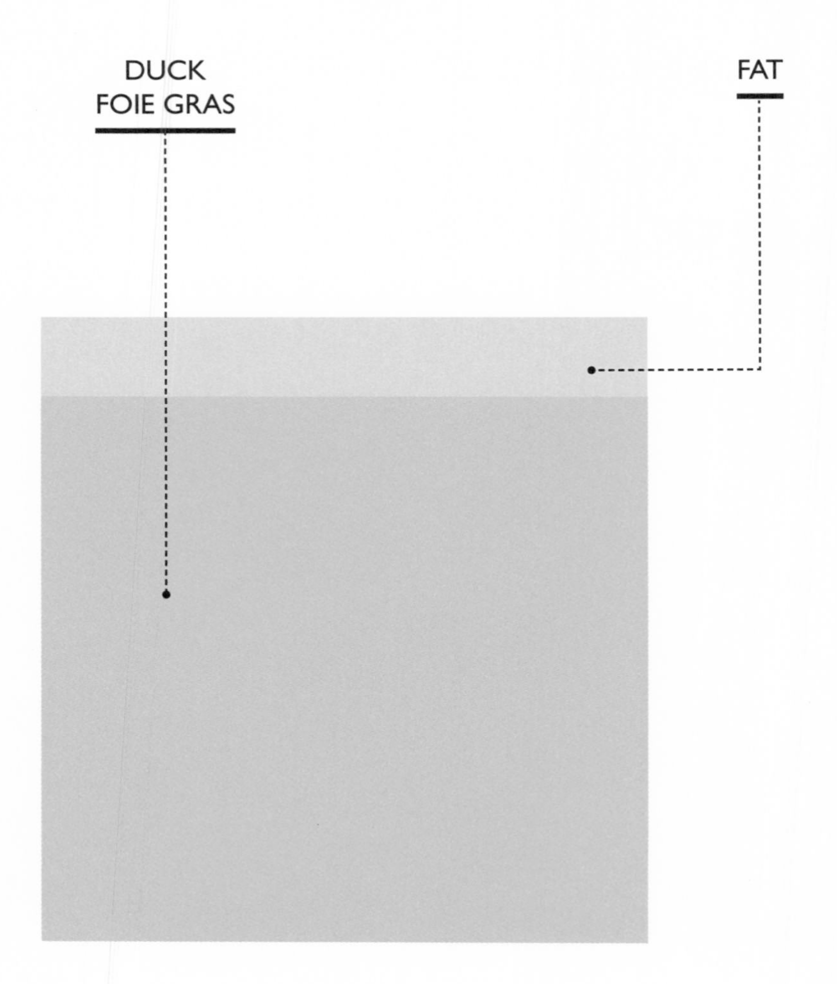

WHAT IS IT?
Raw duck liver seasoned with salt, pepper, and vermouth, cooked in a terrine in a water bath

TIME TO MAKE
Preparation: 20 minutes
Cooking: 45 minutes
Resting: 3 hours + 48 hours (at least)

EQUIPMENT
Terrine or loaf pan (8 × 4 inches)
Small rigid tray (to fit inside the terrine) and 1 lb weight, both covered with foil

ADDITIONAL SEASONINGS
White port, Cognac, Calvados, Armagnac
Espelette pepper, paprika, nutmeg

TRICKY ASPECT
Cooking

TECHNIQUE TO MASTER
Deveining foie gras (page 278)

IT'S READY . . .
When the tip of a knife comes out lukewarm after being inserted into the middle for 5–10 seconds (110°F with a probe thermometer).

STORAGE
1 week in the refrigerator in the sealed terrine

NOTE
Adjust the cooking and seasoning to the weight: 8–10 minutes per 3½ oz foie gras; 1½ teaspoons salt, 2 teaspoons pepper, and 2 tablespoons vermouth per 2 lb 3 oz foie gras.

WHY USE A WATER BATH?
It allows gentle cooking because its temperature never rises above 212°F. This prevents the fat in the foie gras from melting.

WHY "LIGHTLY COOKED"?
Because it is cooked to 110°F at the core (120°F once out of the oven), unlike preserved foie gras (cooked to 210°F at the core).

SERVES 4

FOIE GRAS

one 1 lb 2 oz lobe cold duck foie gras

SEASONING

1 teaspoon fine salt
freshly ground black pepper (15 turns)
1 tablespoon dry vermouth

TO SERVE

fleur de sel
crushed black pepper (page 280)

1 Remove the foie gras from the refrigerator for 1 hour so it is at 54–57°F. Preheat the oven to 250°F. Mix the salt and pepper. Devein the foie gras (page 278). Season the two open faces of the liver with the salt and pepper mixture. Sprinkle with the vermouth.

2 Place the pieces in the terrine, smooth side out, add any seasoning that fell to the side, and tamp down with the back of your hand to remove any trapped air.

3 Place the terrine in a baking dish, add boiling water to reach halfway up the sides, and put the lid on the terrine. Bake for 45 minutes, then let cool to room temperature.

4 When the center of the foie gras is at 90–95°F, place the small tray on top and press to make the fat rise. Tip the terrine over a fat separator and pour off the fat and blood that comes with it. Separate and discard the blood. Set the fat aside. Place the weight on the small tray. Refrigerate for at least 3 hours, or until the foie gras has solidified.

5 Remove the weight and the tray, smooth the surface with a spoon, then pour back the reserved fat. If it has solidified too much, liquefy in a hot water bath without overheating. Refrigerate for at least 48 hours.

6 Run the blade of a knife under hot water, dry it, then cut the terrine into slices ¾ inch thick. Sprinkle with the fleur de sel and the crushed pepper.

VOL-AU-VENTS

Understand

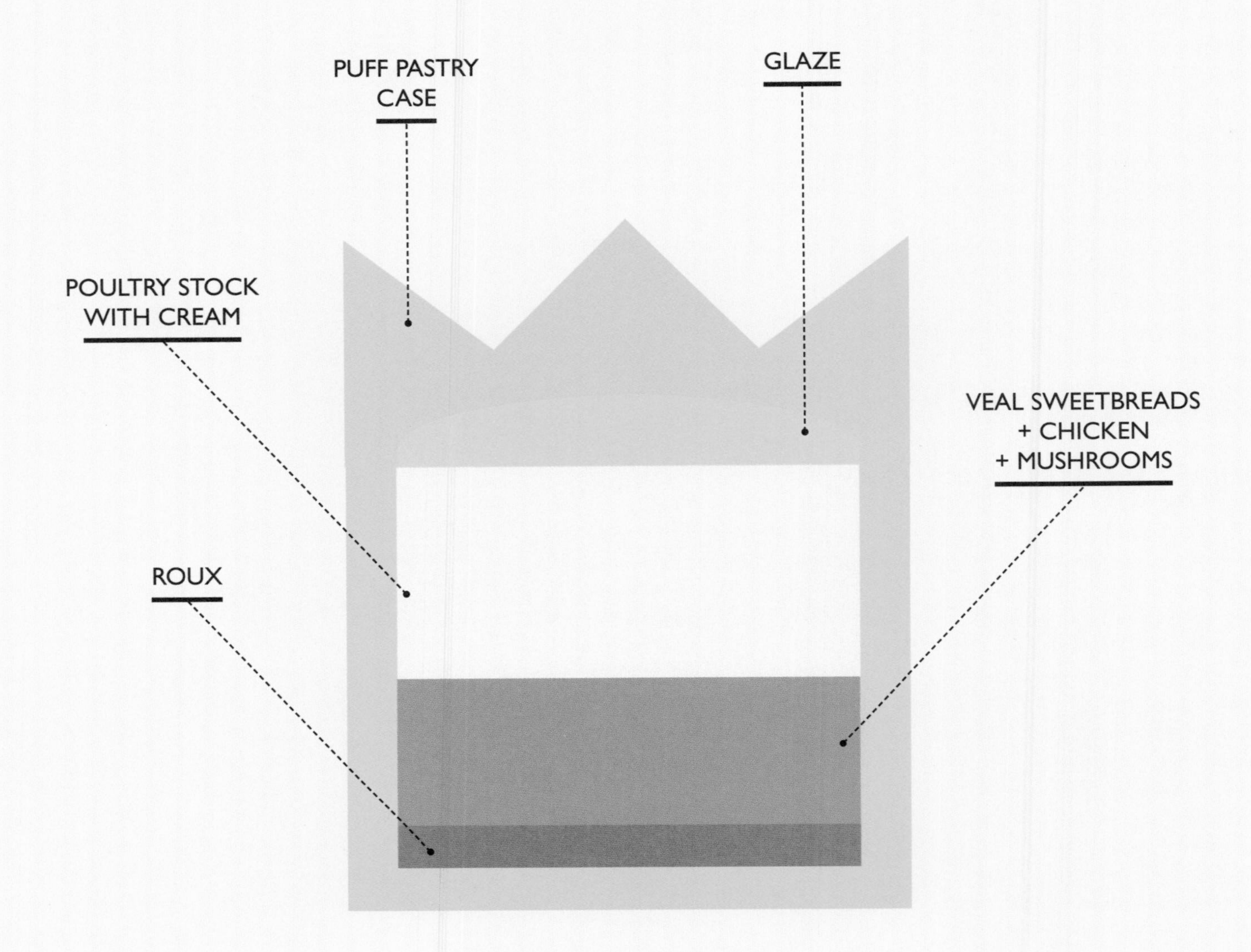

WHAT ARE THEY?

Puff pastry shells filled after cooking with a salpicon (see below) of chicken, veal sweetbreads, and mushrooms, bound with a creamy bechamel sauce

DEFINITIONS

- Vol-au-vent: traditionally, a puff pastry shell of 6–8 inches, filled with a salpicon.
- Bouchée à la reine: mini puff pastry shell filled with a creamy chicken purée or a salpicon of chicken and mushrooms. These days, the two are used interchangeably.
- Salpicon: diced mixture, bound with a sauce.

TIME TO MAKE

Preparation: 45 minutes
Cooking: 1 hour
Resting: 20–30 minutes

EQUIPMENT

Rolling pin
Round cookie cutter (2 inch diameter)
Round cookie cutter (4 inch diameter)

TRICKY ASPECT

Baking the pastry shells

TIP

The puff pastry must be very cold. Refrigerate it for 20–30 minutes before baking, to prevent it from collapsing during cooking.

STORAGE

2 days for the filling (in the refrigerator) and the shells (at room temperature). Assemble and reheat for 8–10 minutes in a 300°F oven.

THEY'RE READY . . .

When the puff pastry is golden and the sauce thick and creamy.

Learn

SERVES 4

1 PASTRY

1 lb 7 oz (1 recipe) puff pastry (page 46)

2 FILLING

2 cups white poultry stock (page 10)
6 oz veal sweetbreads, no membrane
6 oz chicken breast
12 oz white mushrooms
3 tablespoons butter
¼ cup all-purpose flour
½ cup heavy cream

3 GLAZE

1 egg yolk beaten with 1 teaspoon water

4 SEASONING

1 teaspoon fine salt
freshly ground black pepper (6 turns)

Making vol-au-vents

1 Preheat the oven to 390°F. Roll the pastry out to ⅛ inch thick, regularly dusting the pastry, work surface, and rolling pin with flour to prevent it sticking.

2 Cut out four 4-inch disks. Place them on a baking sheet lined with parchment paper. Cut out eight more 4-inch disks, then cut out the centers with a 2-inch cookie cutter to create rings.

3 Brush the pastry disks with the egg glaze, then place one ring on top of each disk, pressing gently to make it stick. Glaze the whole surface of the pastry. Place a second ring on top of the first, pressing gently. Glaze. Firm up the pastry by refrigerating for 20–30 minutes. Bake for 20 minutes. Reduce the temperature to 320°F after 10 minutes.

4 Pour the poultry stock into a saucepan and immerse the veal sweetbreads and chicken breast in it. Bring to a simmer and cook for 25 minutes.

5 Remove the stems from the mushrooms, then peel the caps and cut them into quarters. Add them to the stock and cook for another 5 minutes. Reserving the stock, scoop out the sweetbreads, chicken, and mushrooms using a skimmer or slotted spoon, and keep warm.

6 Make a roux (page 18) with the butter and flour in a large saucepan. Gradually incorporate the stock, whisking constantly. Add the cream and let it simmer for 10 minutes while whisking. Adjust the seasoning.

7 Cut the sweetbreads and chicken in small dice. Add them to the sauce along with the mushrooms.

8 Using a paring knife, pull off the little pastry caps from the first layer of pastry without piercing the bottom, and set aside. Fill the shells with the cream filling and reheat in the oven for 5 minutes.

9 Serve the vol-au-vents topped with their pastry "lids."

GOUGÈRES

Understand

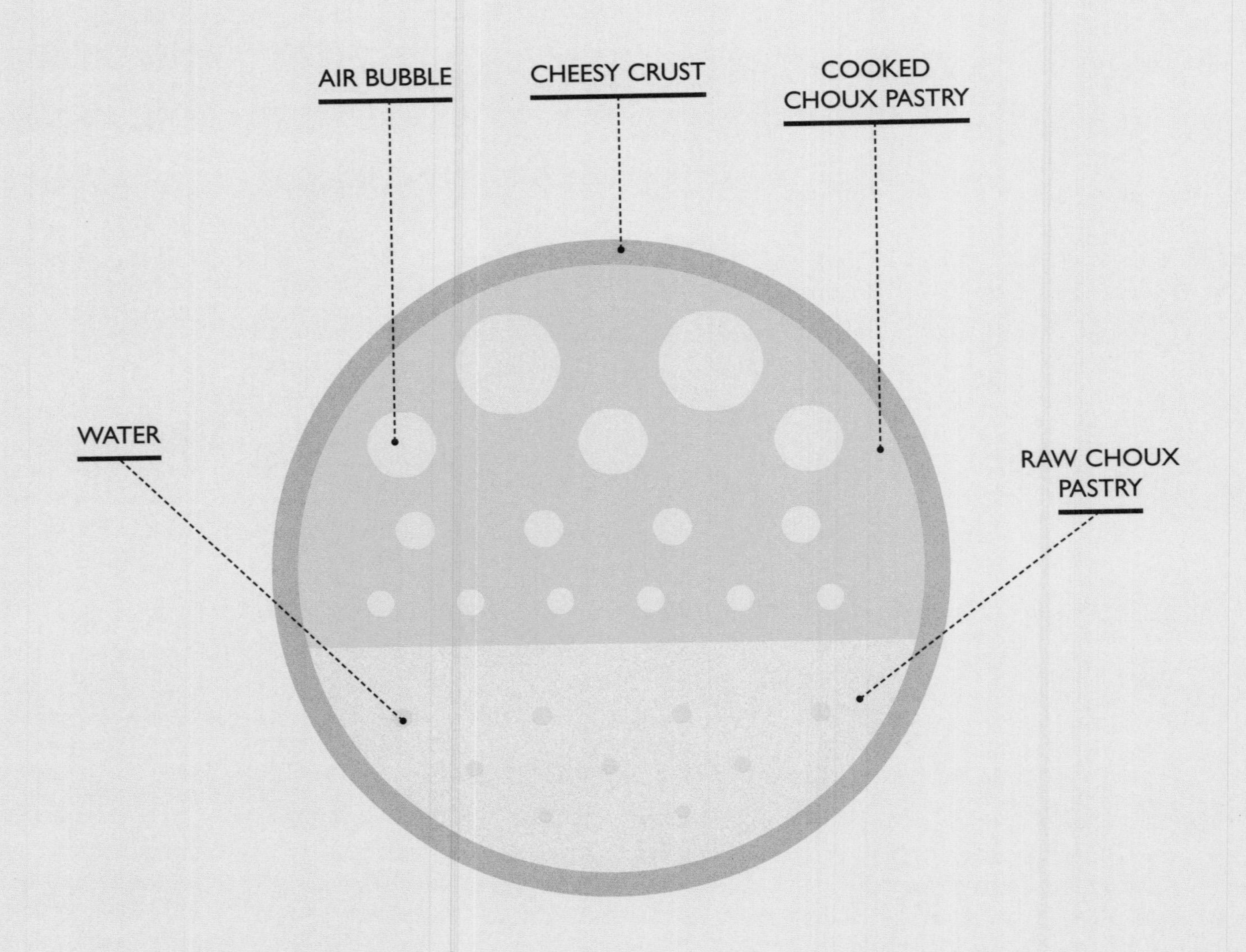

WHAT ARE THEY?
Savory cheese choux pastry, piped into balls and baked

TIME TO MAKE
Preparation: 30 minutes
Cooking: 25–30 minutes

EQUIPMENT
Pastry bag + plain ½-inch decorating tip
Baking sheet

VARIATION
Piping in a ring to make a wreath

TRICKY ASPECT
Baking

TECHNIQUES TO MASTER
Drying out choux pastry (page 119)
Making a panade (page 119)
Piping (page 281)

TIP
Don't open the oven door before the gougères have browned: there's a risk they will sink.

STORAGE
The gougères can be reheated for 2 minutes in a 300°F oven.

HOW DO THE GOUGÈRES PUFF?
During baking at 300°F, the water in the pastry turns into steam, which is trapped by the dough, causing the pastry to inflate.

WHY DO THEY SINK IF THE OVEN IS OPENED TOO SOON?
Because when the temperature of the oven drops, the steam becomes water again, which takes up less volume, and so the gougères fall.

Learn

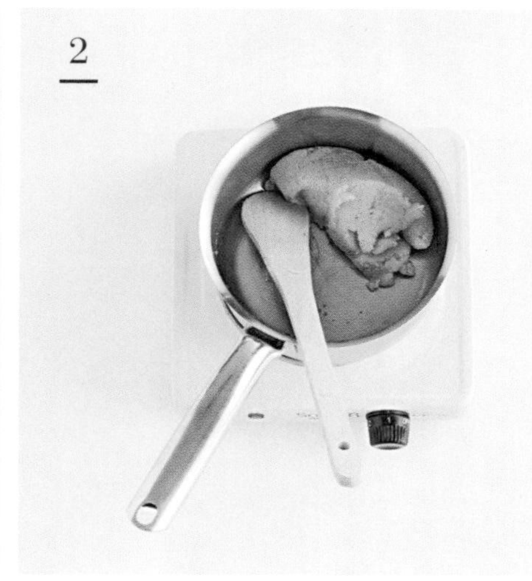

MAKES 30

CHEESE CHOUX PASTRY

½ cup all-purpose flour
¼ cup water + ¼ cup milk
3½ tablespoons butter, cut into dice
2 eggs, lightly whisked
about 1 cup finely grated Comté or Gruyère

SEASONING

pinch of paprika
pinch of cayenne pepper
pinch of freshly grated nutmeg
freshly ground black pepper (6 turns)
large pinch of fine salt

1 Preheat the oven to 360°F. In a bowl, mix the flour with the spices and set aside. In a saucepan, combine the water, milk, butter, and salt and place the pan over medium heat. Stir the mixture with a wooden spoon until the butter melts, then bring everything to a boil; let it boil for 2–3 seconds.

2 Remove the saucepan from the heat, add all the flour at once and stir the mixture with a wooden spoon to form a moist dough, called a panade. Return the saucepan to the stove and, over medium heat, continue to stir the panade until the edges pull away from the sides of the saucepan. This will dry out the panade.

3 Transfer the panade to the bowl of an electric mixer and mix for a few seconds to cool it down, or stir it with a wooden spoon. Once the panade has cooled, gradually add the whisked eggs, stopping after you have added two-thirds. This will create the choux pastry dough. If the choux pastry sticks to the spoon and falls off to form one (or several) points, it is ready; if not, keep adding more of the eggs.

4 Add the cheese to the pastry dough and stir.

5 Using a pastry bag fitted with a plain ½-inch decorating tip, pipe 30 gougères 1¼ inches in diameter, spacing them at least 1¼ inches apart, on a baking sheet lined with parchment paper. Smooth them out (using your finger or a pastry brush) with the remaining beaten egg or water.

6 Bake for 25–30 minutes, until the gougères are golden. Cool on a wire rack and serve warm.

CHEESE SOUFFLÉ

Understand

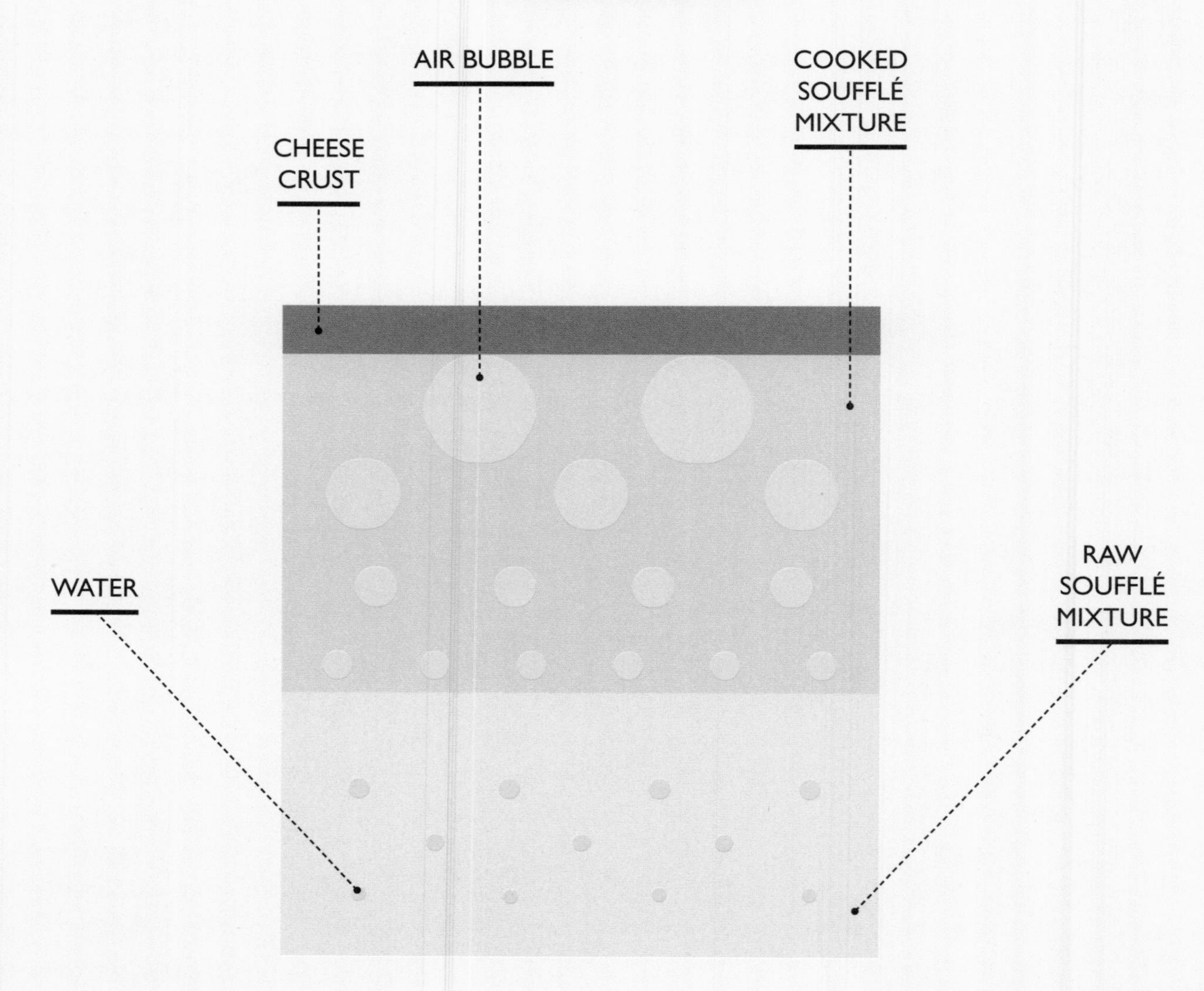

WHAT IS IT?

Mixture of Mornay sauce (bechamel sauce with cheese and egg yolks) and beaten egg white that inflates during cooking

TIME TO MAKE

Preparation: 30 minutes
Cooking: 45–50 minutes
Resting: 10 minutes

EQUIPMENT

Electric mixer (a stand mixer ensures a better structure in the beaten egg white)
Soufflé dish (8 inch diameter)

VARIATIONS

Crab soufflé, sweet soufflés (with pastry cream instead of bechamel sauce)

TRICKY ASPECT

Baking

TECHNIQUES TO MASTER

Bechamel sauce (page 22)
Mincing (page 280)

TIP

If the soufflé sinks, rebake for 5 minutes. It will swell up and lose only ⅜ inch of its height.

IT'S READY . . .

When the soufflé is nicely browned and has risen, but has stopped rising.

Learn

HOW DOES THE SOUFFLÉ INFLATE?

The water in the mixture expands with heat. The air bubbles make the mixture rise, while at the same time are captured by the hardening of the egg proteins.

WHY DO SOUFFLÉS SINK?

Because the steam cools and condenses. As the water takes up less volume and the structural network formed by the hardened egg proteins isn't rigid enough, the soufflé sinks.

SERVES 4

SOUFFLÉ MIXTURE (MORNAY SAUCE)

3–4 Italian parsley sprigs
¼ cup all-purpose flour
¼ teaspoon paprika
½ teaspoon fine salt
pinch of cayenne pepper
pinch of black pepper
pinch of freshly grated nutmeg
3 tablespoons butter
1½ cups milk
1½ cups grated Comté or Gruyère
3 tablespoons finely grated Parmesan
6 egg yolks

EGG WHITES

6 egg whites

FOR THE SOUFFLÉ DISH

1 tablespoon butter, softened
3 tablespoons finely grated Parmesan

Making cheese soufflé

1 Preheat the oven to 360°F. Generously butter an 8-inch soufflé dish with the softened butter. Sprinkle the grated Parmesan around the inside, tipping the dish to spread it around. Refrigerate.

2 Wash, dry, pick, and mince the parsley. Mix the flour, paprika, salt, cayenne pepper, black pepper, and nutmeg in a mixing bowl. Melt the butter in a small saucepan over medium heat. Add the flour mixture and cook for 1 minute, whisking, to make a roux. Pour in all the milk at once, continuing to whisk, and cook for 1 minute to make a bechamel sauce. Remove from the heat.

3 Add the grated Comté and the Parmesan (reserving 1 teaspoon), stirring with a spatula until the cheese has melted. Let the mixture cool for 10 minutes.

4 Incorporate the egg yolks and the parsley to complete the Mornay sauce.

5 Whip the egg whites to stiff peaks using an electric mixer. Add the Mornay sauce and beat for 15 seconds.

6 Pour the mixture into the prepared soufflé dish, leaving 1¼ inches free at the top of the dish. Sprinkle with the reserved Parmesan.

7 Bake for 45–50 minutes, reducing the oven temperature to 320°F after 20 minutes. Check if the soufflé is cooked by inserting a thin-bladed knife in the center (going in from the side): the blade should come out dry.

SOUFFLÉED CREPES

Understand

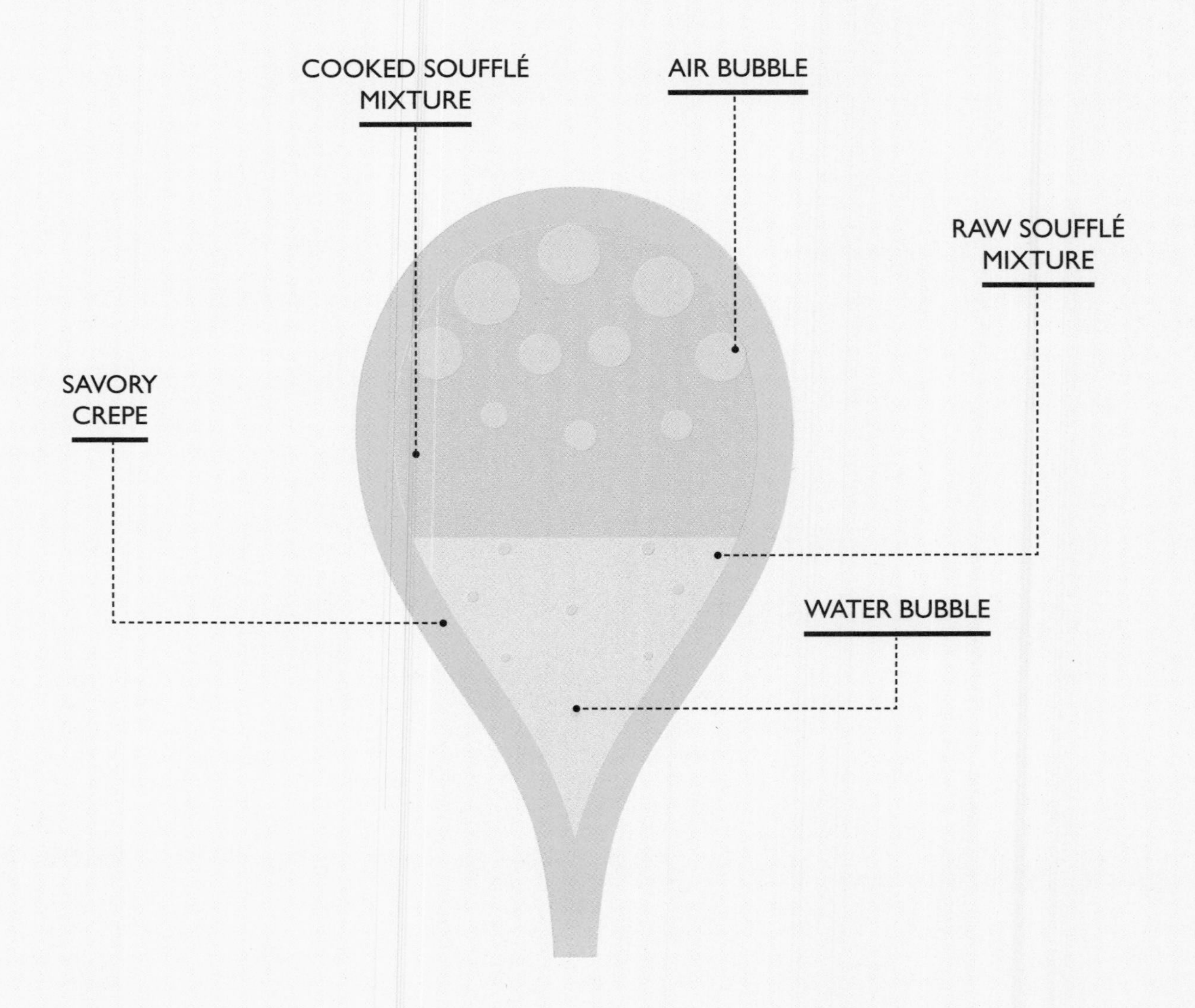

WHAT ARE THEY?

Crepes filled with a cheese soufflé mixture and mushrooms, then baked in the oven

TIME TO MAKE

Preparation: 45 minutes
Cooking: 10–12 minutes
Resting: 10 minutes

EQUIPMENT

1 crepe pan (10 inch diameter)
2 baking sheets
Electric mixer (a stand mixer ensures a better structure in the beaten egg white)

VARIATION

Souffléed crepes with Roquefort and walnuts

TRICKY ASPECTS

- Making thin crepes
- Incorporating the bechamel sauce into the beaten egg white

TECHNIQUES TO MASTER

Finely chopping (page 280)
Cutting in scallops (page 280)

STORAGE

1 day in the refrigerator, covered in plastic wrap. Reheat for 5 minutes in a 300°F oven.

THEY'RE READY . . .

When the crepes are slightly swollen and the soufflé mixture is cooked (a skewer inserted in the middle should come out clean).

Learn

SERVES 4

1 CREPE BATTER

½ cup all-purpose flour
2 eggs (at room temperature)
½ teaspoon fine salt
⅔ cup milk (at room temperature)
2 tablespoons beurre noisette (page 53)
1 teaspoon peanut oil

2 SOUFFLÉ MIXTURE

¼ cup all-purpose flour
½ teaspoon fine salt
pinch of cayenne pepper
freshly ground black pepper (3 turns)
pinch of freshly grated nutmeg
3 tablespoons butter
softened butter for the baking sheets
1 cup milk
5 eggs, separated

3 FILLING

1 garlic clove
7 oz white mushrooms
3 tablespoons butter
¼ teaspoon fine salt
freshly ground black pepper (3 turns)
1 cup grated Emmental cheese

Making souffléed crepes

1 Prepare the crepe batter. Make a well in the center of the flour in a large mixing bowl. Break the eggs into the well, add the salt and whisk. Gradually add half the milk, whisking until the batter is smooth. Add the beurre noisette, mix, then pour in the remaining milk.

2 Heat a crepe pan over very high heat. Grease it using a paper towel soaked with the peanut oil. Pour a half-ladleful of batter into the center and spread it out by tipping the pan. Turn the crepe over when the edges unstick and the bottom has colored. Leave for a few seconds then turn out onto a plate, with the side last cooked on top. Reduce the heat a little and repeat to make seven more crepes, oiling the pan between each if necessary.

3 To make the filling, peel, crush, then finely chop the garlic. Remove the stems from the mushrooms, then peel the caps and cut them in four to eight scallops, depending on their size.

4 Sweat the mushrooms in the 3 tablespoons butter over medium heat, until they lose some of their water. Stir in the garlic, then cook for 30 seconds to 1 minute. Season with the salt and pepper.

5 Preheat the oven to 430°F with racks in the upper and lower thirds. Butter two baking sheets. Prepare the soufflé mixture. Mix the flour, salt, cayenne pepper, black pepper, and nutmeg in a mixing bowl. Make a bechamel sauce (page 22) with 3 tablespoons butter, the flour mixture, and the milk. Remove from the heat, add the Emmental and the mushrooms, stirring with a spatula. Let the mixture cool for 10 minutes. Beat the egg whites to stiff peaks. Incorporate the egg yolks into the soufflé (mushroom) mixture, then pour everything into the beaten egg whites and whisk together.

6 Slide four crepes onto each baking sheet (let them hang over the edge of the sheet a little, with the intention of folding them in half later), the best-looking side down (the side cooked first). Fill half of each crepe with the soufflé mixture. Fold the crepe over without pressing. Put in the oven, reduce the temperature to 390°F and bake for 10–12 minutes. Reduce the temperature to 300°F halfway through the cooking time.

SEARED
FOIE GRAS

Understand

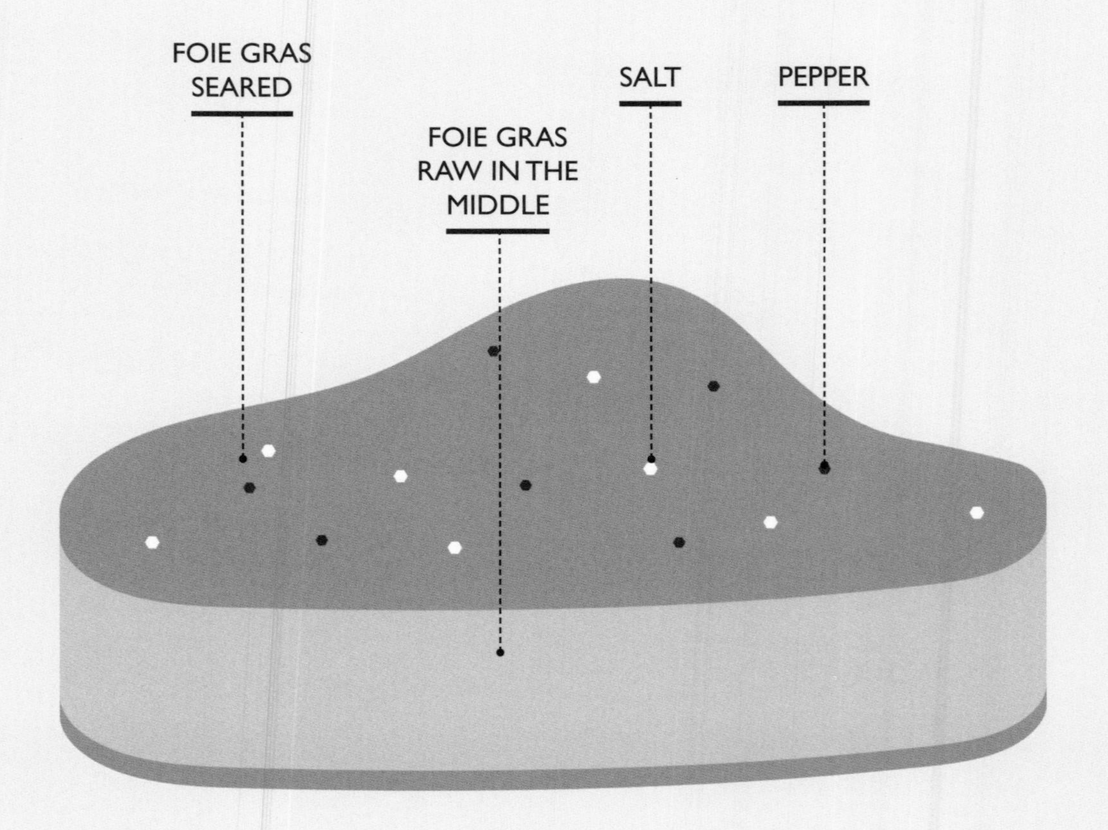

WHAT IS IT?

Slices of raw foie gras seared in a skillet, served with a brunoise of apricots in port or Madeira

TIME TO MAKE

Preparation: 25 minutes
Cooking: 10 minutes
Resting: 1 hour

EQUIPMENT

Ovenproof skillet
Wire rack
French-style zester

VARIATIONS

Filling: fresh or dried figs
Serving: brunoise in a ring

TECHNIQUES TO MASTER

Degreasing a skillet (page 283)
Whisking in butter (page 282)
Cutting in brunoise (page 36)
Reducing a sauce (page 283)

TIPS

- Time the cooking of the foie gras
- Use frozen slices of foie gras to avoid loss during cooking

IT'S READY . . .

When the foie gras is golden and the sauce shiny.

FOIE GRAS OPTIONS

- Frozen slices of raw foie gras (to use as is)
- Whole lobe of foie gras bought from a specialty butcher (ask for slices)
- Vacuum-packed whole lobe of foie gras (separate the two parts and cut them in slices—without deveining)

WHY DOES THE FOIE GRAS "MELT" DURING COOKING?

The foie gras contains lots of fat. The fat melts very rapidly with the rise in temperature, which can cause a significant loss of mass.

Learn

SERVES 4

FOIE GRAS

8 slices raw duck foie gras
½ teaspoon fine salt
freshly ground black pepper (3 turns)

SAUCE

½ cup dried apricots
1 cup port or Madeira
1 lemon
freshly ground black pepper (6 turns)
1 tablespoon olive oil
3 tablespoons butter
½ teaspoon fleur de sel

1 Place the foie gras slices on a large plate lined with plastic wrap, then cover with plastic wrap. Freeze for 1 hour. Preheat the oven to 320°F. Cut the dried apricots in brunoise (page 36). Leave them to marinate for 5 minutes in the port or Madeira. Wash and dry the lemon, then remove the zest in long strips using a French-style zester; chop the zest roughly.

2 Drain the apricots, reserving the wine. Mix the apricots, lemon zest, pepper, and olive oil.

3 Brown the foie gras pieces for 30 seconds on each side in a hot nonstick skillet. Season with the salt and pepper. Transfer the pan to the oven for 5 minutes. Turn off the oven. Transfer the foie gras slices to a wire rack set over a baking sheet and return to the oven.

4 Degrease the skillet. Add the apricots and brown them over high heat, stirring constantly. Deglaze the pan with the reserved wine. Reduce to three-quarters. Cut the butter into dice. Gradually whisk the butter into the sauce (page 282), then adjust the seasoning.

5 Serve the foie gras slices with 2 spoonfuls of the brunoise. Season with the fleur de sel.

ROASTED BONE MARROW

Understand

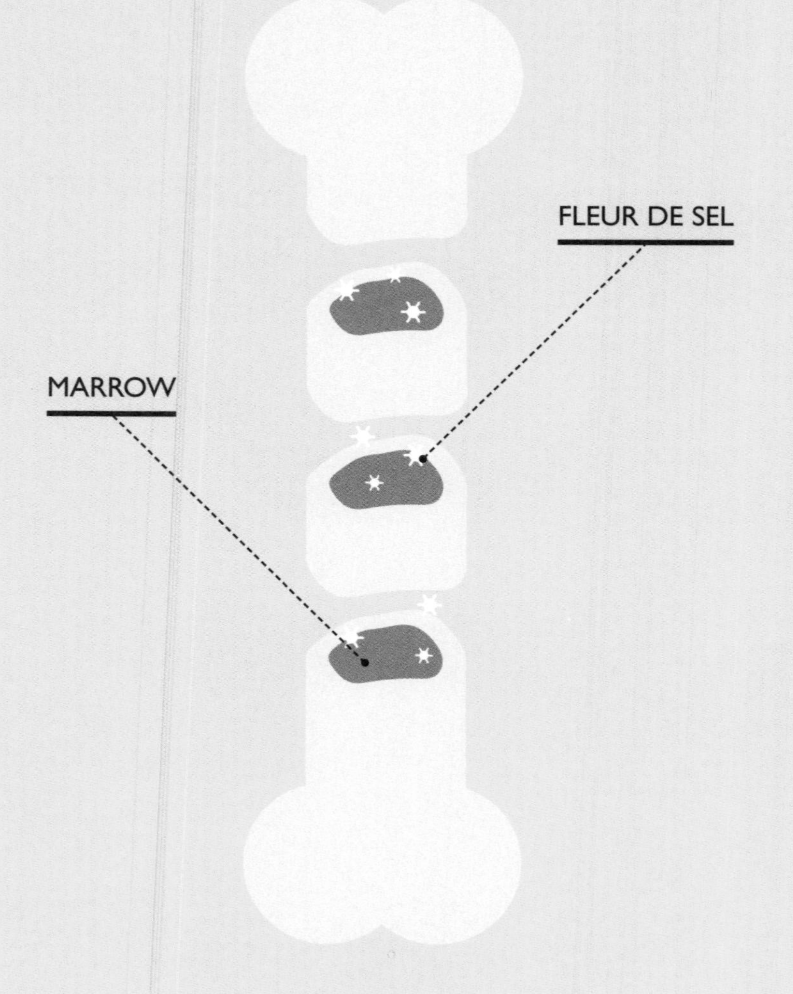

WHAT IS IT?

Cylindrical bones (beef or veal shank) filled with soft marrow

TIME TO MAKE

Preparation: 10 minutes
Cooking: 20 minutes

VARIATIONS

- Bones cut in "canoe-cut"—i.e, halved lengthwise (same cooking time)
- Replace the fleur de sel with a salt flavored with herbs or shallot

TRICKY ASPECT

Cooking: overcooked marrow turns into oil

TIP

Rubbing the marrow with fleur de sel, at either end of the bone, prevents the marrow from coming out during cooking.

IT'S READY . . .

When the marrow has puffed up and browned.

STORAGE

Cooked: eat immediately
Raw: 2–3 days in the refrigerator or several weeks in the freezer

WHAT IS MARROW MADE OF?

Marrow is about 60 percent fat. The remainder is made up of proteins and water.

WHY COVER THE MARROW WITH SALT?

The salt absorbs the water that is released from the marrow as steam while it is cooking. This prevents the marrow from protruding from the bone.

SERVES 4

MARROW BONE

1 teaspoon olive oil
8-inch-long marrow bone (cut crosswise by your butcher into 2-inch segments)
fleur de sel
freshly ground black pepper, to taste

TOAST

½ baguette

1 Preheat the oven to 450°F. Coat a baking sheet with the oil using a paper towel.

2 Rub the marrow with fleur de sel, at either end of each bone segment, pressing hard to ensure it gets in.

3 Bake the bones for 20 minutes, until the marrow is slightly puffed.

4 Cut the baguette on a sharp angle into eight slices. Toast them in the oven for 3–4 minutes, turning them once.

5 Check that the marrow is cooked by inserting the blade of a knife in the middle: it should not meet any resistance and should come out warm. Remove the bones from the oven and serve with the toasted baguette slices. Marrow should be scooped out and eaten on the bread, sprinkled with fleur de sel and pepper.

FOIE GRAS RAVIOLI

Understand

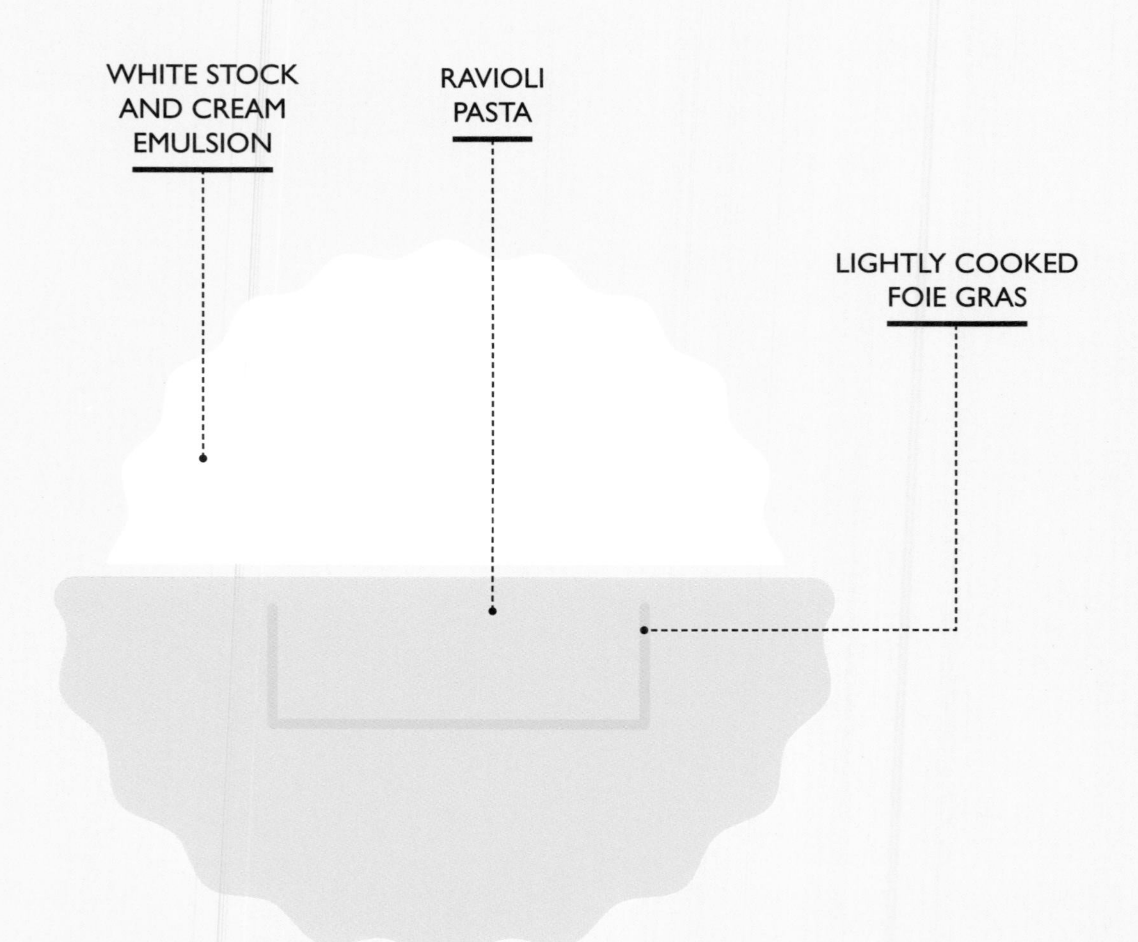

WHAT IS IT?
Squares of pasta, stuffed with foie gras and formed into half-moons, served in poultry stock with cream and flavored with truffle oil

TIME TO MAKE
Preparation: 20 minutes
Cooking: 10 minutes
Resting: 1–2 minutes

EQUIPMENT
Hand-held blender
Pastry brush
Round cookie cutter (2½ inch diameter)

TRICKY ASPECTS
Making and cooking the ravioli

TECHNIQUES TO MASTER
Reducing a sauce (page 283)
Mincing (page 280)

IT'S READY . . .
When the ravioli are al dente and the cream foamy.

SERVES 4

STUFFING
5⅝ oz (about ⅓ recipe) lightly cooked duck foie gras (page 112)
½ teaspoon fleur de sel
freshly ground black pepper (4 turns)
4 teaspoons truffle oil

PASTA
16 square wonton wrappers

Learn

SAUCE

3 cups white poultry stock (page 10)
¼ cup heavy cream

TO SERVE

5 chives
4 teaspoons truffle oil
½ teaspoon fleur de sel
freshly ground black pepper (4 turns)

1 Cut the foie gras into sixteen equal cubes. Season the foie gras cubes with the fleur de sel and pepper. Drizzle ¼ teaspoon truffle oil over each cube.

2 Lay the wonton wrappers on a work surface with one corner facing you. Moisten the top half of the wonton wrappers using a pastry brush dipped in water. Place a cube of foie gras on each wrapper in one corner. Fold the wrapper into a triangle, leaving one side open. Press on the other edges to seal them and push out any trapped air, then seal the open side. Using a ½-inch round cookie cutter, trim the ravioli into half-moons.

3 Bring the poultry stock to a boil in a medium saucepan and add the ravioli. Reduce the heat to a simmer and cook for 1 minute, or until al dente. Remove the ravioli from the stock using a skimmer or slotted spoon, and set aside in four soup bowls. Return the stock to a boil and reduce it by half.

4 Add the cream and reduce again, until you have a creamy but thick liquid. Foam the sauce using a hand-held blender.

5 Wash and dry the chives, then mince. Pour the sauce over the ravioli and sprinkle with the chives. Drizzle with truffle oil, sprinkle with the fleur de sel, and finish each plate with one turn of freshly ground black pepper.

EGGS IN RED WINE

Understand

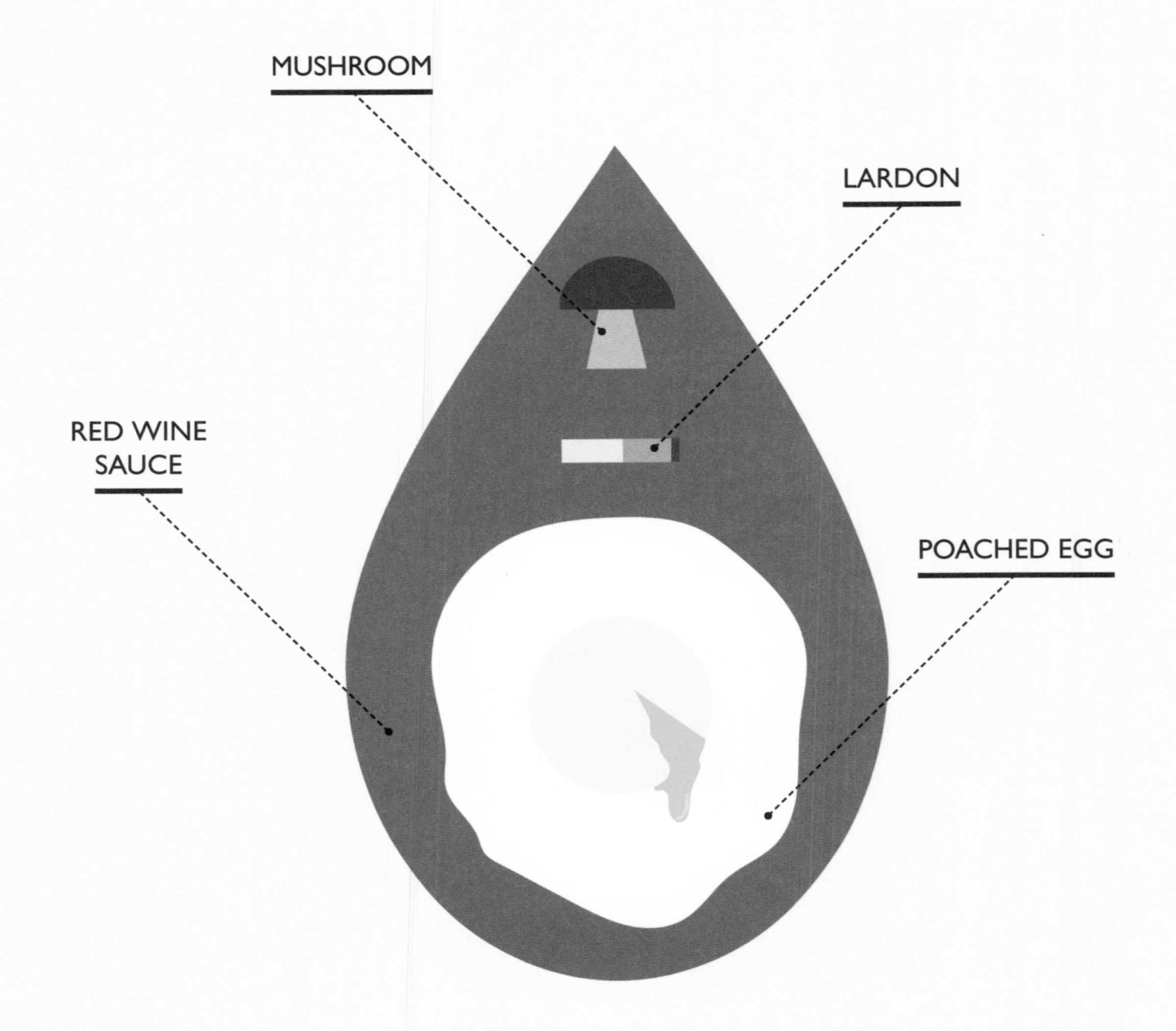

WHAT ARE THEY?
Eggs poached in a red wine sauce, served topped with the sauce and accompanied by lardons of bacon, mushrooms, and toasted bread

TIME TO MAKE
Preparation: 40 minutes
Cooking: 20–25 minutes

EQUIPMENT
Fine-mesh sieve
Skimmer or finely slotted spoon

VARIATIONS
Eggs benedict: replace the red wine sauce with hollandaise sauce (page 30) and the mushrooms and lardons with smoked salmon

TRICKY ASPECTS
- Poaching eggs in an opaque sauce
- Incorporating the beurre manié (butter and flour mixture) into the sauce

TECHNIQUES TO MASTER
Mincing (page 280)
Skimming (page 283)
Cutting in scallops (page 280)
Draining egg whites (page 69)
Straining through a sieve (page 281)
Sweating (page 282)

NOTE
Use a full-bodied, tannin-rich wine (Côtes du Rhône, Bordeaux Supérieur, or Languedoc, etc.).

THEY'RE READY . . .
When the reduced sauce is thick and the garnish browned.

Learn

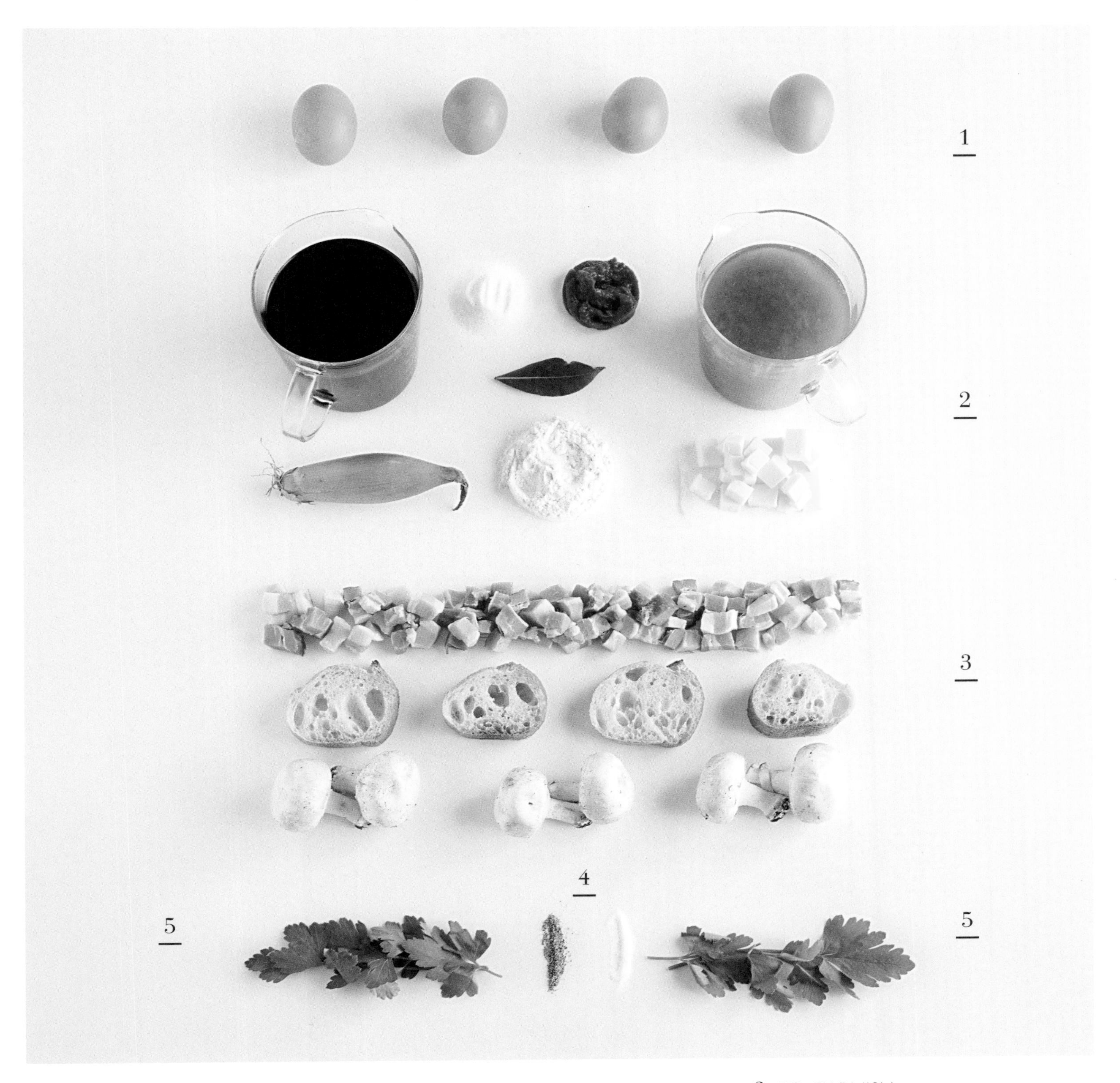

HOW DOES THE SAUCE THICKEN?

Thanks to the beurre manié (butter + flour). During cooking, the starch in the flour swells up with the water in the sauce (it gelatinizes), then bursts and releases two molecules (amylose and amylopectine) that thicken the mixture.

SERVES 4

1 EGGS

4 extra-fresh eggs

2 SAUCE

1 shallot
4 tablespoons butter, softened
1 tablespoon tomato paste
2 cups red wine
2 cups brown veal stock (page 12)
2 teaspoons sugar
1 bay leaf
2 tablespoons all-purpose flour

3 TO GARNISH

5 or 6 slices thick-cut bacon, cut into lardons
5½ oz white mushrooms
4 slices baguette

4 SEASONING

¼ teaspoon fine salt
freshly ground black pepper, to taste

5 TO SERVE

2 Italian parsley sprigs, minced

Making eggs in red wine

1 Peel and mince the shallot. Melt 1 tablespoon of the butter in a medium saucepan. Sweat the shallot with the salt, stirring constantly. Add the tomato paste and cook for 30 seconds, stirring constantly.

2 Add the wine, stock, sugar, bay leaf, and pepper (three turns), then reduce by half, 10–15 minutes, skimming from time to time.

3 Cook the lardons in a single layer in a skillet: Cover them with water, bring to a boil, and reduce the heat to medium. Let the water evaporate, then cook the lardons until they color. Remove the lardons from the pan with a skimmer or slotted spoon and drain on a paper towel. Remove the stems from the mushrooms, then peel the caps and cut them in two or four slices, depending on their size. Add 1 tablespoon of the butter to the pan and brown the mushrooms for 2–3 minutes. Add black pepper (three turns) and remove from the heat.

4 In a small bowl, mix the remaining butter into the flour using a spoon, until the mixture is smooth (this is a beurre manié). Refrigerate. Toast the bread and place a slice on each plate.

5 One by one, break each egg into its own ramekin and drain off the liquid egg white using a skimmer or finely slotted spoon, keeping only the thick part of the white attached to the yolk. Discard the liquidy whites and return the egg to its ramekin. Transfer the stock and wine mixture to a small saucepan. Bring to a boil, then reduce the heat to low and make a small vortex by stirring the liquid with a spatula. Pour an egg into the center and cook for 2 minutes over low heat, gently pushing the white over the yolk.

6 Remove from the heat and remove the egg using a skimmer or slotted spoon. Rest the skimmer on a paper towel, then repeat for the remaining eggs. Place each drained egg on a slice of toast.

7 Strain the sauce through a fine-mesh sieve, then return it to the small saucepan and bring to a boil.

8 Add the beurre manié in small pieces while whisking the sauce to thicken it. Adjust the seasoning.

9 Pour the sauce over the poached eggs and around the slices of toast using a soup spoon. Add the mushrooms and lardons, and sprinkle with the parsley.

STUFFED MUSSELS

Understand

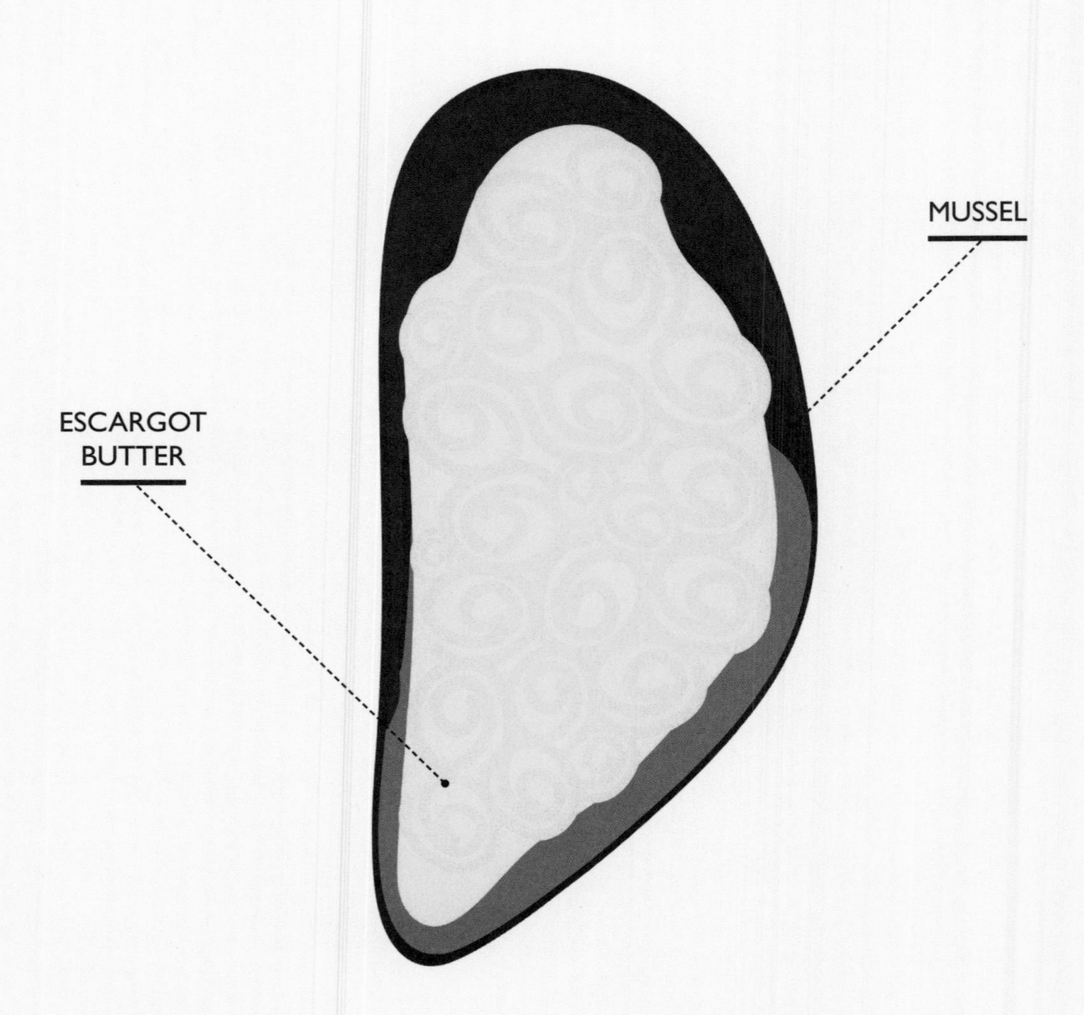

WHAT ARE THEY?

Mussels cooked in white wine, then stuffed with an escargot butter and browned in the oven

TIME TO MAKE

Preparation: 45 minutes
Cooking: 10 minutes

EQUIPMENT

Chef's knife
Metal spatula

VARIATION

Stuffed razor clams

TRICKY ASPECT

Cooking the mussels: they toughen when overcooked

TECHNIQUES TO MASTER

Cleaning mussels (page 139)
Mincing (page 280)

THEY'RE READY . . .

When the top is lightly browned and the butter very soft.

ORGANIZATION

Stuff the mussels 1–2 hours in advance, then refrigerate. Brown them at the last minute.

WHY NOT CLEAN THE MUSSELS IN A BOWL OF WATER?

Because they could open and release their sea water, which adds flavor during cooking.

Learn

SERVES 4

MUSSELS

1 lb 12 oz large mussels (blue or green-lipped)
2 shallots
3 tablespoons white wine
freshly ground black pepper (6 turns)

ESCARGOT BUTTER (PAGE 41)

1 shallot
1 small bunch Italian parsley
2 garlic cloves
1 slice day-old white bread (no crusts)
11 tablespoons butter, softened
½ teaspoon fine salt
freshly ground black pepper (8 turns)

1 Wash the mussels under a trickle of cold water, removing the beards and discarding any that are cracked or half-open. Drain.

2 Peel and mince the two shallots. Make the escargot butter (page 41).

3 Combine the mussels, shallots, white wine, and pepper in a large saucepan. Cook over very high heat for 5–6 minutes, stirring frequently. Remove from the heat when the mussels have opened. Drain and set aside in the refrigerator.

4 Preheat the broiler. Remove the top shell of the mussels. Cover each mussel with a little of the butter. Smooth the top with a metal spatula.

5 Brown under the broiler for 2–3 minutes.

SCALLOPS
WITH ORANGE BUTTER

Understand

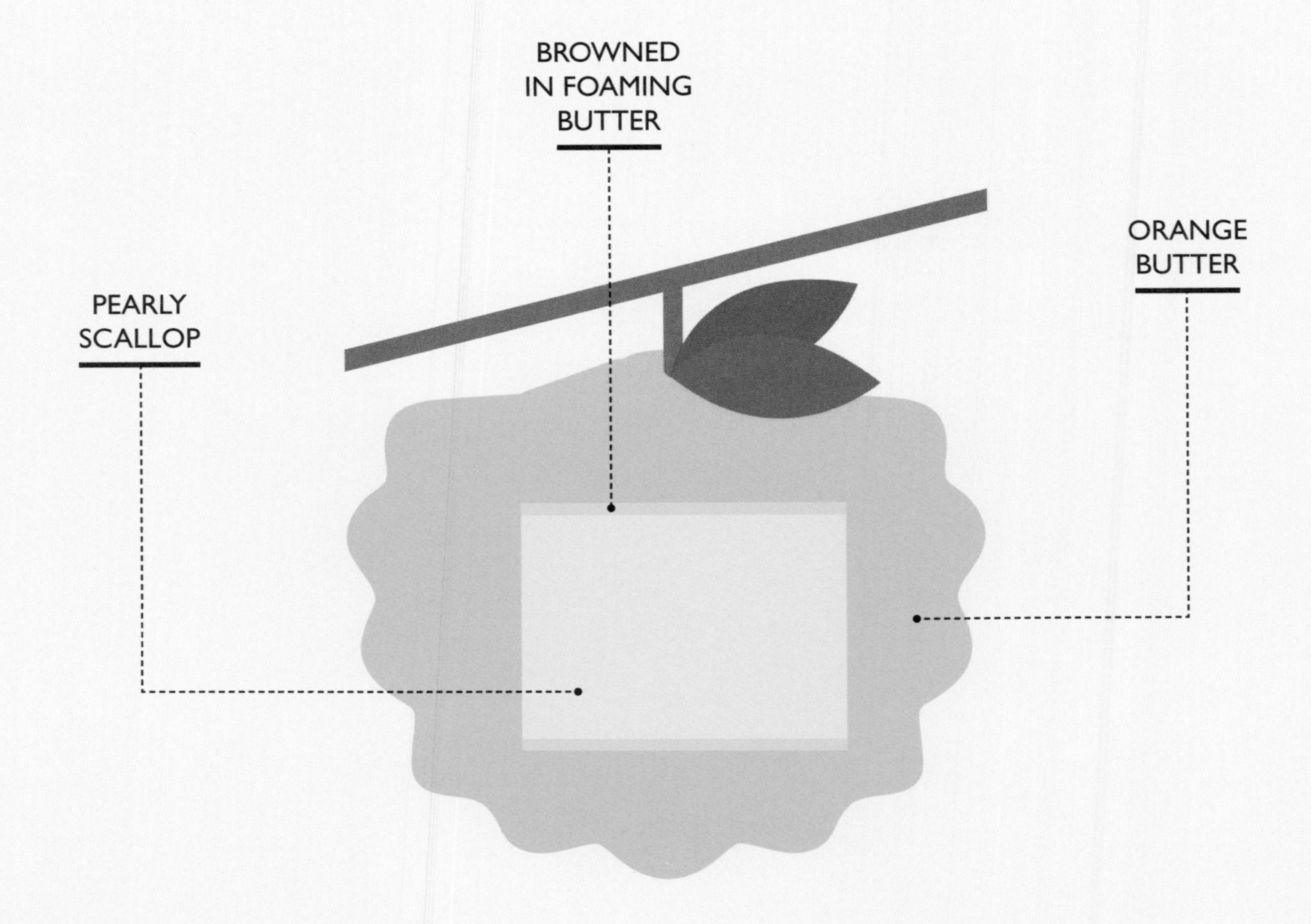

WHAT ARE THEY?
Pan-fried scallops, served with a sauce of reduced orange juice thickened with butter

TIME TO MAKE
Preparation: 20 minutes
Cooking: 5–10 minutes

EQUIPMENT
Nonstick skillet

VARIATION
Scallops in beurre blanc (page 28)

TRICKY ASPECT
Cooking the scallops: overcooked, they become rubbery

TECHNIQUES TO MASTER
Whisking in butter (page 282)

TIP
The scallops must be well-dried to brown during cooking.

HOW DOES THE ORANGE JUICE BECOME A SYRUP?

During reduction, the water evaporates, which results in the juice thickening to a syrupy texture.

WHY DOES THE BUTTER FOAM?

As it heats, the water in the butter begins to release steam. The proteins in the butter surround the steam, forming bubbles.

Learn

SERVES 4

SCALLOPS

16 sea scallops
1 teaspoon olive oil
2 tablespoons butter
½ teaspoon fine salt
freshly ground black pepper (8 turns)

ORANGE BUTTER

3 oranges
4 tablespoons butter, diced

TO FINISH

½ teaspoon fleur de sel

1 Wash the scallops and dry them with paper towels.

2 To make the orange butter, squeeze the oranges to obtain about ¾ cup juice. Bring to a boil in a small saucepan and continue boiling until it has a syrupy consistency (you should end up with about 2 tablespoons juice).

3 Over medium heat, add the 4 tablespoons of butter piece by piece, swirling the pan to spread the butter around, or whisking, until almost melted. Cover and keep warm (over very low heat: 120°F maximum) until ready to serve.

4 Heat the oil in a skillet over very high heat and quickly sear the scallops (1 minute on each side).

5 Reduce the heat to medium, add the 2 tablespoons butter and let it foam. Baste the scallops with the butter for 1–2 minutes. Season with salt and pepper.

6 Place the scallops on serving plates, sprinkle with the fleur de sel, and add a ribbon of orange butter.

FLAMBÉED SHRIMP

Understand

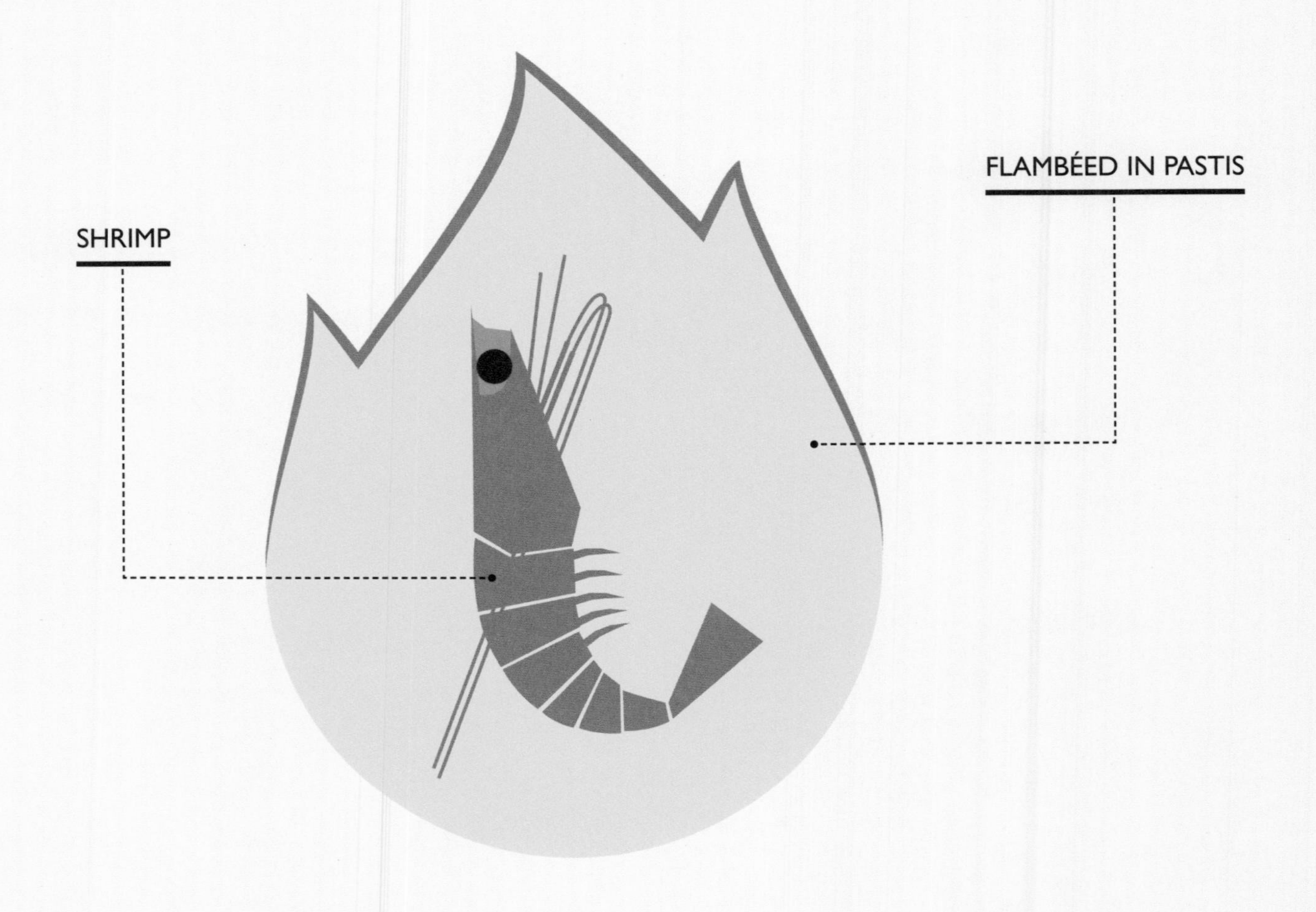

WHAT IS IT?
Shrimp marinated in herbs and garlic, pan-fried and flambéed in pastis

TIME TO MAKE
Preparation: 25 minutes
Cooking: 5 minutes

EQUIPMENT
Large nonstick skillet

VARIATIONS
Flambéed in whiskey or Cognac

TECHNIQUES TO MASTER
Shelling and deveining shrimp (page 279)
Thinly slicing (page 280)
Mincing (page 280)
Flambéing (page 282)
Zesting (page 280)

WHAT HAPPENS DURING FLAMBÉING?
The alcohol vapors are set on fire. This accelerates its evaporation, and leaves aromatic notes of alcohol in the dish.

Learn

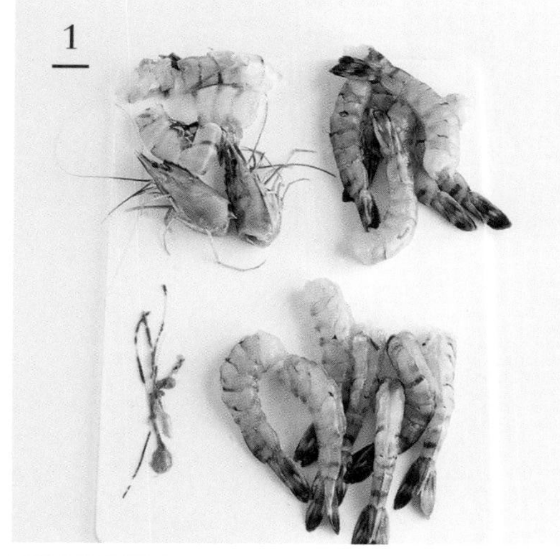

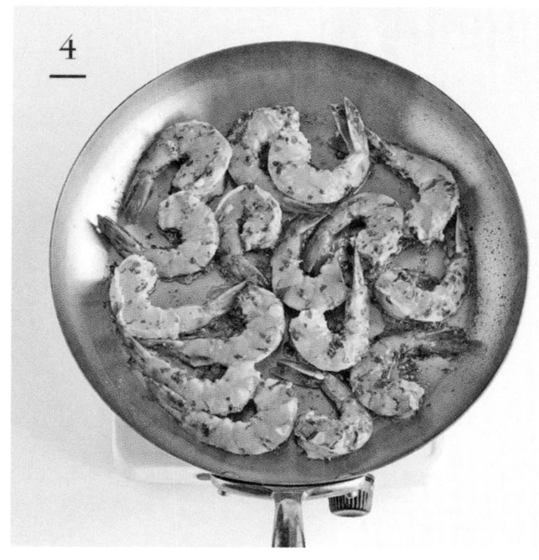

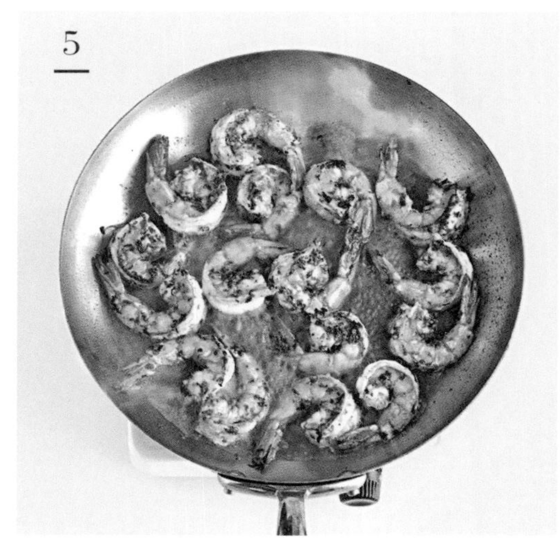

SERVES 4

FLAMBÉED SHRIMP

20 large raw frozen shrimp
3 tablespoons pastis

MARINADE

8 Italian parsley sprigs
6 cilantro sprigs
1 large garlic clove
1 lemon
¼ teaspoon Espelette pepper
1 teaspoon fine salt
2 tablespoons olive oil

1 Thaw the shrimp in the refrigerator. Wash, shell, and devein them (page 279), but leave the tails on. Set them aside in an airtight container in the refrigerator while you prepare the marinade.

2 Wash and dry the parsley and cilantro. Cut off the stems. Peel and de-germ the garlic. Wash, dry, and zest the lemon, then squeeze it. Purée the garlic, Espelette pepper, and salt in a food processor. Add the herbs and blend to a rough paste. Add the lemon juice and the olive oil, stirring with a fork. Add half the lemon zest to the marinade.

3 Pour the marinade over the shrimp.

4 Heat a large nonstick skillet over high heat. Reserving the marinade, pull the shrimp out of the marinade with tongs and add to the pan in a single layer. Cook for 1 minute on each side.

5 Sprinkle with 2 tablespoons of the pastis, then flambé (light it on fire).

6 Transfer the shrimp to a plate. Deglaze the pan with the remaining pastis. Stir in the remaining marinade. Return the shrimp to the pan. Sprinkle with the remaining lemon zest.

CRAYFISH À LA NAGE

Understand

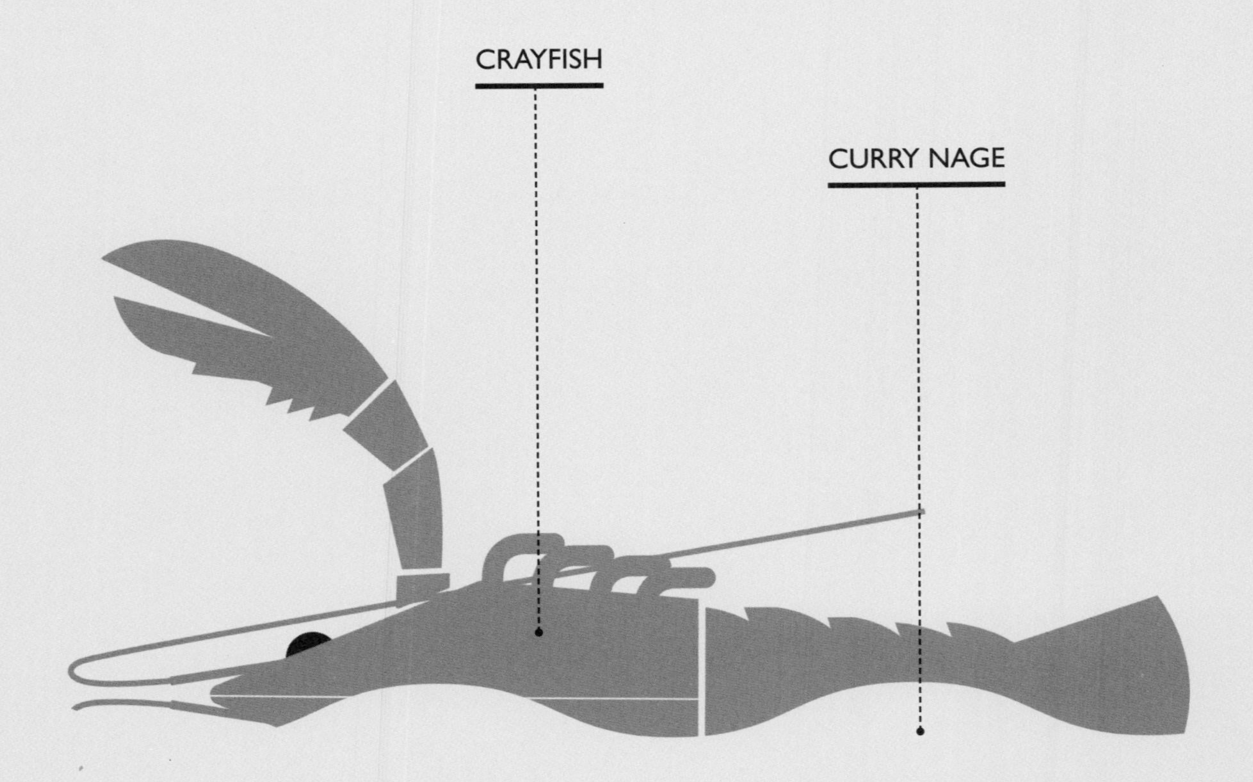

WHAT IS IT?

Crayfish poached in a court bouillon flavored with white wine, served with the cooking liquid flavored with curry and foamed with butter

TIME TO MAKE

Preparation: 15 minutes
(not including the court bouillon)
Cooking: 5–10 minutes

EQUIPMENT

Sieve
Hand-held blender

VARIATIONS

Traditional recipe: served with cooked turned carrots and onion rings
Scallops à la nage
Langoustines à la nage

TRICKY ASPECT

Cooking the crayfish

TECHNIQUES TO MASTER

Deveining crayfish (page 279)
Straining through a sieve (page 281)
Pushing through a sieve (page 281)

TIP

Devein just before cooking, otherwise the meat will pull away from the shell.

IT'S READY . . .

When the crayfish are cooked (taste one).

WHAT IS THE DIFFERENCE BETWEEN NAGE AND COURT BOUILLON?

Court bouillon is a base, nage is the style of dish. The recipe is the same.

Learn

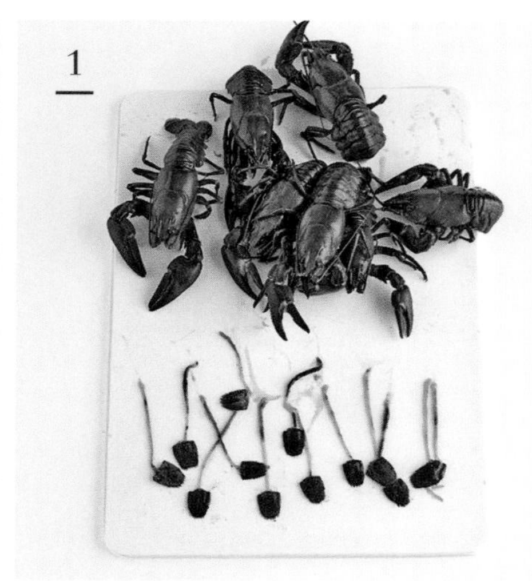

SERVES 4

CRAYFISH

2 lb 3 oz raw crayfish
1 quart (4 cups) court bouillon (page 16), made with ⅔ cup white wine instead of the vinegar, unstrained

SAUCE

4 tablespoons butter
½ teaspoon red curry paste

1 Wash and drain the crayfish. Just before cooking, devein them.

2 Bring the court bouillon to a boil and add the crayfish. Return to a boil, then cook for 5–10 minutes, depending on the size of the crayfish, stirring frequently.

3 Remove the crayfish from the nage and keep warm. Strain the nage through a sieve without pushing on the solids. Peel the crayfish.

4 Melt 2 teaspoons of the butter in a medium saucepan, then add the curry paste. Mix by rubbing the paste against the bottom of the saucepan for 1 minute. Stir in the nage, then bring to a boil. Cut the remaining butter in pieces. Remove the pan from the heat, add the remaining butter, then foam for a few seconds using a hand-held blender.

5 Pour the nage into serving bowls and set the crayfish in it.

ROASTED LOBSTER

Understand

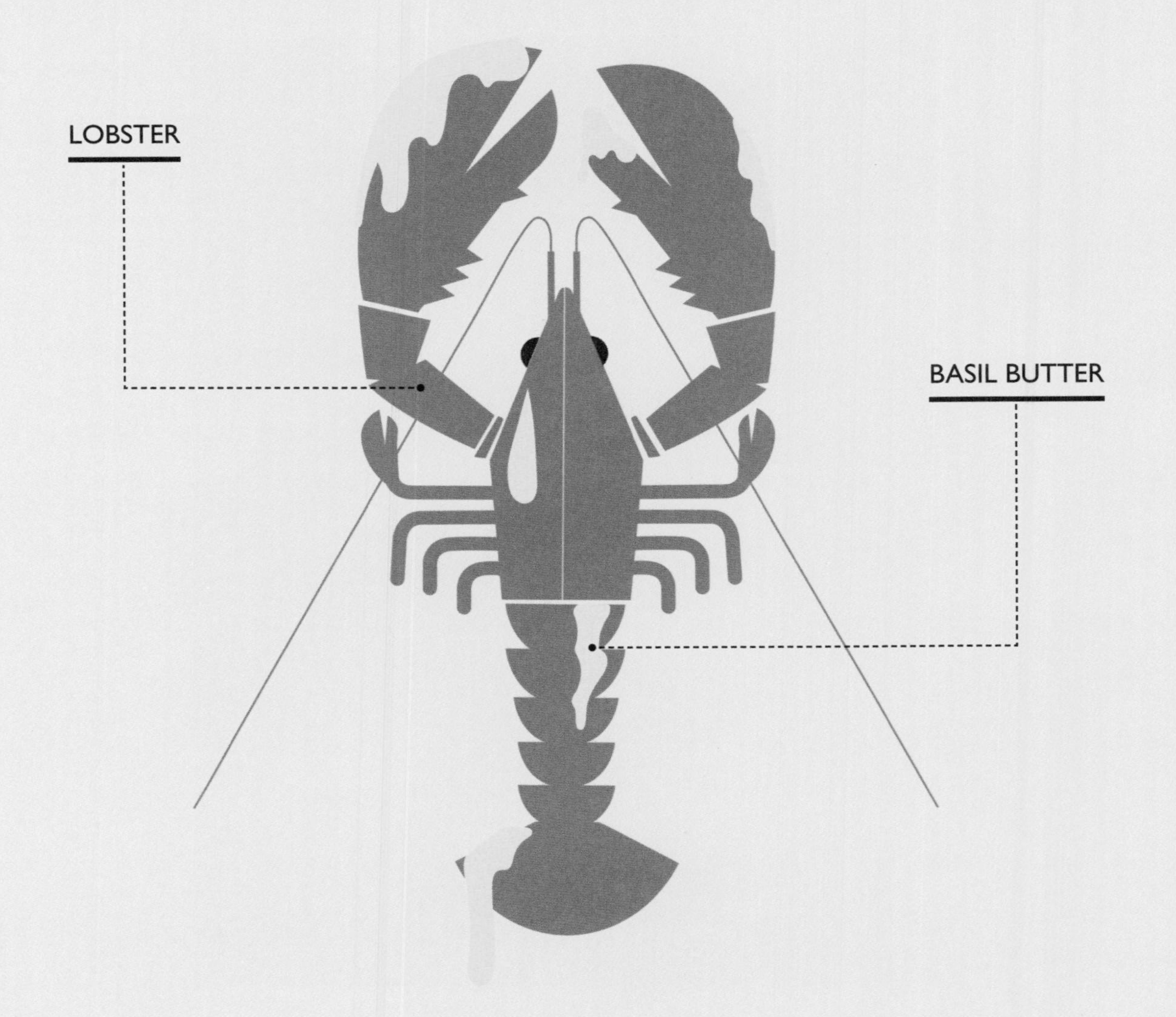

WHAT IS IT?
Lobster cut in half, filled with a basil and mustard butter, pan-fried, then roasted

TIME TO MAKE
Preparation: 20 minutes
Cooking: 7–8 minutes

EQUIPMENT
Thick-bladed knife
2 large ovenproof sauté pans or
2 large sauté pans and 1 roasting pan

TRICKY ASPECT
Cutting the lobster

TECHNIQUES TO MASTER
Mincing (page 280)
Finely chopping (page 280)

TIP
Use the little cross in the middle of the lobster's head as a guide for inserting the blade of your knife.

IT'S READY . . .
When the flesh of the claws is cooked (which takes a bit longer than the flesh of the tail) but before the shell turns completely red.

SERVES 4

LOBSTERS
four 1 lb 2 oz to 1 lb 5 oz live lobsters
1½ tablespoons olive oil

BASIL BUTTER
1 large basil sprig
4 sun-dried tomatoes
8 tablespoons butter, softened
5 tablespoons grainy mustard

Learn

SEASONING

1 teaspoon fine salt
freshly ground black pepper (6 turns)
pinch of Espelette pepper

TO FINISH

1 teaspoon fleur de sel
pinch of Espelette pepper

1 Start by making the basil butter. Pick, wash, dry, and mince the basil leaves. Finely chop the tomatoes. Mix with the butter and the mustard. Season with salt and pepper, and add the Espelette pepper. Mix to make a uniform paste.

2 Kill the lobsters by inserting a knife in the middle of the head in one swift, sharp movement. Cut the lobsters in half lengthwise, from head to the end of the tail. Remove the gut, roe, tomalley (green liver), any creamy parts, and the gravel pouch in the head. Crack the claws with the back of a knife to help them cook.

3 Preheat the oven to 390°F. Lift the tail meat of each lobster from the shell using a spoon, starting at the end of the tail. Put a layer of basil butter at the bottom of the shell then replace the meat. Reserve 2 tablespoons of the butter to serve and distribute the rest among the lobster bodies.

4 Heat the olive oil in two sauté pans over high heat. Put the lobsters in, flesh side down, and leave for 1 minute, until lightly golden. Turn the lobsters over onto a roasting pan. Roast in the oven for 6–7 minutes.

5 Sprinkle with the fleur de sel and Espelette pepper. Serve with the reserved basil butter.

STUFFED SQUID

Understand

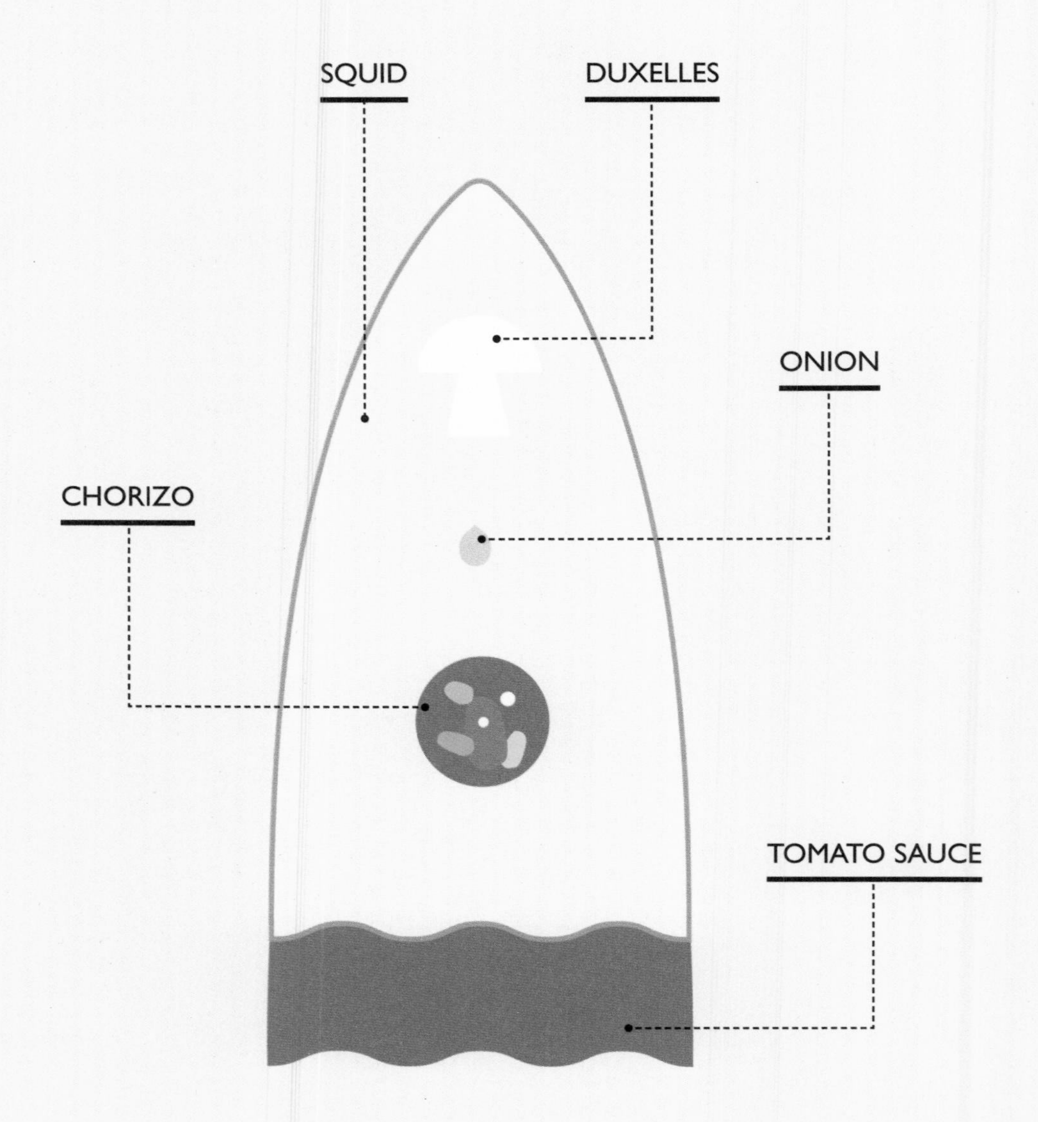

WHAT IS IT?
Whole squid stuffed with chorizo duxelles, pan-fried, then roasted in the oven and served with a tomato sauce

TIME TO MAKE
Preparation: 30 minutes
Cooking: 17–18 minutes

EQUIPMENT
Ovenproof skillet
4 toothpicks
Pastry bag

TRICKY ASPECTS
– Cooking the squid
– Stuffing the squid

TECHNIQUES TO MASTER
Finely chopping (page 280)

VARIATION
To intensify the squid taste, pan-fry the tentacles in olive oil with a little garlic, then chop and add to the duxelles

IT'S READY . . .
When the stuffed squid are golden and the flesh has softened.

SERVES 4

SQUID
4 squid bodies (about 8 inches long when whole), cleaned
¼ teaspoon fine salt
3 tablespoons olive oil

CHORIZO DUXELLES

3 shallots
3 tablespoons butter
10 ½ oz white mushrooms
1 garlic clove, peeled and chopped
1 cup heavy cream
1 ½-inch piece Spanish chorizo
¼ teaspoon fine salt
freshly ground black pepper (3 turns)

ACCOMPANIMENT

1 ½ cups tomato sauce (page 24)

1 Preheat the oven to 360°F. Make duxelles (page 43) with the shallots, butter, and mushrooms. Add the garlic, then stir for 30 seconds, until fragrant. Add the cream, bring to a boil, then simmer for about 10 minutes over low heat, stirring from time to time, until the mixture is smooth and thick.

2 Peel the chorizo and cut into thin slices, then small dice. Season the duxelles with salt and pepper, then add the chorizo. Transfer to another container.

3 Wash the squid and stuff with three-quarters of the duxelles, using a well-filled pastry bag. Close each squid by weaving a toothpick through the open end.

4 Sprinkle the salt over the squid and heat the olive oil in a skillet over very high heat. When the oil starts to smoke, brown the squid for 1 minute, then turn over one by one, with the help of the toothpicks.

5 Remove the squid from the pan, degrease, then deglaze with ¼ cup water. Add the tomato sauce and bring to a boil. Add the squid and transfer the skillet to the oven for 7–8 minutes. Season with pepper. Serve one squid per person with tomato sauce spooned on one side of the plate.

SOLE MEUNIÈRE

Understand

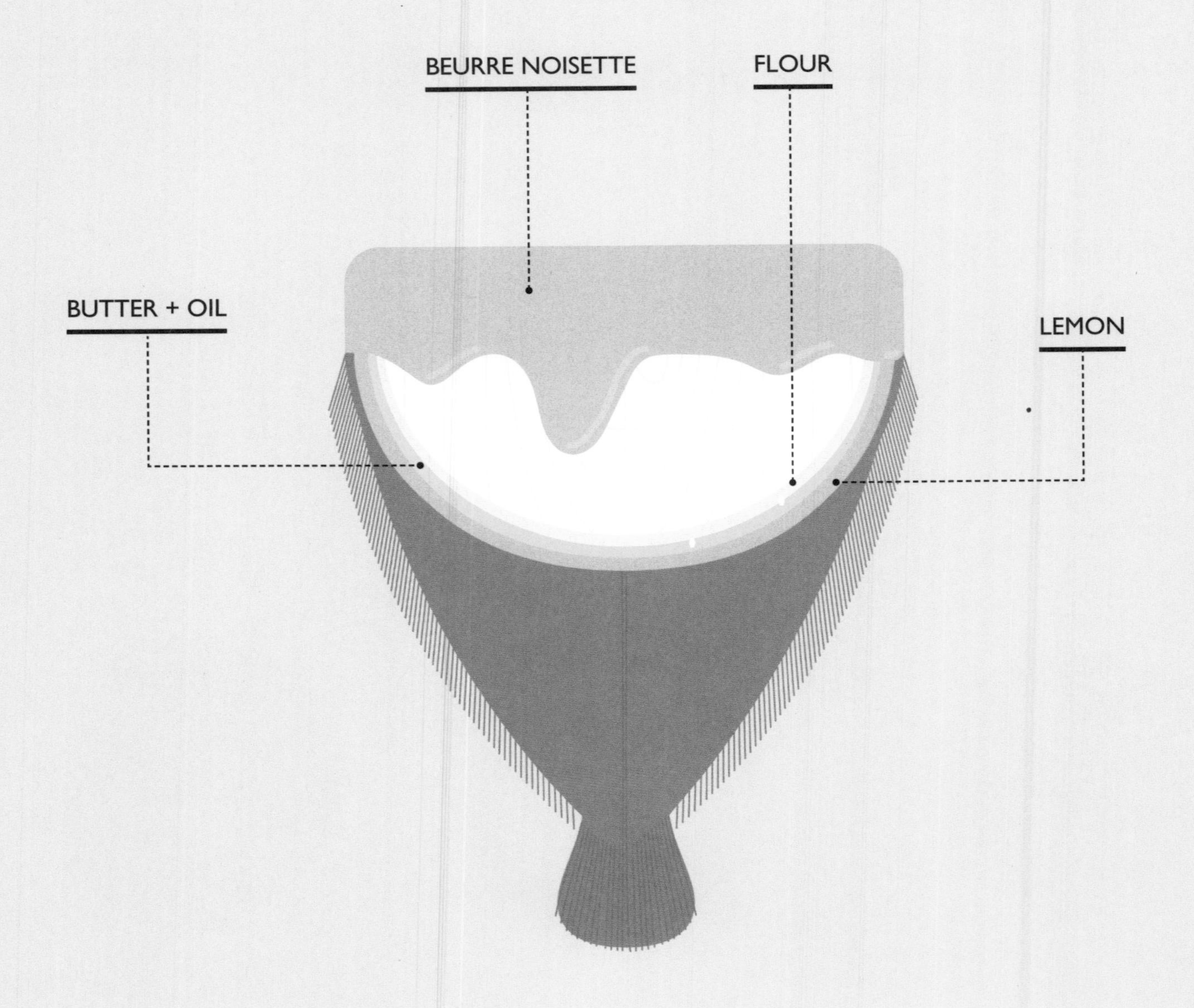

WHAT IS IT?
Sole dusted with flour and pan-fried, sprinkled with beurre noisette, lemon juice, and parsley

TIME TO MAKE
Preparation: 15 minutes
Cooking: 5 minutes

EQUIPMENT
Two large skillets

VARIATION
Trout meunière with almonds

TRICKY ASPECTS
– Cooking
– Plating (sole is fragile after cooking)

TECHNIQUES TO MASTER
Making a beurre noisette (page 53)
Mincing (page 280)

TIP
To ensure the sole is well seared, dust it with flour just before cooking (otherwise the flour will absorb too much moisture and form a paste).

IT'S READY . . .
When pressing a finger into the base of the head (at the level of the gills) separates the fillets.

NOTE
A dressed sole has had the fins removed, and is skinned (white skin scaled and gray skin removed) and gutted.

WHAT DOES THE FLOUR DO?
The starch in the flour absorbs the water on the surface of the fish, then gelatinizes and dries with the application of heat. The dried flour adds to the crispness of the dish.

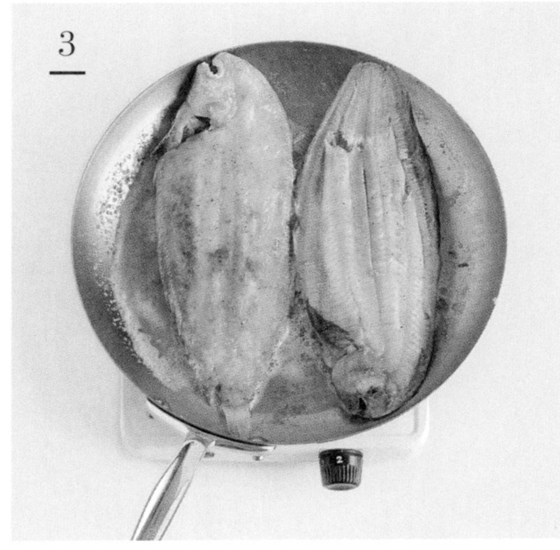

SERVES 4

FISH

four 9 oz Dover sole
½ teaspoon fine salt
freshly ground black pepper (8 turns)
½ cup all-purpose flour
3 tablespoons butter
2½ tablespoons peanut oil
½ lemon

BEURRE NOISETTE (PAGE 53)

6 tablespoons butter

TO SERVE

a few Italian parsley sprigs

1 Wash, dry, pick, and mince the parsley leaves. Wash the sole carefully and dry with a paper towel. Season with salt and pepper.

2 Dust both sides of the sole with flour and tap gently to remove any excess.

3 Heat the butter and oil together in two large skillets over high heat. When the butter foams and turns slightly blond, brown the sole on the white-skinned side for 1–2 minutes.

4 Carefully turn the sole over using a spatula. Finish cooking over low heat for 2 minutes.

5 Transfer the sole to serving plates, white-skinned side up. Squeeze the lemon juice on top. Make a beurre noisette (page 53) and pour over the fish. Sprinkle with the parsley.

SKATE GRENOBLOISE

Understand

WHAT IS IT?

Poached skate, served with beurre noisette, vinegar, capers, croutons, and diced lemon

TIME TO MAKE

Preparation (not including the court bouillon): 30 minutes
Cooking (not including the court bouillon): 10–15 minutes

TRICKY ASPECTS

- Browning the croutons
- Cooking the skate

TECHNIQUES TO MASTER

Peeling citrus for segments (page 280)
Supreming citrus (page 280)

VARIATION

Replace the court bouillon with salted water (2 teaspoons salt per 4 cups water) brought to a boil then cooled and lemon juice added (the juice of 2 lemons per 4 cups)

IT'S READY . . .

When the flesh of the skate comes away easily from the spine.

WHY MUST FISH BE COOKED AT A SIMMER RATHER THAN A VIGOROUS BOIL?

To prevent the flesh falling apart in the high heat.

Learn

SERVES 4

1 FISH

four 9-oz skate wings or 4 fillets on the bone (thin skin left and thick skin removed)
2 tablespoons red wine vinegar

2 BEURRE NOISETTE (PAGE 53)

6 tablespoons butter

3 COURT BOUILLON

2 carrots
2 quarts (8 cups) water
1 scant cup vinegar
1 small bunch Italian parsley
6 thyme sprigs
2 bay leaves
2 yellow onions
1 teaspoon black peppercorns
4 teaspoons coarse sea salt

4 CROUTONS

4 slices day-old white bread (crusts removed)
2 tablespoons butter
2 tablespoons olive oil
¼ teaspoon fine salt

5 TO GARNISH

1 lemon
¼ cup capers

Making skate grenobloise

1 Make the court bouillon (page 17) and let it cool.

2 Cut the bread into ⅜-inch dice. Heat the butter and olive oil together in a large skillet over medium heat. When the butter stops foaming, add the bread cubes and stir for 5 minutes, until the croutons are golden. Drain on paper towels and season with the salt.

3 Peel the lemon, supreme the segments, and cut them into ⅓-inch dice. Wash and drain the capers.

4 Wash the skate wings to remove all trace of slime.

5 Immerse the wings in the cold court bouillon, then bring to a boil and simmer for 10–15 minutes.

6 Make the beurre noisette.

7 Drain the skate wings and transfer to serving plates. Remove the skin. Distribute the capers evenly over the fish and coat it in the beurre noisette. Deglaze the beurre noisette pan with the vinegar and pour immediately over the fish. Sprinkle with the croutons and the diced lemon.

TURBOT
BONNE FEMME

Understand

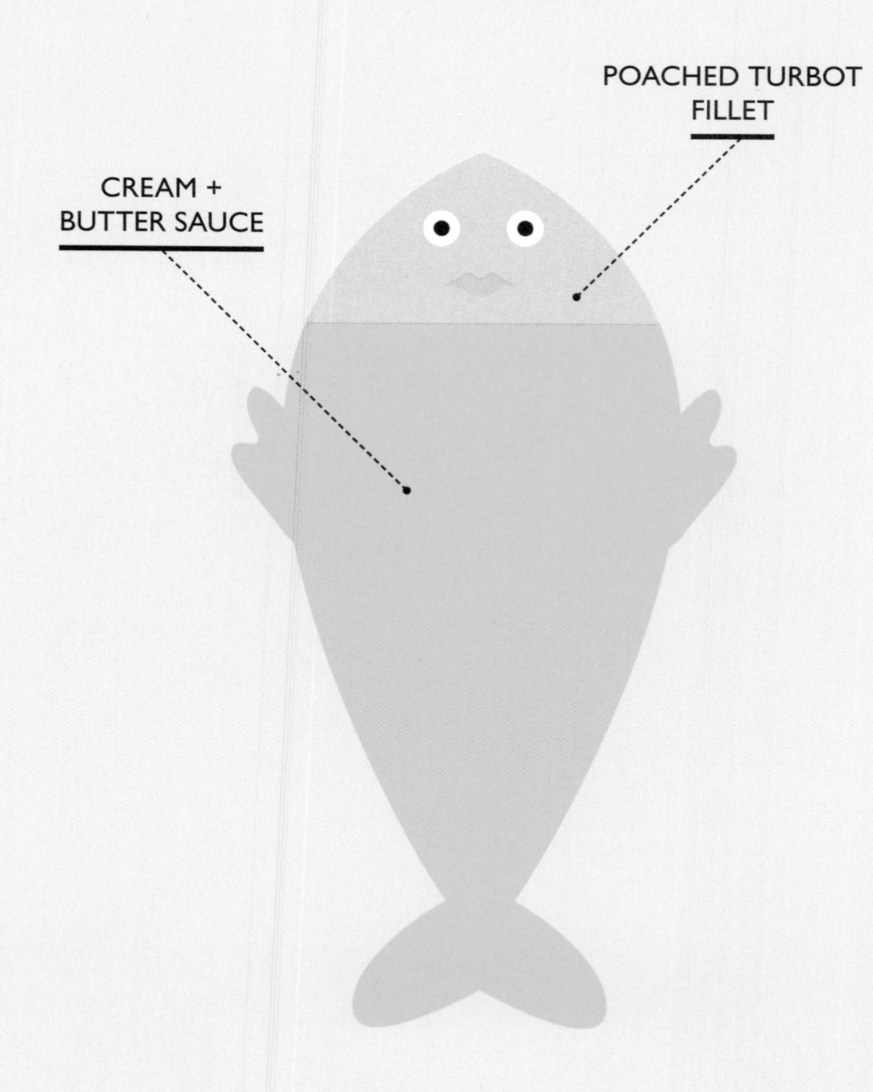

WHAT IS IT?
Turbot fillets poached "housewife style" in a court mouillement, then covered in the reduced cooking liquid, thickened with cream, foamed with butter, and browned under the broiler

TIME TO MAKE
Preparation: 20 minutes
Cooking: 7–9 minutes

EQUIPMENT
Roasting pan or ovenproof skillet
Sieve

VARIATION
Sole bonne femme

TRICKY ASPECT
Cooking the fish

TECHNIQUES TO MASTER
Whisking in butter (page 282)
Mincing (page 280)
Thinly slicing (page 280)
Straining through a sieve (page 281)
Pushing through a sieve (page 281)
Reducing a sauce (page 283)

IT'S READY . . .
When the fish fillets are firm and the sauce browned.

WHAT IS COOKING IN A COURT MOUILLEMENT?
*Cooking in a limited volume of liquid—the fish is just covered (*court mouillement *is French for "shallow broth").*

WHAT IS THE RIGHT COOKING TEMPERATURE?
The fish should be cooked to 120°F in the center. At 320°F, this is reached very quickly, so the cooking phases must both be short: 4–5 minutes in the oven then 3–4 minutes under the broiler.

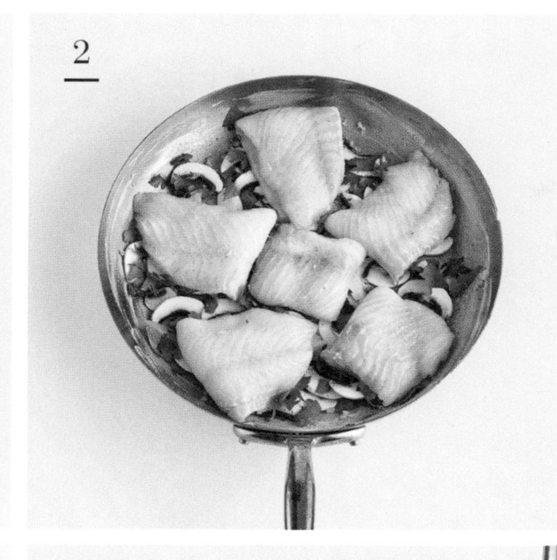

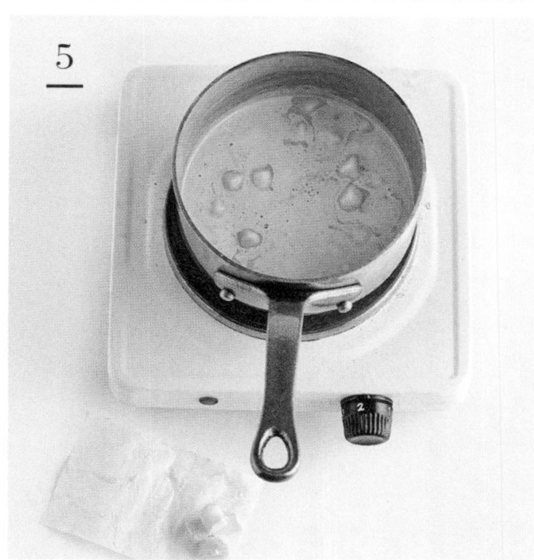

SERVES 4

FISH

two 2 lb 3 oz or one 4 lb 8 oz turbots, filleted

BROTH

1 shallot
1 small bunch Italian parsley
3½ oz white mushrooms
1 teaspoon butter
1 teaspoon fine salt
freshly ground black pepper (4 turns)
½ cup white wine
½–1 cup water

BONNE FEMME SAUCE

1 cup crème fraîche
6 tablespoons butter

1 Preheat the oven to 320°F. Peel and mince the shallot. Wash, dry, and roughly chop the parsley. Remove the stems from the mushrooms, then peel the caps and slice them thinly.

2 Butter a skillet or flameproof roasting pan. Sprinkle in ¾ teaspoon of the salt, the pepper, and the shallot. Add the parsley and mushrooms. Sprinkle the fillets with the remaining salt, fold them in half, and arrange in the pan. Pour in the wine, then enough water to reach three-quarters of the height of the fish. Cover with a sheet of parchment paper cut to fit and bring to a boil on the stovetop.

3 Transfer to the oven for 4–5 minutes, until you meet resistance if you push on the fish with a finger.

4 Remove the fillets with a skimmer. Strain the cooking liquid, without pressing on the solids, through a sieve into a small saucepan, then return the fillets to the empty skillet. Cover with the parchment paper and set aside.

5 Preheat the broiler. Bring the cooking liquid to a boil. Reduce it to 3–4 tablespoons. Dice the butter for the sauce.

6 Add the crème fraîche to the reduced liquid and reduce again until it covers the back of a spoon. Whisk in the butter over medium heat.

7 Pour the sauce over the fillets and brown under the broiler for 3–4 minutes.

MONKFISH À L'AMÉRICAINE

Understand

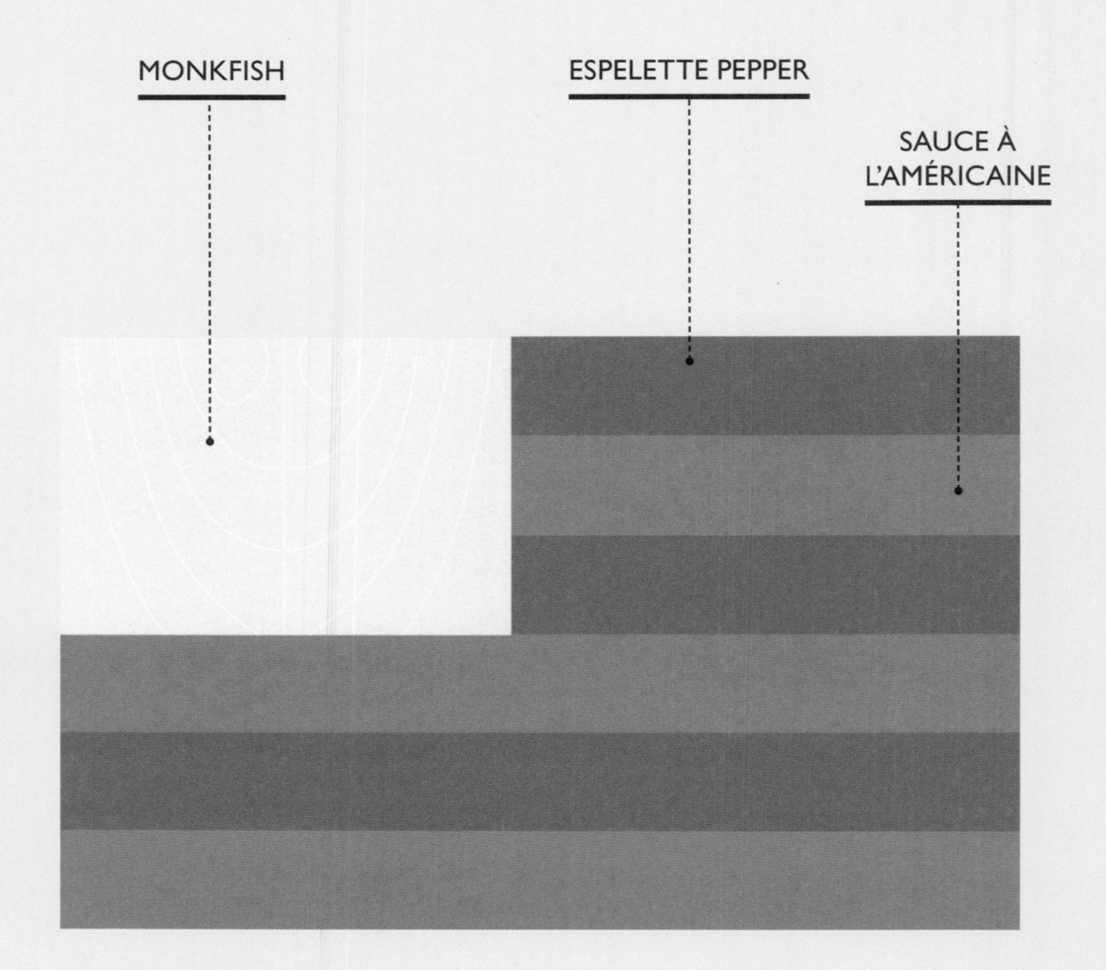

WHAT IS IT?

Monkfish and tomato stew: browned monkfish fillets, deglazed with Cognac, then cooked in a tomato sauce

TIME TO MAKE

Preparation: 35 minutes
Cooking: 30–35 minutes

EQUIPMENT

Chef's knife
Fine-mesh sieve

VARIATION

Sauce à l'américaine made with shellfish

TRICKY ASPECT

Cooking the monkfish in two phases

TECHNIQUES TO MASTER

Browning (page 282)
Reducing a sauce (page 283)
Whisking in butter (page 282)
Straining and pushing through a sieve (page 281)
Mincing (page 280)
Zesting (page 280)

IT'S READY . . .

When the monkfish is firm enough, and the sauce is smooth and creamy.

SAUCE À L'ARMORICAINE . . .

Is the same as sauce à l'américaine.

WHY USE ULTRA-PASTEURIZED CREAM?

The acidity provided by the wine, along with the reduction of the cream sauce, can curdle the cream. Ultra-pasteurized cream is more stable during cooking.

SERVES 4

1 FISH

2 lb 3 oz headless, skinless monkfish, filleted (ask for the spine)
½ teaspoon fine salt
2 tablespoons butter
2 tablespoons peanut oil
¼ cup Cognac

2 SAUCE À L'AMÉRICAINE

4–7 shallots
¼ teaspoon fine salt
1 garlic clove
2 tablespoons tomato paste
1 cup dry white wine
1½ cups canned tomato purée
freshly ground black pepper (3 turns)
pinch of cayenne pepper
½ cup ultra-pasturized heavy cream
2 tablespoons butter

3 TO SERVE

4–6 Italian parsley sprigs
1 lemon
pinch of Espelette pepper

Making monkfish à l'américaine

1 Chop the monkfish spine into pieces. Peel and mince the shallots and garlic. Cut each monkfish fillet into four pieces. Dry the cut fillets with paper towels and sprinkle with the salt.

2 Heat the butter and the peanut oil in a Dutch oven over very high heat and brown the fish on all sides. Pour in the Cognac and let it almost completely evaporate.

3 Remove the fish pieces. To make the sauce, add the shallots and salt to the Dutch oven and fry over medium heat. Add the monkfish spine and sweat for 1–2 minutes, then add the garlic. Stir for 30 seconds, mix in the tomato paste, then cook for about 1 minute. Pour in the wine and let it reduce by half.

4 Add the tomato purée, pepper, and cayenne pepper, then simmer, uncovered, for 15–20 minutes. Remove the spine pieces. If necessary to warm them through, return the fillet pieces to the pan, then cover and simmer for 2–3 minutes.

5 Remove the fillets and keep them warm. Strain the sauce through a fine-mesh sieve, pushing it through. Reduce it over high heat to about half. Reduce the heat to medium and stir in the cream, then reduce until thickened. Whisk in the butter. Adjust the seasoning.

6 Wash, dry, pick, and mince the parsley leaves. Wash, dry, and zest half the lemon. Return the fillets to the pan and sprinkle with the Espelette pepper, lemon zest, and parsley.

COD
WITH AN HERB CRUST

Understand

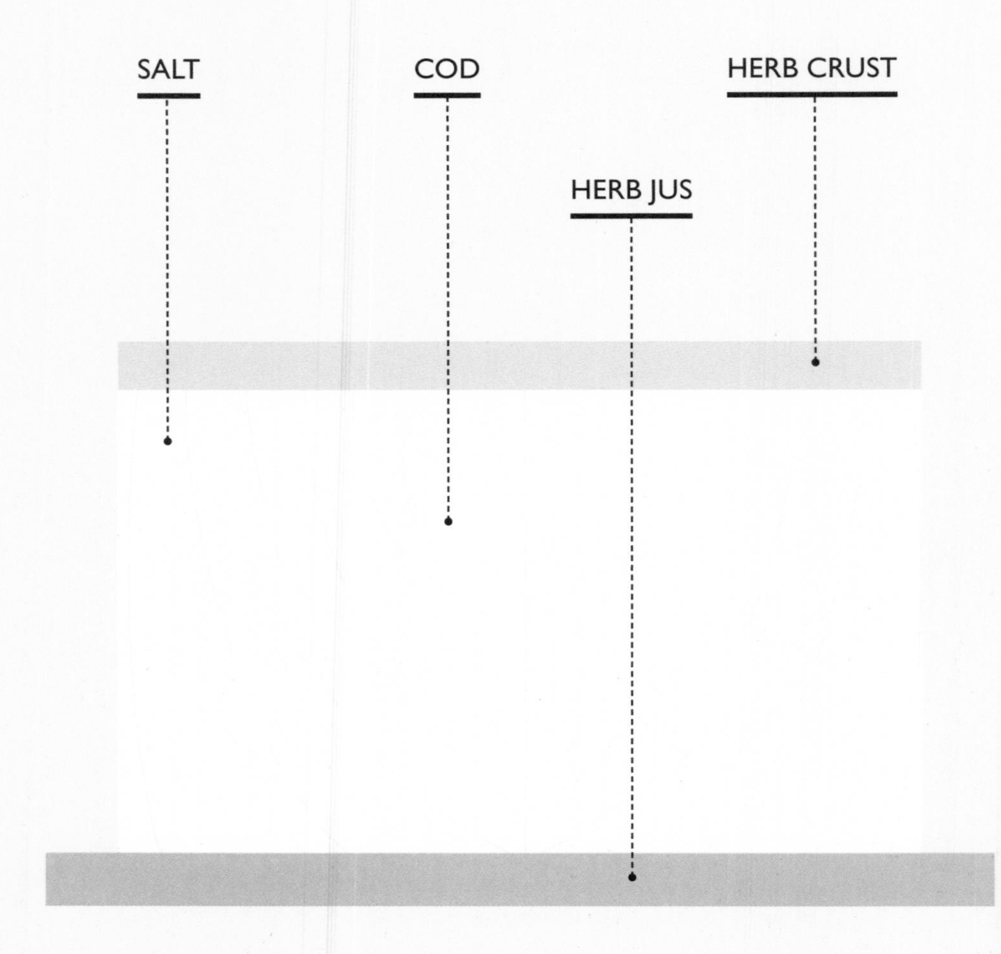

WHAT IS IT?
Semi-salted cod fillet (precooked in a marinade of salt and sugar), pan-fried, then coated with an herb butter and browned

TIME TO MAKE
Preparation: 35 minutes
Cooking: 5 minutes
Resting: 50 minutes

EQUIPMENT
Food processor
Rolling pin

VARIATION
Chorizo crust: replace the herbs with 3½ oz chorizo mixed with fresh breadcrumbs

TRICKY ASPECT
Coating with the herb crust

TECHNIQUES TO MASTER
Mincing (page 280)
Finely chopping (page 280)

IT'S READY . . .
When the herb butter is golden.

STORAGE
Freeze the herb butter for 3 weeks, covered with parchment paper and plastic wrap.

WHY "PRECOOK" IN SALT?
The salt absorbs water from the surface of the fish. The flesh of the fish firms up slightly and holds together better during cooking.

WHY "SEMI-SALTED"?
The precooking is called semi-salting because the fish remains fresh (unlike salt cod, for example).

Learn

SERVES 4

1 FISH

⅓ cup coarse sea salt
2 teaspoons sugar
1 lb 5 oz skinless cod fillet
4 teaspoons olive oil
3½ tablespoons butter
½ teaspoon fleur de sel

2 HERB CRUST

4 slices day-old white bread (no crusts)
2 shallots
1 bunch Italian parsley
1 small bunch tarragon
3 large basil sprigs
14 tablespoons butter, softened
¾ teaspoon fine salt
freshly ground black pepper (6 turns)

3 GREEN JUS

1 bunch Italian parsley
1 teaspoon coarse sea salt
freshly ground black pepper (4 turns)

Making cod with an herb crust

1 Make the herb crust: process the bread to fine crumbs. Peel and mince the shallots. Wash, dry, pick, and chop the herbs. Mix with all the remaining ingredients in a bowl. Using a rolling pin, roll the herb crust between two sheets of parchment paper to a ¼-inch thickness. Freeze for at least 30 minutes to harden.

2 For the fish, mix the coarse sea salt with the sugar. Spread a thin layer of the mixture in a baking dish. Place the cod fillet on top. Cover with the remaining salt mixture. Cover with plastic wrap and refrigerate for 20 minutes to firm up the flesh.

3 To make the green jus, wash and pick the parsley leaves. Plunge the leaves into boiling water with the salt added. Cook for 2 minutes. Drain, reserving 1 teaspoon of the cooking water. Process the cooked leaves with the reserved cooking water to form a smooth liquid. Push through a fine-mesh sieve. Adjust the seasoning.

4 Wash the cod under cold water. Dry with paper towels. Cut into four equal slices. Preheat the broiler. Heat the olive oil in a skillet over high heat and brown the cod pieces for 1 minute. Reduce the heat to low, turn the cod over, add the butter, and cook for 5–6 minutes, basting the cod constantly with the foaming butter. Transfer to a wire rack.

5 Cut the crust into four pieces slightly larger than the cod slices. Place one on each piece of cod using a thin spatula.

6 Broil the cod until the crust is golden. Sprinkle with the fleur de sel. Serve on a pool of the green jus.

SLOW-COOKED COD

Understand

120°F IN THE CENTER

140°F AT THE SURFACE

WHAT IS IT?
Cod roasted at low temperature, served with fried shrimp and a warm olive vinaigrette

TIME TO MAKE
Preparation: 25 minutes
Cooking: 30 minutes
Resting: 20 minutes

EQUIPMENT
Roasting pan
Large saucepan and frying basket
Thermometer

TRICKY ASPECT
The low oven temperature.

TECHNIQUES TO MASTER
Using a probe thermometer (page 282)
Finely chopping (page 280)
Mincing (page 280)

INGREDIENT TIP
You can use raw shrimp—just fry them longer.

COOKING TIP
Use a digital probe thermometer to check if the fish is cooked: the core temperature should reach 120°F.

WHY COOK AT LOW TEMPERATURE?
The flesh cooks while staying soft and moist.

SERVES 4

1 ROAST COD

1 lb 2 oz skinless cod fillet, cut into 4 pieces
¾ teaspoon fine salt
2 tablespoons olive oil

2 VINAIGRETTE

¼ cup pitted kalamata olives
1 small shallot
5 Italian parsley sprigs
½ lemon
½ teaspoon fine salt
freshly ground black pepper (6 turns)
¼ cup olive oil

3 FRIED SHRIMP

2 cups peanut oil
7 oz cooked small shrimp, head and shell on
1 cup milk
1 teaspoon fine salt
½ cup all-purpose flour
½ teaspoon fleur de sel
freshly ground black pepper (3 turns)

Making slow-cooked cod

1 Wash the fish and cut into four equal portions. Let it warm up to room temperature on a paper towel for 20 minutes. Preheat the oven to 200°F with a roasting pan on a lower rack. Season the fish with the salt, brush it with the olive oil, and place it in the hot roasting pan in the oven. Cook for 15–30 minutes. The fish should be opaque on the outside and translucent in the middle.

2 To make the vinaigrette, cut the olives in thin slices. Peel and mince the shallot. Wash, dry, pick, and chop the parsley leaves. Squeeze the lemon. Dissolve the salt in the lemon juice. Mix all the vinaigrette ingredients except the olive oil.

3 To make the fried shrimp, pour the peanut oil into a heavy-bottomed saucepan and heat to 360°F. Rinse and drain the shrimp, then dry on a clean dish towel. Soak the shrimp in the milk, then drain and season with the fine salt.

4 Coat them in the flour, then pour them into the frying basket and shake off the excess flour. Plunge the basket of shrimp into the hot oil for 10 seconds. Remove the basket and return the oil to 360°F. Plunge the shrimp into the oil again for 5 seconds, to make them really crisp. Drain.

5 Season the shrimp, in the basket, with the fleur de sel and the pepper. Mix, then drain on paper towels.

6 For the warm vinaigrette, heat the olive oil in a small saucepan over medium heat. Add the other vinaigrette ingredients and stir.

7 Place each piece of cod on a warm serving plate, then top with the hot vinaigrette and arrange the fried shrimp on the side.

SEARED TUNA

Understand

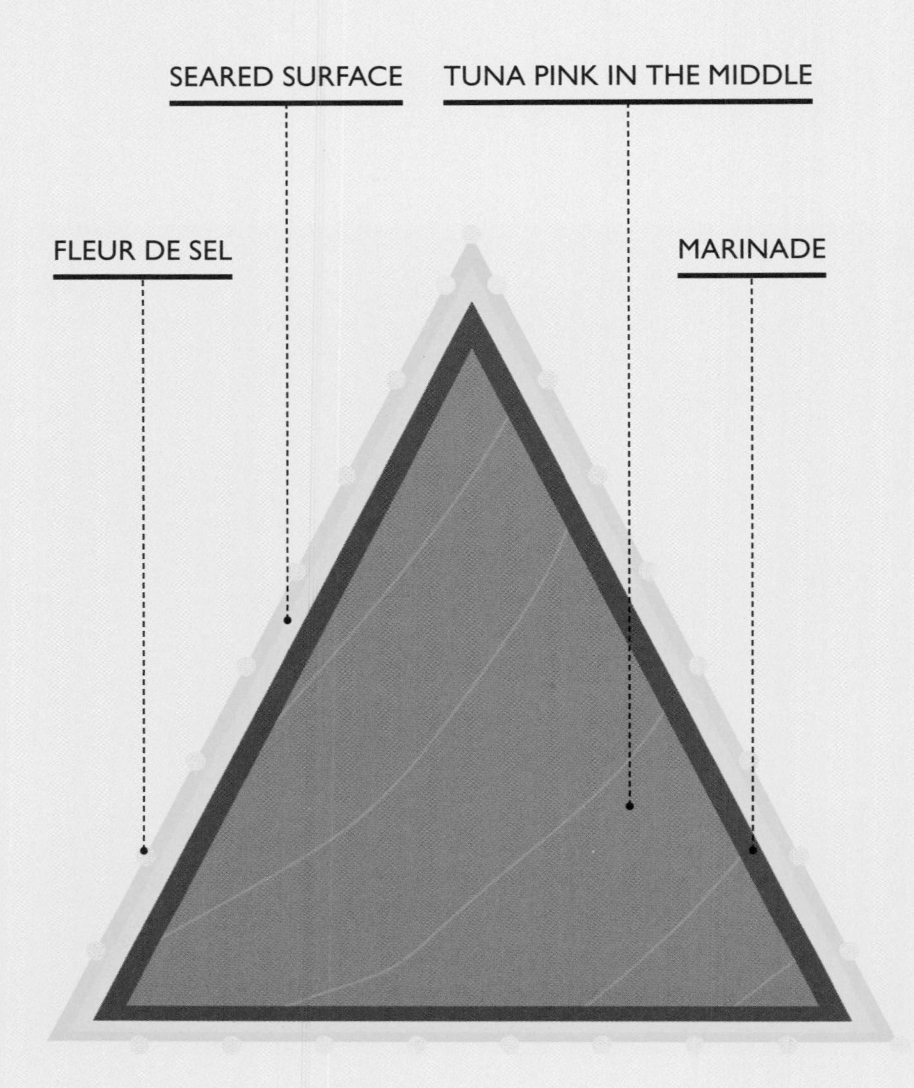

WHAT IS IT?

Marinated tuna seared on all sides and left raw in the middle

TIME TO MAKE

Preparation: 30 minutes
Cooking: 5 minutes, Resting: 30 minutes

EQUIPMENT

Microplane grater

TRICKY ASPECTS

– Cooking: searing the tuna to form a crust without cooking in the middle
– Cutting: if the triangles are too large, the flesh won't be warm in the middle

TECHNIQUES TO MASTER

Zesting (page 280)
Thinly slicing (page 280)
Cutting a parchment paper disk (page 285)

IT'S READY . . .

When the tuna is browned on the outside and warm in the middle.

HOW DOES THE MARINADE AFFECT THE FISH?

It flavors the fish but doesn't precook it because it contains no acid.

SERVES 4

FISH

1 lb 5 oz bluefin or yellowfin tuna top loin, cut in 3 triangular pieces 2¾–4 inches on a side

MARINADE

½ cup soy sauce
¼ cup peanut oil or grapeseed oil
¼ cup toasted sesame oil
1½ tablespoons sesame seeds
freshly ground black pepper (6 turns)

Learn

SALAD

1 fennel bulb
$1\frac{1}{3}$ packed cup arugula leaves
1 lime

SEASONING

$\frac{1}{2}$ teaspoon fleur de sel
freshly ground black pepper, to taste
2 tablespoons olive oil

1 In a large baking dish, coat the tuna pieces with the soy sauce. Add the oils, sesame seeds, and pepper. Coat the fish again, then cover with plastic wrap and leave to marinate for 20 minutes at room temperature.

2 Cut the fennel in half lengthwise, then in half again. Remove the core, then cut the fennel into very thin slices using a knife or a mandoline. Plunge the fennel slices into ice water, then drain.

3 Wash and drain the arugula. Grate the lime zest, then squeeze the lime.

4 Drain the tuna, reserving the marinade. Heat a skillet, lined with a disk of parchment paper cut to fit, over very high heat for 1–2 minutes. Brown each side of the tuna, then reduce the heat to low and cook for 2–3 minutes, turning the pieces regularly. You want the middle to stay pink, almost raw. Cut each piece into 4 slices.

5 Mix the marinade with the lime zest and juice, then add the fennel and the arugula.

6 Arrange the tuna on one side of the plate and the salad on the other. Sprinkle with the fleur de sel and pepper, then drizzle with the olive oil.

SALMON CONFIT

Understand

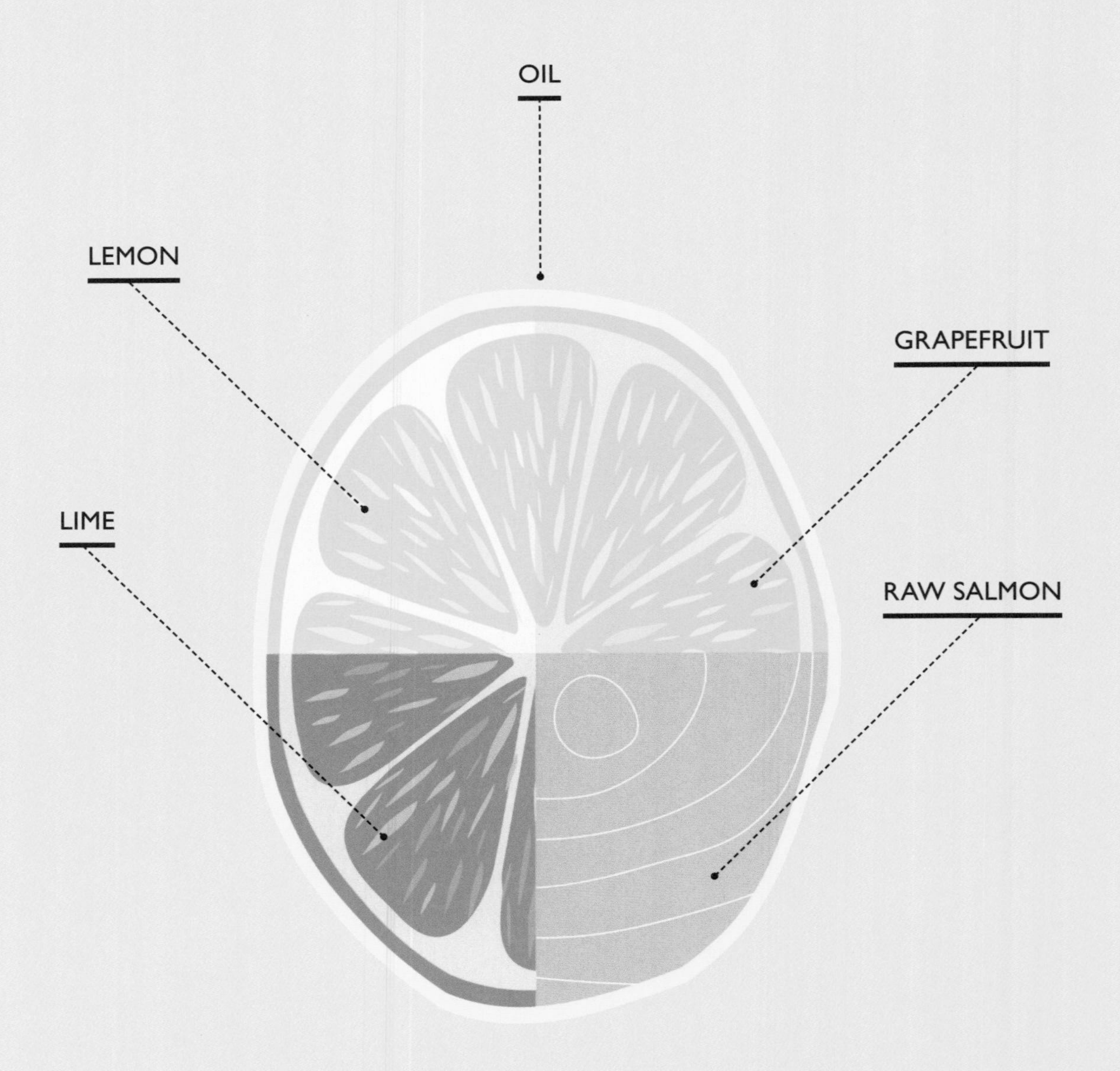

WHAT IS IT?

Salmon cooked in an oil bath at 200°F, served with thin strips of raw vegetables and citrus segments

TIME TO MAKE

Preparation: 25 minutes
Cooking: 40 minutes

EQUIPMENT

Ovenproof saucepan or baking dish (to fit all the fish pieces side by side)
Microplane grater
Mandoline

VARIATION

Confit of cod

TECHNIQUES TO MASTER

Peeling citrus for segments (page 280)
Supreming citrus (page 280)
Using a mandoline (page 284)
Zesting (page 280)

STORAGE

The salmon can sit in the oil for 30 minutes after cooking. Eat at room temperature.

IT'S READY . . .

When the flesh of the salmon is slightly paler and very soft.

WHY COOK IN OIL?

Oil and water don't mix, so the water in the flesh of the fish remains concentrated, which prevents it from drying out.

WHY COOK AT LOW TEMPERATURE?

This minimizes contraction of the muscles and so prevents the flesh from toughening.

WHAT IS "CONFITING"?

Cooking slowly in sugar or fat until the cooking liquid (syrup or oil) penetrates to the center of the food.

Learn

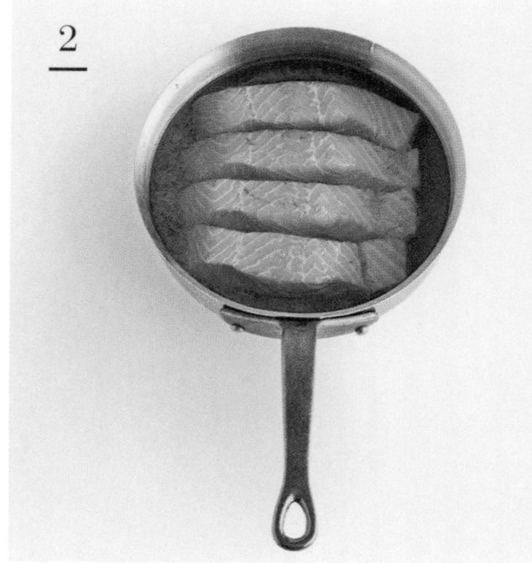
2

3

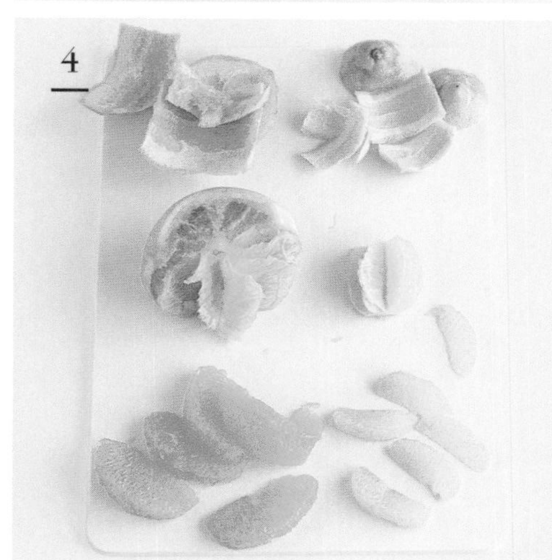
4

6

5

SERVES 4

FISH

four 5 ½ oz skinless salmon fillets
1 ¼–2 cups olive oil

ACCOMPANIMENT

1 lemon
1 lime
1 grapefruit
about 15 red radishes
2 spring onions

SEASONING

2 pinches of Espelette pepper
½ teaspoon each of fine salt and fleur de sel

1 Preheat the oven to 200°F. Wash and zest the citrus fruits using a Microplane. Place the salmon fillets side by side in an ovenproof saucepan. Pour in enough olive oil just to cover. Remove the salmon from the oil and drain over a dish, then set aside on a paper towel. Mix the citrus zests into the oil in the saucepan and season with half the Espelette pepper. Put the pan in the oven for 15–20 minutes.

2 Immerse the salmon in the oil and return to the oven for another 15–20 minutes. Remove from the oven and leave the salmon in the pan.

3 Squeeze half of the lime for its juice, then dissolve the fine salt in it. Add the remaining Espelette pepper and pour in 3 tablespoons of the oil used to cook the salmon. Stir.

4 Peel the lemon and grapefruit for segments, then supreme (page 280) the whole lemon and half the grapefruit. Cut them in half lengthwise if the segments are too thick.

5 Trim and wash the radishes. Cut off half the green tops of the onions. Using a mandoline, slice the vegetables into very thin slices, then mix them with the citrus segments. Add some of the lime juice dressing.

6 Drain the salmon fillets. Place them whole or cut into cubes on one side of the serving plates with the salad on the other side. Season with the remaining vinaigrette and the fleur de sel.

COULIBIAC

Understand

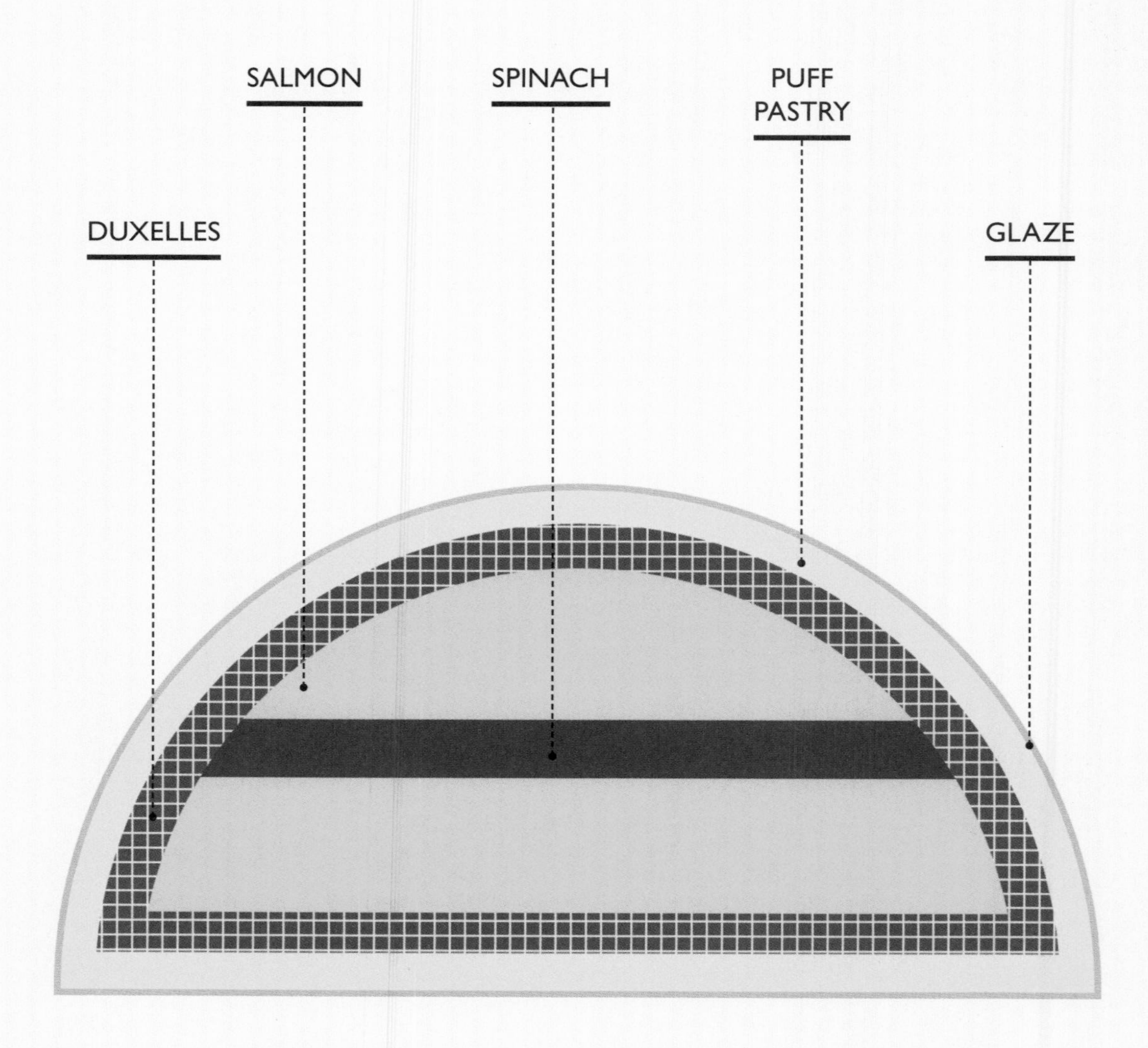

WHAT IS IT?
Salmon in a puff pastry crust stuffed with spinach and mushroom duxelles

TIME TO MAKE
Preparation: 50 minutes
Cooking: 30 minutes
Resting: 1 hour 5 minutes

EQUIPMENT
Fishbone tweezers
Rolling pin
Pastry brush
Lattice pastry roller

VARIATIONS
Traditional stuffing: hard-boiled eggs and cooked rice
Assembly: laying a crepe between the stuffing and the puff pastry to avoid moistening the latter

TRICKY ASPECT
Assembling the pastry

TIPS
– Roll out the pastry in a cold room to prevent it from sticking.
– If you don't have a lattice roller, create the decoration by hand (see beef Wellington, page 232).

STORAGE
2 days in the refrigerator; reheat for 10 minutes in a 300°F oven.

ACCOMPANIMENT
Beurre blanc (page 28)

Learn

SERVES 4

1 SALMON

1 lb 12 oz skinless salmon top loin, cut in half lengthwise (making two 12 × 3¼-inch pieces)

2 STUFFING

7 oz spinach leaves
1 garlic clove
2 tablespoons olive oil
¼ teaspoon fine salt
freshly ground black pepper (3 turns)

3 CRUST

1 lb 7 oz (1 recipe) puff pastry (page 46)
2 egg yolks
2 teaspoons water

4 DUXELLES

10½ oz (about 2½ recipes) duxelles (page 42)
pinch of cayenne pepper
grated zest of 1 lemon
1 small bunch dill, finely chopped
2 teaspoons fine salt
freshly ground black pepper (8 turns)
2 teaspoons sugar

Making coulibiac

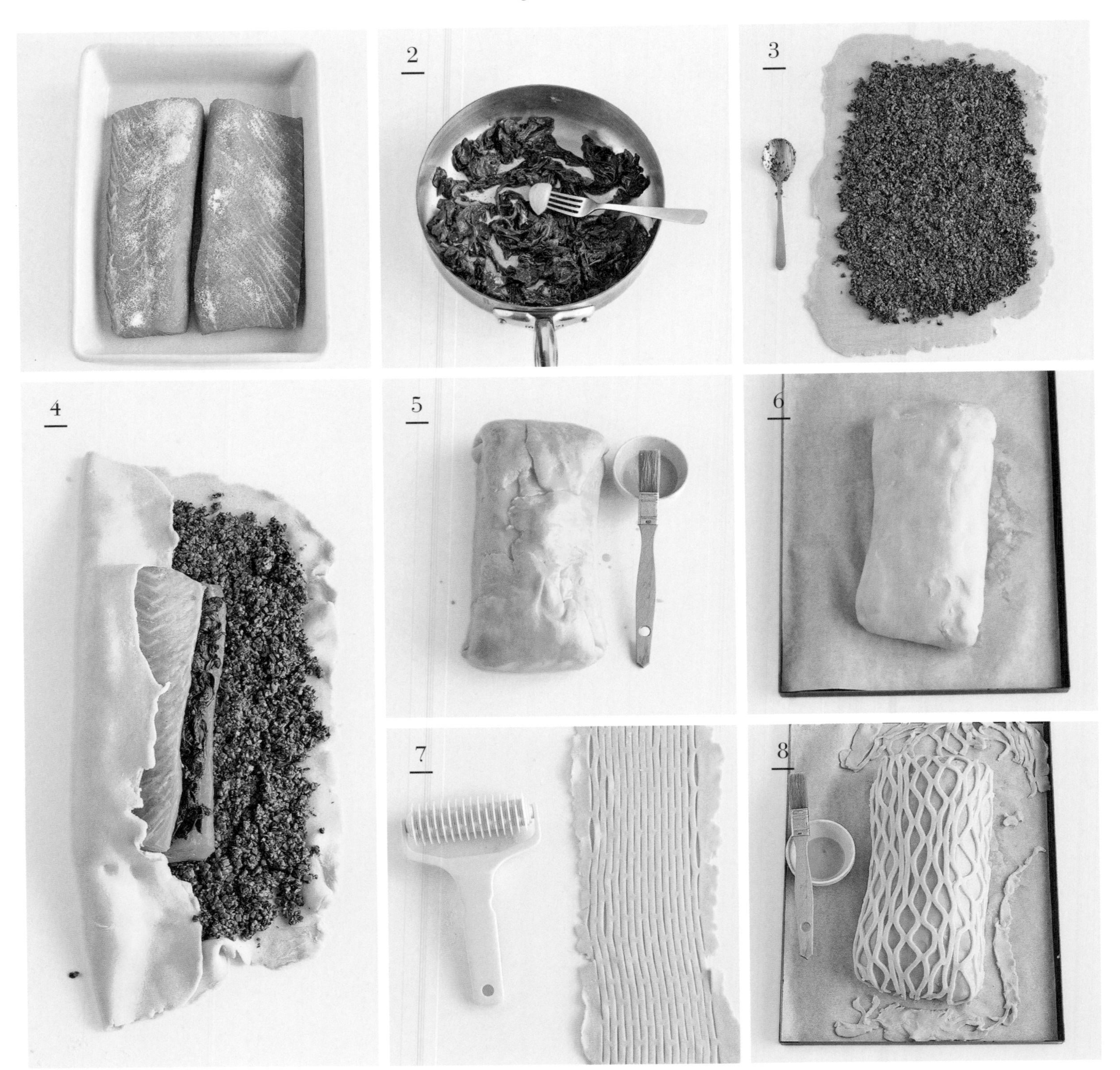

1 At the end of cooking the duxelles (page 42), add the cayenne pepper, lemon zest, and dill. Season with the salt, black pepper, and sugar. Refrigerate for 1 hour. Preheat the oven to 400°F.

2 Wash the spinach in plenty of water, then remove the stems and any tough fibers. Wilt the spinach as follows: stick the peeled garlic clove on the end of a fork and make an incision with the point of a knife. Heat the olive oil in a large skillet over high heat and add the spinach. Stir and rub with the garlic fork. When the spinach has wilted, remove from the heat, then season with the salt and pepper. Stir with the garlic fork. When the spinach is lukewarm, squeeze it with your fingers to remove as much water as possible.

3 Wash the salmon under a trickle of water, then drain on paper towels. Cut the puff pastry into two pieces, a larger one of 1 lb and a smaller one of 7 oz. Set the smaller piece aside in the refrigerator. Dust a work surface with flour and roll out the larger piece into a rectangle ⅛ inch thick and large enough to comfortably cover the two salmon pieces stacked on top of each other. Spread the duxelles over the pastry, leaving a 1¼-inch border around the edges.

4 Set a piece of salmon in the middle of the pastry then cover with the spinach. Set the second piece of fish on top. Enclose the salmon in the pastry, ensuring there are no air bubbles.

5 Mix the egg yolks and water. Using a pastry brush, glaze the pastry with the egg wash.

6 Line a baking sheet with parchment paper. Transfer the coulibiac to the prepared baking sheet, with the pastry seam on the bottom. Set aside in the refrigerator.

7 Roll out the smaller piece of puff pastry into a rectangle as wide as your lattice pastry roller (about 4¾ inches). Run the roller over the whole length of the pastry, pressing hard.

8 Brush the pastry of the coulibiac with egg wash once more, then place the latticed rectangle over the top. Trim and glaze. Bake at 400°F for 30 minutes (the pastry must be golden). Let it rest for 5 minutes before cutting into thick slices.

FISH AND CHIPS

Understand

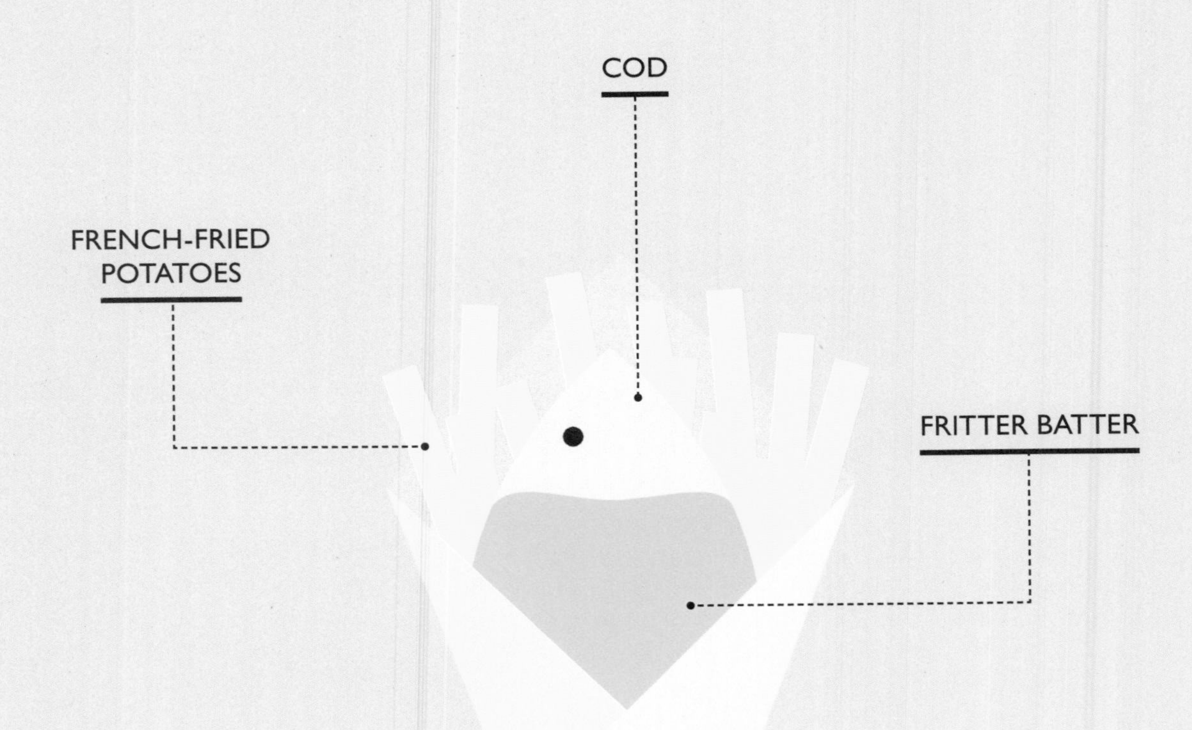

WHAT IS IT?
Battered cod served with French fries and tartar sauce

TIME TO MAKE
Preparation: 40 minutes
Cooking: 10 minutes
Resting: 30 minutes

EQUIPMENT
Large saucepan
Pastry brush (preferably long)
Thermometer

VARIATIONS
Battered whiting or pollock

TRICKY ASPECTS
– Cooking the fries
– Cooking the fish

TECHNIQUES TO MASTER
Finely chopping (page 280)
Mincing (page 280)

TIP
Reheat the fried potatoes by plunging them into an oil bath at 360°F for a few seconds.

IT'S READY . . .
When the battered fish and the fries are golden and crisp.

WHAT DOES THE BEER DO?
It adds gas to the batter, which aerates the mixture, making it light and crisp.

WHY MARINATE THE FISH IN COARSE SEA SALT?
To season the flesh of the fish deeply and to firm it up. In addition, the salt dries the surface of the fish and makes the batter stick more easily.

Learn

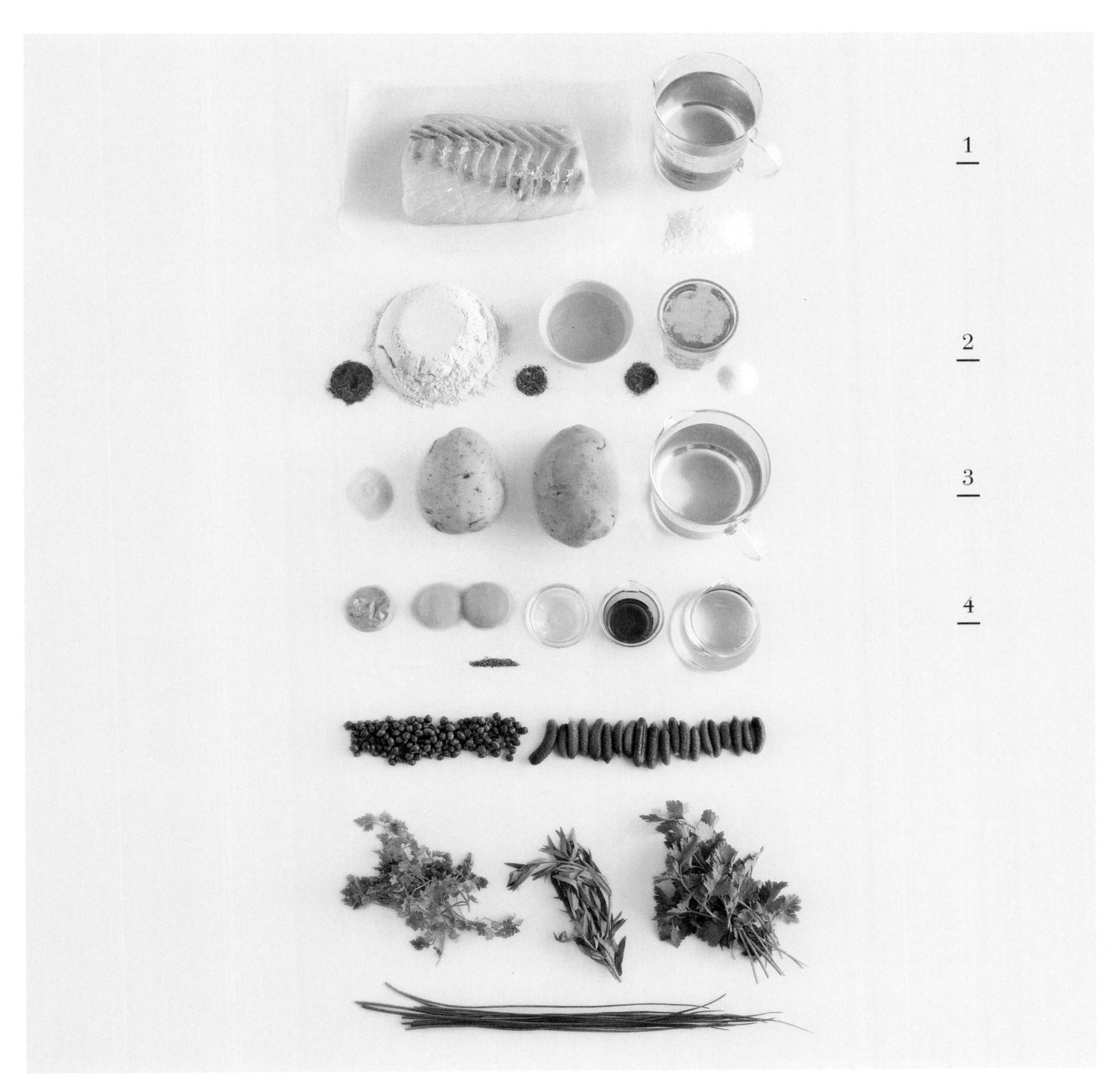

SERVES 4

1 FISH

2 tablespoons coarse sea salt
1 lb 7 oz skinless cod fillet
2 cups peanut oil

2 BATTER

1⅓ cups all-purpose flour
1 teaspoon paprika
½ teaspoon cayenne pepper
¼ teaspoon ground black pepper
2 teaspoons fine salt
1 cup beer
2 egg whites

3 FRENCH-FRIED POTATOES

2 lb 3 oz baking potatoes (russet)
6 cups peanut oil
1 teaspoon fine salt

4 TARTAR SAUCE

Mayonnaise
1 tablespoon water
1 tablespoon Dijon mustard
4½ teaspoons vinegar
½ teaspoon fine salt
¼ teaspoon ground black pepper
2 egg yolks
1¼ cups peanut oil

Tartar flavoring
1 small bunch Italian parsley
a few chervil sprigs
a few tarragon sprigs
a few chives
¼ cup capers
8–10 cornichons

Making fish and chips

1 Sprinkle the bottom of a baking dish with half the coarse sea salt. Cut the piece of cod in half, set the cod on top of the salt, then sprinkle with the remaining coarse sea salt. Cover with plastic wrap and refrigerate for 30 minutes.

2 To make the tartar sauce, wash, pick, and finely chop the parsley, chervil, and tarragon leaves. Wash and mince the chives. Cut the capers into small pieces and finely chop the cornichons. Make a mayonnaise using the technique on page 27, but replace the lemon juice with the mustard and vinegar. Stir in the herbs, capers, and cornichons, then cover with plastic wrap and refrigerate.

3 Cut the potatoes for French fries (page 59) and fry them as directed on page 87. Drain on paper towels. Add 2 more cups of peanut oil to the saucepan and bring the temperature of the oil back up to 360°F.

4 To make the batter, mix the flour, paprika, cayenne pepper, black pepper, and salt in a large mixing bowl. Add the egg whites and beer, then mix just enough for the batter to be smooth but still very foamy.

5 Wash the fish under cold water and carefully pat dry with a paper towel. Cut into strips $3\frac{1}{4}$–4 inches long and $\frac{5}{8}$–$\frac{3}{4}$ inch wide.

6 Using tongs, dip each piece of fish into the batter, then drop carefully into the oil without crowding. Cook the fish in several batches. Let the oil temperature fall when you add the fish and fry for 5 minutes. Drain on paper towels. Return the oil to 360°F before adding the next batch.

7 Serve the fish very hot, with the fries and tartar sauce.

BOEUF BOURGUIGNON

Understand

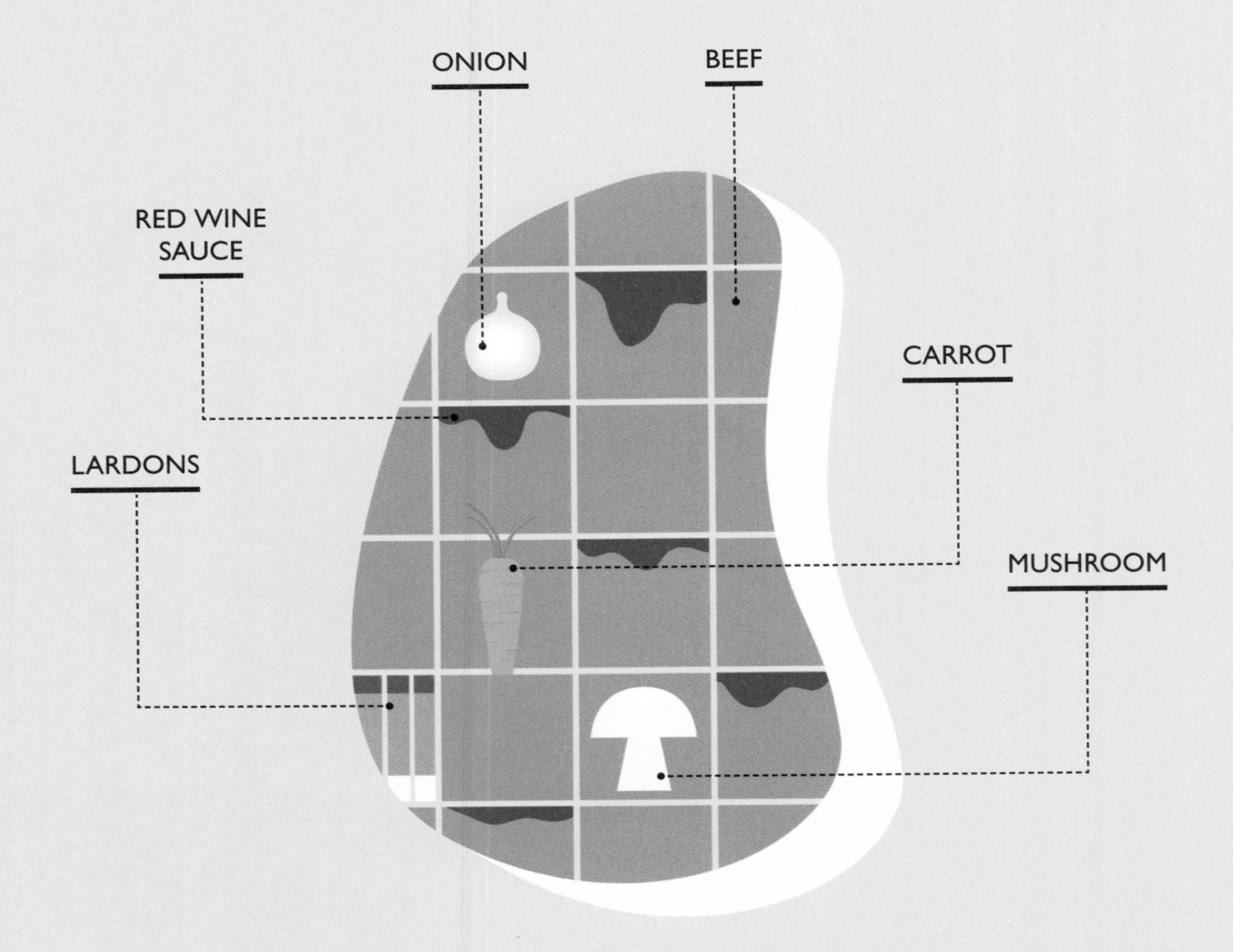

WHAT IS IT?
Brown beef stew: pieces of beef slowly cooked in a brown sauce with a red wine base

TIME TO MAKE
Preparation: 40 minutes
Cooking: 2 hours 30 minutes to 3 hours

EQUIPMENT
Fine-mesh sieve
Dutch oven

TRICKY ASPECTS
– Not burning the bits stuck to the bottom
– Retaining sufficient sauce

TECHNIQUES TO MASTER
Degreasing a skillet (page 283)
Transferring (page 282)
Browning (page 282)
Scraping up stuck-on bits (page 283)
Reducing a sauce (page 283)
Straining through a sieve (page 281)
Adding flour to stews (page 282)
Toasting flour (page 281)
Cutting in scallops (page 280)
Cutting in mirepoix (page 34)

IT'S READY . . .
When the sauce is smooth and thick.

STORAGE
Refrigerate the meat, covered by the sauce.

NOTE
Use a full-bodied, tannin-rich wine (Côtes du Rhône, Bordeaux Supérieur, Languedoc, etc.).

ACCOMPANIMENT
Brown-glazed baby onions (page 252) (added with the mushrooms)

WHAT DOES CHOCOLATE ADD?
Rounded aromatic notes.

Learn

SERVES 4

1 BEEF

1 onion
1 carrot
1 celery stalk
1 orange
¾ teaspoon fine salt
2½ tablespoons peanut oil
2 lb 3 oz chuck steak, cut into 2-inch cubes
2 tablespoons all-purpose flour
1½ cups full-bodied red wine
1½ cups water
1 tablespoon tomato paste
⅜ oz bittersweet chocolate (70% cacao)

2 AROMATICS

½ teaspoon ground ginger
½ teaspoon paprika
pinch of freshly grated nutmeg
1 bay leaf
1 thyme sprig

3 GARNISH

5½ oz white mushrooms
5 or 6 slices thick-cut bacon, cut into lardons
1 cup water
2 teaspoons peanut oil
¼ teaspoon fine salt
freshly ground black pepper (3 turns)

Making boeuf bourguignon

1 Preheat the oven to 360°F (with the rack in the bottom position). Peel the onion and cut in mirepoix. Peel the carrot and cut in half lengthwise, then into ¼-inch slices. Cut the celery into ½-inch slices. Zest half the orange. Pat the meat dry with paper towels, then season with ½ teaspoon of the salt.

2 Heat 2 tablespoons of the oil in a Dutch oven over high heat. Brown the pieces of beef on all sides. Remove the meat, degrease the Dutch oven, then pour in the remaining oil. Add the carrot and onion, then season with the remaining salt. When the onion is soft, sprinkle in the flour and toast in the oven for 5 minutes.

3 Heat the wine with the water in a saucepan until simmering. Remove the Dutch oven from the oven, mix the vegetables well, and reduce the oven temperature to 300°F. Add the tomato paste, ginger, paprika, and nutmeg, then cook for 1 minute over high heat on the stovetop, stirring constantly. Stir in the meat.

4 Cover the meat to three-quarters of its height with the wine and water mixture. Add the celery, orange zest, thyme, and bay leaf. Scrape the bottom of the Dutch oven to remove any stuck-on bits. Bring to a simmer, then cover and transfer to the oven for 2½ to 3 hours, until the meat is tender. After 1½ hours, add more of the reheated wine and water mixture or hot water if necessary. Stir from time to time and check the concentration of the sauce every 45 minutes.

5 Put the lardons in a nonstick skillet and cover with the water. Bring to a boil and let the water almost completely evaporate. Add half the oil and brown the lardons over medium heat, stirring frequently. Drain in a colander.

6 Cut the stems off the mushrooms, then peel the caps and cut them into two or four slices, depending on their size. In the same skillet, cook the mushrooms, adding the remaining oil if necessary. Add the ¼ teaspoon salt and the pepper.

7 With a skimmer or slotted spoon, lift the beef and carrots out of the pan and set aside. Strain the sauce through a sieve into a bowl. Off the heat, return the meat and carrots to the pan, along with the bacon and the mushrooms. Cover. Add the chocolate to the sauce and let it melt. Adjust the seasoning, then pour over the meat.

POT-AU-FEU

Understand

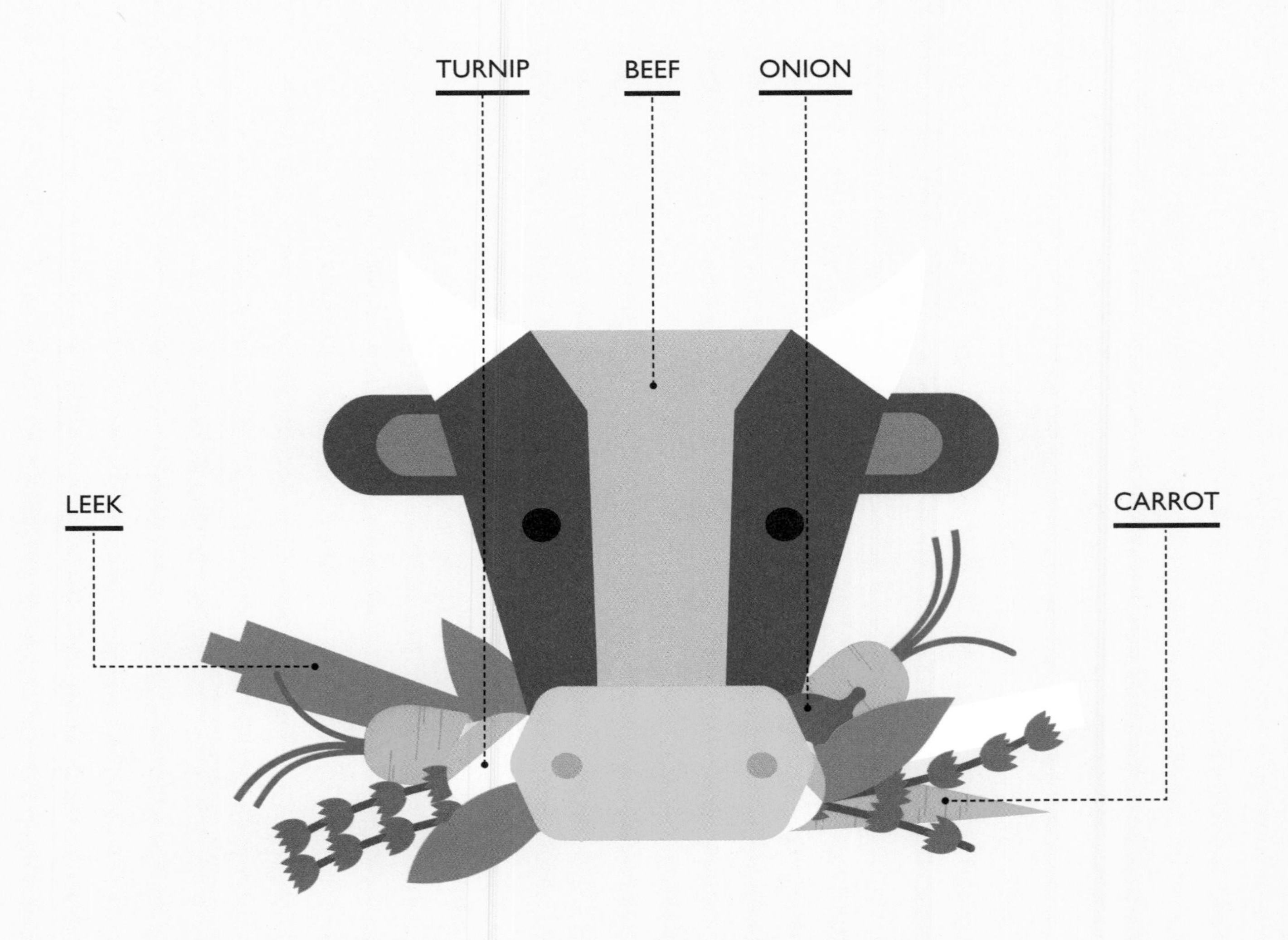

WHAT IS IT?

Beef poached in an aromatic broth over very low heat, served with the vegetables it was cooked with, plus a condiment

TIME TO MAKE

Preparation: 30 minutes
Cooking: 3–4 hours

VARIATIONS

Replace the herb cream with traditional condiments: mustards (Dijon and grainy), cornichons, and fleur de sel (or coarse sea salt)

TECHNIQUES TO MASTER

Skimming (page 283)
Mincing (page 280)
Finely chopping (page 280)
Crushing garlic (page 280)
Making a bouquet garni (page 34)

TIP

To flavor and color the broth, add a burnt onion (cut in half and blackened on foil in a skillet over very high heat)

IT'S READY . . .

When the stock is clear and the meat and vegetables are tender.

SERVES 4

BEEF

2 lb 3 oz beef: chuck steak and short ribs

BROTH

1 bay leaf
3–4 Italian parsley leaves
2 thyme sprigs
4 small leeks
2½ quarts (10 cups) water
8 carrots with trimmed tops

Learn

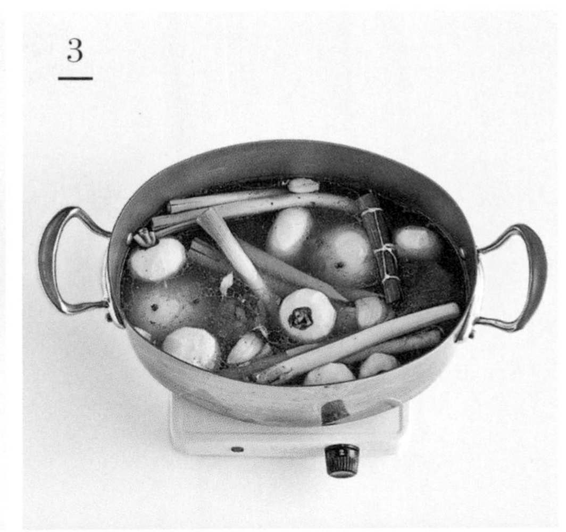

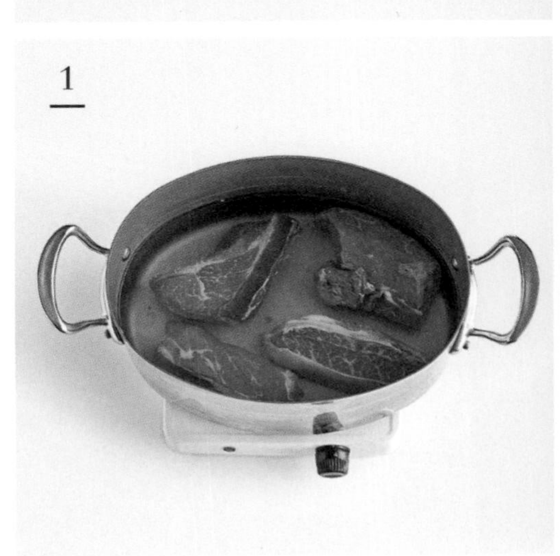

2 onions
6 whole cloves
4 garlic cloves
1 tablespoon coarse sea salt
4 black peppercorns
8 small turnips

HERB CREAM

¾ cup fromage blanc
10 chives, minced
10 Italian parsley leaves, finely chopped
¼ teaspoon fine salt
freshly ground black pepper (6 turns)

SEASONING

½ teaspoon fleur de sel
freshly ground black pepper (6 turns)

1 Prepare a bouquet garni (page 34) with the bay leaf, parsley leaves, and thyme sprigs. Wrap them inside one green leaf from a leek and tie into a bundle with kitchen string. Put the pieces of meat in a Dutch oven and cover with the water. Bring to a boil, then reduce the heat and let it simmer. Skim all the foam off the surface.

2 Peel the carrots and onions. Stud the onions with the cloves, pushing them in near the root end. Peel, de-germ, and crush the garlic cloves. Add these vegetables to the pan with the salt, peppercorns, and bouquet garni. Skim off any foam and leave it to simmer, uncovered, for 3–4 hours, until the meat is tender.

3 Peel the turnips and trim and wash the leeks, then add them whole to the pan. Cook for at least 1 hour.

4 To make the herb cream, mix the fromage blanc with the chives and parsley. Season with the salt and pepper, then set aside in the refrigerator.

5 Cut the meat and serve with the vegetables. Sprinkle with the fleur de sel and pepper. Serve with the herb cream.

BLANQUETTE OF VEAL

Understand

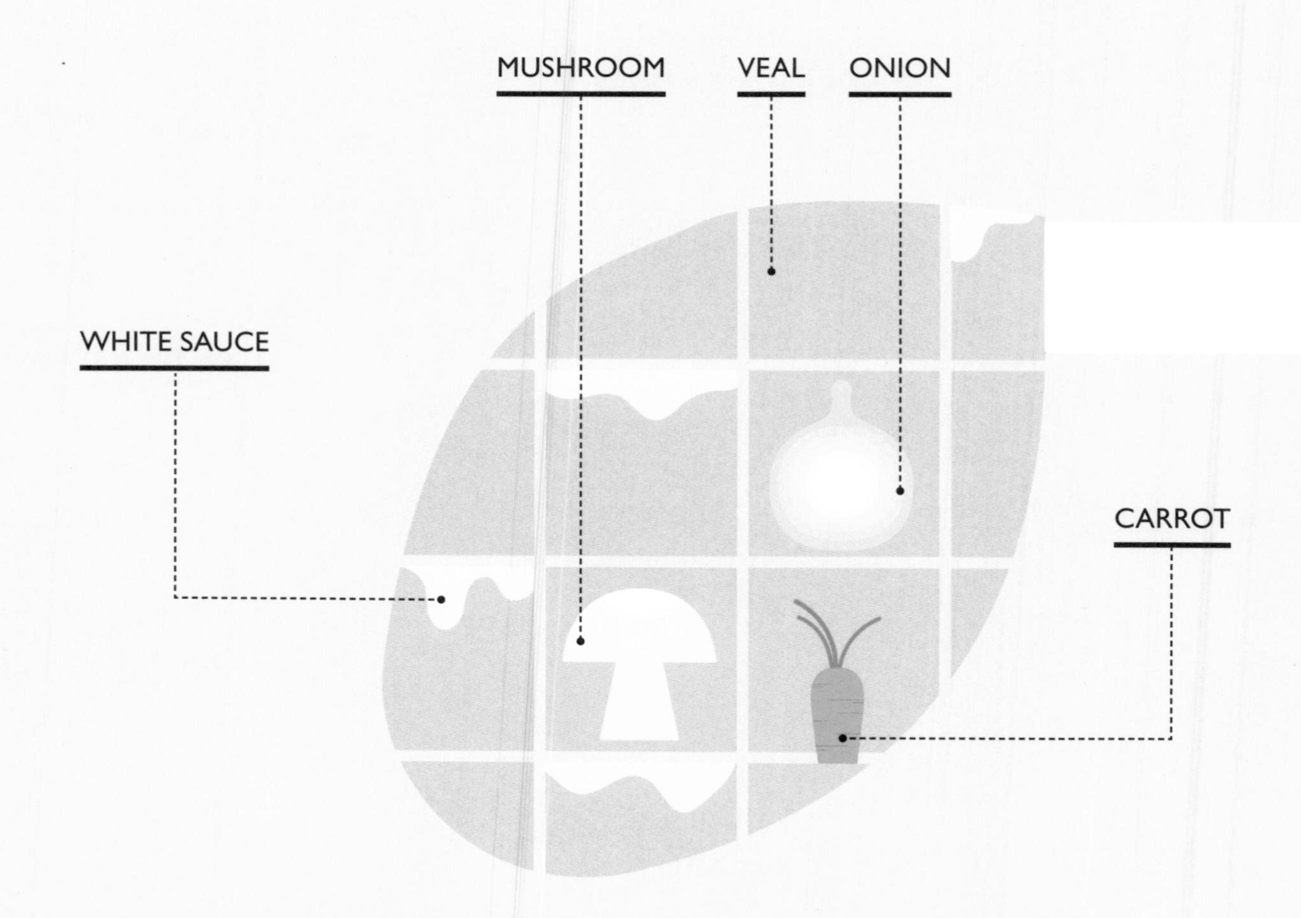

WHAT IS IT?
Veal stew: pieces of browned veal, poached in an aromatic stock, then served with a white sauce made with roux and the cooking broth, thickened with cream and egg yolk

TIME TO MAKE
Preparation: 45 minutes
Cooking: 1 hour 55 minutes

EQUIPMENT
Fine-mesh sieve
Whisk

VARIATION
Traditional recipe: meat blanched, then poached in cold water (no browning)

TRICKY ASPECTS
– Browning the meat
– Thickening the sauce

TECHNIQUES TO MASTER
Mincing (page 280)
Making a roux (page 18)
Scraping up stuck-on bits (page 283)
Skimming (page 283)
Cutting in scallops (page 280)
Transferring (page 282)
Straining through a sieve (page 281)
Cutting a parchment paper disk (page 285)

IT'S READY . . .
When the sauce is velvety.

STORAGE
2 days in the refrigerator.

HOW CAN THE CREAM BOIL WITHOUT THE EGG YOLKS COAGULATING?
When the yolk is mixed into the cream, it is diluted in the liquid. The proteins are more widely spaced, so the risk of coagulation is reduced. Adding the velouté sauce gradually heats the cream and egg yolk mixture gently and dilutes the preparation.

Learn

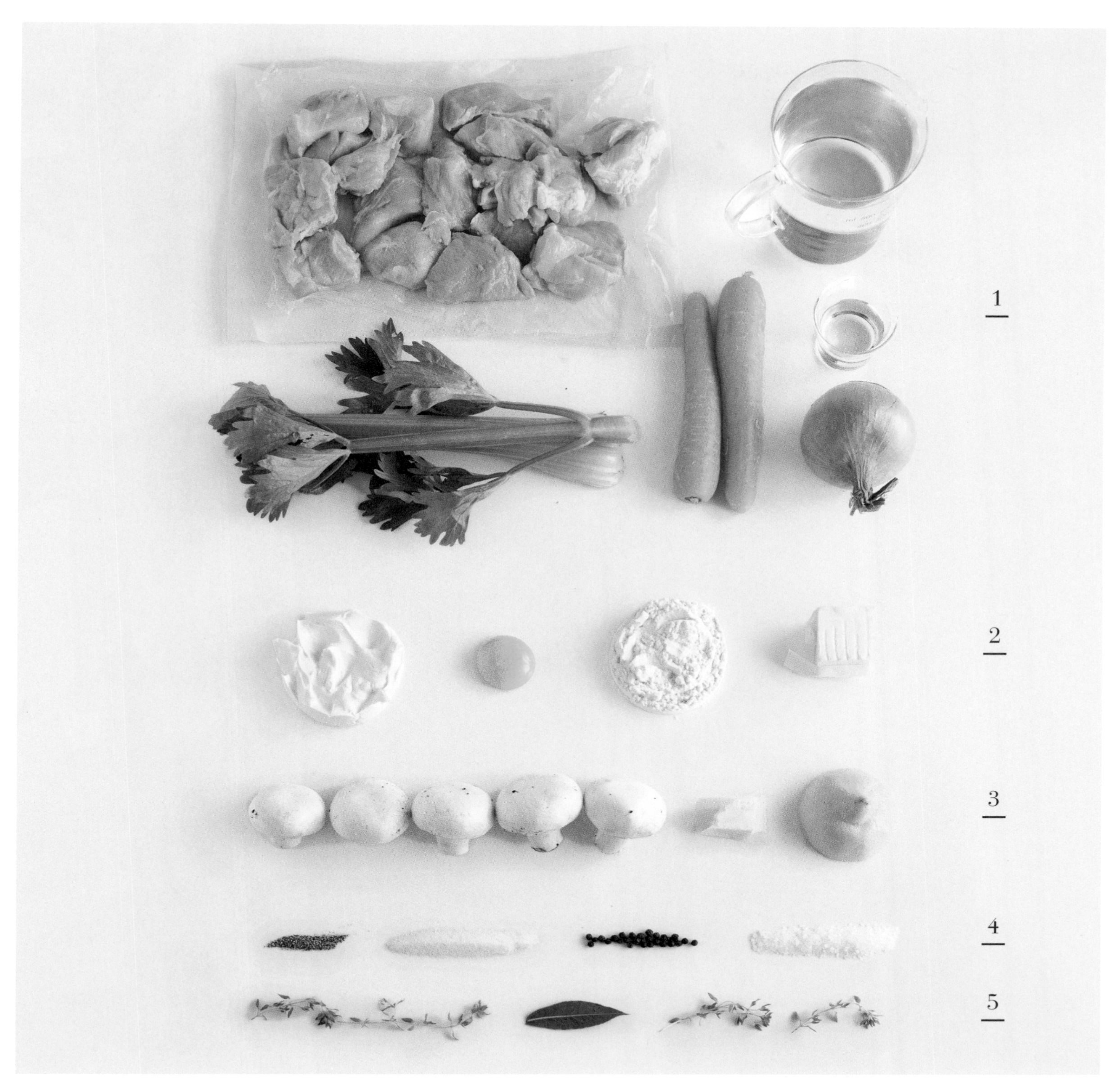

SERVES 4

1 VEAL

1 onion
2 carrots
1 celery stalk
1 lb 12 oz veal shoulder, cut into 2-inch chunks
2 tablespoons peanut oil
1¼ quarts (5 cups) water

2 THICKENING

3½ tablespoons butter
⅓ cup all-purpose flour
1 egg yolk
½ cup crème fraîche

3 MUSHROOMS

9 oz white mushrooms
1 tablespoon butter, diced
½ lemon

4 SEASONING

1 teaspoon fine salt
1 teaspoon coarse sea salt
½ teaspoon black peppercorns
freshly ground black pepper, to taste

5 AROMATICS

2 thyme sprigs
1 bay leaf

Making blanquette of veal

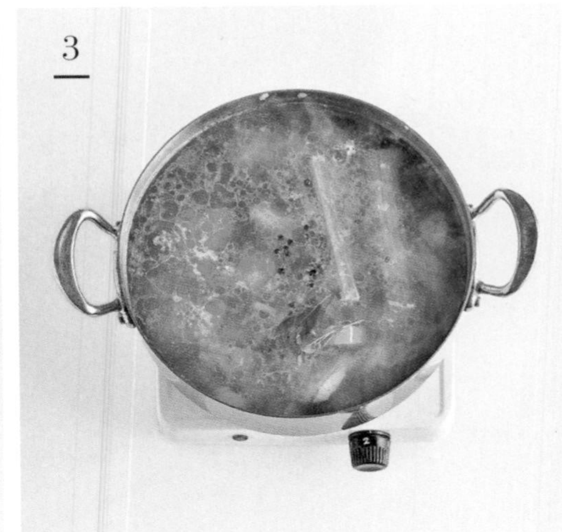

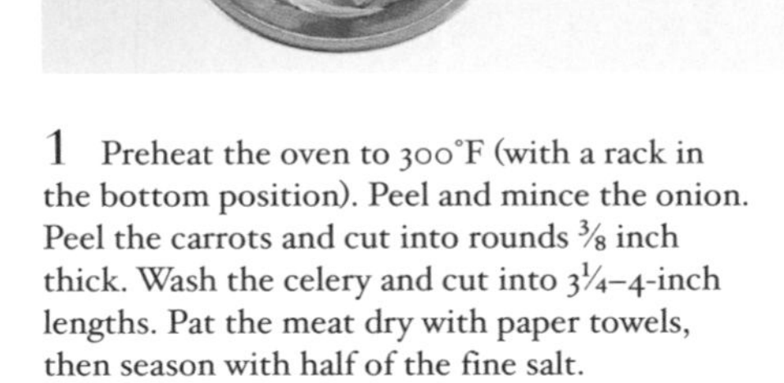

1 Preheat the oven to 300°F (with a rack in the bottom position). Peel and mince the onion. Peel the carrots and cut into rounds 3/8 inch thick. Wash the celery and cut into 3¼–4-inch lengths. Pat the meat dry with paper towels, then season with half of the fine salt.

2 Heat the oil in a Dutch oven over very high heat and brown the meat on all sides. With tongs, pull the meat out of the pan and set aside. Add the onion, carrots, and the remaining fine salt to the pan. Reduce the heat to medium and sweat the vegetables.

3 Return the meat to the pan, stir, then pour in the water. Increase the heat to very high and bring to a simmer, scraping the bottom to get up any stuck-on bits. Skim. Add the coarse sea salt, thyme, bay leaf, celery, and peppercorns. Cover and transfer to the oven for 1½ hours.

4 Cut the stems off the mushrooms, then peel the caps and cut them into two or four slices, depending on their size. Put the mushrooms in a sauté pan and cover with 1½ cups of the cooking liquid from the veal. Add the butter and 1 teaspoon of juice from the lemon half. Bring to a boil, then simmer for 10 minutes, covered with a disk of parchment paper cut to fit and vented (page 285). Drain the mushrooms, reserving the liquid.

5 With a skimmer or slotted spoon, lift the meat and vegetables out of the Dutch oven and set aside. Discard the celery, thyme, bay leaf, and peppercorns. Strain the cooking liquid through a sieve. Return the meat, vegetables, and mushrooms into the covered Dutch oven.

6 Make a roux with the butter and flour (page 18). Add the strained cooking liquid (about 2 cups), along with the reserved mushroom-cooking liquid. Bring to a boil while whisking. Let it thicken into a velouté sauce over low heat for 15 minutes.

7 Mix the egg yolk and crème fraîche in a small bowl, then add a little of the velouté sauce. Off the heat, gradually add this mixture to the hot velouté sauce. Return to the heat and bring to a boil, then let it boil for a few seconds while whisking. Check the thickness of the sauce and adjust the seasoning. Add a few drops of lemon juice, if desired.

8 Pour the sauce over the veal. Simmer for 5 minutes, then keep over very low heat until ready to serve.

ROLLED LAMB
WITH SPICES

Understand

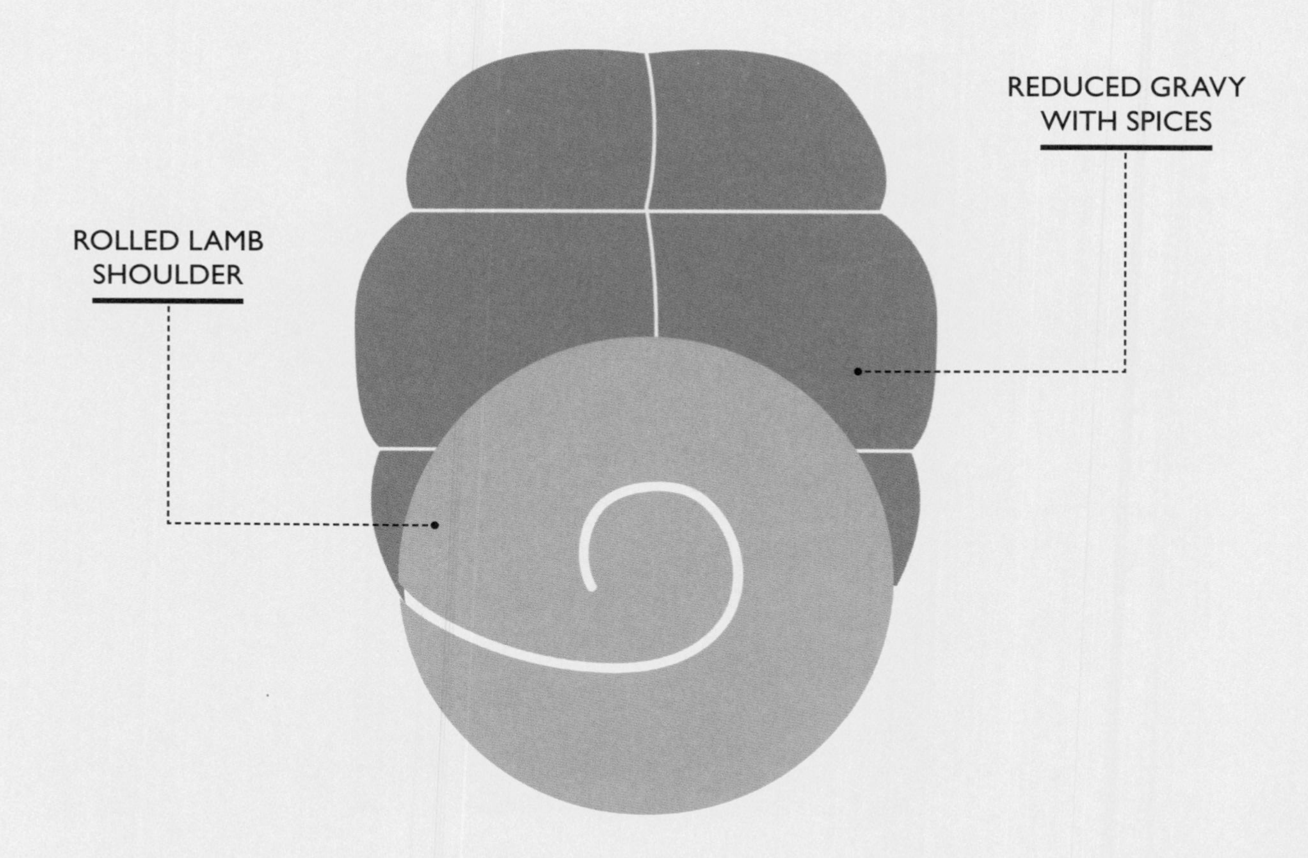

WHAT IS IT?
Lamb shoulder rolled with spices, cooked in gentle heat, and basted regularly with the cooking liquid until almost completely reduced

TIME TO MAKE
Preparation: 25 minutes
Cooking: 2 hours 35 minutes

EQUIPMENT
Kitchen string

VARIATION
Seven-hour leg of lamb: longer cooking time (7 hours), more gentle heat (250°F), and covered

TRICKY ASPECT
Not burning the bits stuck to the bottom

TECHNIQUES TO MASTER
Tying a roast (page 278)
Mincing (page 280)
Sweating (page 282)

IT'S READY . . .
When the meat has a nice shiny crust and the sauce is well concentrated.

ACCOMPANIMENT
Couscous (page 236)

WHY COOK UNCOVERED?
To obtain a shiny sauce at the end of cooking.

SERVES 4

1 LAMB

one 1 lb 12 oz–2 lb 3 oz boned lamb shoulder (3½ lb before boning)

2 MARINADE

½ teaspoon ras el hanout
½ teaspoon fine salt
¼ cup olive oil

3 TO COOK

⅓ cup raisins
1-inch piece fresh ginger
1 onion
1 garlic clove
1 tablespoon olive oil
4 teaspoons honey
2 pinches of ground saffron
1¼ cups white poultry stock (page 10)

4 TO FINISH

⅓ cup blanched almonds
freshly ground black pepper (6 turns)

Making rolled lamb with spices

1 Roll the meat tightly and secure with kitchen string. Set in a baking dish to catch the marinade. Sprinkle with the ras el hanout and the salt, then coat with the ¼ cup olive oil. Preheat the oven to 300°F. Soak the raisins in warm water.

2 Peel and grate the ginger. Peel and mince the onion. Peel, de-germ, and crush the garlic. Drain the raisins.

3 Heat the 1 tablespoon of olive oil in a Dutch oven over high heat. Reserving the marinade, add the lamb shoulder and brown on all sides. Remove from the pan.

4 Reduce the heat to medium and add the onion to the pan. Sweat the onion for a few seconds. Stir in the ginger, reserved marinade, and the honey.

5 Return the meat to the Dutch oven, then add the saffron, garlic, and raisins. Pour in half the poultry stock. Transfer to the oven and cook, uncovered, for 2–2½ hours, basting the meat occasionally with the cooking liquid. The juices should reduce and become shiny by the end of cooking; add the remaining stock if they evaporate too quickly.

6 Toast the almonds in a dry skillet over medium heat and roughly chop.

7 Remove the string from the lamb. Sprinkle with the almonds, season with the pepper, and coat the lamb in the reduced juices.

NAVARIN OF LAMB

Understand

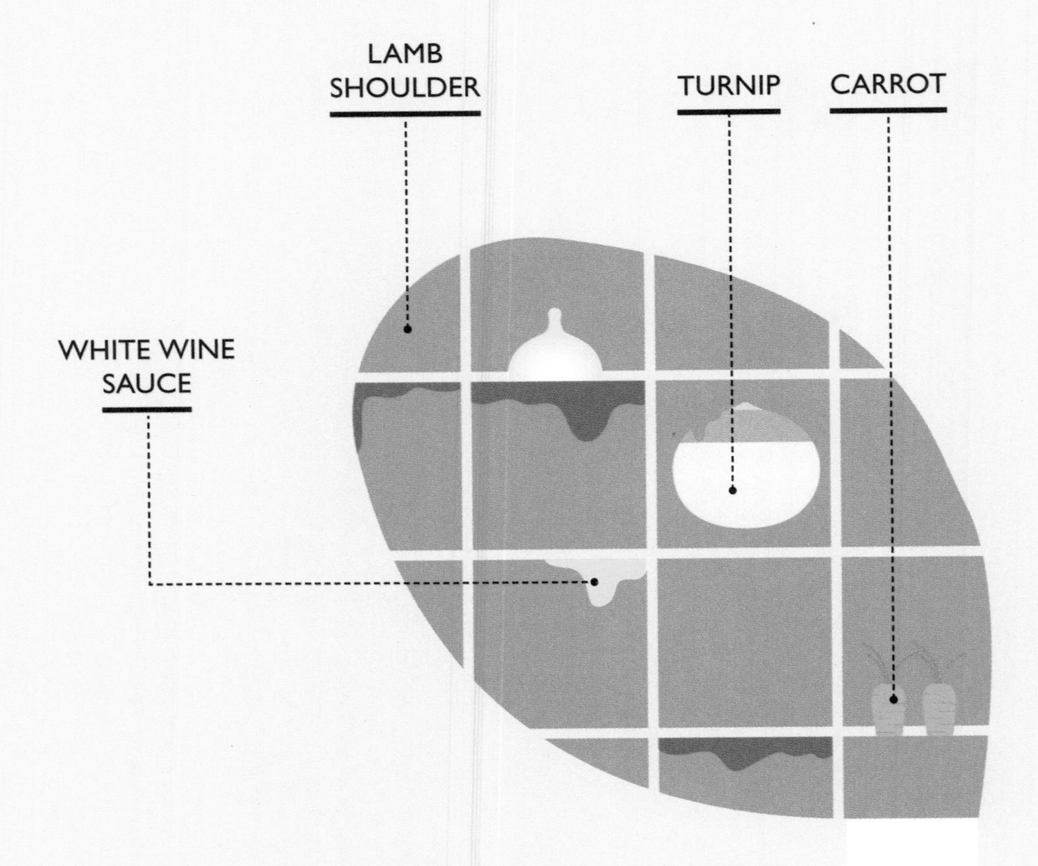

WHAT IS IT?

Brown lamb stew: a piece of lamb shoulder browned, cooked slowly in a white wine sauce, and served with spring vegetables

TIME TO MAKE

Preparation: 25 minutes
Cooking: 1 hour 30 minutes
to 1 hour 45 minutes

VARIATION

The original recipe is served with turnips (hence the name navarin, from *navet*: "turnip"). Adding spring vegetables like carrots and peas makes it *navarin printanier* (spring stew).

TRICKY ASPECT

The sauce: it must be thick without adding flour or reduction

TECHNIQUES TO MASTER

Mincing (page 280)
Scraping up stuck-on bits (page 283)
Transferring (page 282)
Browning (page 282)

TIP

If the vegetables are prepared in advance, keep them in the refrigerator under damp paper towels to prevent them from drying out.

IT'S READY . . .

When the meat is tender, the vegetables soft, and the sauce thick and smooth.

STORAGE

3 days in the refrigerator. Reheat, covered, over low heat with a little added water.

WHY REDUCE THE WINE?

To concentrate the sugars it contains, which makes it seems less acidic (in fact, its acidity is unchanged, but is camouflaged by the sugar).

Learn

SERVES 4

1 LAMB

1 garlic clove
1 onion
1 boned lamb shoulder (about 2 lb 14 oz), cut into 15 pieces
¼ cup olive oil
1 tablespoon tomato paste
⅓ cup dry white wine
1 cup water

2 VEGETABLES

5 or 6 thin carrots with trimmed tops
5 round turnips with trimmed tops
10½ oz firm-fleshed potatoes, such as Yukon Gold

3 AROMATICS

1 bay leaf
1 thyme sprig

4 SEASONING

1½ teaspoons fine salt
freshly ground black pepper (6 turns)

Making navarin of lamb

1 Preheat the oven to 300°F (with a rack in the bottom position). Peel the garlic, cut in half, and remove the germ. Peel and mince the onion. Pat the meat dry with paper towels, then season with ½ teaspoon of the salt.

2 Heat the oil in a Dutch oven over very high heat and brown the pieces of lamb. With tongs, transfer the meat to a plate and set aside.

3 Reduce the heat to medium and add the onion, garlic, and another ½ teaspoon salt, then sweat, stirring frequently. Add the tomato paste and stir for 1–2 minutes.

4 Return the lamb to the pan and stir. Pour in the wine and let it reduce while scraping up any stuck-on bits from the bottom of the dish: you should have 2–3 tablespoons of liquid. Pour in the water, add the bay leaf and thyme, then bring to a boil. Cover and transfer to the oven for 1 hour.

5 Peel and wash the carrots, turnips, and potatoes. Cut the carrots on an angle into 1¼-inch lengths. Cut the turnips in half or quarters depending on their size. Cut the potatoes into 1¼-inch pieces. Season with the remaining ½ teaspoon salt.

6 Remove the garlic, bay leaf, and thyme from the Dutch oven, then stir in the vegetables. Return to the oven for another 30–45 minutes, until the vegetables are tender. Add the pepper and more salt if necessary.

LACQUERED DUCKLING

Understand

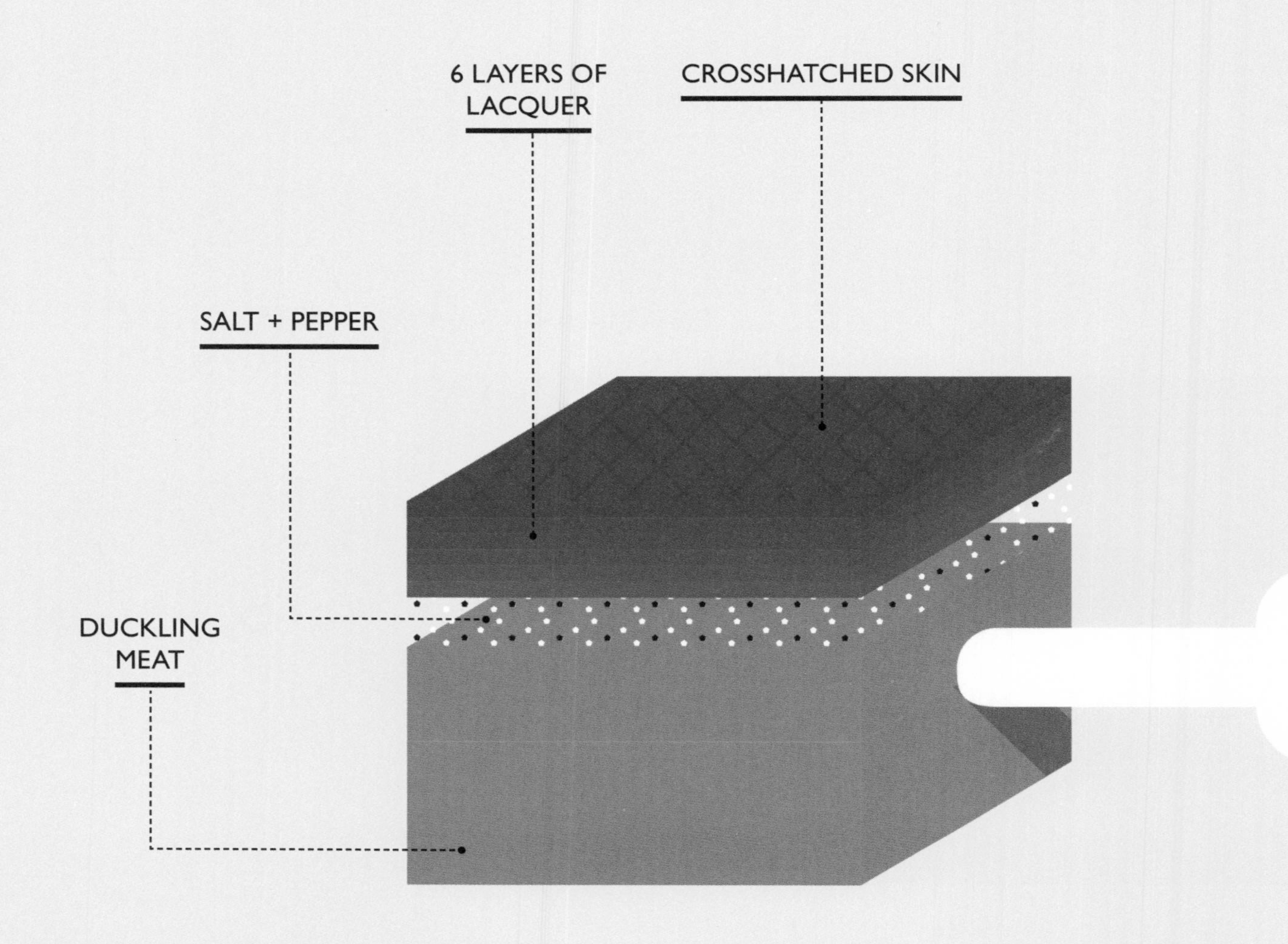

WHAT IS IT?
Roast duckling that is glazed (lacquered) with sugar + vinegar syrup during cooking

TIME TO MAKE
Preparation: 35 minutes
Cooking: 1 hour 10 minutes

EQUIPMENT
Pastry brush
Baking dish or roasting pan

VARIATION
Lacquered duck (adapted to serve 8)

TRICKY ASPECT
Preparing the lacquer

TECHNIQUE TO MASTER
Scraping up stuck-on bits (page 283)

TIPS
- Use the natural pattern of the skin to help you crosshatch it evenly.
- The roasting pan shouldn't be too large or the bird might burn.

IT'S READY . . .
When the skin is dark and shiny, but not burnt.

WHAT MAKES THE LACQUER SHINE?
At high temperatures, the sugar caramelizes, which adds a sheen.

WHY IS IT NECESSARY TO CROSSHATCH THE SKIN?
To create small spaces that trap the lacquer before it caramelizes in the oven.

Learn

SERVES 4

1 DUCK

one 3 lb 5 oz–4 lb duckling

2 LACQUER

⅔ cup muscovado sugar
⅔ cup sherry vinegar
1 teaspoon fine salt

3 SEASONING

½ teaspoon fine salt
1 tablespoon coarse sea salt
½ teaspoon freshly ground black pepper

Making lacquered duckling

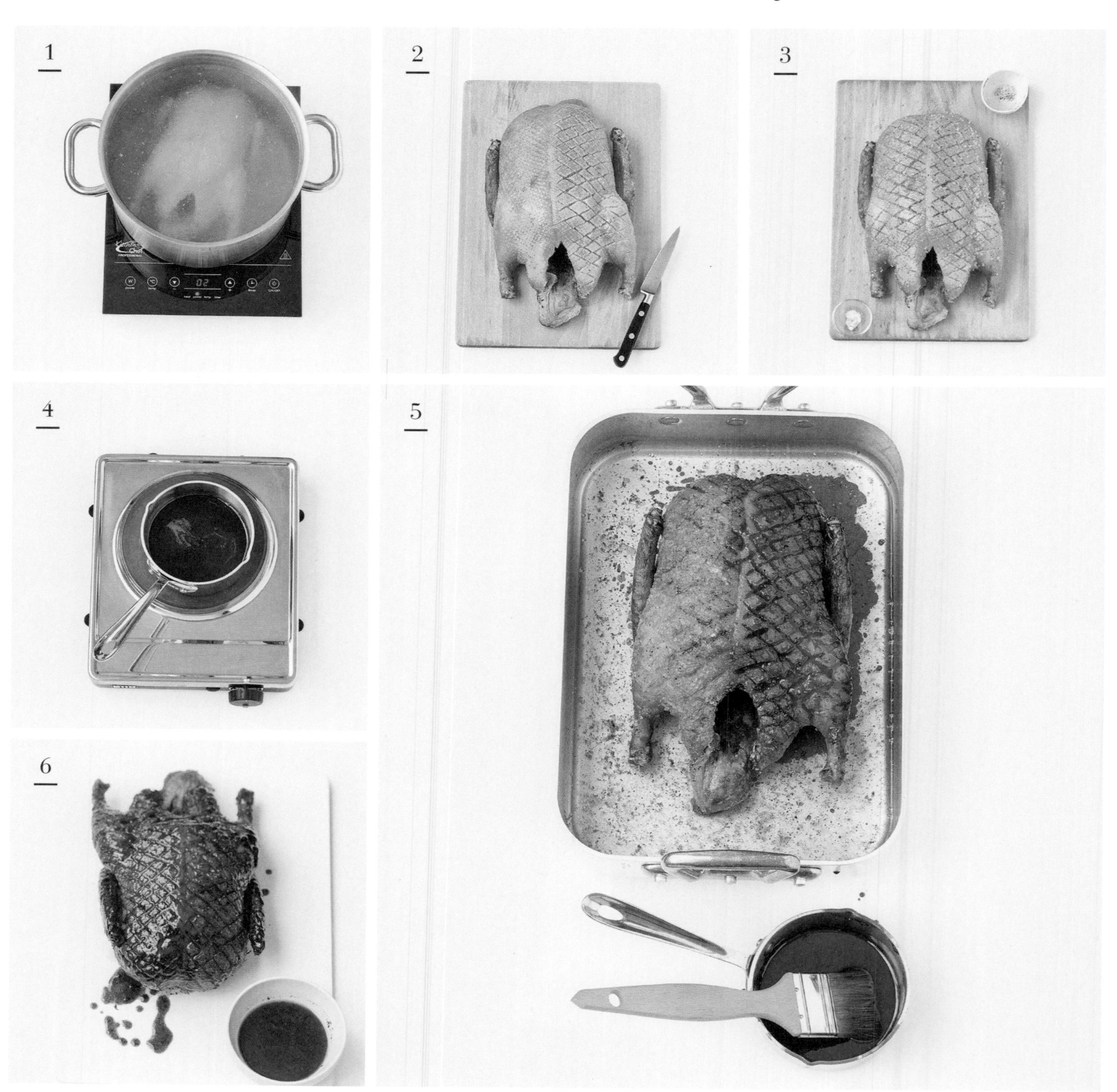

1 Preheat the oven to 360°F. Prepare a stockpot of simmering water, then turn off the heat and plunge the duckling into the water for 5 minutes.

2 Remove the duckling from the water by inserting a spatula into the rear end. Drain, shaking it a little. Crosshatch the skin with a thin-bladed knife.

3 Place the bird in a roasting pan and season the cavity with the ½ teaspoon of fine salt. Mix the coarse sea salt with the pepper. Rub the skin with this mixture. Roast for 30 minutes.

4 Prepare the lacquer. Mix the sugar, vinegar, and salt in a small saucepan and bring to a boil, then simmer for about 15 minutes, until the mixture becomes syrupy. You should have about ⅔ cup.

5 Increase the oven temperature to 430°F. Using a pastry brush, give the duckling two coats of the lacquer then roast for 5 minutes. Repeat this procedure four times. Increase the oven temperature to 520°F (or the oven's highest setting) and lacquer one last time with two coats. Roast for just 5 minutes, watching carefully as it colors.

6 Remove the duckling from the pan. Discard the grease and any burnt residue. Pour in about 1¼ cups of hot water and scrape up the stuck-on bits from the bottom with a spatula. Transfer this liquid to a small saucepan and reduce until the sauce has the desired concentration.

DUCK BREAST
WITH ORANGE SAUCE

Understand

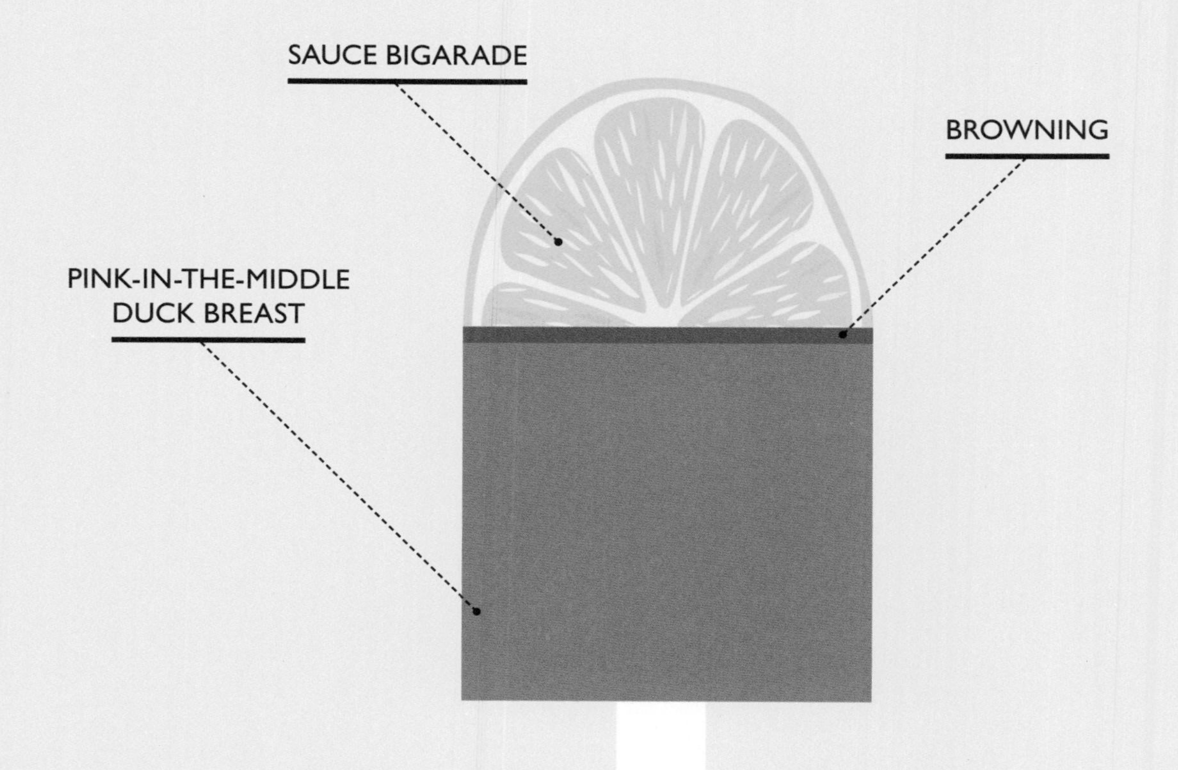

WHAT IS IT?
Duck breast fillets pan-fried, then roasted in the oven, served with a sweet citrus sauce

TIME TO MAKE
Preparation: 20 minutes
Cooking: 20 minutes

EQUIPMENT
Ovenproof skillet
French-style zester
Small fine-mesh sieve

TRICKY ASPECT
Cooking the caramel: if it is too dark it will be bitter

TECHNIQUES TO MASTER
Zesting citrus (page 280)
Crushing spices (page 280)
Reducing a sauce (page 283)
Deglazing (page 283)
Degreasing a skillet (page 283)
Making a gastrique (page 55)

TIP
Use a skillet with a pale interior (stainless steel) for the caramel, to make it easier to judge the change in color.

WHY COOK THE SKIN OF THE DUCK FIRST?
To partially melt the fat, so it can be used to cook the breast later on.

WHY TWO COOKING PHASES (SKILLET, THEN OVEN)?
Cooking in the skillet allows browning (and the development of aromatic notes); roasting in the oven allows cooking to the center.

SERVES 4

DUCK

two 14 oz duck breast fillets with skin on

ORANGE SAUCE

1 orange
1 lemon
3 tablespoons sugar
2 tablespoons sherry vinegar

SEASONING

10 black peppercorns
¾ teaspoon fine salt
freshly ground black pepper (4 turns)
½ teaspoon fleur de sel

1 Wash, dry, and zest the orange and lemon. Squeeze them separately. Strain the juice and reserve ⅓ cup of orange juice and 2½ tablespoons of lemon juice.

2 Make a gastrique (page 55) with the sugar and vinegar in a small skillet. Finish the orange sauce by adding the orange and lemon juices. Let it reduce by half over medium heat for 8–10 minutes. Add the zests. Remove from the heat. Preheat the oven to 460°F. Crush the peppercorns.

3 Remove the membrane, the fatty parts on the flesh side, and any superfluous fat on the duck. Crosshatch the skin on the diagonal. Season with ½ teaspoon of the fine salt and half the ground pepper.

4 Heat an ovenproof skillet over medium heat then cook the breasts, skin side down, for 2 minutes. Season the flesh side with the remaining salt and ground pepper. Turn the breasts and transfer the pan to the oven for 6–8 minutes: they should be pink in the middle. Set them on a paper towel.

5 Degrease the pan and deglaze with 3 tablespoons water. Let it reduce until almost dry. Strain through a fine-mesh sieve and return to the pan. Stir in the orange sauce, then remove from the heat.

6 Cut the breasts into ¼-inch slices. Arrange them on a plate, flesh side down. Remove the zests from the orange sauce and spread them over the meat. Coat with the sauce. Sprinkle with the fleur de sel and the crushed peppercorns.

PULLED PORK

Understand

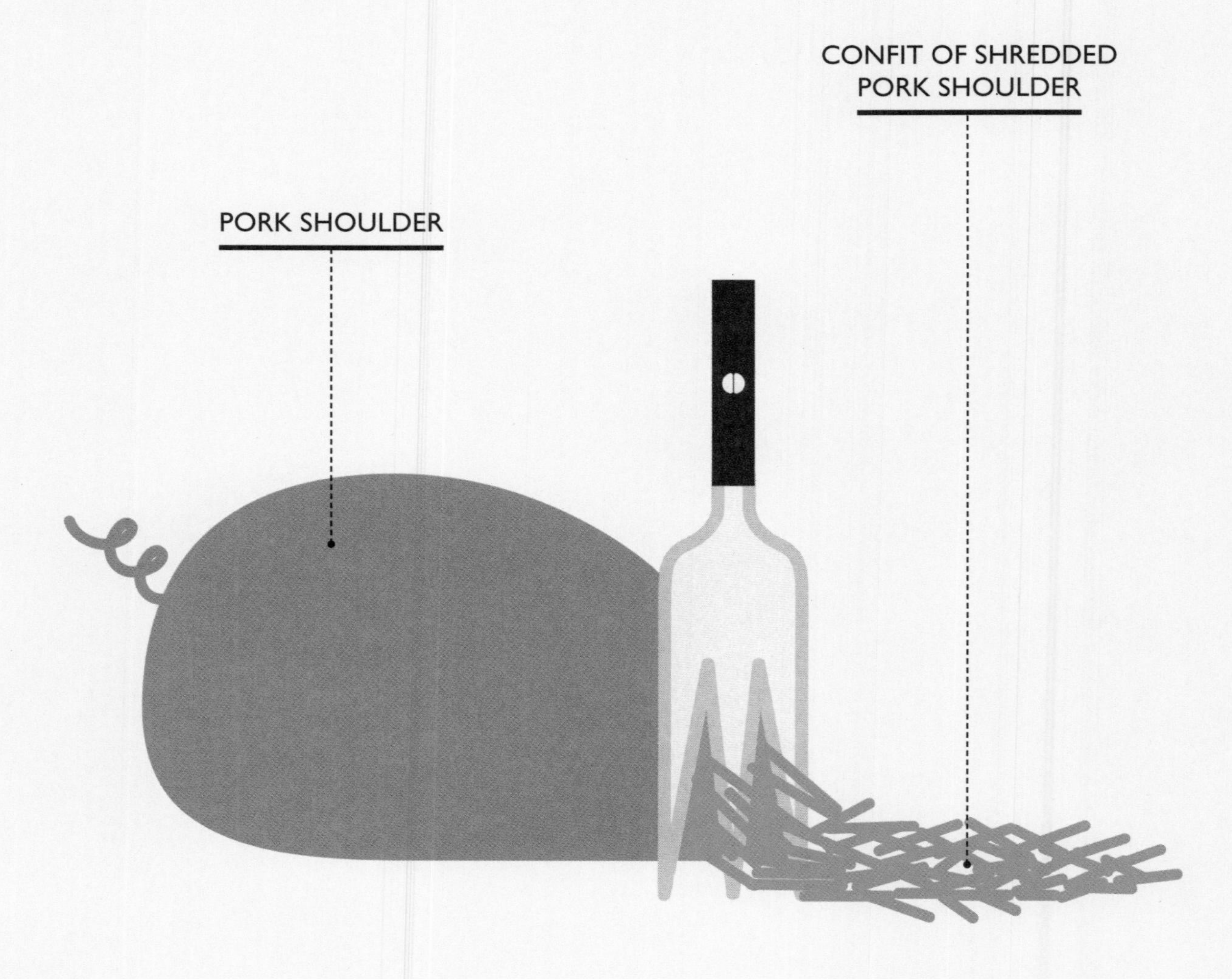

WHAT IS IT?
Piece of pork shoulder slow-roasted at low heat, then broiled, shredded, and served with barbecue sauce

TIME TO MAKE
Preparation: 30 minutes
Cooking: 2 hours 10 minutes

EQUIPMENT
Ovenproof saucepan

TECHNIQUES TO MASTER
Transferring (page 282)
Reducing a sauce (page 283)
Straining through a sieve (page 281)

VARIATION
Whole shoulder: rub it with mustard, sprinkle with paprika, salt, black pepper, sugar, and cayenne. Cook for 3 hours in the saucepan, then 1½ hours in the oven on a wire rack over a roasting pan.

IT'S READY . . .
When the top of the meat is well browned (but not burnt) and the corners crisp

STORAGE
In the refrigerator, tightly covered, for 3–4 days. Reheat for 10 minutes at 300°F.

ACCOMPANIMENT
Roasted squash (page 254)

WHY START COOKING IN COLD WATER?
Starting from cold means the cooking time is longer, which allows for the extraction of the aromatic components of the meat into the cooking liquid, without overcooking the meat. When this liquid is then reduced to be mixed with the meat and to make the sauce, it adds extra depth of flavor.

Learn

SERVES 4

1 PORK

1 small yellow onion
1 orange
2 lb 3 oz boneless pork shoulder (with a ¼-inch layer of fat), cut into 2-inch pieces
1 teaspoon fine salt
½ teaspoon freshly ground balck pepper
1 bay leaf
2 tablespoons lime juice
1¾ cups water

2 BARBECUE SAUCE

½ cup ketchup
2 tablespoons molasses
1½ teaspoons Worcestershire sauce
½–1 teaspoon hot sauce (sriracha or Tabasco)
pinch of smoked paprika
large pinch of fine salt
freshly ground black pepper (10 turns)

Making pulled pork

1 Preheat the oven to 300°F. Peel the onion and cut it in half. Wash and squeeze the orange. In a large ovenproof saucepan, combine the meat, salt, pepper, bay leaf, onion, lime juice, juice and whole rind of the orange (seeds removed), and enough of the water to just cover the meat. Place over high heat and stir from time to time until it simmers.

2 Cover and transfer to the oven for 2 hours, until the meat is tender. Turn the pieces over halfway through the cooking time.

3 With a skimmer or slotted spoon, lift the meat out of the cooking liquid and set aside. Discard the orange rind, onion, and bay leaf. Reduce the liquid over high heat until it is syrupy. Strain 2½ tablespoons of this syrup through a fine-mesh sieve and set aside. Reserve the remainder of the syrup. Preheat the broiler with a rack in the lowest position in the oven.

4 Break each piece of meat in half using two forks. Mix the syrup from the saucepan with the meat. Adjust the seasoning.

5 Spread the pieces of meat on a wire rack set in a rimmed baking sheet. Brown under the broiler for 8–10 minutes. Turn the meat over after 4 minutes.

6 Whisk the reserved 2 ½ tablespoons syrup with all the barbecue sauce ingredients until very smooth. Serve the meat in pieces or completely shredded with the sauce on the side.

RABBIT
WITH MUSTARD

Understand

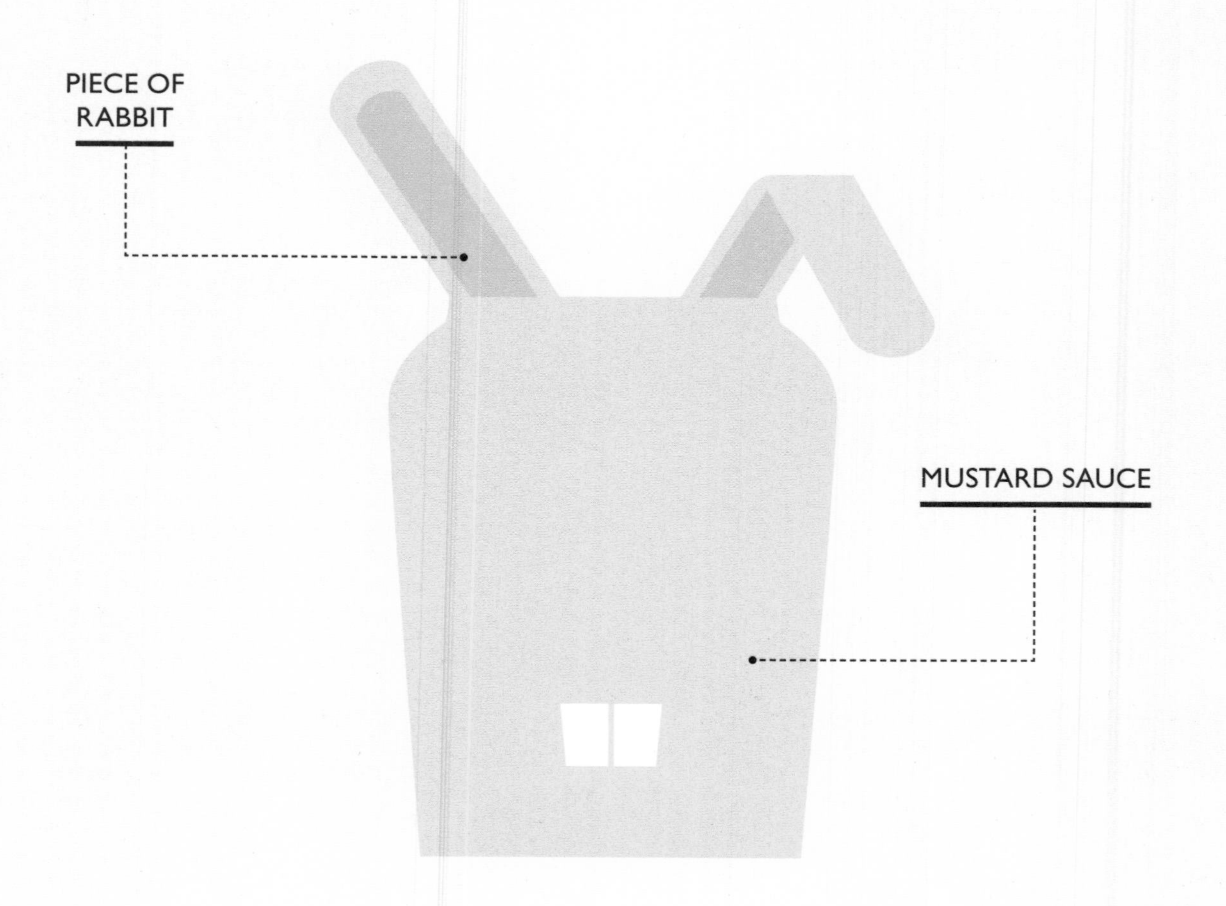

WHAT IS IT?
Brown rabbit stew: browned pieces of rabbit, covered and cooked in a mustard sauce, then coated in the reduced cooking liquid mixed with cream

TIME TO MAKE
Preparation: 25 minutes
Cooking: 30 minutes

EQUIPMENT
Sieve
Large, deep, straight-sided skillet

TRICKY ASPECT
Browning the rabbit meat without burning it

TECHNIQUES TO MASTER
Mincing (page 280)
Thinly slicing (page 280)
Crushing garlic (page 280)
Transferring (page 282)
Deglazing (page 283)
Reducing a sauce (page 283)
Straining through a sieve (page 281)
Pushing through a sieve (page 281)
Browning (page 282)

ACCOMPANIMENT
Mashed potatoes (page 60)

SERVES 4

RABBIT
1 rabbit, cut into 6 pieces (ribcage removed) and the saddle cut in half and tied together with kitchen string
2 tablespoons olive oil
3 tablespoons Dijon mustard
3 tablespoons grainy mustard
⅔ cup dry white wine
1 ¼ cups water
1 cup crème fraîche

Learn

AROMATICS

2 garlic cloves
2 shallots
1 thyme sprig
1 bay leaf

SEASONING

1½ teaspoons fine salt
freshly ground black pepper (6 turns)

TO FINISH

3 Italian parsley sprigs

1 Preheat the oven to 360°F. Peel, de-germ, and crush the garlic. Peel and thinly slice the shallots. Wash, dry, pick, and mince the parsley leaves. Remove any fatty bits or blood from the rabbit pieces, then season with 1 teaspoon of the salt.

2 Heat 1 tablespoon of the olive oil in a deep skillet over medium heat. Brown the rabbit pieces without burning them. Work in several batches to avoid overcrowding the pan.

3 With tongs, pull the rabbit pieces out of the pan and set aside. Add the remaining olive oil and sweat the shallots with ¼ teaspoon of the salt. Stir, then cook until tender. Add the garlic and cook until fragrant, about 30 seconds. Stir in the two mustards.

4 When the mustard starts to stick a little, deglaze the pan with the wine and let it reduce to almost dry, still over medium heat.

5 Return the rabbit to the pan, stir, then add enough of the water to come two-thirds of the way up. Add the thyme and bay leaf, bring to a boil, then cover and simmer for 30 minutes. Transfer all pieces but the thighs to a hot platter, and continue simmering the thighs for another 10 minutes.

6 Transfer the thighs to the platter. Strain the cooking liquid through a sieve without pushing on the solids, then pour into a saucepan and reduce by half. Whisk in the crème fraîche and bring to a simmer. Reduce until it coats the back of a spoon. Adjust the seasoning and add a little extra grainy mustard if desired.

7 Return the rabbit pieces to the pan, coat them in the sauce, then sprinkle with the parsley.

ROAST CHICKEN
WITH HERB BUTTER

Understand

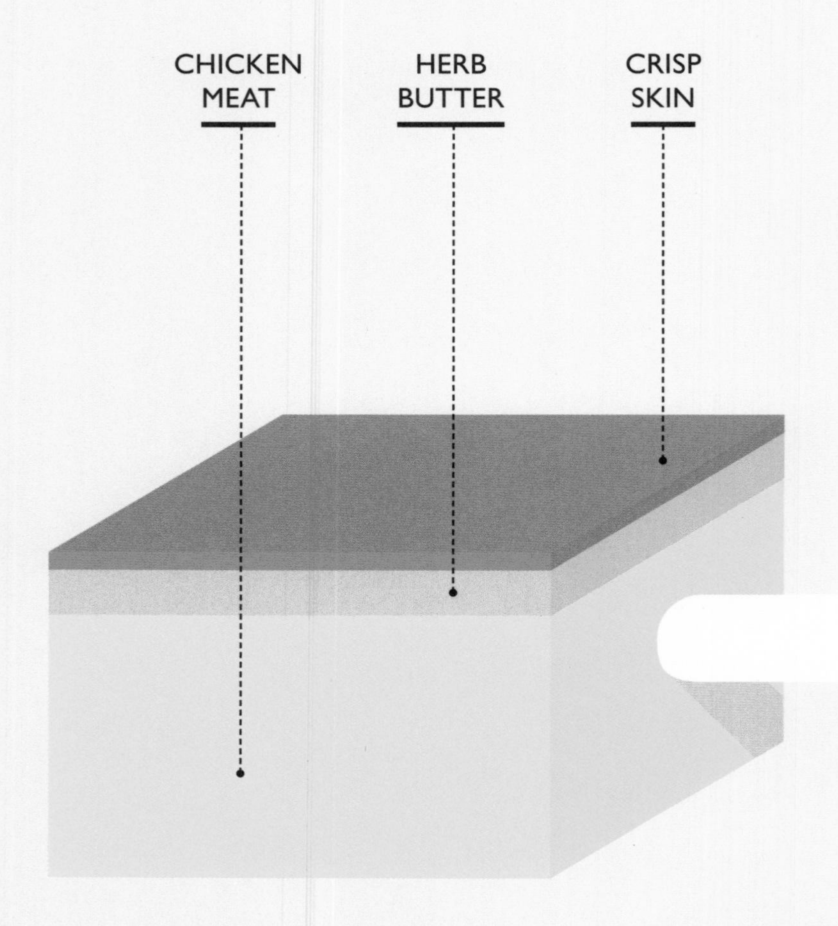

WHAT IS IT?
Chicken stuffed under the skin with an herb butter, roasted with potatoes and served with chicken jus

TIME TO MAKE
Preparation: 45 minutes
Cooking: 40 minutes
Resting: 10 minutes

EQUIPMENT
Dutch oven
Fine-mesh sieve
Pastry bag + plain ⅜-inch decorating tip
Wire rack

TRICKY ASPECT
Stuffing under the skin

TECHNIQUES TO MASTER
Mincing (page 280)
Finely chopping (page 280)
Degreasing a skillet (page 283)
Deglazing (page 283)
Scraping up stuck-on bits (page 283)
Reducing a sauce (page 283)
Straining through a sieve (page 281)

IT'S READY . . .
When the skin is well browned and the juices run clear.

TIPS
- To stuff without a pastry bag: work quickly with your fingers to avoid melting the butter.
- Use a turkey baster to baste the chicken.

WHY START COOKING THE CHICKEN ON ITS SIDE?
To protect the breast, which cooks at a lower temperature than the thighs.

Learn

SERVES 4

1 CHICKEN

3 lb 5 oz whole chicken
2 teaspoons fine salt
freshly ground black pepper (8 turns)
6 tablespoons butter

2 POTATOES

1 lb 2 oz firm-fleshed potatoes
(such as fingerlings)
1 garlic bulb
⅔ cup white poultry stock (page 10)

3 HERB BUTTER

1 shallot
1 small bunch Italian parsley
1 small bunch chervil
1 tarragon sprig
1 small bunch chives
14 tablespoons butter, softened
1 teaspoon fine salt
freshly ground black pepper (3 turns)

Making roast chicken with herb butter

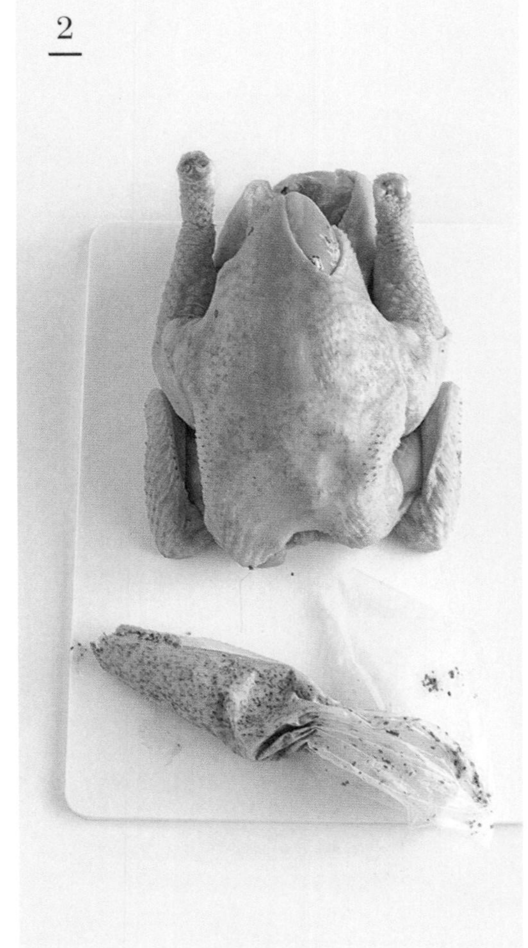

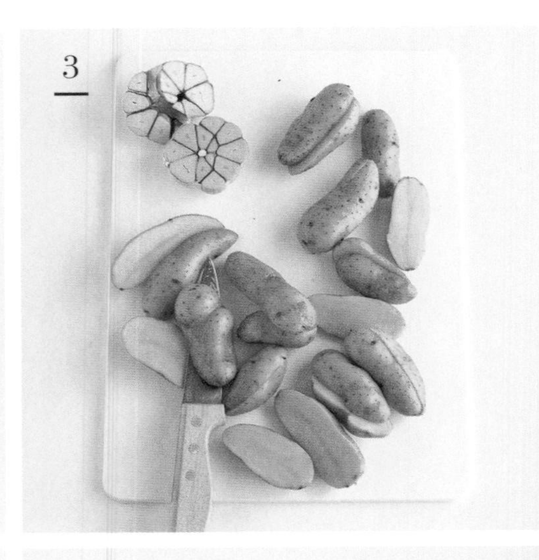

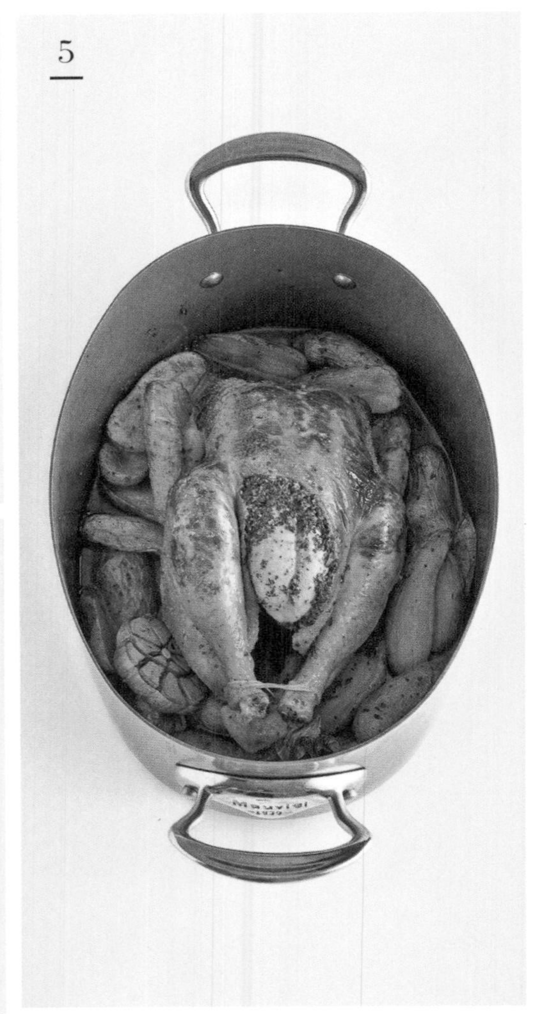

1 Preheat the oven to 430°F. To make the herb butter, peel and mince the shallot. Wash, dry, pick, and finely chop the parsley, chervil, and tarragon. Wash, dry, and mince the chives. Incorporate the herbs into the butter, then add the shallot. Season with the salt and pepper.

3 Wash the potatoes and cut in half lengthwise. Cut the garlic bulb in half horizontally.

4 Grease a Dutch oven with 1 tablespoon of the butter, put the chicken in, resting on one thigh, then arrange the potatoes and the halved garlic bulb around it. Dot the potatoes with the remaining butter cut into pieces. Roast for 15 minutes.

5 Baste the chicken with the cooking butter and turn it onto its other thigh. Roast for another 15 minutes. Baste again. When the potatoes start to turn golden, season them with salt and turn them over. Turn the chicken onto its back and roast for another 10 minutes. Check if it is cooked by lifting and letting the juices in the cavity run out: they should be clear. Rest the chicken on a wire rack for 10 minutes.

6 Remove the potatoes and garlic using a slotted spoon. Degrease the pan. Deglaze with the poultry stock. Bring to a boil, scraping up any stuck-on bits from the bottom. Reduce to the desired consistency. Strain through a fine-mesh sieve and check the seasoning.

7 Carve the chicken into pieces and serve with the potatoes, roasted garlic, and the sauce.

CHICKEN IN A POT

Understand

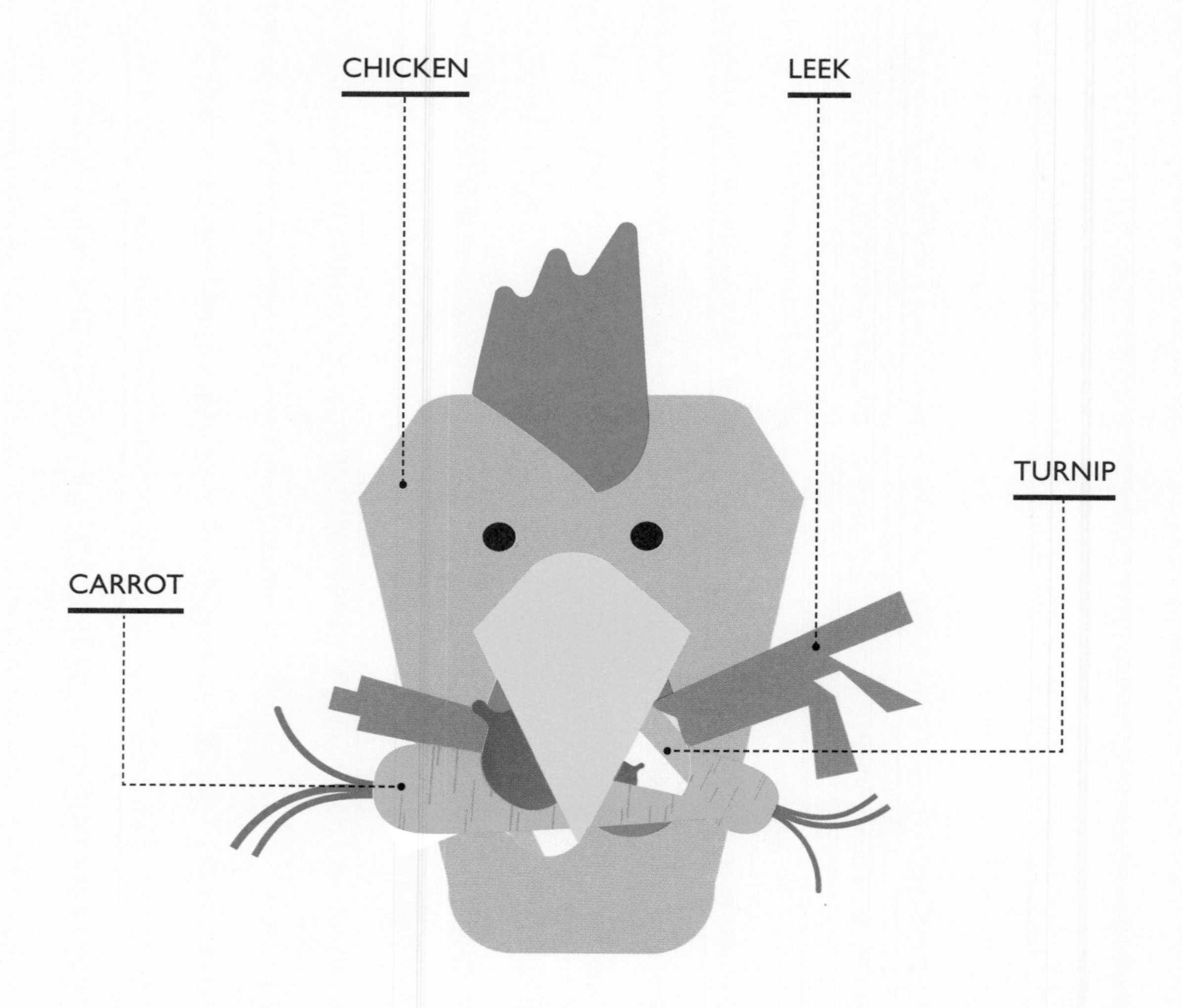

WHAT IS IT?

Chicken poached over very low heat in an aromatic cooking liquid, served with the vegetables with which it is cooked

TIME TO MAKE

Preparation: 20 minutes
Cooking: 3 hours

EQUIPMENT

Dutch oven

VARIATION

Pot-au-feu (page 186)

TECHNIQUES TO MASTER

Making a bouquet garni (page 34)
Turning vegetables (page 38)
Skimming (page 283)

DEGREASING THE BROTH

Let it rest for 5 minutes, then remove the grease that has risen to the surface. Refrigerate overnight, then remove the fat that has congealed on the surface.

STORAGE

48 hours in the refrigerator (meat and vegetables submerged in the broth). Reheat by bringing to a boil, then simmering for at least 15 minutes.

SERVES 4

CHICKEN

4 lb 7 oz chicken

VEGETABLES

2 yellow onions
6 leeks
8 carrots
6 large turnips
7 spring onions

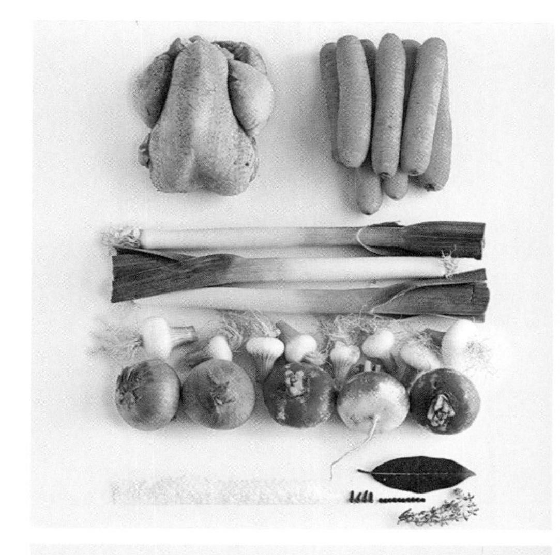

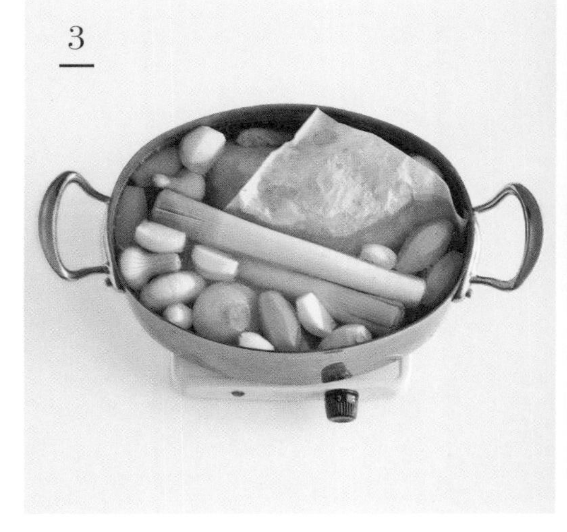

AROMATICS

4 whole cloves
1 bay leaf
1 thyme sprig

SEASONING

10 black peppercorns
4½ teaspoons coarse sea salt

1 Peel the yellow onions and stud them with the cloves. Discard the outer leaf from each leek. Separate the white and green parts of the leeks. Retain the white parts and one green leaf. Make a bouquet garni (page 34) by wrapping the green leek leaf around the bay leaf, thyme, and peppercorns and tying it into a bundle with kitchen string. Insert the bouquet garni into the cavity of the chicken.

2 Peel and wash the carrots and turnips. Cut the turnips into quarters and the carrots into 2½-inch lengths, then turn the carrot and the turnip pieces (page 38). Discard the outer leaf from the spring onions, cut off the roots, and wash.

3 Place the chicken and clove-studded onions in a large Dutch oven. Pour in about 4 quarts of water, to mostly cover the chicken. Bring to a boil on the stovetop, then add the sea salt, reduce the heat, and simmer for 3 hours, skimming regularly. Cover the part of the chicken sticking out of the water with a piece of parchment paper.

4 After 2 hours of cooking, add all the vegetables. Simmer until the vegetables are tender. Drain the chicken and carve it into pieces. Transfer the vegetables to a serving dish with the cooking liquid.

5 Serve in bowls with a piece of chicken and the vegetables from the pot: turnips, carrots, leeks, and spring onions.

STUFFED
ROASTER CHICKEN

Understand

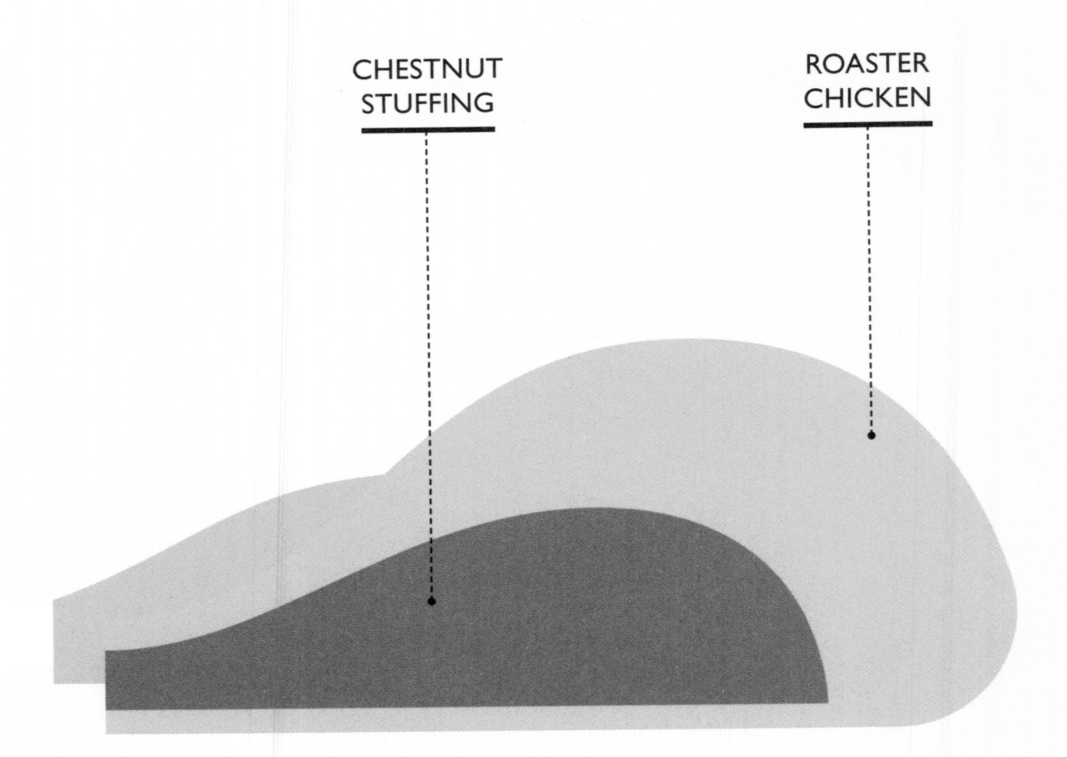

WHAT IS IT?

Chicken stuffed with a poultry mousseline with chestnuts, browned in a skillet, then finished in the oven

TIME TO MAKE

Preparation: 55 minutes
Cooking: 1 hour 20 minutes

EQUIPMENT

Deep, covered ovenproof skillet
Food processor
Trussing needle and kitchen string

VARIATION

Turkey stuffed with chestnuts

TRICKY ASPECT

The mousseline stuffing

TECHNIQUES TO MASTER

Trussing (page 278)
Degreasing a skillet (page 283)
Deglazing (page 283)
Scraping up stuck-on bits (page 283)
Browning (page 282)
Basting (page 283)
Straining through a sieve (page 281)
Scraping out (page 281)

WHAT HAPPENS BETWEEN THE BIRD AND THE STUFFING DURING COOKING?

The stuffing is protected from overcooking and drying out by the ribcage of the bird, and the meat captures the flavors of the stuffing.

Learn

SERVES 4

1 CHICKEN

3 lb 5 oz roaster chicken
2 teaspoons fine salt
freshly ground black pepper (6 turns)
2 tablespoons olive oil
4 tablespoons butter

2 STUFFING

Poultry mousseline
⅓ cup heavy cream
7 oz skinless chicken breast
5 tablespoons butter
1 egg white
½ teaspoon fine salt
freshly ground black pepper (3 turns)
pinch of cayenne pepper

Flavoring
8 oz roasted shelled chestnuts
5½ oz (1¼ recipes) mushroom duxelles (page 42)

3 CHESTNUT PURÉE

2 garlic cloves
3 cups white poultry stock (page 10)
1½ lb roasted shelled chestnuts
3 tablespoons butter

Making stuffed roaster chicken

1 To make the poultry mousseline stuffing, refrigerate the bowl of your food processor and the measured-out cream. Remove any fat and sinew from the chicken breasts, if necessary. Cut them into lengthwise strips then into ¾-inch cubes. Cut the butter into ¾-inch cubes.

2 Process the chicken with the egg white, salt, black pepper, and cayenne. Gradually add the butter and cream, alternating between the two. Process for about 3 minutes, until the mixture is smooth. Using a silicone spatula, transfer to a bowl, scraping the sides of the processor and smoothing the top. Cover with plastic wrap touching the surface and refrigerate.

3 To make the chestnut purée, peel and de-germ the garlic cloves. Bring the poultry stock to a boil and add the chestnuts, garlic cloves, and 1 tablespoon of the butter. Return to a boil, then simmer for 20 minutes. Remove from the heat and leave the chestnuts, covered, in the stock.

4 Roughly chop the chestnuts for the stuffing. Mix them with the duxelles and the poultry mousseline, then set aside in the refrigerator.

5 Massage the skin of the chicken with half the salt. Season the cavity with the remaining salt and the pepper. Stuff the chicken using a spoon (or a pastry bag), pushing it in well.

6 Truss the chicken (page 278). Cut the string and secure the two ends with a double knot.

7 Preheat the oven to 400°F. Heat the olive oil in a deep, oven-proof skillet and brown the chicken on all sides, starting with the thighs, then the breast, then the back.

8 Turn the chicken onto its breast. Add the butter, let it foam, then spoon it over the chicken. Cover and transfer to the oven for 1 hour 15 minutes to 1 hour 20 minutes. Halfway through cooking, turn the chicken onto its back and baste.

9 Drain the chestnuts for the purée and reserve the cooking liquid. Process the chestnuts with 2–3 ladlefuls of the cooking liquid, until you have a smooth, creamy purée. Add the remaining butter and process again. Cover and set aside.

10 Remove the chicken. Degrease the skillet, retaining the fat. Deglaze with the reserved chestnut purée. Bring to a boil, scraping up any stuck-on bits from the bottom. Reduce by half. Strain through a fine-mesh sieve, add 2 tablespoons of the reserved fat, then stir and adjust the seasoning. Carve the chicken and serve with the stuffing, sauce, and chestnut purée.

CHICKEN BALLOTINES

Understand

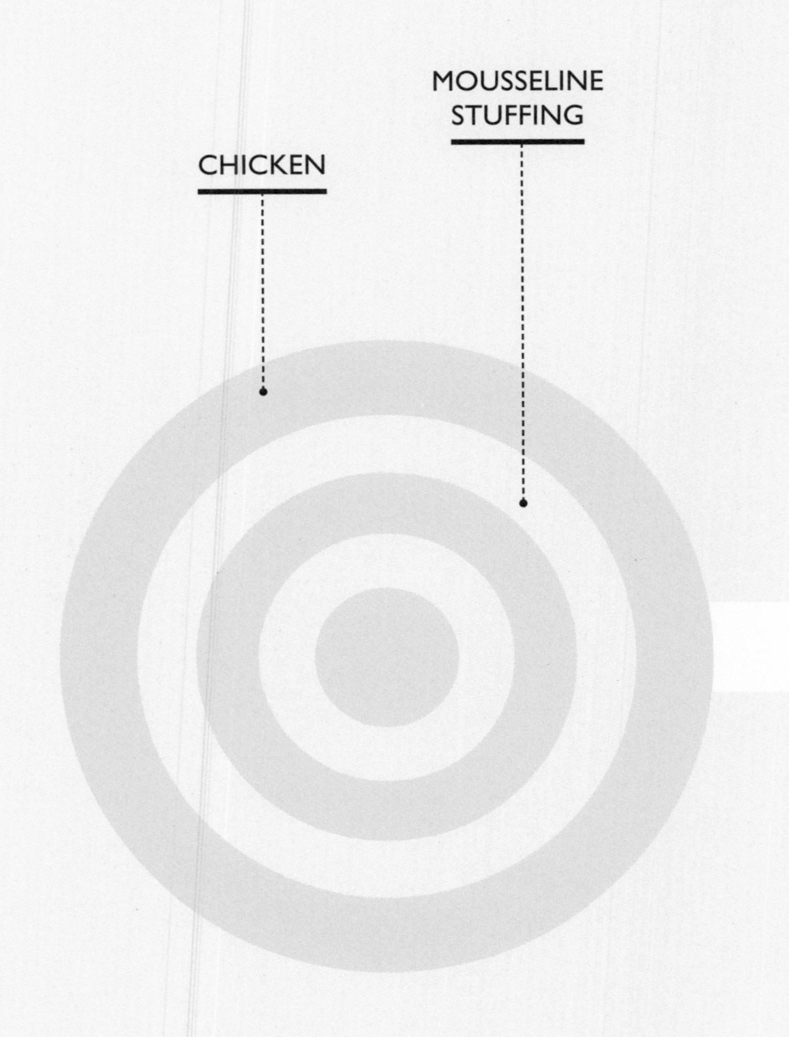

WHAT IS IT?
Boned chicken legs, rolled and stuffed with a poultry mousseline, then poached and served with a morel sauce

TIME TO MAKE
Preparation: 55 minutes
Cooking: 1 hour

EQUIPMENT
Food processor
Kitchen string
Nonstick skillet

VARIATIONS
Mousseline stuffing made with veal, fish, or shellfish.

TECHNIQUES TO MASTER
Mincing (page 280)
Scraping out (page 281)
Deglazing (page 283)
Scraping up stuck-on bits (page 283)
Boiling in hot water (page 84)
Degreasing a skillet (page 283)

IT'S READY . . .
When the ballotines are browned on the outside and soft in the middle.

TIP
Get your butcher to bone the chicken legs.

TO USE DRIED MORELS
Rehydrate 1⅜ oz dried morels in hot water for 30 minutes. Squeeze to remove the water, but reserve 3 tablespoons liquid to add to the pan when you sweat the shallots and morels.

WHY COOK AS BALLOTINES?
To ensure well-cooked thighs (the proteins of which coagulate at higher temperatures than those of the breast) while maintaining tenderness in the breast meat.

Learn

SERVES 4

1 CHICKEN

four whole chicken legs (1 lb 12 oz)
1 teaspoon fine salt
freshly ground black pepper (8 turns)
4 tablespoons olive oil

2 POULTRY MOUSSELINE STUFFING

½ cup heavy cream
10½ oz skinless chicken breast
1 egg white
freshly ground black pepper (4 turns)
pinch of cayenne pepper
8 tablespoons butter

3 MOREL CREAM SAUCE

10½ oz fresh morels
2 shallots
2 tablespoons butter
½ teaspoon fine salt
2½ tablespoons white wine
1 cup heavy cream

Making chicken ballotines

1 To make the mousseline stuffing, refrigerate the bowl of your food processor and the measured-out cream. Trim the chicken breasts if necessary. Cut into strips lengthwise, then into ¾-inch cubes. Process the chicken, egg white, salt, black pepper, and cayenne. Gradually add the butter and cream, alternating between the two, then process for 3–4 minutes, until the mixture is smooth. Using a silicone spatula, transfer to a bowl, scraping the sides of the processor and smoothing the top of the stuffing. Cover with plastic wrap touching the surface and refrigerate.

2 To bone the chicken legs, stick the knife into the joint between the two bones (tibia in the drumstick and femur in the thigh). Cut the length of the thigh to the bone, then scrape the bone to release the flesh. Lift the bone and scrape off the remaining flesh. Continue scraping until you reach the joint. Twist at the joint and cut through the nerves and tendons to separate the bone. Repeat for the tibia.

3 Lay the legs skin side down on a large cutting board. Season with the salt and pepper. Spread the mousseline stuffing over the meat. Roll into a cylinder around the stuffing. Tightly roll each ballotine in several layers of plastic wrap. Tie up the ends with kitchen string.

4 Poach the ballotines in simmering water for 40 minutes.

5 Cut the morels in half lengthwise. Wash under a trickle of water using a pastry brush. Gently squeeze them all at once, then dry with paper towels. Peel and mince the shallots, then sweat them in the butter in a medium saucepan over medium heat. Add the morels and the salt, then cover and cook for 20 minutes.

6 Remove the plastic wrap from the ballotines and brown them a little with the olive oil in a skillet over high heat. Remove them from the pan, then degrease the pan and deglaze with the white wine, scraping up any stuck-on bits from the bottom.

7 Transfer the deglazed pan juices to the saucepan with the morels and stir in the cream. Bring to a boil and reduce until the sauce is thick enough to coat a spoon.

8 Trim off the ends of the ballotines, then cut them into thick slices. Serve them with the morel cream sauce to one side.

VENISON
IN WINE SAUCE

Understand

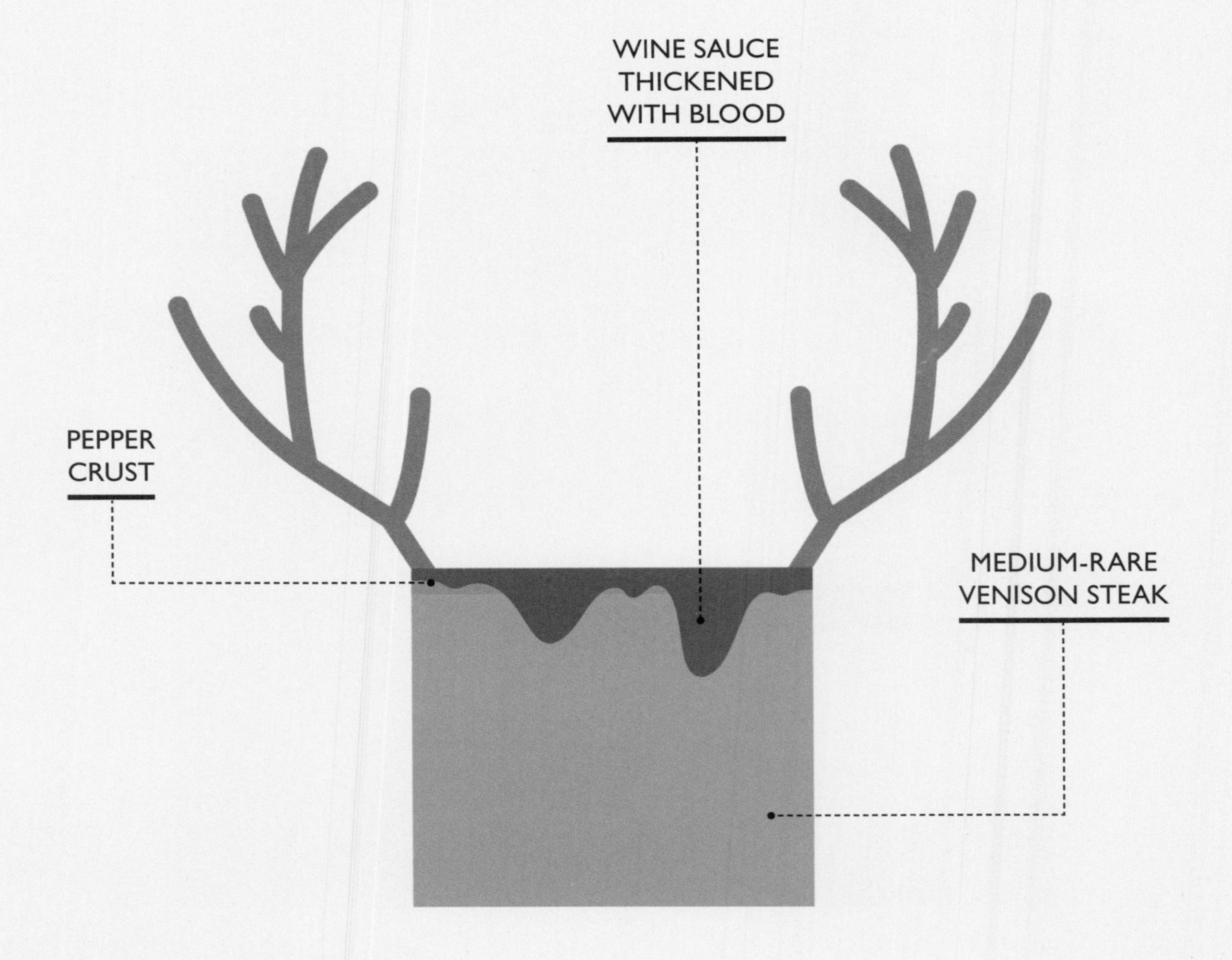

WHAT IS IT?
Pan-fried venison steak served with a red wine sauce made by deglazing the pan and thickening with blood

TIME TO MAKE
Preparation: 35 minutes
Cooking: 1 hour 50 minutes

EQUIPMENT
Large sauté pan
Fine-mesh sieve

VARIATION
Grand veneur sauce: red wine and red currant jelly sauce thickened with blood

TRICKY ASPECT
Thickening with blood

TECHNIQUES TO MASTER
Crushing spices (page 280)
Degreasing a skillet (page 283)
Mincing (page 280)
Cutting in brunoise (page 36)
Reducing a sauce (page 283)
Deglazing (page 283)
Scraping up stuck-on bits (page 283)
Whisking in butter (page 282)
Straining through a sieve (page 281)
Skimming (page 283)
Flambéing (page 282)
Basting (page 283)
Foaming butter (page 283)

STORAGE
Keep unthickened sauce in the refrigerator (24 hours maximum) and thicken it at the last moment.

WHY USE MODERATE HEAT FOR THICKENING WITH BLOOD?
Above 170°F, the blood proteins coagulate and create a grainy texture.

SERVES 4

1 VENISON

four $5\frac{1}{2}$ oz venison steaks, with trimmings
freshly ground black pepper
2 tablespoons olive oil
2 tablespoons butter
1 teaspoon fine salt

2 WINE SAUCE

1 carrot
3 large white mushrooms
6 small shallots
$\frac{3}{4}$ teaspoon black peppercorns
$2\frac{1}{2}$ tablespoons olive oil
1 tablespoon butter
2 tablespoons Cognac
1 thyme sprig
1 small bay leaf
1 tablespoon white wine vinegar
2 cups red wine
$3\frac{1}{4}$ cups water
2 teaspoons aged wine vinegar
3 juniper berries
$\frac{1}{2}$ teaspoon fleur de sel
$2\frac{1}{2}$ tablespoons game blood
(may substitute pig's blood)

Making venison in wine sauce

1 To make the sauce, peel and wash the carrot. Remove the stems from the mushrooms and peel the caps. Peel and mince the shallots. Cut the vegetables in brunoise. Crush the peppercorns.

2 Heat the 2½ tablespoons olive oil in a saucepan and brown the venison trimmings over very high heat at first, then over low heat for 2–3 minutes.

3 Degrease the pan, then melt the 1 tablespoon butter and sweat the vegetable brunoise with the crushed pepper for 2–3 minutes. Flambé with the Cognac. Add the thyme and the bay leaf, then reduce the liquid completely. Deglaze with the white wine vinegar. Reduce until dry, using a spatula to scrape up any stuck-on bits.

4 Add the red wine and reduce by half over medium heat, skimming regularly. Pour in 3 cups of the water, then simmer for 1½ hours, skimming occasionally. At the end of cooking, the sauce should have reduced by one-third. If not, bring to a boil over medium heat and let it reduce.

5 Push through a fine-mesh sieve and set aside.

6 To prepare the meat, lightly sprinkle the venison steaks with pepper.

7 Heat the 2 tablespoons olive oil in a sauté pan over high heat. Reduce the heat to medium and sear the venison steaks for 2 minutes on each side. Add 1 tablespoon of the butter, then let the steaks brown for 3 minutes more on each side, regularly spooning the foaming butter over them. Drain the steaks on a wire rack and cover them with foil to keep them hot.

8 Discard the cooking fat and deglaze the pan with the aged wine vinegar and the remaining ¼ cup water. Add the wine sauce. Bring to a boil, skim, then cook over low heat for 5–10 minutes. Adjust the seasoning, then whisk in the remaining tablespoon of butter to make the sauce shiny and smooth. Crush the juniper berries, then sprinkle them into the sauce along with the fleur de sel. Strain the sauce through the fine-mesh sieve.

9 Return the sauce to the saucepan, bring to a simmer, then remove from the heat. Gently whisk in the blood. Adjust the seasoning.

10 Serve a venison steak on each plate, setting each in a pool of sauce.

CALF'S LIVER
WITH RAISINS

Understand

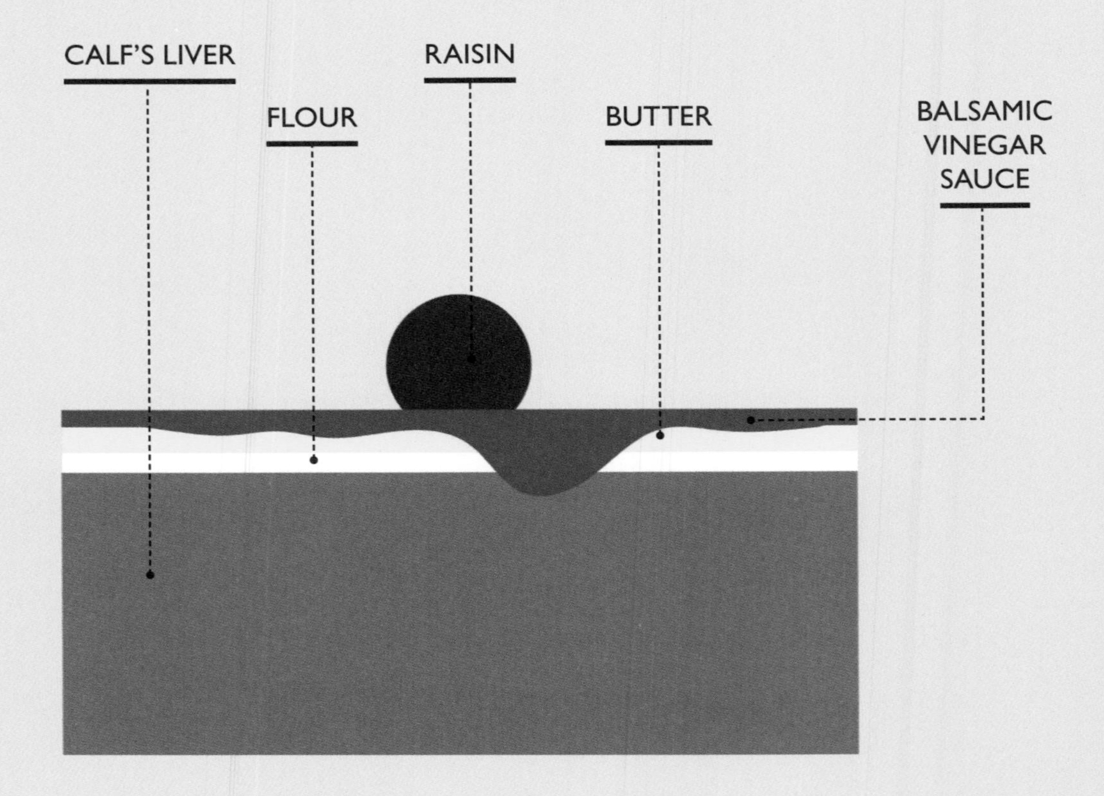

WHAT IS IT?
Slices of calf's liver sautéed in butter and served with a vinegar-and-raisin sauce

TIME TO MAKE
Preparation: 15 minutes
Cooking: 10 minutes

EQUIPMENT
Wire rack

VARIATION
Calf's liver with bacon (sautéed calf's liver + bacon + beurre noisette)

TRICKY ASPECT
Cooking the liver: the center must be pink

TECHNIQUE TO MASTER
Mincing (page 280)
Deglazing (page 283)
Scraping up stuck-on bits (page 283)
Reducing a sauce (page 283)
Whisking in butter (page 282)

ACCOMPANIMENT
Mashed potatoes (page 60)

WHY DUST THE LIVER SLICES WITH FLOUR?
The starch in the flour absorbs moisture from the liver, which improves the browning of the liver (Maillard reaction, page 282).

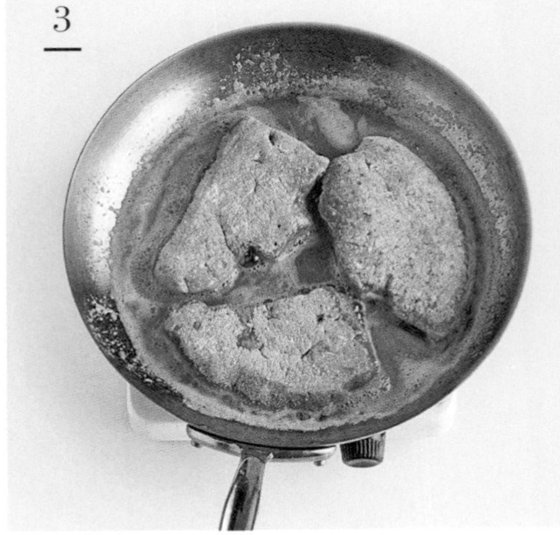

SERVES 4

CALF'S LIVER

½ cup water
½ cup raisins
2 shallots
two 10½ oz slices calf's liver
2 tablespoons all-purpose flour
4 tablespoons butter
¼ cup balsamic vinegar

SEASONING

1 teaspoon fine salt
freshly ground black pepper (4 turns)
½ teaspoon fleur de sel

1 Bring the water to a boil and add the raisins off the heat. Peel and mince the shallots.

2 Cut the liver slices in half. Pat dry with paper towels, season with salt, then dust with flour. Tap gently to remove any excess flour.

3 Heat half the butter in a large skillet until lightly golden. Add the liver pieces and brown for 3 minutes over medium heat. Turn them over, add another ½ tablespoon of butter and cook for 2–3 minutes, spooning the butter over the liver pieces constantly. Transfer to a wire rack, then season with the pepper and sprinkle with the fleur de sel.

4 Sweat the shallots for 1 minute in the same pan. Deglaze with the balsamic vinegar, scraping any stuck-on bits from the bottom. Add the raisins with their soaking water. Reduce the sauce until slightly thickened. Dice the remaining 1½ tablespoons butter and whisk it into the sauce (page 282).

5 Return the liver to the pan and coat with the sauce.

BEEF WELLINGTON

Understand

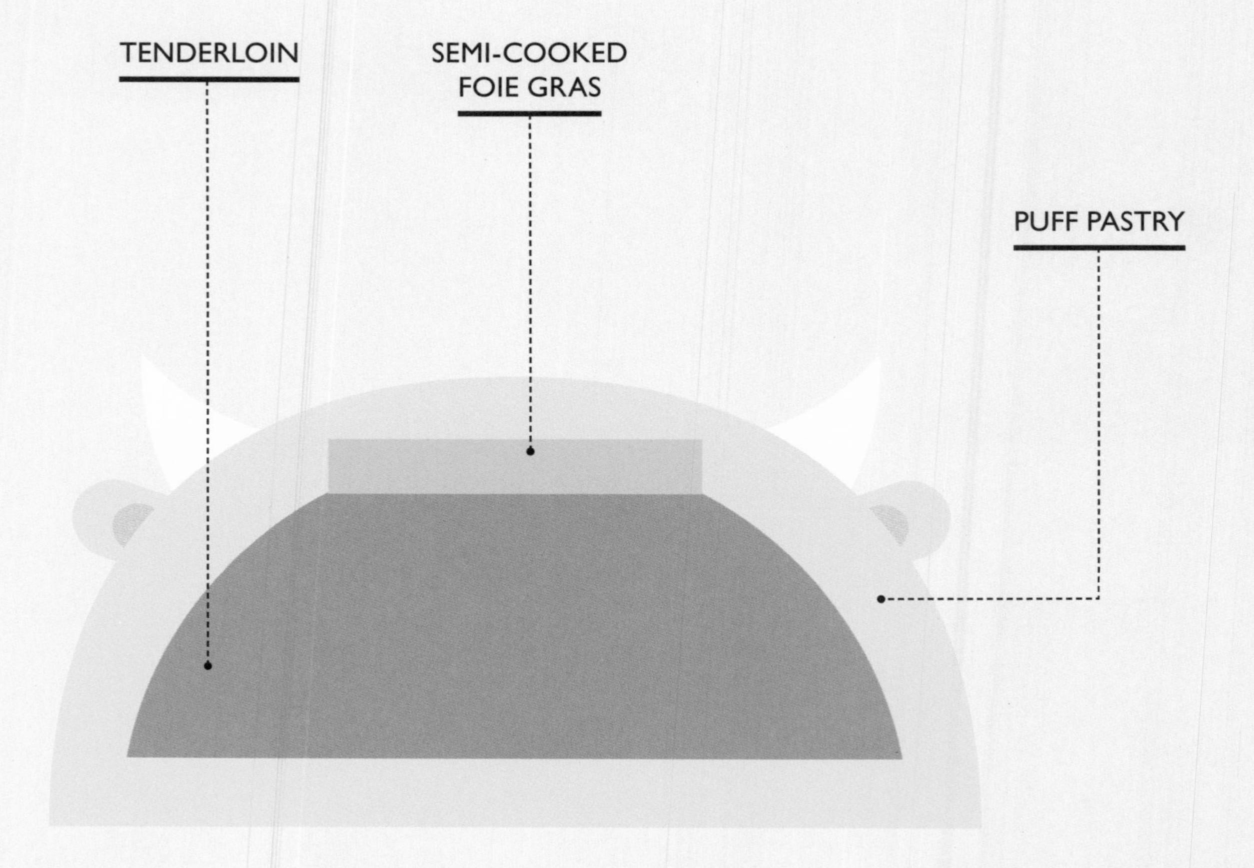

WHAT IS IT?

Roast beef in a puff pastry crust, stuffed with foie gras

TIME TO MAKE

Preparation: 35 minutes
Cooking: 25 minutes
Resting: 15 minutes

EQUIPMENT

Rolling pin
Pastry brush
Large pizza cutter with a thin blade

VARIATIONS

Crust made with pie crust pastry
Boeuf en croûte: Beef Wellington also stuffed with mushroom duxelles

TRICKY ASPECT

Working with the puff pastry

TECHNIQUES TO MASTER

Browning (page 282)
Deglazing (page 283)
Scraping up stuck-on bits (page 283)
Degreasing a skillet (page 283)
Straining through a sieve (page 281)

WHAT DOES THE PASTRY CRUST DO?

It protects the meat from overcooking and allows the core temperature to remain at 130°F, despite a very high cooking temperature.

Learn

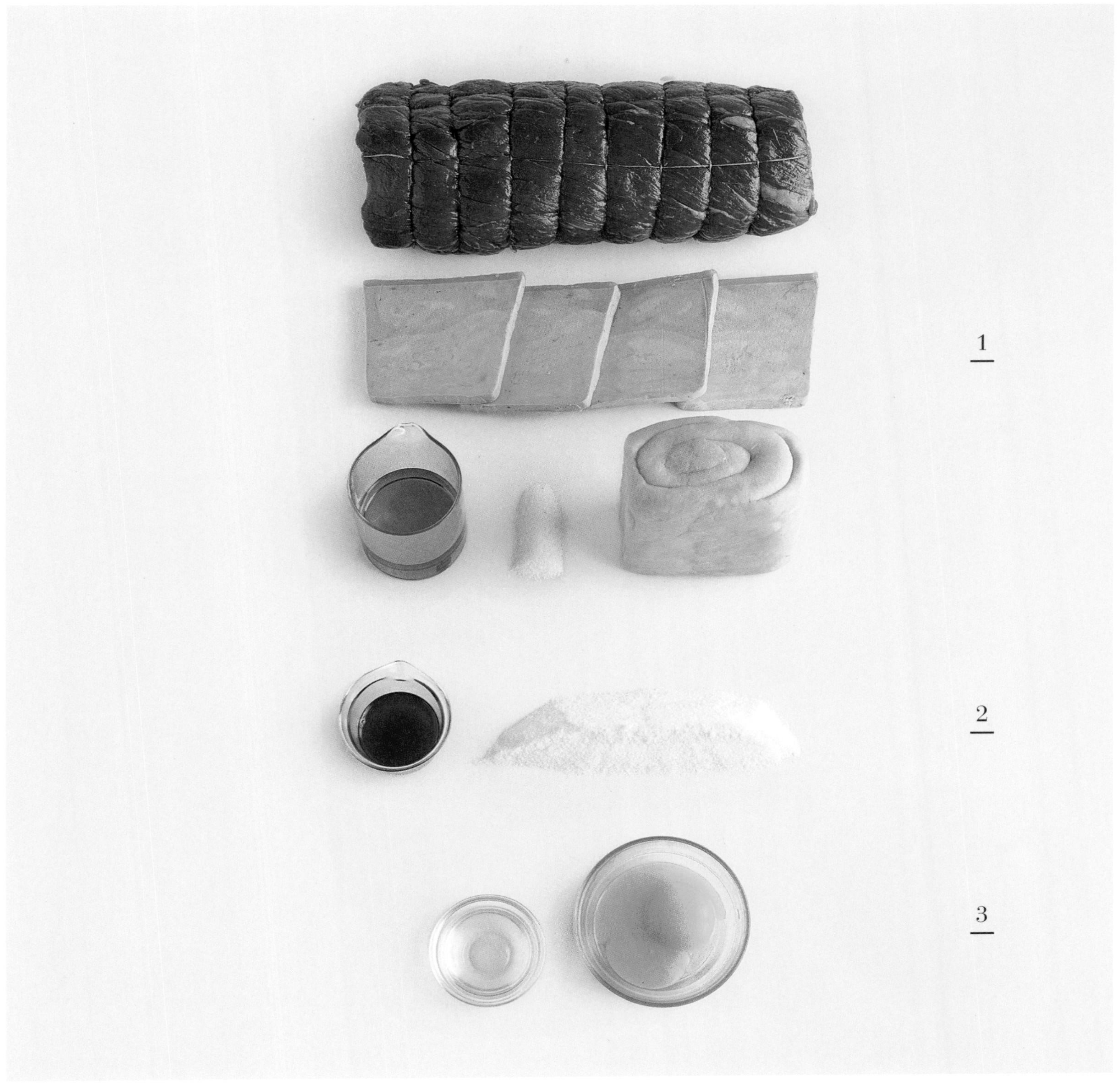

SERVES 4

1 MEAT

one 3 lb 5 oz rolled and tied beef tenderloin
1½ teaspoons fine salt
2½ tablespoons olive oil
1 lb 7 oz (1 recipe) puff pastry (page 46)
8–10½ oz (about ½ recipe) lightly cooked foie gras (page 112), cut into 3–4 slices that will together cover the length of the rolled roast

2 GASTRIQUE

½ cup sugar
3 tablespoons sherry vinegar

3 GLAZE

2 egg yolks
2 teaspoons water

Making beef Wellington

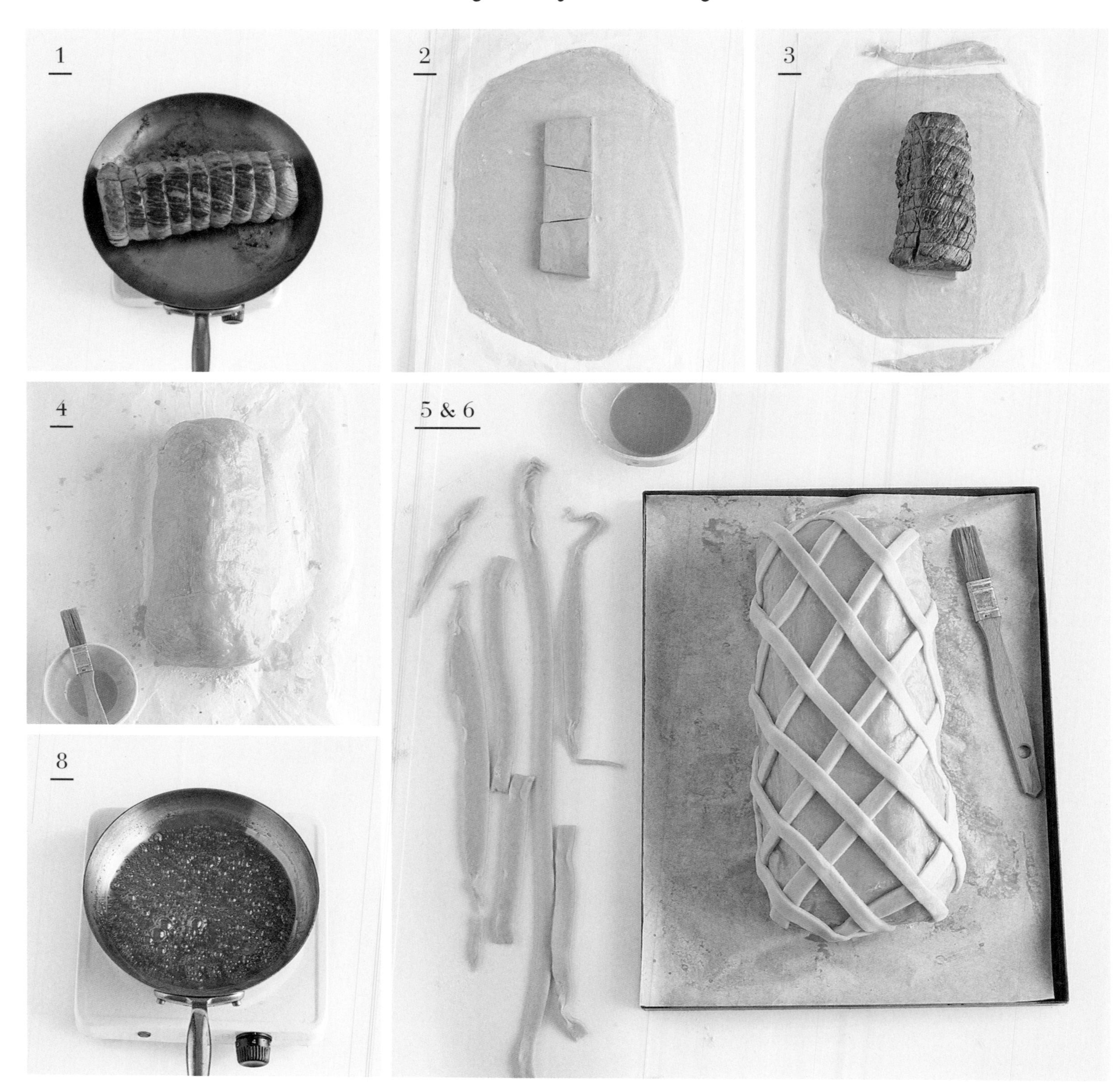

1 Pat the meat dry with paper towels. Season with the salt. Heat the olive oil in a skillet over very high heat and brown the roast on all sides. Let it cool on a wire rack. Set aside the skillet with its stuck-on bits for the sauce.

2 Preheat the oven to 460°F with a rack in the bottom position. Line a baking sheet with parchment paper. Cut the pastry into one large piece (about four-fifths) and one small piece (the remaining one-fifth). Roll out the large piece with a rolling pin into a rectangle 1/8–3/16 inch thick and large enough to comfortably envelop the roast. Arrange the foie gras slices in a vertical line down the center of the pastry.

3 Remove the string from the roast and place on top of the foie gras.

4 Wrap the pastry around the meat, taking care to push out any air bubbles. Mix the egg yolks with the water and glaze the pastry using a pastry brush. Transfer the beef to the prepared baking sheet, with the seam on the bottom. Set aside in the refrigerator.

5 Roll out the second piece of pastry into a rectangle the same length as the roast and 1/8–3/16 inch thick. Cut into strips 3/8–5/8 inch wide with the pizza cutter.

6 Remove the beef from the refrigerator and glaze the pastry again. Arrange the pastry strips on top in a criss-cross pattern. Glaze.

7 Reduce the oven to 430°F and bake for 25 minutes. Remove from the oven and let it rest for 15 minutes before serving.

8 Make the gastrique (page 55) with the sugar and vinegar. Remove from the heat.

9 Degrease the pan you seared the beef in and heat over very high heat. Deglaze with 1/4 cup water, scraping the bottom of the pan to incorporate any stuck-on bits. Strain this liquid through a fine-mesh sieve into the pan containing the gastrique, then reheat and stir. Cut thick slices of the roast and coat with the sauce.

COUSCOUS

Understand

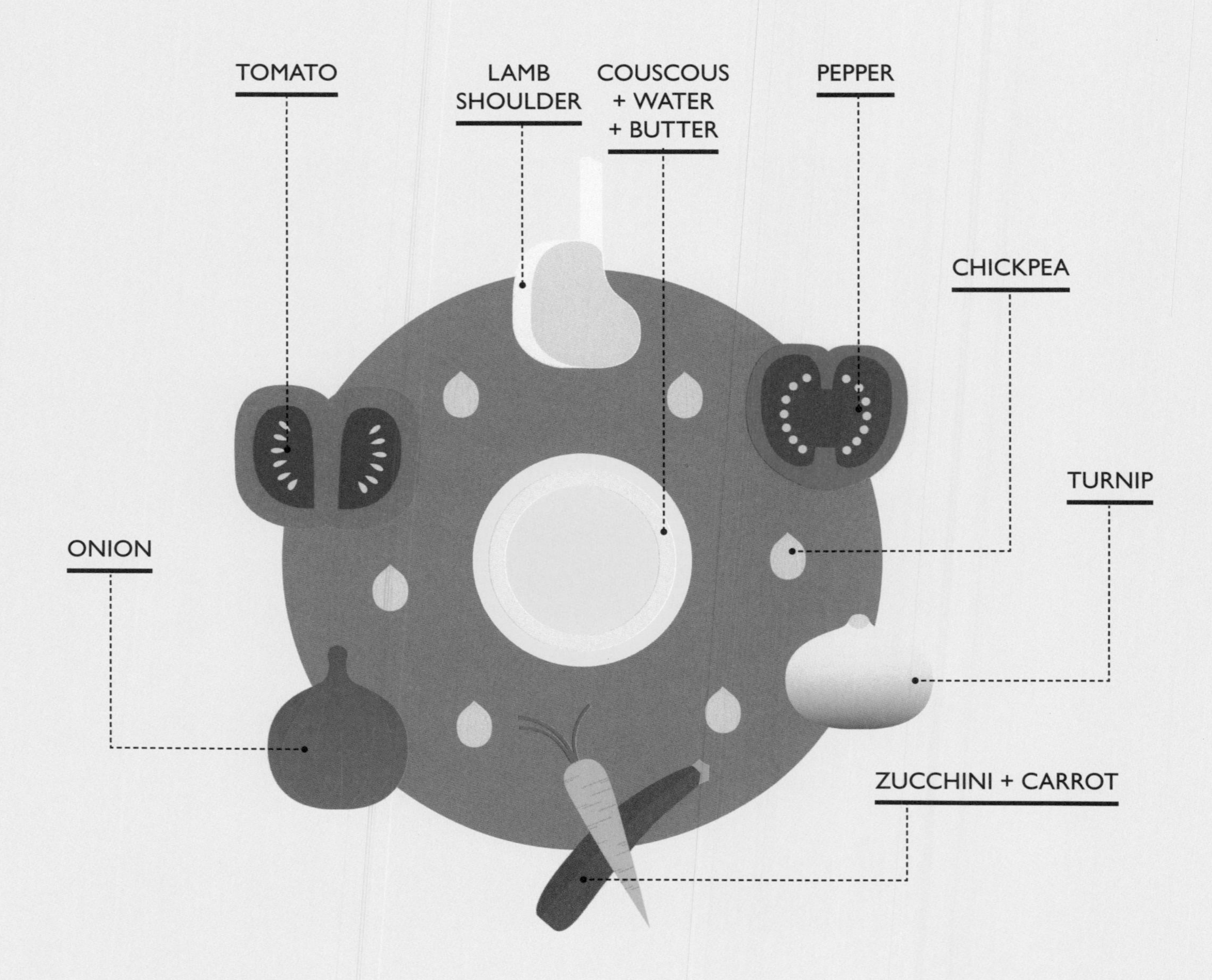

WHAT IS IT?

Couscous cooked in water, served with a lamb stew with seven vegetables and a spiced broth

TIME TO MAKE

Preparation: 40 minutes
Cooking: 1 hour 25 minutes
Resting: 5 minutes

EQUIPMENT

Couscous pan (or stockpot + steaming basket)

TRICKY ASPECTS

- Not burning the bits stuck to the bottom
- Cooking the vegetables
- Preparing the couscous (cooking and separating the grains)

TECHNIQUES TO MASTER

Thinly slicing (page 280)
Browning (page 282)
Degreasing broth (page 283)
Transferring (page 282)

IT'S READY . . .

When the zucchini and the lamb are tender.

STORAGE

Store in the refrigerator no more than three days. Remove the fat solidified on the surface before reheating.

VARIATION

WITH DRIED CHICKPEAS

Soak ⅔ cup chickpeas in a large volume of water for 12 hours with ½ teaspoon baking soda. Drain and rinse. Cover with water in a small saucepan, bring to a boil, then cook over low heat, covered, for 1 hour. Add 1 teaspoon salt 5 minutes before the end of cooking.

SERVES 4

1 LAMB AND BROTH

1 red onion
1 lamb shoulder (about 2 lb 14 oz), boned and cut into 15 pieces
1 teaspoon fine salt
4 tablespoons olive oil
1 teaspoon harissa
½ tablespoon tomato paste
2 cups water

2 VEGETABLES

2 carrots
3–6 turnips
1 green bell pepper
2 tomatoes
1 zucchini
9 oz canned chickpeas

3 COUSCOUS

1 lb fine-grained instant couscous
1½ teaspoons coarse sea salt
2 cups boiling water
4 tablespoons butter

Making couscous

1 Peel and slice the onion. Pat the meat dry with paper towels, then season with half the salt.

2 Heat the olive oil in a couscous pan (or stockpot) over high heat and brown the lamb pieces, working in several batches. With tongs, transfer the lamb to a plate.

3 In the same pan, fry the onion over medium heat until golden, then add the remaining salt, the harissa, and the tomato paste, stirring for 1–2 minutes.

4 Return the lamb to the pan. Pour in the water and bring to a boil. Reduce the heat, then simmer, covered, for 1 hour.

5 Peel the carrots and cut them in half lengthwise, then slice on a slight angle into three pieces. Peel the turnips and cut into quarters. Remove the ends of the pepper, remove the seeds and cut into rounds (not too thin), then cut each round in half. Wash the tomatoes, remove the stems, cut into quarters, and seed. Wash the zucchini, cut off each end, then cut into half or thirds lengthwise (depending on its thickness), then on an angle into three slices.

6 Add to the couscous pan the carrots, turnips, pepper, and chickpeas, along with the liquid from the can. Bring to a simmer and cook, uncovered, for 15 minutes. Add the zucchini and tomatoes. Cook for 10 minutes. Degrease regularly.

7 Put the couscous in a large baking dish. Add the salt to the boiling water, then pour it over the couscous and stir immediately with a spoon. Smooth the surface and let it swell for 5 minutes. Cut the butter into pieces, then add to the couscous. Rub the butter into the couscous to spread through the grains and separate them.

8 Transfer the couscous to the top part of the couscous pan (or a steamer basket). When ready to serve, place a quarter of the couscous into a bowl, and ladle the lamb and vegetables over top.

HAMBURGERS

Understand

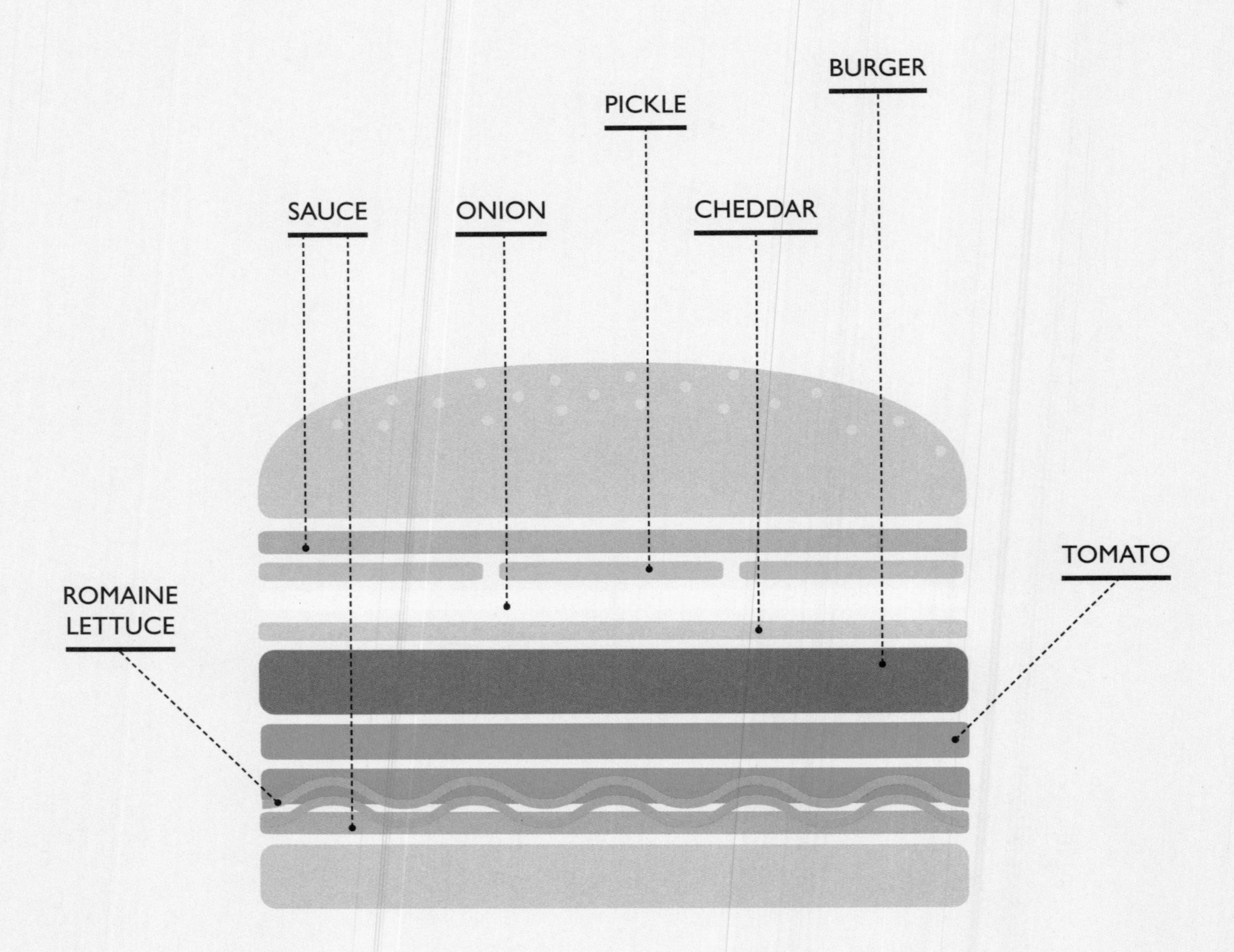

WHAT IS IT?
Hot sandwich made with a brioche-style bun, ground beef (short rib + sirloin), cheese, crisp vegetables, and a lightly sweetened sauce

TIME TO MAKE
Preparation: 35 minutes
Cooking: 15 minutes

EQUIPMENT
Large skillet
Thin spatula
Wire rack

TRICKY ASPECT
Cooking the meat: making a good crust on the outside without burning while retaining a rare center

TECHNIQUES TO MASTER
Straining through a sieve (page 281)
Pushing through a sieve (page 281)
Transferring (page 282)

TIP
If your butcher cannot grind the beef, cut it into ¾-inch dice and grind with a grinder or a food processor with the blade attachment. For a food processor, chill the meat in the freezer for 15 minutes, then grind by pulsing several times.

Learn

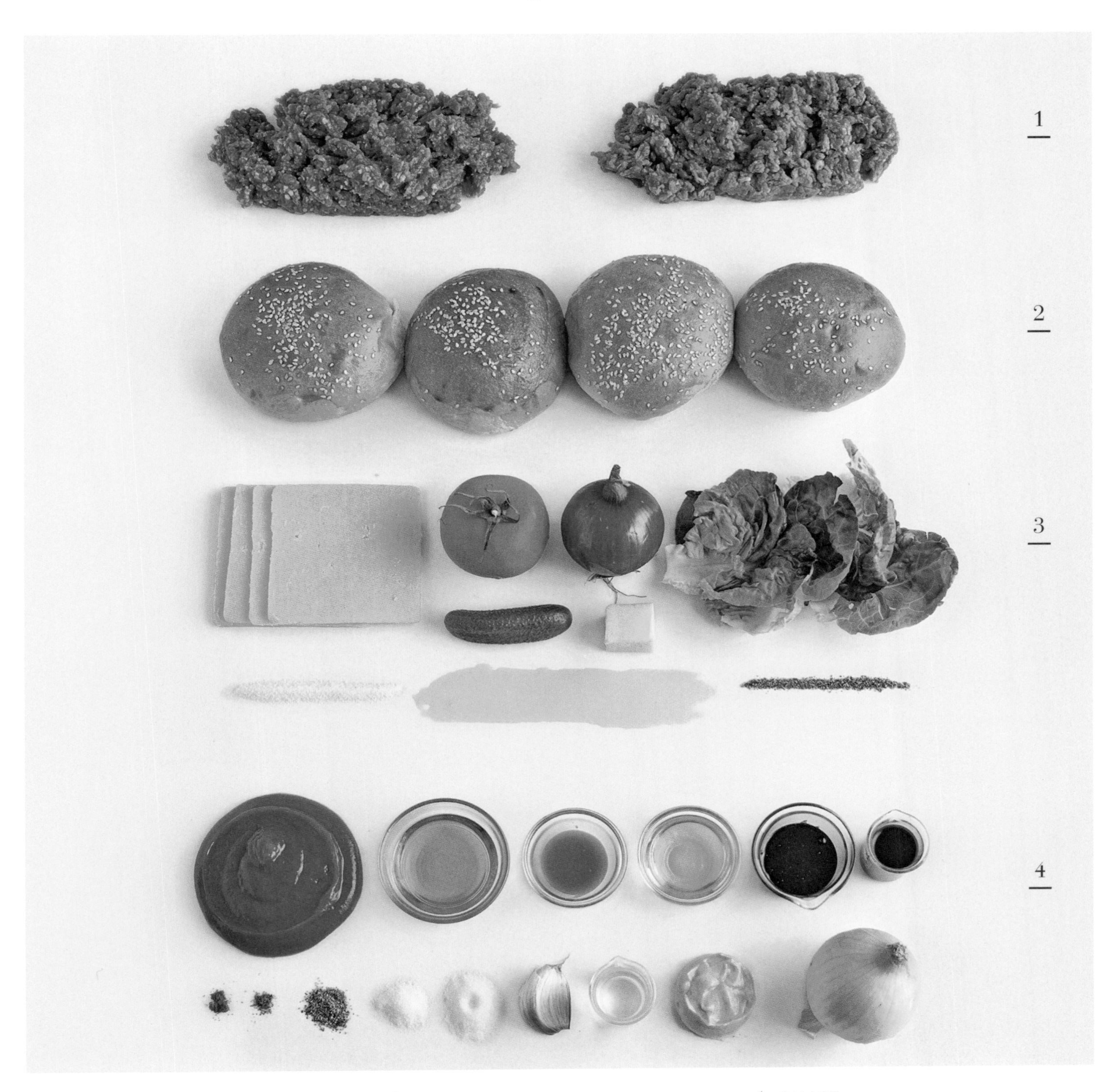

SERVES 4

1 PATTIES

14 oz freshly ground beef, mixed (not tightly packed): 7 oz short rib and 7 oz sirloin
1 teaspoon fine salt
1 teaspoon olive oil

2 BREAD

4 hamburger buns (3½–4 inch diameter)
1 tablespoon butter

3 GARNISHES

4 large lettuce leaves
1 tomato
1 small red onion
1 pickle or cornichon
4 slices cheddar cheese
1 teaspoon fine salt
freshly ground black pepper (8 turns)

4 SAUCE

1 yellow onion
2½ tablespoons water
1 cup ketchup
3 tablespoons molasses
2 tablespoons apple cider vinegar
2 tablespoons Worcestershire sauce
2 scant tablespoons Dijon mustard
½ teaspoon Tabasco sauce
1 teaspoon sugar
freshly ground black pepper (8 turns)
1 garlic clove
2 tablespoons olive oil
½ teaspoon Espelette pepper
pinch of cayenne pepper

Making hamburgers

1 To make the sauce, blend the onion with the water in a food processor until it forms a smooth cream (about 30 seconds). Push this through a fine-mesh sieve. Measure out ½ cup of the strained purée. Mix this with the ketchup, molasses, vinegar, Worcestershire sauce, mustard, Tabasco, sugar, and black pepper.

2 Peel and finely chop the garlic. Heat the oil in a medium saucepan over medium heat. Add the garlic and the Espelette and cayenne peppers. Cook for about 30 seconds or until fragrant. Add the ketchup mixture and bring to a boil. Simmer, uncovered, for about 25 minutes, until the sauce thickens.

3 To prepare the garnishes, wash the lettuce leaves and cut in half. Cut eight slices of tomato. Peel the red onion and cut in thin rings. Cut the pickle lengthwise into four slices about ⅛ inch thick. Cut each slice in half crosswise. Salt and pepper to taste.

4 To prepare the patties, on a cutting board, gently divide the ground beef into four equal piles. Without lifting them, form each pile into a round the diameter of the buns and ⅜–⅝ inch thick. Don't smooth the surface. Season the patties with half the salt, then turn them over using a spatula and season the other side with the remaining salt.

5 Heat the oil in a skillet over the highest possible heat. When the oil starts to smoke, cook the patties, without disturbing them, for about 1 minute, so they form a dark crust. Turn them over with a spatula, reduce the heat to medium, place a slice of cheddar on each one, and let it melt, for 1 minute. Transfer the patties to a wire rack.

6 Split the buns. Melt half the butter in a skillet over medium heat until it turns golden. Brown both cut sides of two buns. Repeat with the remaining butter and buns.

7 Spread 1 tablespoon of the sauce on each side of the buns. On each bottom half, layer a lettuce leaf, two slices of tomato, a patty with the cheese, several onion rings and two pieces of pickle. Set the other half of the bun on top. Serve the rest of the sauce on the side.

DAUPHINE POTATOES

Understand

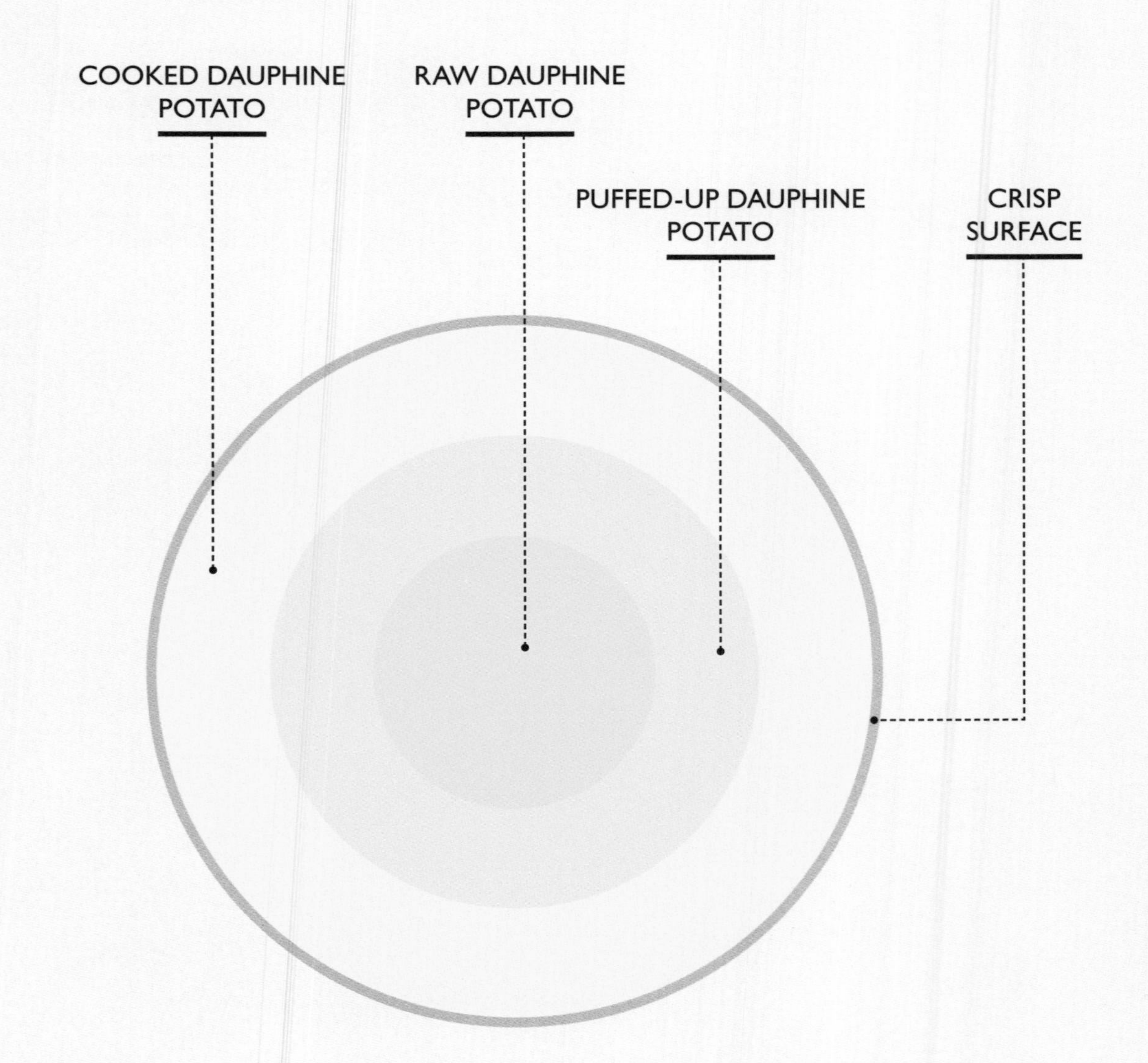

WHAT ARE THEY?
Mixture of mashed potato and choux pastry, shaped into little balls and fried

TIME TO MAKE
Preparation: 45 minutes
Cooking: 40 minutes to 1 hour

EQUIPMENT
Fine-mesh sieve + dough scraper
(or potato masher or food mill)
Kitchen scale
Pastry bag and plain ¾-inch decorating tip
Thermometer
Skimmer or slotted spoon

TRICKY ASPECT
The texture of the mashed potato

TECHNIQUE TO MASTER
Piping (page 281)

THEY'RE READY . . .
When they are golden and puffy.

STORAGE
To reheat: 3 minutes in the oven at 400°F; add salt after. To make in advance: freeze raw, then fry an extra 3 minutes.

NOTE
You must have half as much choux pastry as mashed potatoes. Using a kitchen scale, weigh each before combining.

TO ACCOMPANY
Roast meats, roast poultry, lacquered duckling (page 200), hamburgers (page 240)

Learn

HOW DO THE DAUPHINE POTATOES PUFF UP?

When heated, steam is released from the water in the mixture, causing them to swell.

WHY DO THEY FLOAT TO THE SURFACE?

As the steam dissipates, the balls become less dense and rise to the surface.

MAKES 40

1 MASHED POTATO

1 lb 2 oz potatoes (russet or Yukon Gold)
coarse sea salt

2 CHOUX PASTRY

4 tablespoons butter
½ cup water
½ teaspoon fine salt
½ cup all-purpose flour
2 eggs, lightly whisked

3 SEASONING AND TO COOK

fine salt
freshly ground black pepper
pinch of freshly grated nutmeg
4 cups peanut oil

Making dauphine potatoes

1 Wash the potatoes and place in a large saucepan with some coarse sea salt and cold water. Bring to a boil. Simmer for 20–40 minutes, depending on their size, until tender.

2 To make the choux pastry, melt the butter with the water and salt in a saucepan over medium heat, stirring. Bring to a boil, then boil for 2–3 seconds.

3 Remove from the heat, add the flour all at once, and stir to incorporate it, gently at first. When the pastry pulls together, mix vigorously.

4 Dry the pastry by stirring for 30 seconds to 1 minute over medium heat. Remove from the heat from time to time to prevent it burning on the bottom. Stop when the pastry no longer sticks.

5 Process the dried pastry for a few seconds in a food processor to cool it down (or stir it with a wooden spoon). Gradually add two-thirds of the eggs. If the pastry sticks to the spoon, then falls to form one (or several) peaks, it's ready; if not, add the remaining egg.

6 Drain the potatoes, then return them to the saucepan over the heat, moving them around so the skin is well dried. Peel.

7 Roughly mash the hot potatoes using a fork, then push through a sieve using a dough scraper (or mash with a potato masher). Season with salt and pepper, and stir in the nutmeg.

8 Mix the choux pastry with the mashed potato using a spatula or a dough scraper. Fill a pastry bag fitted with a ¾-inch plain tip with the mixture (or use a spoon).

9 Pipe about 40 balls onto a cutting board. Heat the peanut oil in a saucepan to 320°F. Cook the pastry balls, eight at a time, in the oil, watching that they don't stick together. They will sink, then rise to the surface again. Cook them for 4 minutes. Remove from the oil using a skimmer, then season with salt and drain on paper towels. Repeat with the remaining potato balls.

SOUFFLÉED POTATOES

Understand

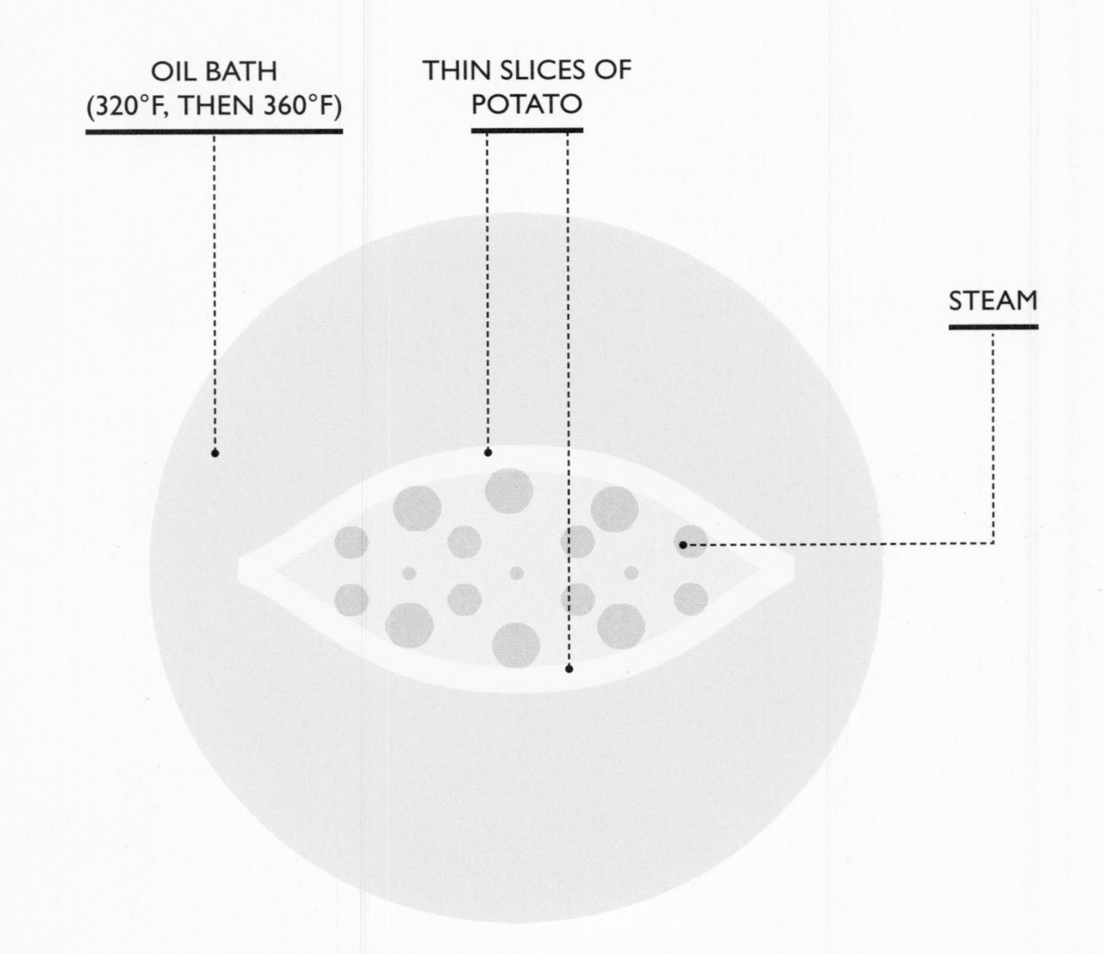

WHAT ARE THEY?

Thin rounds of potato that "soufflé" during cooking: they puff up and turn golden

TIME TO MAKE

Preparation: 15 minutes
Cooking: 30–40 minutes

EQUIPMENT

Two medium saucepans
Thermometer
Mandoline
Small skimmer
Round cookie cutter (2 inch diameter)

TRICKY ASPECTS

- Synchronizing the temperature of the two oil baths
- Transferring the potatoes from one oil bath to the other

THEY'RE READY . . .

When the potato rounds are puffy and lightly browned.

TO ACCOMPANY

A leg of lamb, a duck breast (page 204), or a rack of lamb (page 83)

HOW DOES THE POTATO ROUND PUFF UP?

The heat turns the water in the potato into steam, which puffs up the round.

HOW DOES IT SPLIT IN TWO?

The water vapor lifts the two surfaces of the slices. Once dried by cooking, the two surfaces remain separated.

Learn

MAKES 30–40

peanut oil, for deep-frying
2 large baking potatoes (such as russet), 10½ oz each
1 teaspoon fine salt

1 Prepare two oil baths: one at 320°F and the other at 360°F. Peel the potatoes, wash them under cold water, then dry them with a clean dish towel. Using a mandoline, cut them into 1/16-inch slices.

2 Cut a disk out of the middle of each slice using a 2-inch cookie cutter. Set aside in a bowl of cold water.

3 Wash and dry five to eight slices and immerse them in the 320°F oil bath. Remove the pan from the heat and stir with a heatproof spatula so that the slices are moving constantly.

4 As soon as the slices start to form little blisters on the surface (after 2–4 minutes), remove them from the oil using a small skimmer and transfer immediately to the 360°F oil bath. Stir with a spatula.

5 When the slices have puffed up, browned, and dried (after a few seconds), remove using the skimmer, season with salt and drain on paper towels. Once the first batch is completed, reheat the first oil bath to 320°F and start again with five to eight new slices.

POTATO MILLE-FEUILLES

Understand

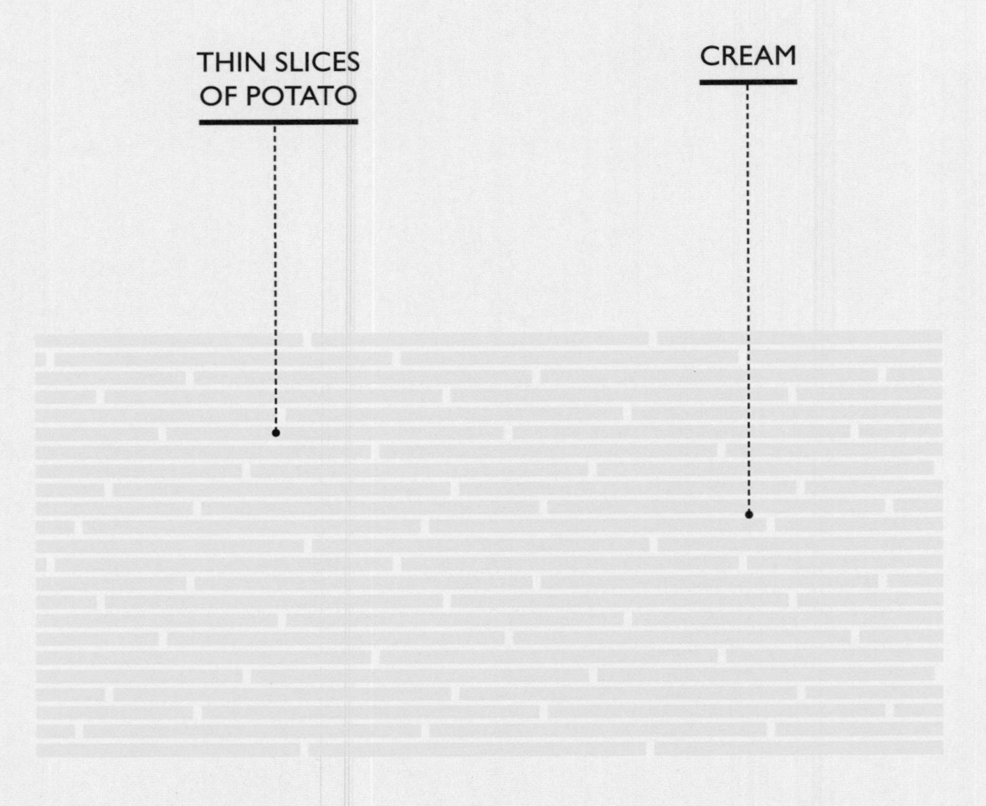

WHAT IS IT?
Thin slices of potato, soaked in cream, arranged in layers, baked in the oven, then compressed

TIME TO MAKE
Preparation: 40 minutes
Cooking: 1 hour
Resting: 6 hours

EQUIPMENT
Loaf pan (about 9 × 5 inches)
Mandoline

VARIATION
Gratin dauphinois (potatoes + milk + cream + garlic)

TRICKY ASPECT
Cutting the potatoes

TECHNIQUES TO MASTER
Using a mandoline (page 284)
Trimming (page 281)

IT'S READY . . .
When an inserted knife meets no resistance.

TO ACCOMPANY
Rolled lamb shoulder (page 192), rack of lamb (page 83), salmon

HOW DO THE POTATOES BECOME TRANSLUCENT AND "MELT"?
During cooking, the starch in the potatoes swells up with water and gelatinizes, which modifies the texture.

Learn

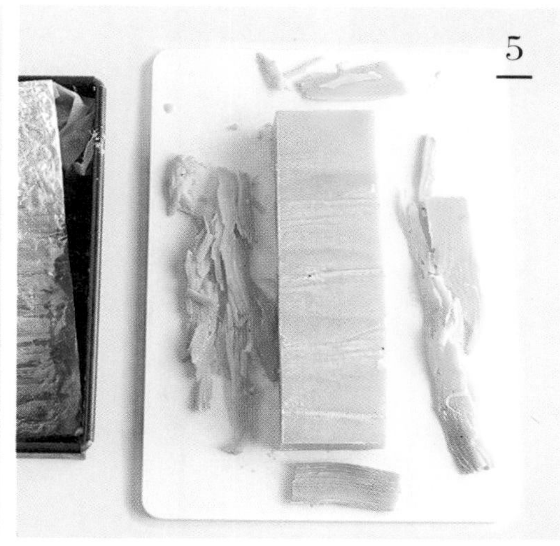

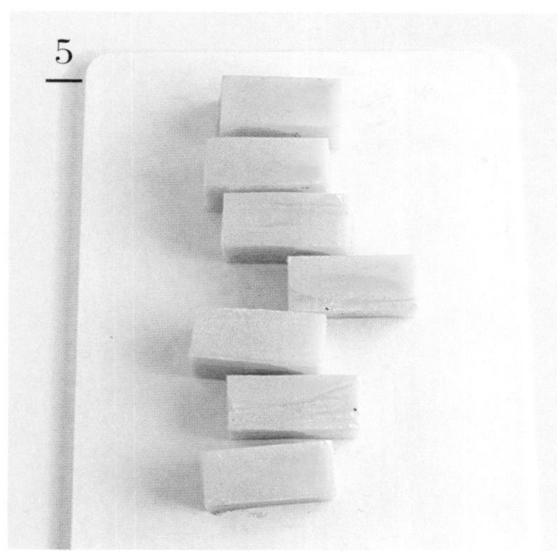

SERVES 4

- 2 lb 10 oz very large starchy and soft-fleshed potatoes (12½–14 oz each) (such as russet or Yukon Gold)
- ¾ cup heavy cream
- 2 teaspoons fine salt
- freshly ground black pepper (12 turns)
- pinch of freshly grated nutmeg
- 2 tablespoons olive oil
- ½ teaspoon fleur de sel

1 Preheat the oven to 340°F. Line a 9 × 5-inch loaf pan with parchment paper, leaving overhang on the two long sides. Mix the cream, half the salt, half the pepper and the nutmeg in a large mixing bowl.

2 Peel and wash the potatoes. Trim them to obtain rectangular blocks the width of the pan (5 inches) then cut into paper-thin slices using a mandoline sitting over the bowl. Stir from time to time to soak the slices in the cream mixture.

3 Arrange the slightly drained potato slices in the pan, in layers, side by side but overlapping if necessary to fill a gap. Season with the remaining salt and pepper every two layers. Cover with the overhanging parchment paper, then with foil, and bake for 1 hour.

4 Cut a rectangle of cardboard a little larger than the pan and wrap in foil. When you take the pan out of the oven, place the cardboard on top of the mille-feuilles, spread out weights on top (about three 1 lb 2 oz weights) and cool to room temperature. Remove the weights and the cardboard, cover with plastic wrap, and refrigerate for at least 6 hours.

5 Turn out the mille-feuilles with the help of the overhanging parchment paper, transfer to a cutting board, remove the paper, trim the edges, and cut into thick slices.

6 Heat the olive oil in a nonstick skillet over medium heat and brown the top and bottom of each mille-feuilles. Serve sprinkled with the fleur de sel.

GLAZED VEGETABLES

Understand

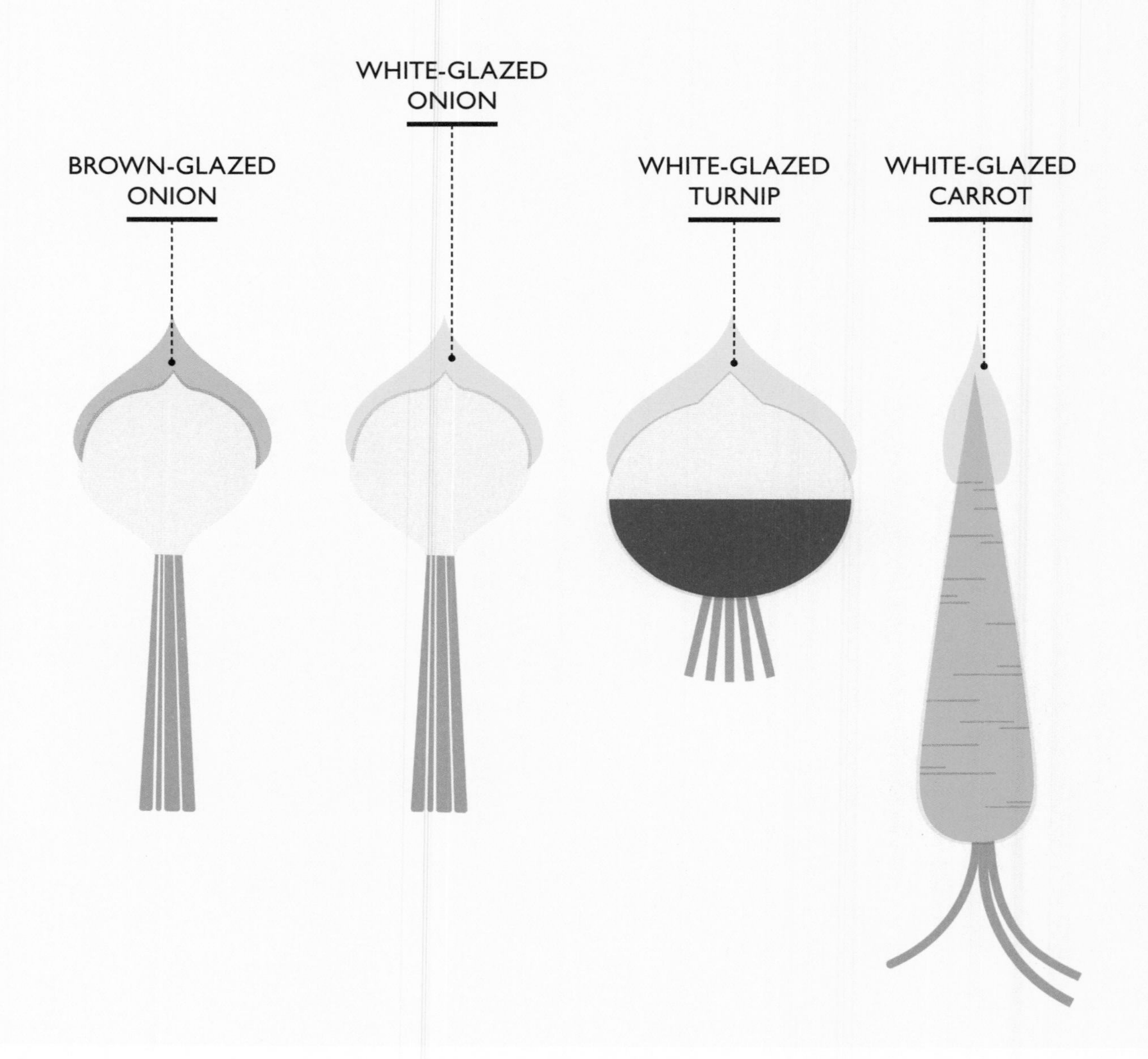

WHAT IS IT?
Small vegetables cooked in water, butter, and sugar to coat them in a shiny clear syrup (white-glazed) or caramelized syrup (brown-glazed)

TIME TO MAKE
Preparation: 20 minutes
Cooking: 10 minutes

EQUIPMENT
Large skillet

TRICKY ASPECT
Cooking the vegetables through by the time the liquid has reduced

TECHNIQUES TO MASTER
Cutting a parchment paper disk (page 285)
Turning vegetables (page 38)

TIPS
- Use peeled and frozen baby onions, and increase the cooking time by 2–3 minutes.
- If the vegetables aren't cooked at the end, add boiling water.
- If they're cooked but the water hasn't evaporated, remove them from the pan, reduce the liquid, then return them to the syrup.

TO ACCOMPANY
Meats in sauce, game, white fish

HOW DO THE ONIONS BROWN?
When the temperature reaches 212°F, the water evaporates, triggering caramelization: brown compounds form and make the onions golden.

WHAT IS THE PURPOSE OF THE PAPER DISK?
To slow down evaporation and retain sufficient water to cook the vegetables.

Learn

SERVES 4

VEGETABLES

6½ oz baby onions (about 25)
or
9 oz baby turnips (about 20)
or
9 oz very thin carrots (about 20)

SYRUP

½ cup water
1 tablespoon butter
1 teaspoon sugar
¼ teaspoon fine salt

1 Peel and wash the vegetables.

2 Place the vegetables in a single layer in a large skillet. Add water to come up halfway, then add the butter, sugar, and salt.

3 Bring to a boil and cover the pan with a disk of parchment paper. Simmer until the water has competely evaporated.

4 Remove the paper disk and cook for 1 minute more, watching the reduction: the butter and sugar should form a shiny syrup. To brown-glaze onions, continue to reduce the syrup until it caramelizes.

5 Gently coat the vegetables in the syrup by swirling the pan.

ROASTED SQUASH

Understand

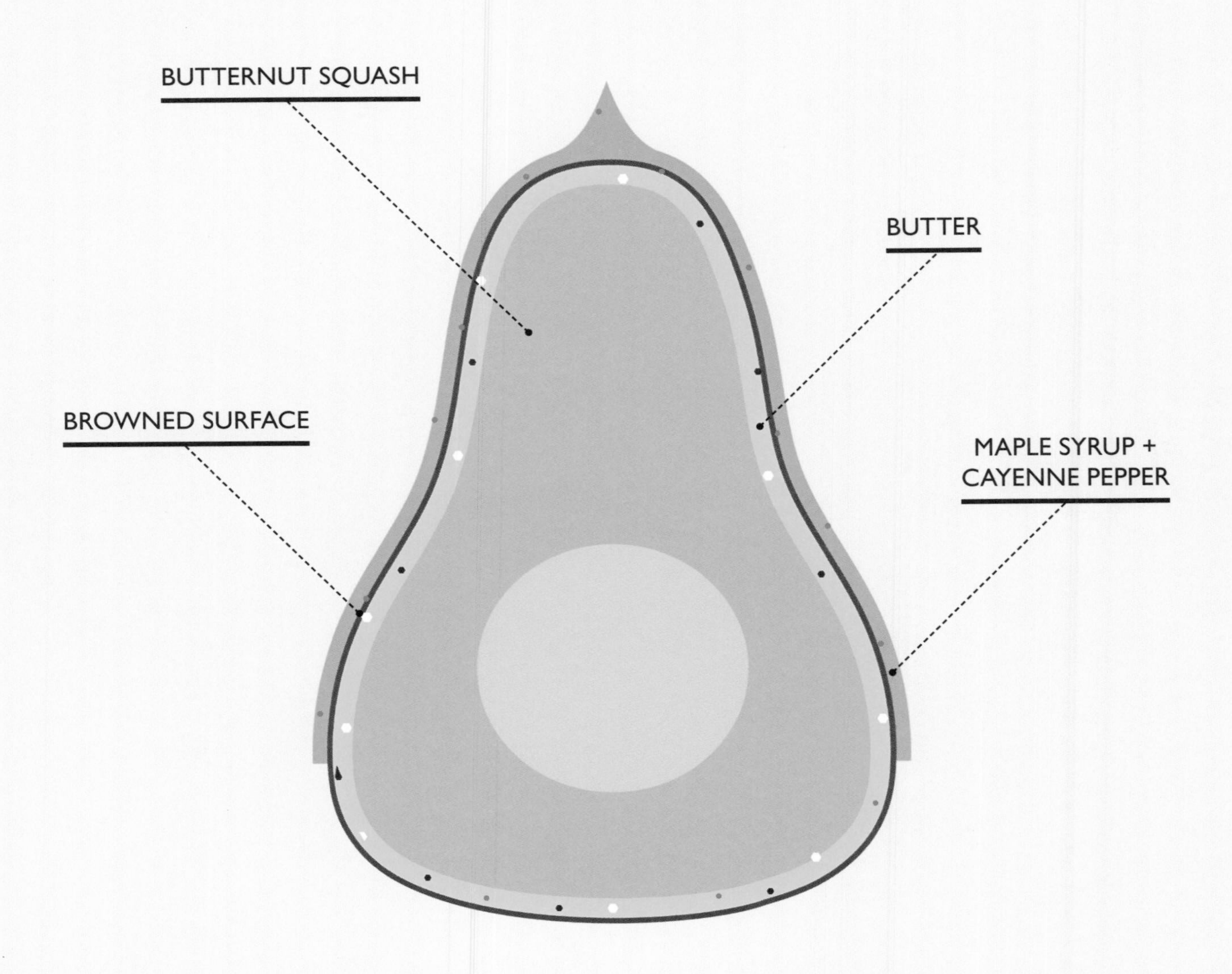

WHAT IS IT?
Roasted slices of butternut squash, served with spiced maple syrup, goat cheese, and pecans

TIME TO MAKE
Preparation: 25 minutes
Cooking: 35–40 minutes

EQUIPMENT
Very sharp vegetable peeler
Baking sheet

TECHNIQUE TO MASTER
Toasting nuts (page 281)

IT'S READY . . .
When the squash is browned on both sides.

TO ACCOMPANY
Eggs, poultry

Learn

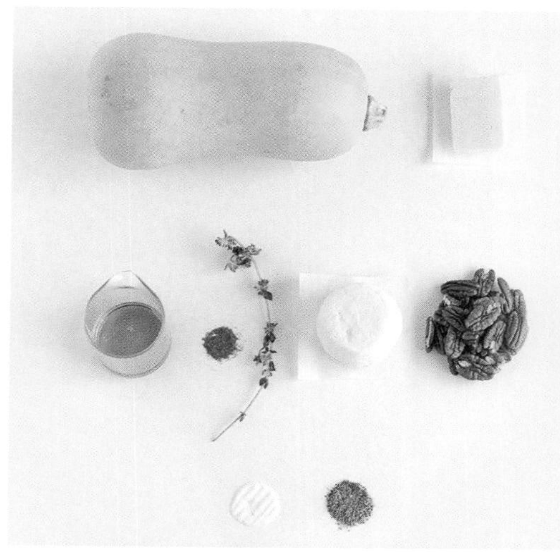

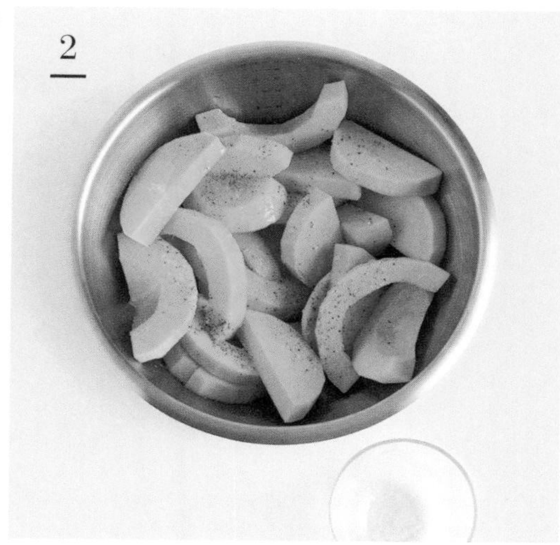

SERVES 4

ROASTED SQUASH

one 1 lb 12 oz butternut squash
3 tablespoons butter
½ teaspoon fine salt
freshly ground black pepper (10 turns)

GARNISH

⅓ cup pecan halves
2 oz goat cheese
¼ cup maple syrup
pinch of cayenne pepper
1 thyme sprig

1 Preheat the oven to 430°F (with a rack in the bottom position). Using a sharp vegetable peeler, peel the squash, also removing the white layer under the skin: the peeled squash should be orange. Cut in half crosswise, separating the thinner neck from the rounded part, then cut in half lengthwise. Use a spoon to remove the seeds and fibers.

2 Melt the butter. With the cut side down, cut each piece of squash into slices ⅝-inch thick. Put them in a large mixing bowl, then add the melted butter, salt, and pepper. Mix well.

3 Place the slices on a baking sheet in a single layer. Roast for 25–30 minutes, until the underside is well browned. Turn each piece over using a spatula. Roast for 10 minutes more: the other side should be browned and the flesh tender.

4 Toast the pecans in a dry skillet then roughly chop them. Dice the goat cheese.

5 Mix the maple syrup and cayenne pepper in a small bowl. Arrange the squash on a platter, then drizzle with the spiced maple syrup. Add the cheese and pecans, then sprinkle with the thyme leaves.

ROASTED CAULIFLOWER

Understand

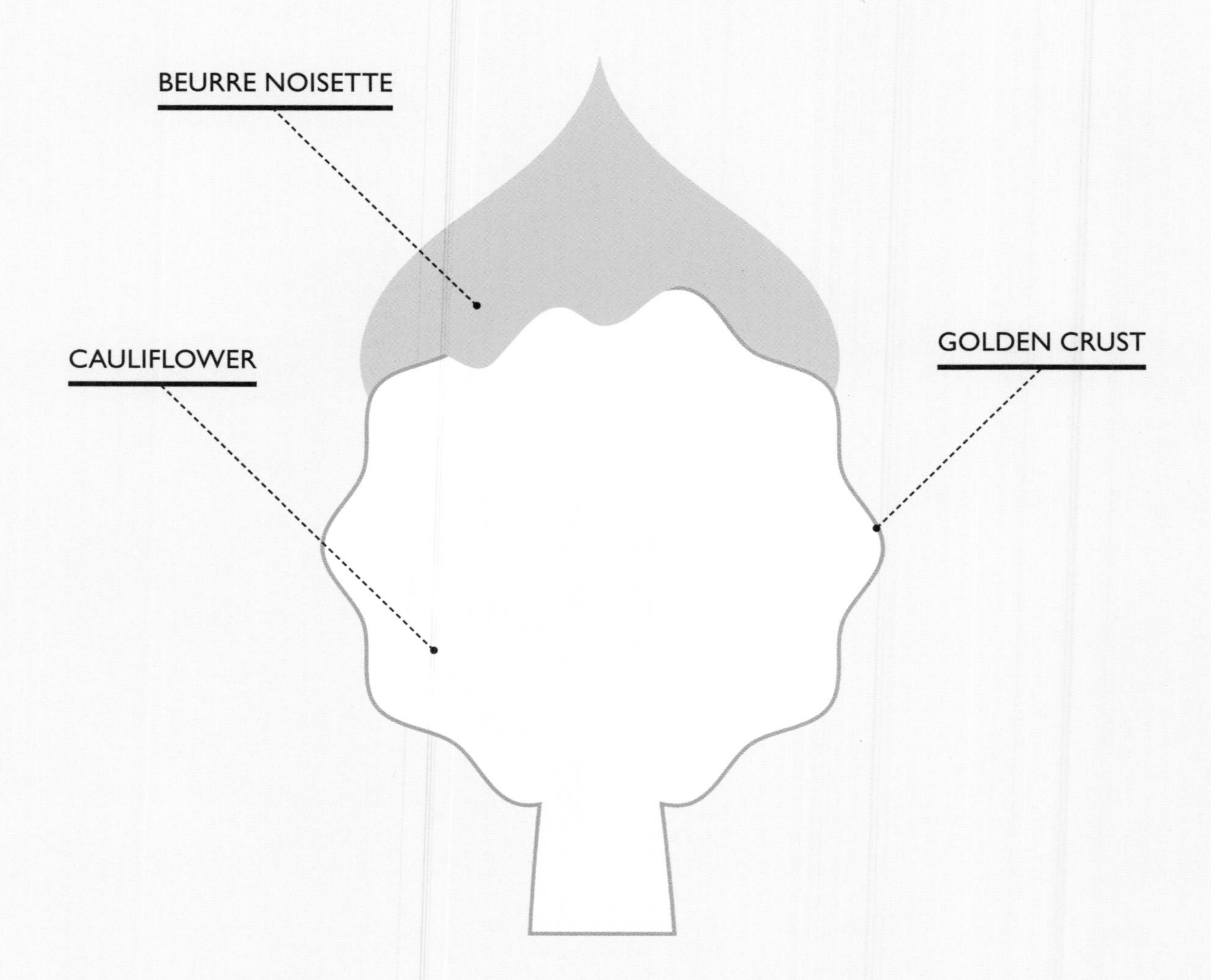

WHAT IS IT?
Cauliflower cooked whole in the oven, regularly basted with melted butter

TIME TO MAKE
Preparation: 10 minutes
Cooking: 1 hour to 1 hour 15 minutes

TRICKY ASPECT
Browning: the cauliflower must not burn

IT'S READY . . .
When the cauliflower is very dark on the outside and tender in the middle.

TO ACCOMPANY
A leg of lamb, rabbit with mustard (page 210), coulibiac (page 174), crayfish à la nage (page 144), turbot bonne femme (page 156)

HOW DO PLANTS GET TENDER?
The structure of plants is characterized by cell walls that provide rigidity. During cooking over 160°F, the cell walls break down and the vegetable softens.

Learn

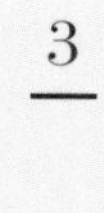

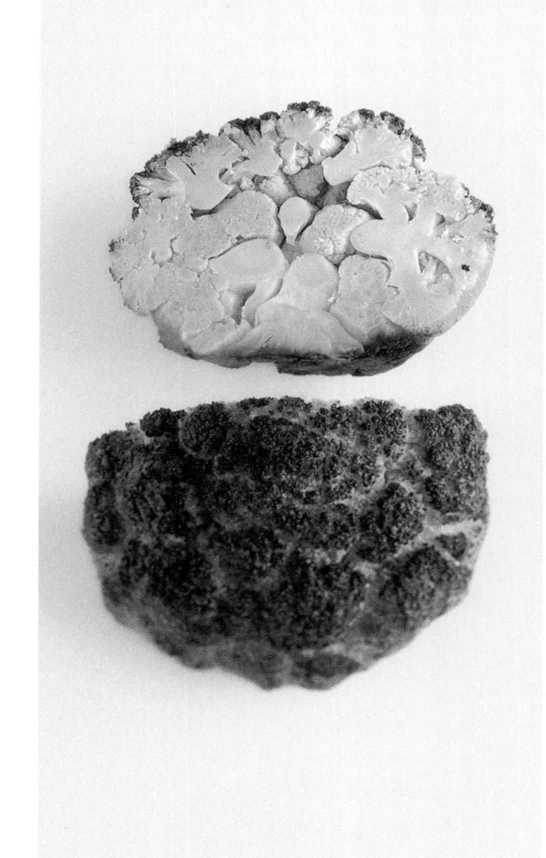

SERVES 4

ROAST CAULIFLOWER

1 cauliflower (about 2 lb 3 oz)
6 tablespoons butter, softened

SEASONING

1 teaspoon fine salt

1 Preheat the oven to 400°F. Cut the stem off the cauliflower and remove the green leaves so that it sits flat. Clean by rubbing with moist paper towels.

2 Put the cauliflower in a small baking dish or an ovenproof skillet. Cover the entire surface of the cauliflower with the butter and season with salt. Transfer to the oven.

3 Roast until the cauliflower is tender, 1 hour to 1 hour 15 minutes, basting it with the butter every 10–15 minutes. Slice at the table.

GLAZED

BRUSSELS SPROUTS

Understand

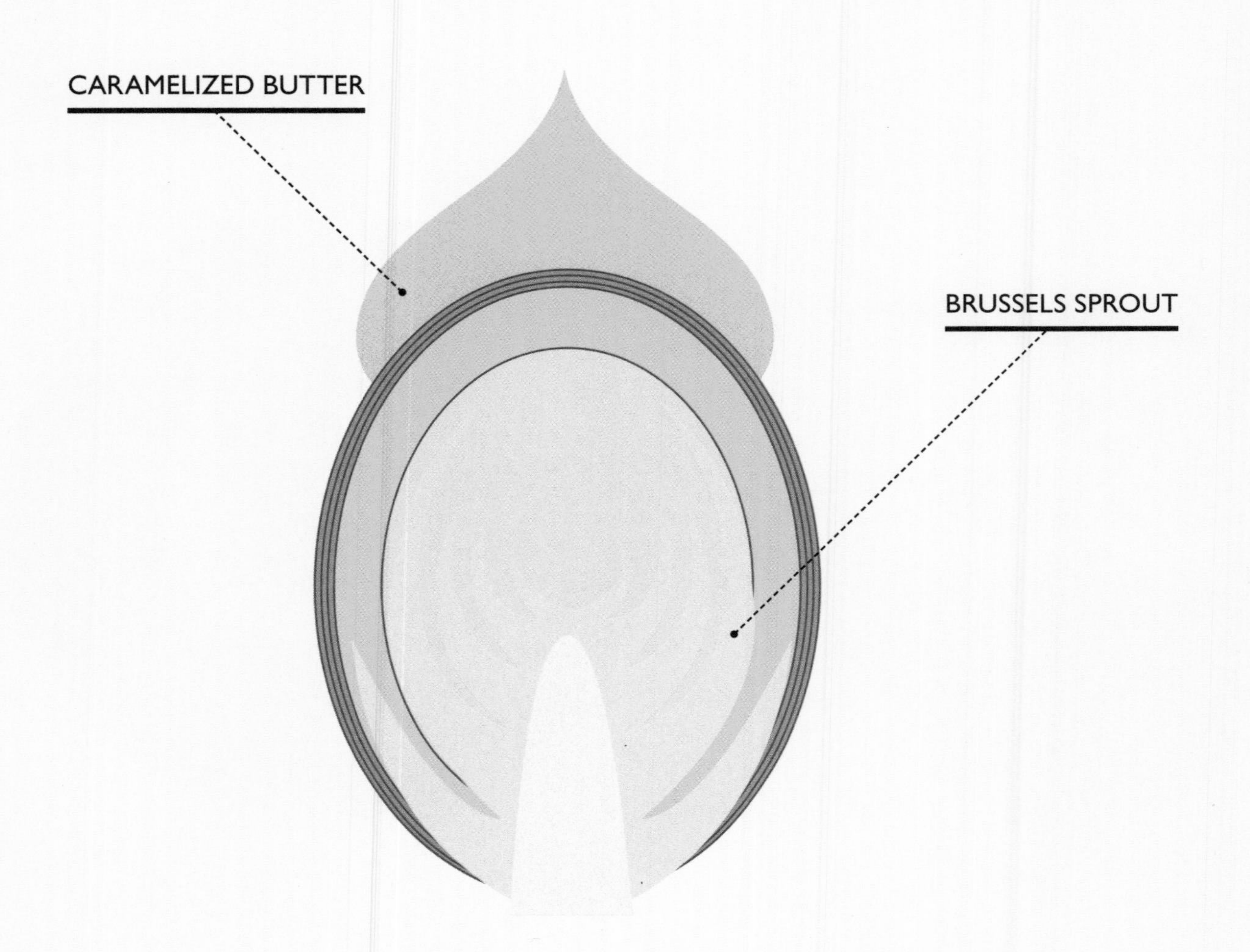

WHAT IS IT?
Brussels sprouts braised, then browned in butter and sugar with hazelnuts

TIME TO MAKE
Preparation: 25 minutes
Cooking: 25 minutes

VARIATION
With cooked and shelled chestnuts (don't roast them)

TRICKY ASPECT
Glazing the hazelnuts: they become bitter if this step is too long

TECHNIQUE TO MASTER
Toasting nuts (page 281)

IT'S READY . . .
When the sprouts are very shiny.

TO ACCOMPANY
Roast pork

WHY DO WE USE THE TERM "GLAZING"?
The sugar and the butter mix to slowly form a viscous and shiny base that coats the nuts and sprouts like a glaze.

SERVES 4

GLAZED BRUSSELS SPROUTS

1 lb 2 oz small brussels sprouts
1 teaspoon fine salt
1 tablespoon butter

GLAZED HAZELNUTS

½ cup hazelnuts
2 tablespoons butter
1 tablespoon sugar

SEASONING

fine salt
freshly ground black pepper (6 turns)

1 Remove the outer leaves of the sprouts and cut the stems level with the bottom of the sprouts. Wash and drain.

2 Put the sprouts and the salt in a saucepan of boiling water. Reduce the heat and simmer, covered, for 10–15 minutes, until the sprouts are easily pierced with the point of a knife.

3 Toast the hazelnuts in a hot dry skillet until browned in places. Chop them roughly with a knife. Drain the brussels sprouts.

4 Melt the 2 tablespoons of butter with the sugar in a skillet over medium heat. Add the hazelnuts and stir to coat. Cook for about 3 minutes, stirring occasionally, until the nuts are shiny and have browned a little.

5 Add the brussels sprouts and 1 tablespoon of the butter. Stir until the sprouts are very hot. Add salt to taste, and season with pepper.

ASPARAGUS
WITH SABAYON

Understand

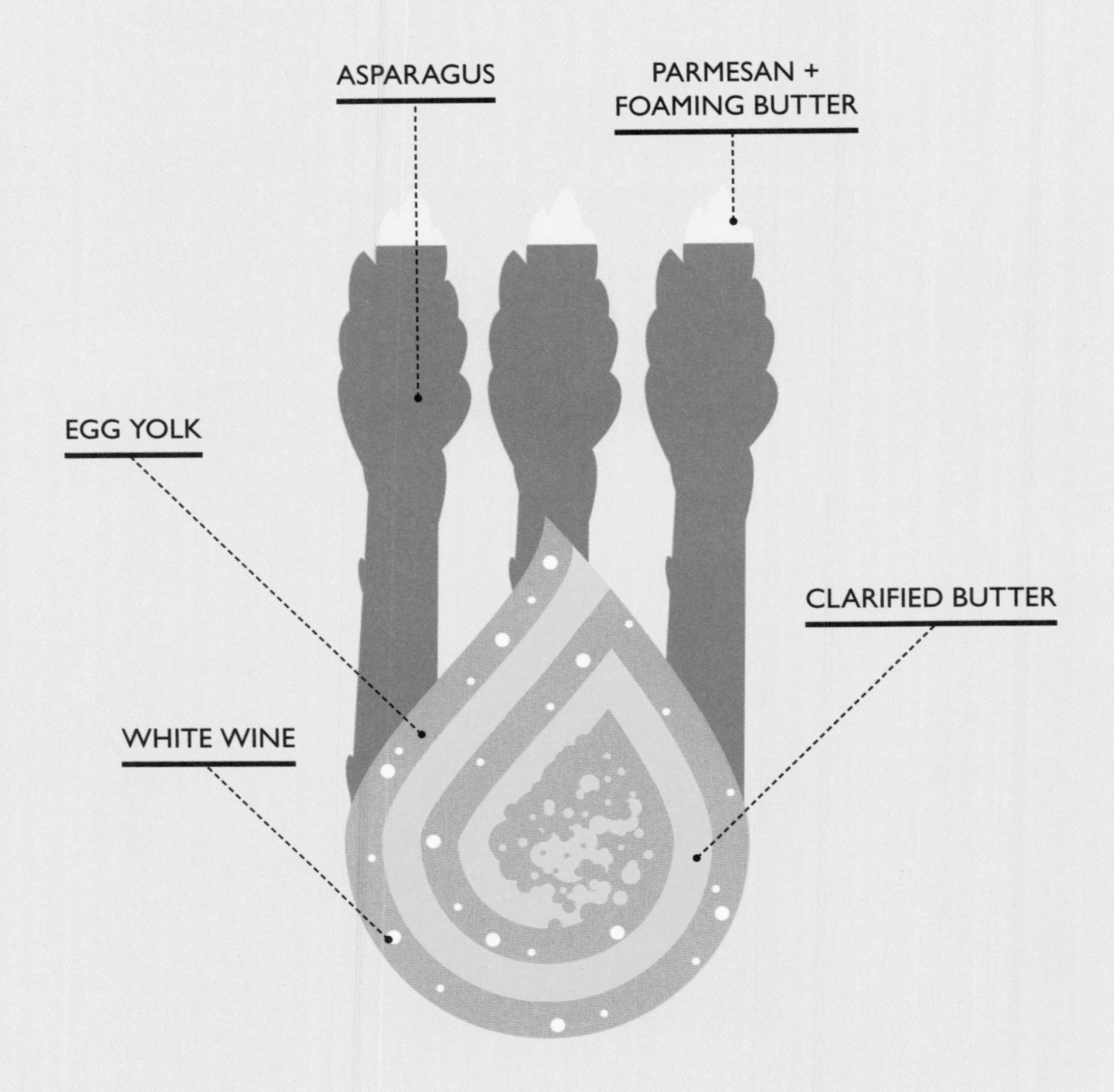

WHAT IS IT?
Poached asparagus, pan-fried in foaming butter with Parmesan, served with an emulsion of egg yolks, white wine, and butter

TIME TO MAKE
Preparation: 35 minutes
Cooking: 15 minutes

EQUIPMENT
Small sauté pan
Large saucepan
Two large skillets
Whisk

TERMS
– Sabayon: technique of whisking egg yolks with a liquid over heat.
– By extension: Italian dessert (thick custard with a wine base of sugar and egg yolk), sauce accompaniment (for asparagus, etc.).

DERIVATIVE OF SABAYON
Hollandaise sauce (page 30)

USES OF SABAYON
To accompany fish and shellfish

TECHNIQUE TO MASTER
Making clarified butter (page 51)

TIP
Use a small sauté pan to make whisking easier, otherwise the egg yolks will coagulate too quickly without increasing in volume.

IT'S READY . . .
When the asparagus is tender and the sauce light.

HOW DOES THE EMULSION TRIPLE IN VOLUME?
By whisking, air is incorporated and the sabayon becomes foamy.

Learn

SERVES 4

1 ASPARAGUS

1½ tablespoons Parmesan cheese
24 thick green asparagus spears (about 3 lb 5 oz)
2 tablespoons coarse sea salt
(2 tablespoons per 4 cups water)
4 tablespoons butter
freshly ground black pepper (2 turns)

2 LEMON SABAYON

11 tablespoons clarified butter (page 51)
1 lemon
5 egg yolks
2 tablespoons white wine
1 teaspoon fine salt
pinch of cayenne pepper

Making asparagus with sabayon

1 Keep the clarified butter warm (about 100°F) in a hot water bath over very low heat. Squeeze the lemon. Grate the Parmesan. Cut 1¼–1½ inches off the bottom of the asparagus spears and discard, then wash the spears.

2 Bring a large saucepan of water to a boil and add the coarse sea salt. Cook the asparagus in the boiling water for 8–10 minutes, until tender. Drain.

3 In a sauté pan off the heat, whisk together the egg yolks and white wine. Cook over low heat, whisking constantly, for 3–5 minutes to thicken the sabayon: it should be creamy and foamy.

4 Remove from the heat and, still whisking, add the clarified butter to the sabayon in a thin, steady trickle. Season with the salt and add the cayenne pepper, then stir. Cover and set aside at room temperature.

5 Divide the 4 tablespoons butter between two skillets over high heat. Divide the asparagus between the pans, coat them with the butter, and cover them with Parmesan.

6 Spoon the foaming butter over the asparagus. Season with pepper. Reheat the sabayon over very low heat, whisking constantly. Add the lemon juice to the sabayon and adjust the seasoning. Serve the asparagus with the sabayon to one side.

PORCINI RISOTTO

Understand

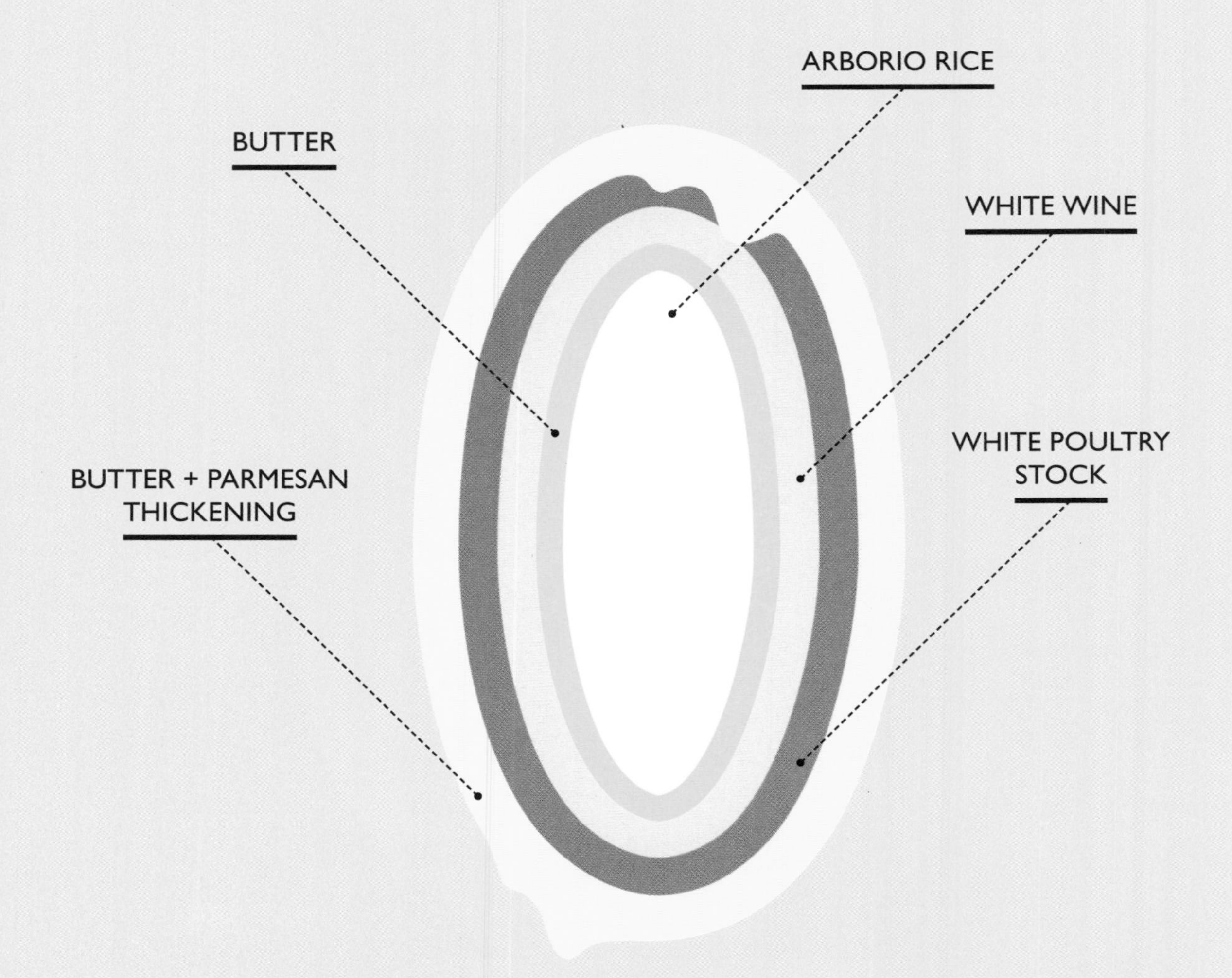

WHAT IS IT?

Short-grain rice sautéed until pearly in butter with onions, deglazed with white wine, then cooked in stock, all flavored with porcini mushrooms, and thickened with butter and Parmesan

TIME TO MAKE

Preparation: 50 minutes
Soaking: 25 minutes
Cooking: 25 minutes

EQUIPMENT

4-inch ring mold
Small and medium saucepans
Nonstick skillet
Ladle

VARIATION

Risotto Milanese: replace the mushrooms with a large pinch of saffron soaked in a ladleful of the stock, added a few minutes before the end of cooking

TRICKY ASPECT

The end of cooking: the rice must be slightly al dente

TECHNIQUES TO MASTER

Making Parmesan tuiles (page 276)
Crushing garlic (page 280)
Mincing (page 280)

TIP

The stock and the rice must simmer at the same intensity for the stock to be well absorbed by the rice.

IT'S READY . . .

When the risotto is creamy and the rice is still slightly al dente.

WHY NOT WASH THE RICE?

To avoid washing away the starch on the surface of the rice grains, which is necessary for the sauce to thicken.

SERVES 4

1 RISOTTO

1 onion
4 cups white poultry stock (page 10)
1 tablespoon butter
1¼ cups risotto rice (Carnaroli or Arborio)
½ cup white wine
fine salt
freshly ground black pepper

2 TO THICKEN

2 oz Parmesan cheese
4 tablespoons butter

3 LACE TUILES

¾ oz Parmesan cheese

4 PORCINI MUSHROOMS

1 garlic clove
¾ oz dried porcini mushrooms
1 cup hot water
1 tablespoon butter
¼ teaspoon fine salt
freshly ground black pepper (3 turns)

Making porcini risotto

1 Finely grate all the Parmesan. Peel, de-germ, and crush the garlic. Peel and mince the onion. Soak the mushrooms in the hot water for 15–30 minutes, until they are supple. Squeeze them over the bowl. Strain the soaking water and mix with the poultry stock. Rinse the mushrooms, then dry with paper towels. Bring the stock to a simmer in a small saucepan.

2 To make the tuiles, heat a small nonstick skillet over medium heat (3 minutes). Remove from the heat, place a 4-inch ring mold in the middle and spread 2 tablespoons of Parmesan inside it. Remove the ring, then return the pan to the heat until the cheese is lightly golden, 1–2 minutes. Remove from the heat and carefully unstick the tuile using a thin spatula. Repeat three more times to make a total of 4 tuiles (without preheating the pan).

3 To prepare the mushrooms, melt the 1 tablespoon butter in a saucepan over medium heat. Fry the mushrooms for a few minutes, stirring regularly. Stir in the garlic, then cook until fragrant (30 seconds). Add the salt and pepper, and a ladleful of the stock, then cook for 2 minutes. Remove from the pan.

4 For the risotto, melt 1 tablespoon of butter in the medium saucepan over medium heat. Fry the onion for 2 minutes, stirring, until translucent. Add the rice and stir frequently for 2 minutes. Pour in the white wine and reduce until dry.

5 Add a ladleful of the simmering stock and stir constantly. Wait until it is absorbed, then add another ladleful. Repeat this procedure until all the stock has been incorporated. Add the mushrooms after 10 minutes.

6 Remove from the heat, then gently stir in 4 tablespoons of butter and the remaining Parmesan. Season with salt and pepper. Serve on plates decorated with a tuile.

SQUID INK RISOTTO

Understand

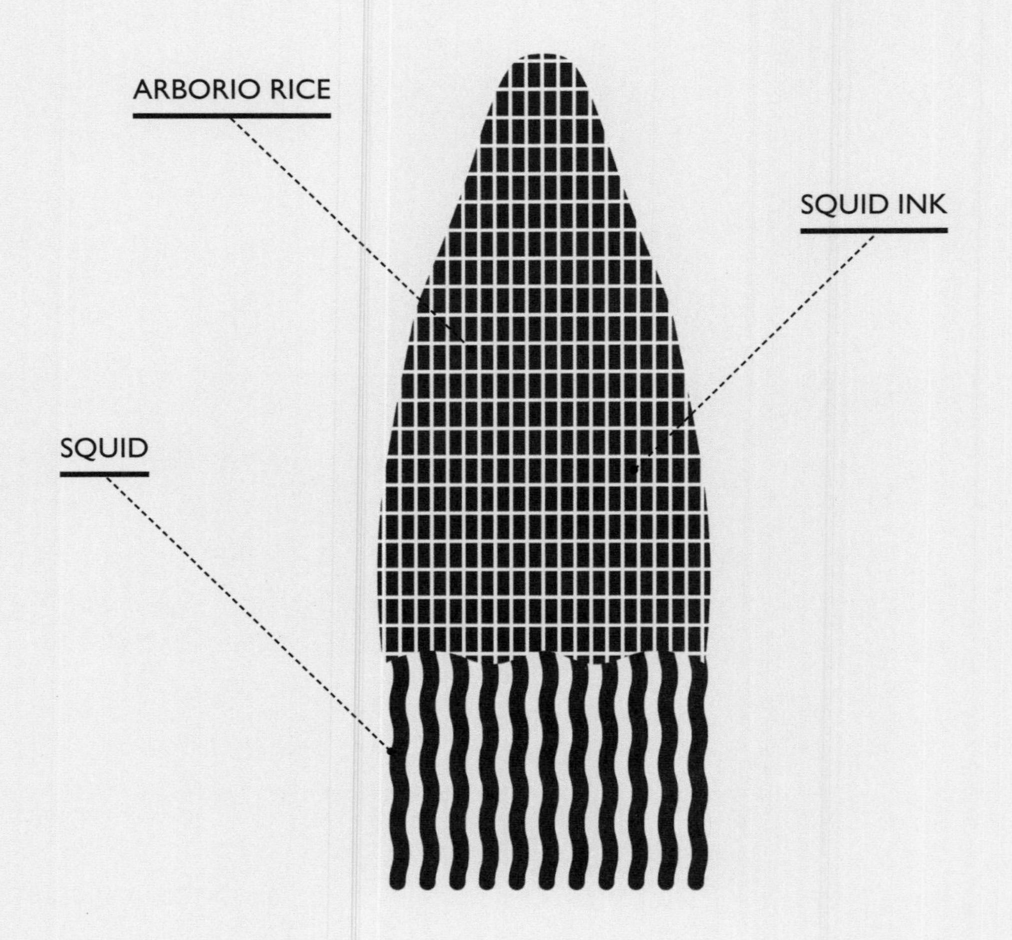

WHAT IS IT?

Short-grain rice sautéed until pearly in butter with onions, deglazed with white wine, then cooked in a squid ink broth

TIME TO MAKE

Preparation: 40 minutes
Cooking: 15 minutes

EQUIPMENT

Two saucepans
Nonstick skillet

VARIATION

Buy whole cuttlefish and set aside the ink sac when cleaning the cuttlefish. You'll need twice as many cuttlefish for this much ink. (The flesh of cuttlefish is less delicate than that of squid.)

TRICKY ASPECT

The end of cooking: the rice must be slightly al dente

TECHNIQUES TO MASTER

Crushing garlic (page 280)
Mincing (page 280)
Reducing a sauce (page 283)

TIP

The broth and the rice must simmer at the same intensity for the broth to be well absorbed by the rice.

IT'S READY . . .

When the risotto is creamy and the rice is still slightly al dente.

WHY ADD THE BROTH GRADUALLY?

To add just the right amount, depending on how the rice absorbs the liquid.

Learn

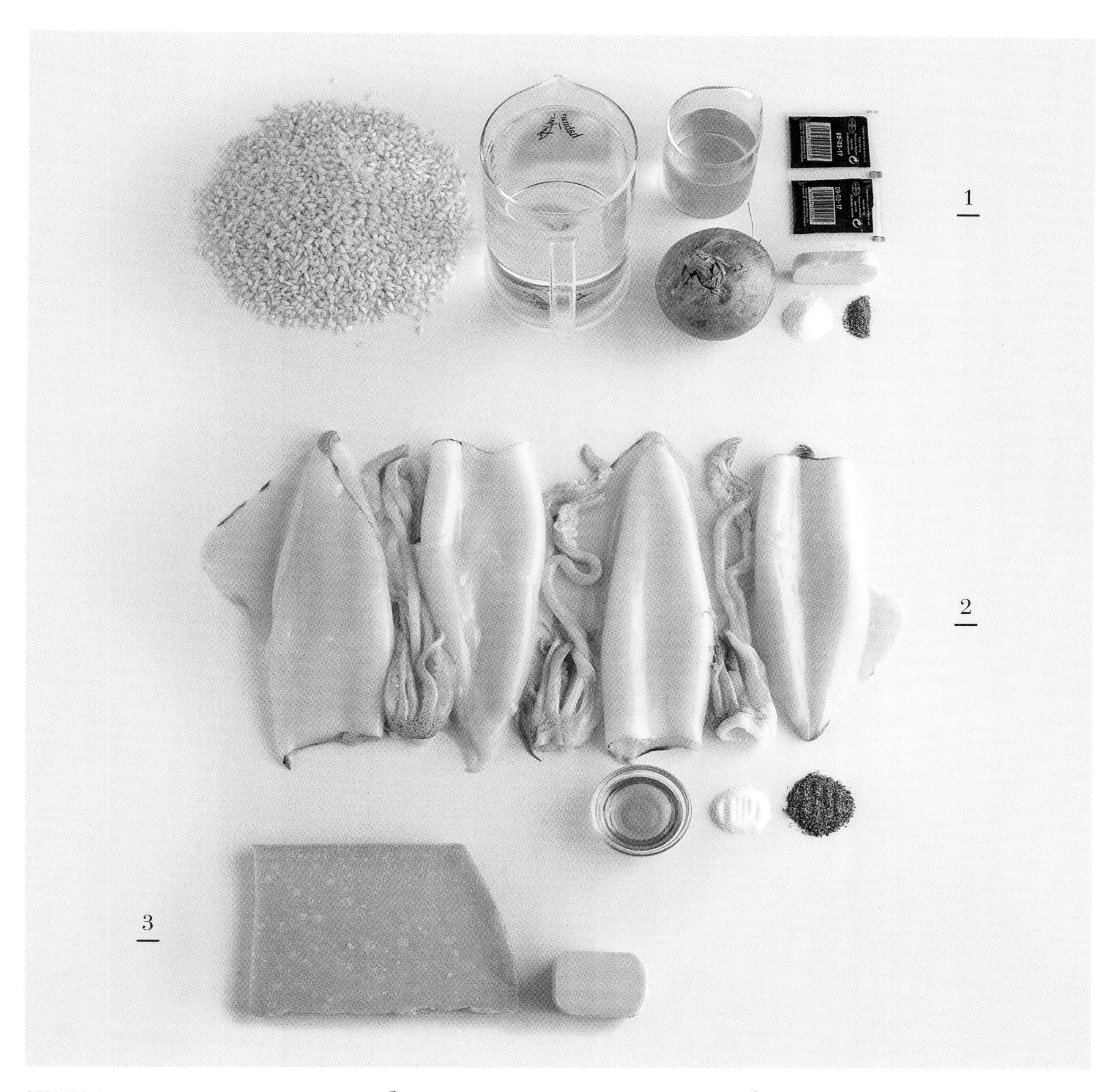

SERVES 4

1 RISOTTO

4 ¼ cups water
1 yellow onion
1 tablespoon butter
1 ¼ cups risotto rice (Carnaroli or Arborio)
½ cup white wine
two 4g packets of squid ink
½ teaspoon fine salt
freshly ground black pepper (3 turns)

2 GARNISH

4 squid (8 inches long), cleaned
½ teaspoon fine salt
1 tablespoon olive oil
freshly ground black pepper (6 turns)

3 TO THICKEN

2 oz Parmesan cheese
4 tablespoons butter

Making squid ink risotto

1 Detach the squid bodies and set aside half the tentacles, reserving the rest for another use. Put the bodies in a saucepan with the water and the salt, then bring to a boil and simmer until the water is fragrant, about 2 minutes. Remove the squid bodies but keep the broth simmering.

2 Finely grate the Parmesan cheese. Peel and mince the onion.

3 Rinse the squid bodies, cut down one side and open them out flat, then dry them with paper towels. Crosshatch both sides of the bodies with the point of a knife.

4 Cut the bodies into strips about ¾ inch wide.

5 Melt the butter for the risotto in a saucepan over medium heat. Fry the onion with the tentacles for 2 minutes, stirring, until the onion is translucent.

6 Add the rice and stir frequently for 2 minutes. Pour in the wine and reduce until dry. Add a ladleful of simmering broth and stir constantly. Wait until it is absorbed, then add another ladleful. Repeat this procedure until the rice is cooked but still al dente.

7 Halfway through cooking, mix the squid ink into a ladleful of the broth and add to the risotto. Mix well.

8 Remove from the heat and gently stir in the 4 tablespoons of butter and the Parmesan cheese. Season with salt and pepper.

9 Heat the olive oil in a skillet over very high heat. Add the strips of squid and cook for 1 minute, until they curl slightly. Adjust the seasoning.

10 Serve the risotto on a plate with the sautéed squid on top. Season with pepper.

CHAPTER 3

ILLUSTRATED GLOSSARY

SERVING A SAUCE OR ACCOMPANIMENT

PLATING

DECORATING

PREPARING MEAT

PREPARING FISH

CUTTING

BASICS

COOKING

UTENSILS

SERVING A SAUCE OR ACCOMPANIMENT

1 SERVING A SAUCE

A. In a comma
With the spoon perpendicular to the plate, drop a dollop of sauce. Then, with the end of the spoon touching the plate, draw out the sauce to give it the shape of a comma.

B. Using a ring mold
Pour the sauce in the middle of the ring, arrange the other elements of the recipe on top and remove the ring just before serving.

C. Simple, using a spoon
Let the sauce run out as you move the spoon quickly across the plate. If the sauce is very runny, serve it in a small vessel on the side.

2 SERVING A PURÉE

A. Using a ring mold
Spread the purée in the middle of the ring, smooth the top with the back of a spoon, and remove the ring.

B. In quenelles
Dip two spoons in a bowl of hot water, take a little of the purée with one spoon, slide the bowl of the second spoon into the first, pushing the purée so that it ends up all in the second spoon. Repeat five to ten times, moving from spoon to spoon, to create a lovely quenelle. Moisten the spoons before starting each new quenelle.

C. Smeared with a spoon
Drop the purée from a spoon, then with the back of the spoon touching the plate, draw a line through the middle of the purée.

3 SERVING AN ACCOMPANIMENT

It must be visible but not dominate. Typically, the sauce is plated first, then the main dish, then the accompaniment.

A. In a line
Arrange the accompaniment and the main element in parallel lines.

B. In a curve
Make the accompaniment follow the curve of the plate.

4 SERVING WITH A PASTRY BAG

Cut off the end of the bag and slide the tip inside, creasing the bag around it to secure it. Fill the bag and twist the end closed, tip pointing upward, until the mixture starts to come out. Hold the bag perpendicular to and above the plate, and push gently to create a swirled mound or rosette.

PLATING

1 USING A RING MOLD

Traditional plate, clean and precise.

The ring allows soft preparations to be molded (purées, tartar sauce), giving them a clean form and height, or to serve recipes in a pile, setting the different preparations that compose the dish on top of one another.

Fill the entire bottom of the ring but not necessarily its whole height. Pack it in using the back of a spoon, then remove the ring.

2 IN A LINE

Very modern plate, very white.

Create a ribbon an inch or two wide with the components of the dish, along the whole length of the plate, using a ruler or a piece of cardboard as a guide.

3 CREATING HEIGHT AND VOLUME

Generous and spectacular plate.

Pile up the differents elements of the dish. For example, a sauce molded in a ring, a piece of fish, and a crown of salad.

4 GRAPHIC

Geometric plate, refined.

Arrange the elements using the geometry of the plate. Compose clean forms and lines: half-moons (A), straight lines (B), a circle facing a straight line, and so on.

5 USING CONTRASTS

Contrasting colors: black olives on white fish.

Contrast in composition: an element with height (fish) versus an element spread out (shrimp).

6 STRUCTURED VS. UNSTRUCTURED

A. Structured
Each element arranged on its own side.

B. Unstrucutured
Disordered elements.

7 THE PRINCIPLES OF COMPOSITION

Start by imagining the final plate. Perhaps draw it, to plan its composition better.

Use the whole plate without overloading it; plan for empty spaces.

Try to create combinations of textures, colors, and temperatures that will please the eye and the palate.

DECORATING

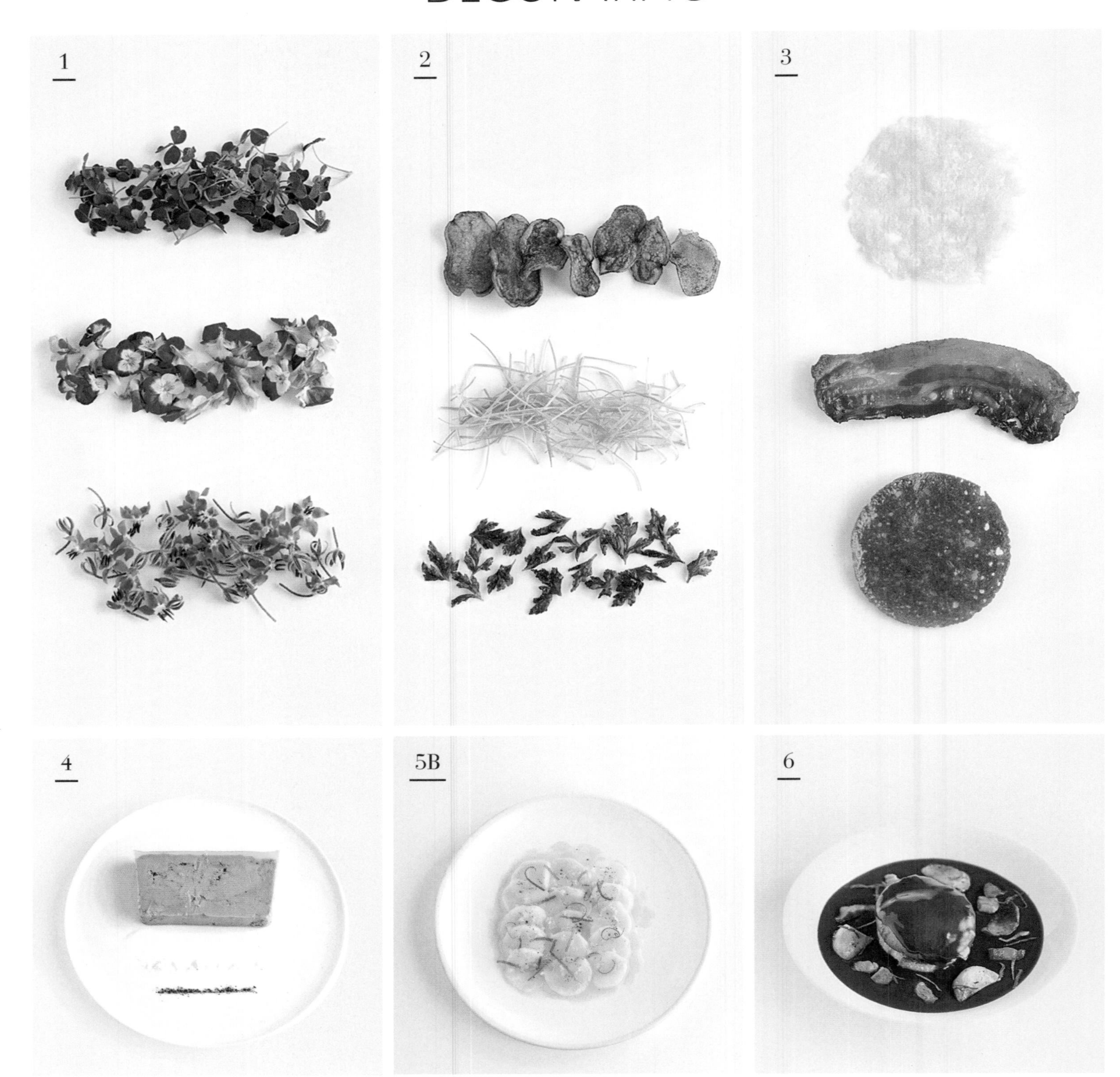

1 FLOWERS AND SPROUTS

Edible flowers (borage, pansy, nasturtium, etc.) or sprouts can be added to a dish to provide color and freshness. Use as small finishing touches, so as not to upset the balance of tastes on a plate. Arrange them carefully, using tweezers.

2 THIN FRIED FOOD

Blue potato chips
Shave blue potatoes into paper-thin slices using a mandoline. Wash, dry, and fry the slices for a few minutes in hot oil until dry, but not for too long (or they will brown). Season with salt.

Leek chips
Remove the overlapping leaves from the white portion only. Cut in fine julienne and fry for a few seconds in ¾–1¼ inches of very hot oil. Season with salt.

Fried parsley
Fry parsley leaves in 1¼ inches of very hot oil for a few seconds, until crisp, but not too long (they darken quickly). Season with salt.

3 TUILES

Parmesan
Heat a nonstick skillet. Remove from the heat, place a ring mold in the middle, and spread grated Parmesan inside it. Remove the ring and return to the heat until the cheese is melted and lightly golden. Remove from the heat, then carefully lift the tuile using a thin spatula.

Bacon
Place thin slices of bacon in a large skillet. Set a weight on top. Cook over medium heat for 3–4 minutes on each side.

Buckwheat crepes
Cut a circle from a crepe using a cookie cutter. Brush with melted butter, then bake for 10 minutes at 360°F.

4 SALT AND PEPPER

Fleur de sel and freshly ground black pepper are the simplest ways to make a dish more appetizing, and add texture and contrast to the composition of a plate.

5 ZESTS

Microplane
Texture almost intangible in the mouth; light decorative element.

French-style zester
Thicker and longer pieces of zest for more crunch and more obvious color.

7

8A

8B

9

6 HERBS

Scattering aromatic minced herbs over a dish adds contrasting green tones that accentuate the dish.

7 DROPS

Syrup
Reduce balsamic vinegar to a syrupy consistency. Let it cool. Dot on the plate using a small spoon (let a drop run off without letting the spoon touch the plate) or a pipette.

Purée
Make a very smooth green bean or carrot purée and add using a pastry bag with a small tip.

8 THINLY SLICED VEGETABLES

Cut very thin slices of vegetables using a mandoline then soak them for 10 minutes in an ice water bath to give them crunch and, depending on the vegetable, make them curl a little.

A. Decoration using height
Gather the slices into a "bouquet" between your hands, then place on the plate.

B. Flat decoration
Arrange the slices in a single layer, as for carpaccio.

9 FOAM

Foam a creamy cooking liquid (or another liquid containing a protein—egg white, gelatin, or stock) in a high, narrow container, using a hand-held blender. Spoon the foam over the dish (soup, nage, fish fillet, etc.).

10 THE PRINCIPLES OF DECORATION

The decorative elements should add elegance to a dish, giving it depth and a note of sophistication. Moderation is the key; the dish itself must be respected and honored.

PREPARING MEAT

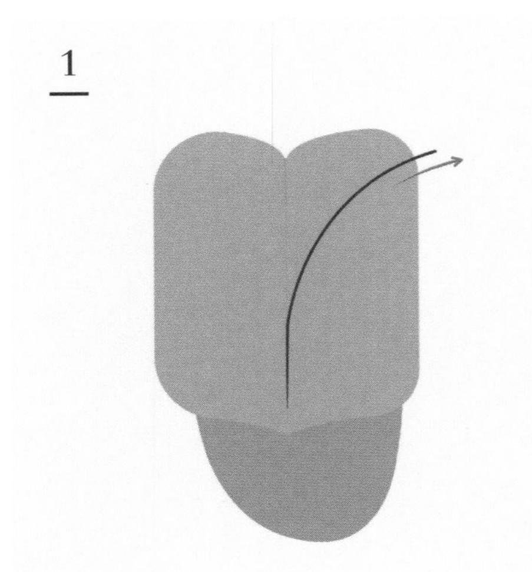

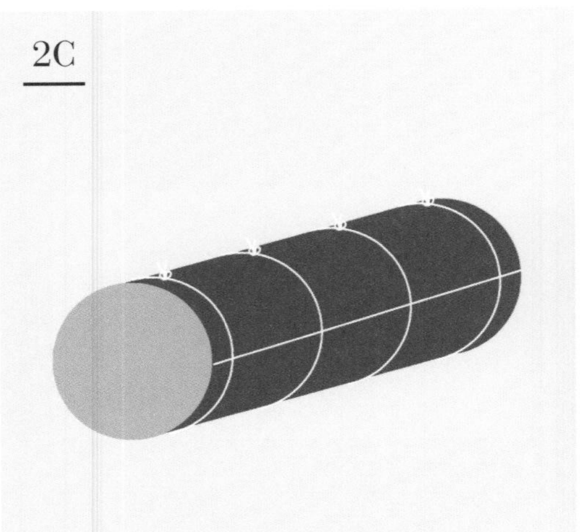

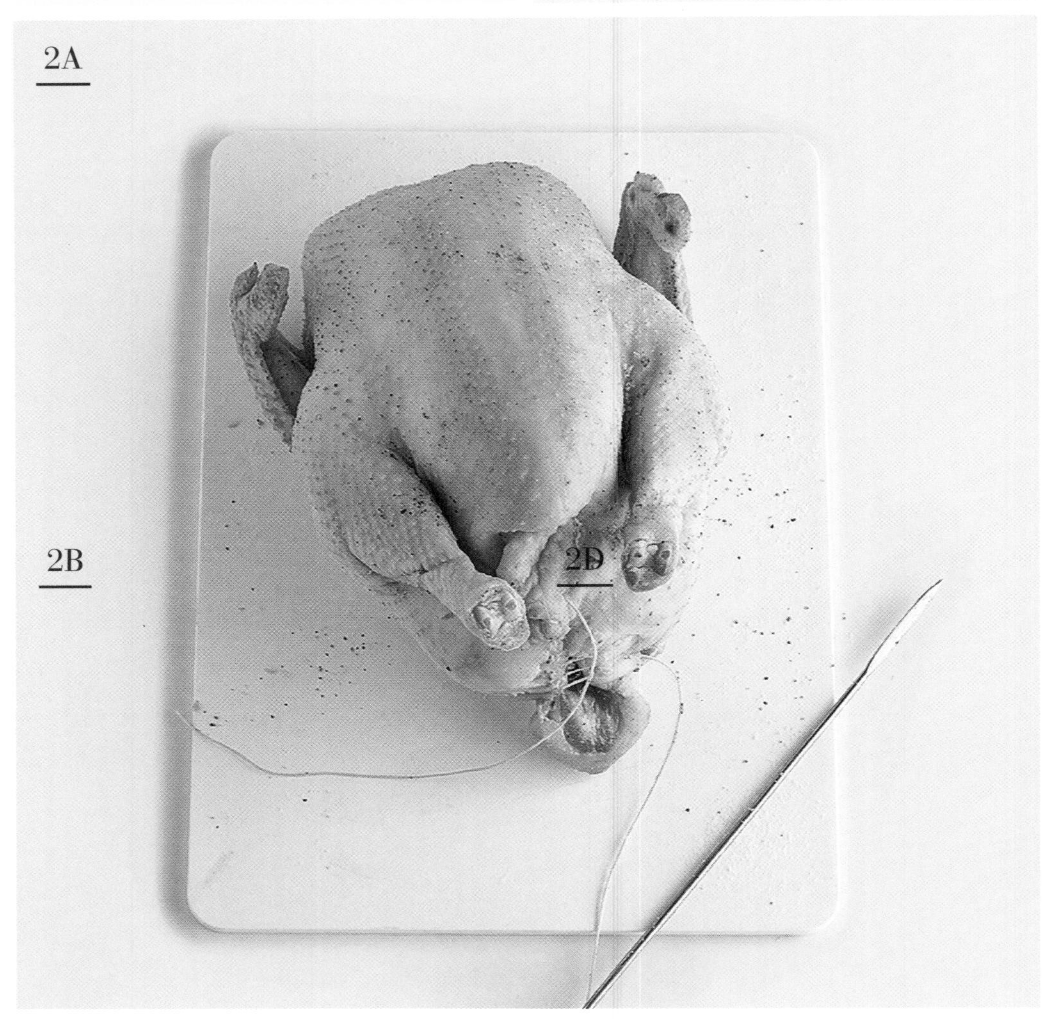

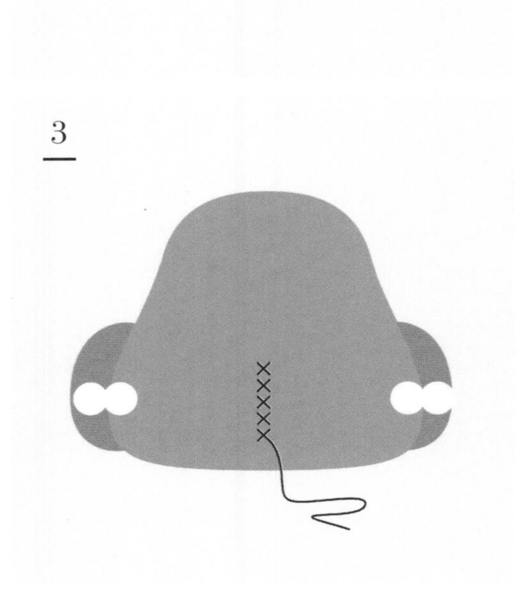

1 DEVEINING FOIE GRAS

Removing the veins from lobes of foie gras. Separate the large piece from the small and gently devein the liver with your fingers or with the rounded handle of a spoon. Open up each piece by cutting down the middle and separating the two cut edges. Remove the first vein at the surface. Remove the second, deeper vein by carefully cutting the liver.

Deveining prevents the texture of the veins from affecting the dish and also makes a better presentation as the red filaments would still be visible even after cooking. It is not necessary to devein foie gras for pan-frying.

2 TYING AND TRUSSING

Tying up a roast or holding the limbs of poultry in place (trussing) allows for neat presentation and uniform cooking. Trussing poultry increases the cooking time by 25 percent because the hot air penetrates the flesh more slowly.

A. AND B. TYING A ROAST
Wind the string around every $\frac{3}{4}$ inch. Wind the first piece of string under one end of the roast. Tie off the two ends securely with a double knot. Continue in this way the entire length of the roast.

C. AND D. TRUSSING STUFFED POULTRY
Stuffed poultry must be sewn up to prevent the stuffing from falling out during cooking. Thread a trussing needle with a length of kitchen string. Sew the opening shut tightly with crossed stitches. Tie off with a double knot.

3 FLATTENING MEAT

Using a meat tenderizer, a rolling pin, or the bottom of a saucepan, hit the meat to flatten it uniformly and tenderize it by breaking some of the muscle fibers.

4 GRADES OF MEAT

PRIME
Tender pieces: rib-eye steak, top round steak, tenderloin steak, skirt steak, hanger steak, sirloin steak, and tri-tip for beef; tenderloin, round, and rump for veal; and chops, leg, and ribs for lamb.

Cooking style: short (pan-frying, broiling) to avoid drying out the meat.

CHOICE OR SELECT
Firm pieces, rich in collagen (tendons): short ribs, brisket, chuck tender, chuck roast, bottom round, and chuck for beef; shoulder and chuck for veal; and shoulder for lamb.

Cooking style: long, to break down the collagen and tenderize the meat.

PREPARING FISH

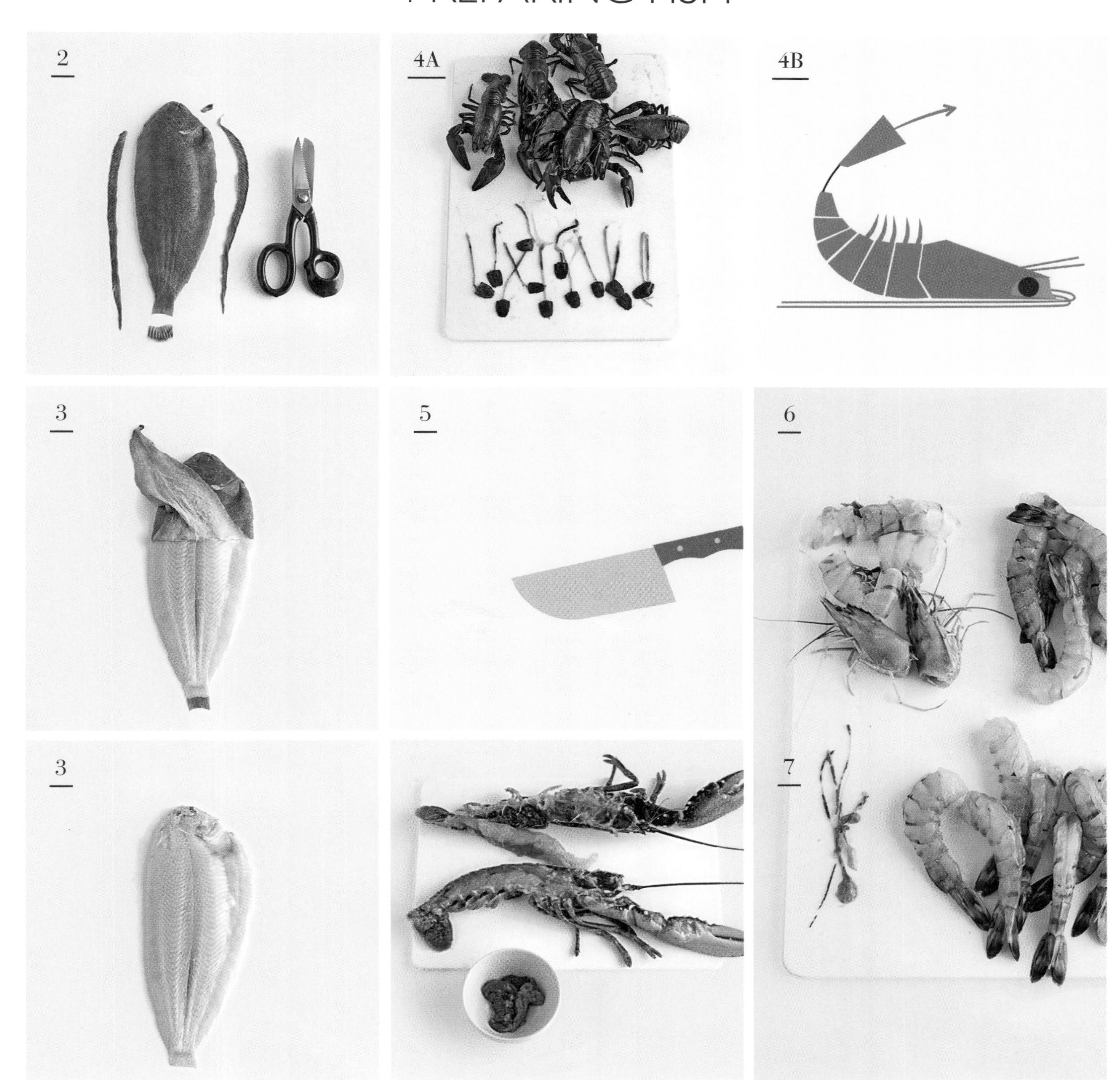

1 DRESSING

Preparing a fish (scaling, cutting off fins, gutting, etc.) before cooking.

2 REMOVING FINS

Starting from the tail and working toward the head, remove all the fins using kitchen shears.

3 SKINNING

Using a knife, lift a sizeable piece of the skin by cutting between the skin and the flesh at the tail end. Hold the tail with one hand and pull the skin toward the head with the other. Discard the skin.

4 DEVEINING CRAYFISH

A. Place the crayfish on a work surface with one hand on the head and legs. Pull gently on the center of the tail fin, twisting it left and right, and pulling.

B. The digestive tract will pull out attached to the tail.

5 SHELLING AND DEVEINING SHRIMP

Remove the head of the shrimp, remove the shell, and then pull out the black digestive tract, cutting along the back with the point of a paring knife.

6 CRUSHING FISH BONES

Roughly chop the spine (and frame), cutting each bone into three or four pieces, depending on size.

7 THE LOBSTER HEAD

This front part of the lobster is also called the cephalothorax. It contains the gravel pouch, the tomalley, and a black digestive tract on each side. Reserve the tomalley (creamy and greenish-gray when raw, red when cooked), to thicken sauces.

CUTTING

1 MINCING

Herbs: make a pile of the leaves, roll them up tight, then chop into tiny bits.

Shallots: cut into fine pieces.

2 FINELY CHOPPING (HERBS, GARLIC)

Chop into very small pieces using a chef's knife.

3 CRUSHING GARLIC

Press down firmly on a garlic clove with the flat of a knife, then peel, de-germ, and crush to a paste with the flat of a knife.

4 THINLY SLICING

Cut a vegetable in thin slices.

5 PEELING CITRUS FOR SEGMENTS

Cut off the two ends of the citrus fruit to the flesh, which gives it a stable base. Peel the sides in an arc using a paring knife, starting from the top. Give the fruit a rounded shape, without leaving any trace of peel or pith.

6 SUPREMING CITRUS

Separate the segments from their dividing membranes using a very sharp knife.

7 PEELING TOMATOES

Remove the skin of tomatoes by plunging them into boiling water for a few seconds, then refreshing them immediately in ice water. Or use a vegetable peeler made for soft fruits and vegetables.

8 ZESTING

Remove the fragrant, colored outer layer of citrus peels, either finely grated or pulled into long, thin slivers.

Microplane grater: this rasp-style tool grates the zest into very fine "snow."

French-style zester: the little holes on this zester are pulled across the peel to create thicker and longer pieces of zest.

9 CUTTING IN SCALLOPS

Cut slices on the bias (diagonally).

10 CRUSHING SPICES

Place seeds in a small skillet and crush them with the bottom of a saucepan.

BASICS

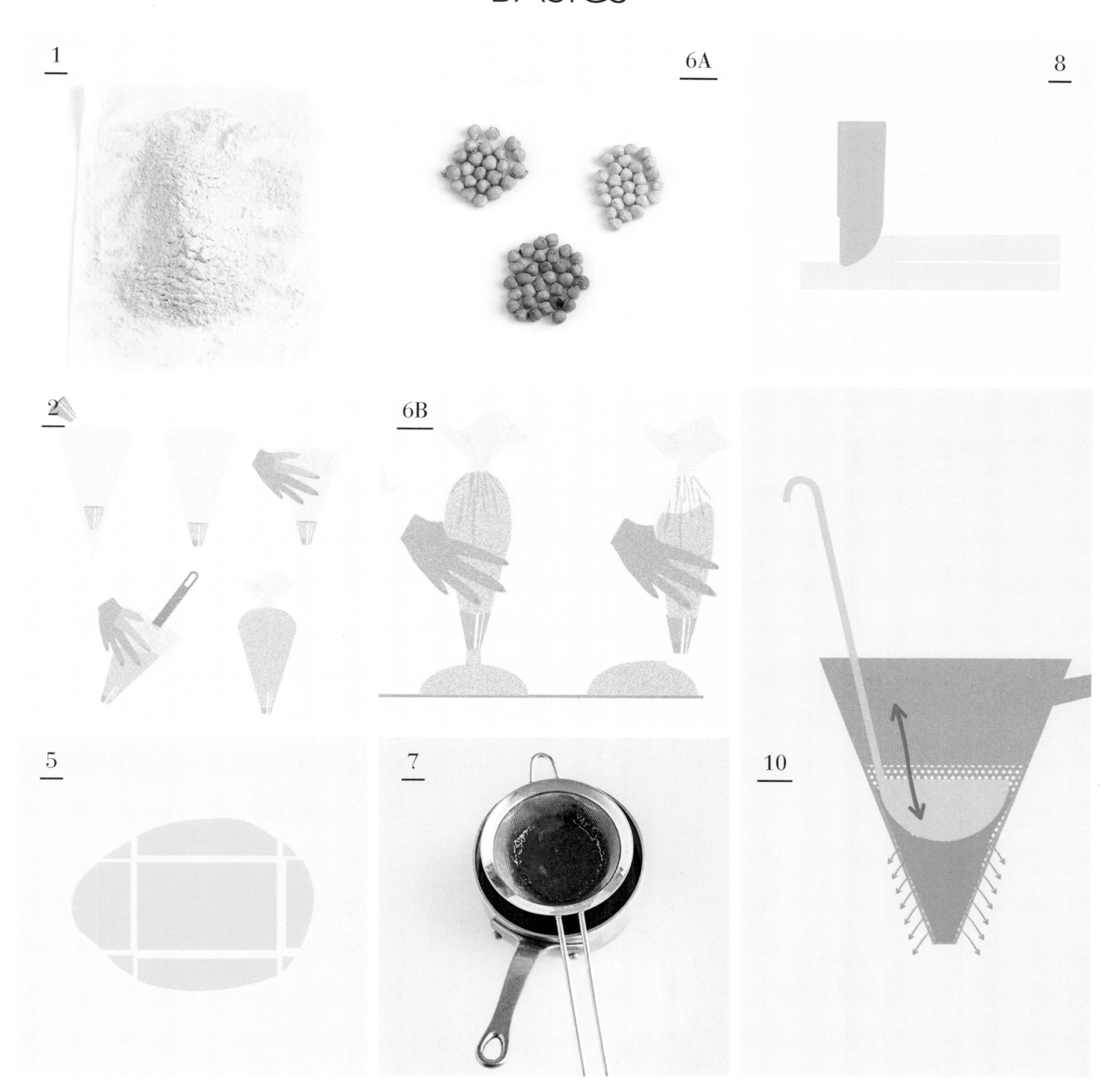

1 RUBBING IN BUTTER

Mix small pieces of butter into flour using fingertips. Coat each flour grain in butter until the color is off-white and the texture is sandy.

2 TOASTING NUTS

Toast nuts in a dry skillet over medium heat, stirring regularly, until they turn brown.

3 TOASTING FLOUR

– Heat flour in a dry skillet over medium heat, stirring constantly.

– Heat flour sprinkled on top of a mixture containing a sauce that needs thickening, in a baking dish, in a 360°F oven for 5–10 minutes, without stirring.

4 SCRAPING OUT

Use a dough scraper or silicone spatula to retrieve as much of the mixture as possible.

5 SEALING PASTRY EDGES

Brush the edges of the dough with water or glaze, then press lightly between two fingers so that they stay together during cooking.

6 PIPING

A. Cut the end off a (disposable plastic) pastry bag and slide in a tip. Crease the bag around it to hold it in place. Fill the bag with the mixture and twist the end of the bag closed, with the tip pointing upward.

B. Hold the bag perpendicular to the surface, ⅜ inch above it, and push. "Cut" the mixture with a quarter-turn, staying as close as possible.

7 STRAINING THROUGH A SIEVE

Pour a mixture into a sieve to obtain a smooth liquid and eliminate the inedible parts.

8 PUSHING THROUGH A SIEVE

Strain a mixture through a sieve while pushing hard on the sides with a ladle or spoon, to extract the maximum amount of liquid.

9 COVERING WITH PLASTIC WRAP

Place plastic wrap so that it touches the surface of the mixture, then press lightly to expel all the air. This preserves the food better.

10 TRIMMING

Give a regular shape to food by removing the unpresentable or inedible parts.

COOKING

1

4

9

2

5

10

3

6

1 MAILLARD REACTION

A chemical reaction between the proteins and sugars in foods. This reaction occurs as soon as there are no more water molecules at the surface (at 230–240°F). It manifests as browning and a powerful enrichment of the taste (aromatic roasted notes).

2 BROWNING

Gives color to a food being cooked. Heat the chosen fat in the cooking vessel. Carefully pat the food dry with paper towels. Cook each side of the food until it browns. Work in several batches if necessary.

3 ADDING FLOUR TO STEWS

Sprinkle a stew with flour before adding liquid, so that the sauce thickens by the end of cooking.

4 TRANSFERRING

Remove a piece of food from the cooking vessel, leaving behind the sauce, using a skimmer or slotted spoon.

5 SWEATING

Remove the water from a vegetable by heating it gently with a fat, avoiding any coloration.

6 STEAMING

Cook a vegetable slowly, covered, in its own juices, with a little butter or water.

7 FLAMBÉING

Douse a boiling preparation with alcohol and, still over the heat, light it on fire. Let the flame die down naturally.

8 USING A PROBE THERMOMETER

To monitor the core temperature of a food during cooking, insert a probe, making sure it lodges in the middle of the food and doesn't touch a bone.

9 THICKENING

Give body to a liquid by adding a thickening element (flour at the beginning of cooking, potato starch or egg yolk at the end).

10 WHISKING IN BUTTER

Incorporating butter into a sauce to increase its volume and creaminess. Dice cold butter and add gradually over medium heat while whisking or swirling the saucepan. Wait for the first pieces to be incorporated before adding the next.

COOKING

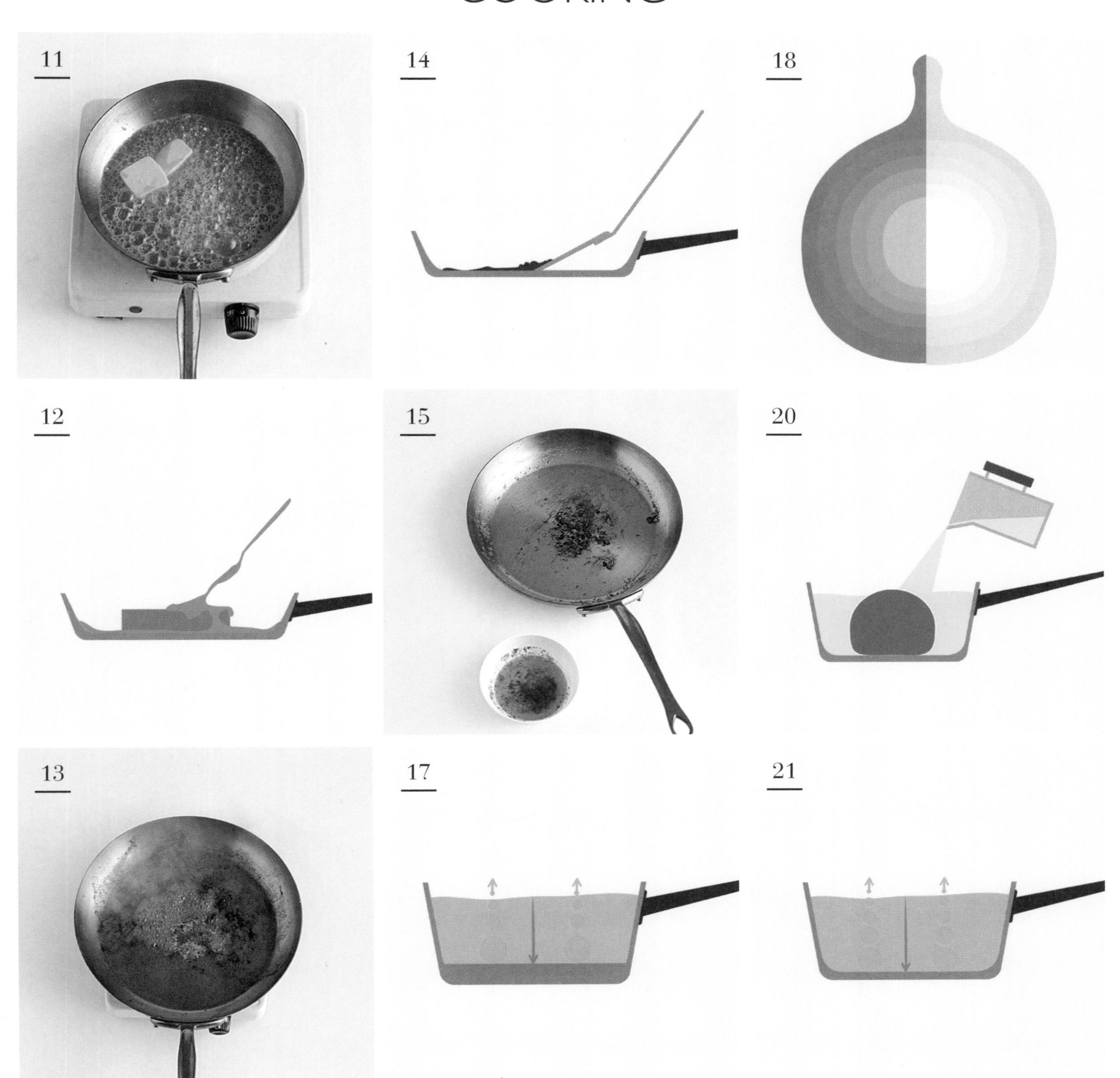

11 FOAMING BUTTER

When melting butter, micro-droplets of water in the fat are transformed into steam, creating bubbles, and thus foam. It can be used to baste a food during cooking and enrich it.

12 BASTING

Pouring a food's own fat or some melted butter over it to prevent it from drying out. Use a spoon or turkey baster. Baste as regularly as possible.

13 DEGLAZING

Liquefying caramelized pieces stuck to the bottom of a cooking vessel. If the vessel is hot, add a cold liquid (water, stock, wine), bring to a boil, and scrape up the pieces with a spatula. If the vessel is cold, pour in boiling water off the heat, then scrape the bottom.

14 SCRAPING UP STUCK-ON BITS

To incorporate the flavorful bits stuck to the cooking vessel, gently scrape the bottom using a flat spatula.

15 DEGREASING A SKILLET

Remove the excess fat by tipping the pan over a bowl so that it runs out.

16 DEGREASING BROTH

Using a spoon, remove the fat that floats to the surface of a liquid. If the liquid is cold, the fat will congeal and be easier to remove.

17 REDUCING A SAUCE

Concentrate a sauce by simmering to evaporate some of its water.

18 REDUCING UNTIL DRY

Bring a liquid (wine, water, another type of alcohol) to a boil and let it evaporate completely.

19 SKIMMING

Using a skimmer, remove the foam or scum that forms on the surface of a boiling or simmering liquid.

20 BROWN AND WHITE METHODS

The degree of coloration of a food being browned. *À blanc* (white): no coloration at all, just increased firmness. *À brun* (brown): the food turns brown.

21 COOKING LIQUID

Liquid (stock, wine, water) added to a preparation to allow it to cook.

UTENSILS

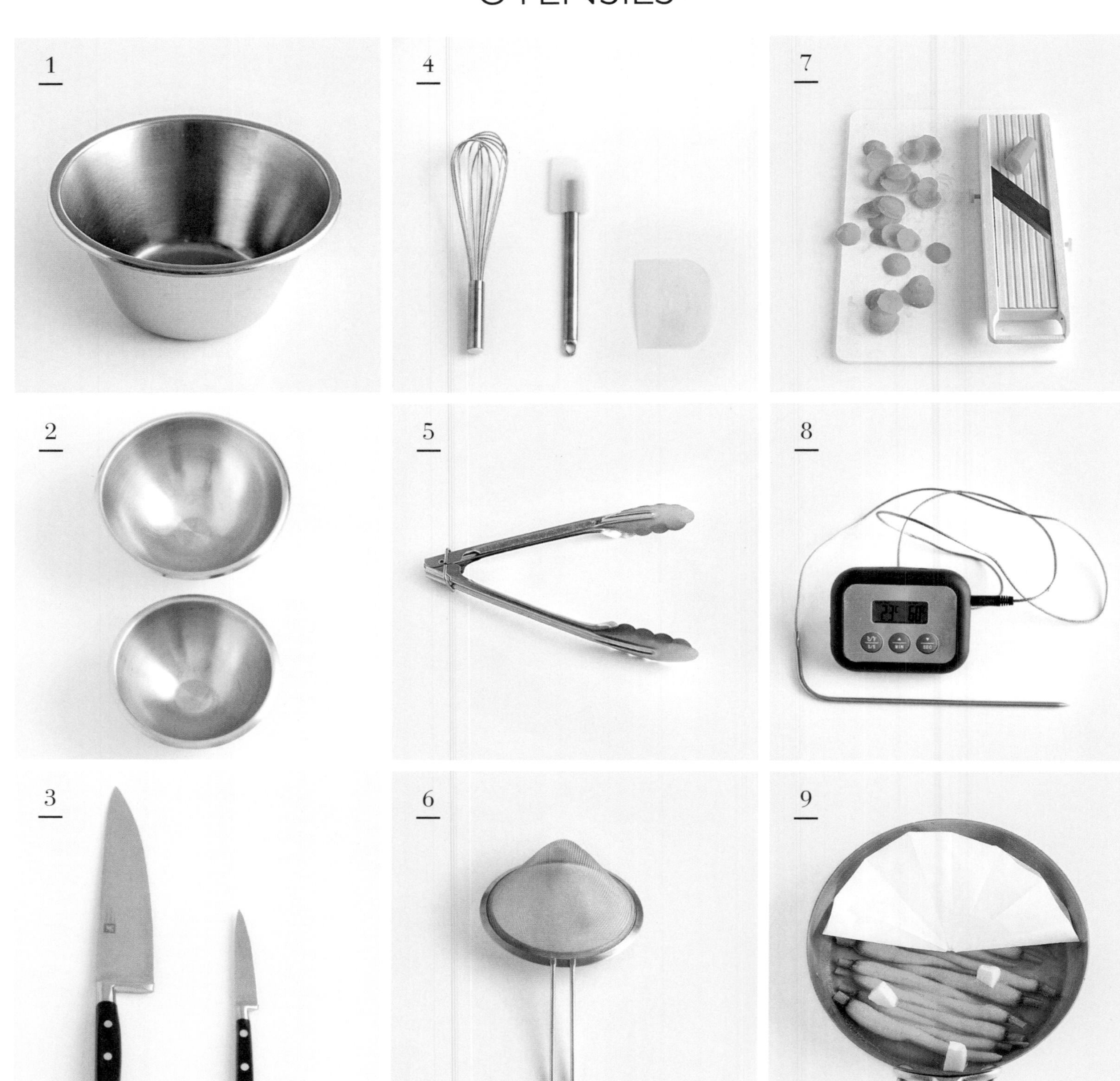

1 FLAT-BOTTOMED BOWL

Stainless-steel bowl with a flat, stable base. For scraps, storing foods, or washing vegetables.

2 MIXING BOWL

Round-bottomed bowl for preparing mixtures. Often used for whisking egg whites to stiff peaks because it allows whisking everywhere, without missing any corners.

3 CHEF'S AND PARING KNIVES

Chef's knife: thick blade 10–12 inches long, with a wide heel. The heel provides extra force for breaking up hard items (e.g., fish bones). Also used for cutting raw meats and chopping finely.

Paring knife: blade 2 ¾–4 inches long, thin tip. Multiple uses.

4 WHISK, SILICONE SPATULA, DOUGH SCRAPER

Whisk: wire utensil used for beating food by hand.

Silicone spatula: flexible heatproof spatula.

Dough scraper: half-moon-shaped, semi-flexible plastic utensil used for scraping cooking vessels and work surfaces.

5 TONGS

Allow delicate handling of foods during cooking.

6 SIEVE

Conical or hemispherical utensil used to strain preparations. Types include: the classic *chinois*, with rigid, small holes; and the *chinois étamine*, with very fine mesh that retains very small particles; and the tamis, a wide, flat-bottomed fine-mesh sieve. It can sometimes be replaced with a fine-mesh strainer.

7 MANDOLINE

Cutting tool: for thin slices, julienne, gaufrettes (waffle chips), chips, etc. Pass the food over the blade in a quick, clean movement, pushing down and using the protective guard or a cut-resistant glove.

8 THERMOMETER WITH PROBE

Tool that allows control of the temperature of an oven, of food, and of frying oil, indispensable in the last case, unless you use an electric deep-fryer. Watch that the thermometer or the probe never touch the bottom of the cooking vessel.

UTENSILS

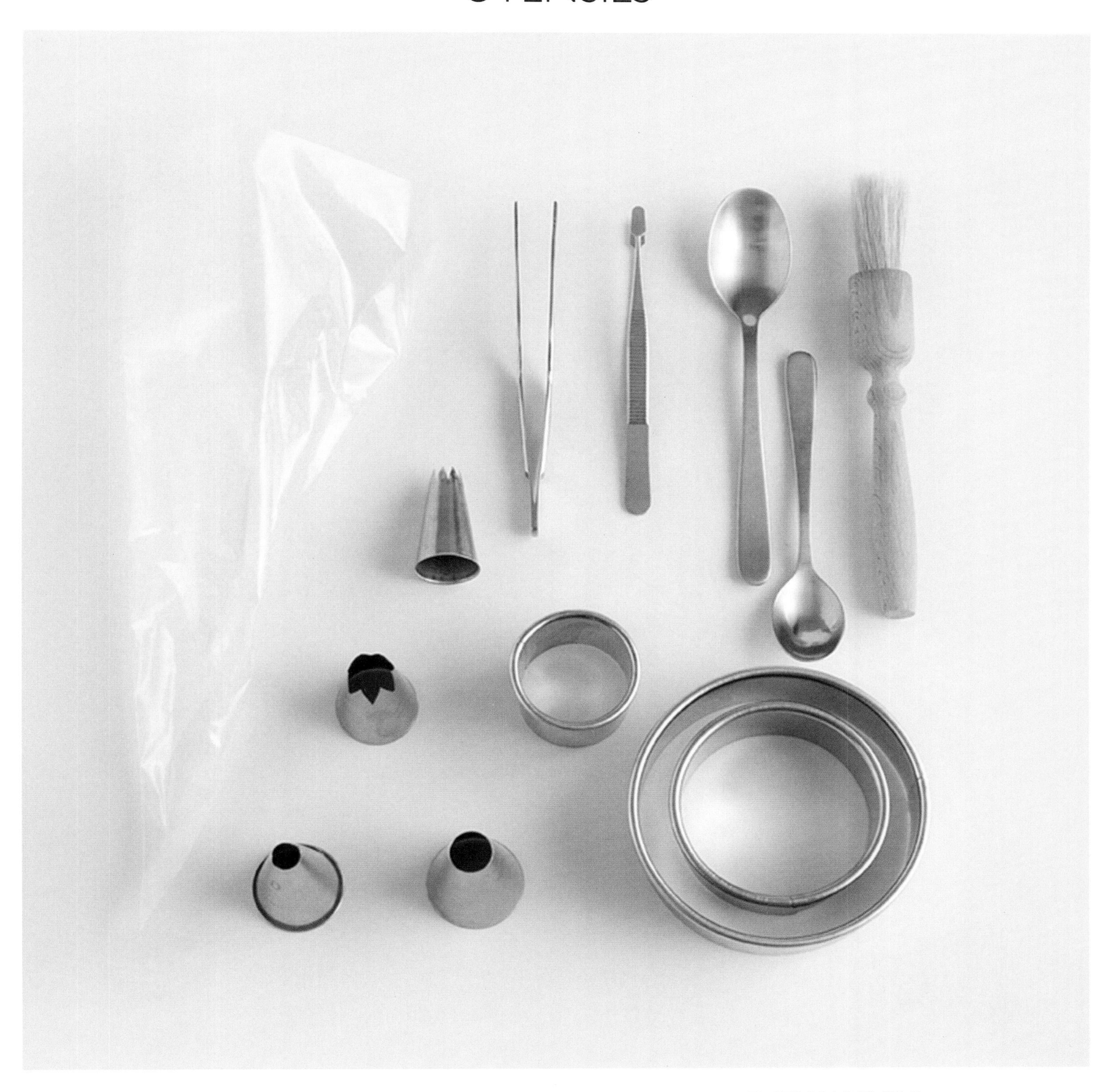

9 PARCHMENT PAPER DISK

Prevents foods from drying out or browning, while also allowing evaporation, thanks to a vent cut in the middle.

Cut a square of parchment paper larger than the cooking vessel. Fold the sheet in half, then in half again to get a square. Fold on the diagonal, folding through the twice-folded corner. You will have a right-angled triangle. Keeping the thrice-folded corner as the tip of your triangle, fold the right-angle side along the hypotenuse (longest side), then repeat twice more. You will have a very thin triangle.

Place the point of the triangle at the center of the pan and cut off the overhang. Unfold the sheet and you will have a disk.

To make a vent, cut about ⅛ inch off the tip of the triangle before unfolding.

STOVETOP TEMPERATURES

The stovetop temperature indications in this book are on a rising scale of strength: very low, low, medium, high, very high.

These indications correspond to induction stovetops, which often allow high and low temperatures above and below those possible with a gas, electric, or ceramic stovetop. If you have a gas stovetop, perhaps use a hot water bath for those recipes that require "very low," and plan for a longer cooking time for "very high" if you have an electric or a ceramic stovetop. Also anticipate the reaction time of your stovetop: electric and ceramic do not change from hot to medium instantaneously (unlike gas or induction stovetops), so prepare two burners at different temperatures if the recipe requires you to move from one to the other quickly.

PLATING UTENSILS

Above (clockwise from upper left): Pastry bag, tweezers (to handle elements carefully or remove unwanted items from a plate), spoons, pastry brush for adding shine, food rings of various sizes, and decorating tips for the pastry bag.

POTS AND PANS

– Saucepan:
Small : 5½ inches; medium: 6¼–7 inches;
Large: 8–8¾ inches

– Skillet or sauté pan:
Small: 8 inches; medium: 8¾ inches; large: 10¼ inches

– Oval baking dish or Dutch oven:
Medium: 8¾ inches; large: 12 inches.

RECIPE LIST

BASE RECIPES

STOCKS

BASIC SAUCES

EMULSIONS

BASIC PREPARATION METHODS AND MIXTURES

PASTRY

BASIC INGREDIENTS

COOKING TECHNIQUES

RECIPES

SOUPS

COLD APPETIZERS

HOT APPETIZERS

SHELLFISH

FISH

MEATS

ACCOMPANIMENTS

ILLUSTRATED GLOSSARY

INGREDIENTS INDEX

MARIANNE'S ACKNOWLEDGMENTS

Immense thanks to Emmanuel Vallois, Rosemarie di Domenico, and Pauline Labrousse for entrusting me with this project.
Thanks also to the passionate cooking team with whom I had the pleasure of writing this book.
More particularly, I would like to thank:
Pauline Labrousse for conceiving this immense project and organizing it with her legendary grace.
Pierre Javelle for his wonderful photos and compositions of ingredients, always created with good humor.
Orathay Souksisavanh for her elegant styling, but also because she is a walking encyclopedia of cooking, and she generously shared her knowledge with me throughout the shoot.
Audrey Génin, who corrected my text while enriching it with her own knowledge of cooking.
Yannis Varoutsikos (illustrator) and Anne Cazor (food technologist), who did me the honor of creating this book with me.
And thanks to Agathe's dad, "Didier the Hunter," who found in his stores what we needed to prepare venison steaks out of hunting season!

ANNE'S ACKNOWLEDGMENTS

Thanks to the whole team who contributed to the creation of this work.

YANNIS'S ACKNOWLEDGMENTS

I knew I should have listened to my grandmothers!
Luckily, my parents knew how to pass on a taste for good food, and good recipes accompanied with all their practical tips.
I hope my little Clémentine will also develop a taste for good food and good recipes.
For Granny Vonnette's delicious ravioli and pesto soup, and Granny Claude's incredible roasts.
And thanks to the team at Marabout for all their good advice.

HarperCollins books may be purchased for educational, business, or sales promotional use. For information please email the Special Markets Department at SPsales@harpercollins.com.

Published in 2018 by
Harper Design
An Imprint of HarperCollins *Publishers*
195 Broadway
New York, NY 10007
Tel: (212) 207-7000
Fax: (855) 746-6023
harperdesign@harpercollins.com
www.hc.com

Distributed throughout North America by
HarperCollins *Publishers*
195 Broadway
New York, NY 10007

ISBN 978-0-06-264107-6

Library of Congress Control Number 2017932171

Printed in China

First Printing, 2018

Graphic design: Yannis Varoutsikos
Styling: Orathay Souksisavanh
Editing: Audrey Genin, Émilie Collet, and Véronique Dussidour
Translation: Nicola Young

First published by Hachette Livre (Marabout) 2015